Reading Corporeality in Patrick White's Fiction

Cross/Cultures

READINGS IN POST/COLONIAL
LITERATURES AND CULTURES IN ENGLISH

Edited by

Gordon Collier
Geoffrey Davis
Bénédicte Ledent

Co-founding editor

†Hena Maes-Jelinek

Advisory Board

David Callahan (*University of Aveira*)
Stephen Clingman (*University of Massachusetts*)
Marc Delrez (*Université de Liège*)
Gaurav Desai (*University of Michigan*)
Russell McDougall (*University of New England*)
John McLeod (*University of Leeds*)
Irikidzayi Manase (*University of the Free State*)
Caryl Phillips (*Yale University*)
Diana Brydon (*University of Manitoba*)
Pilar Cuder-Dominguez (*University of Huelva*)
Wendy Knepper (*Brunel University*)
Carine Mardorossian (*University of Buffalo*)
Maria Olaussen (*University of Gothenburg*)
Chris Prentice (*Otago University*)
Cheryl Stobie (*University of KwaZulu-Natal*)
Daria Tunca (*Université de Liège*)

VOLUME 204

The titles published in this series are listed at *brill.com/cc*

Reading Corporeality in Patrick White's Fiction

An Abject Dictatorship of the Flesh

By

Bridget Grogan

BRILL
RODOPI

LEIDEN | BOSTON

Cover illustration: Robert Hodgins, "The Governess" (2008, lithograph, 72 × 56 cm). © Robert Hodgins Print Archive (Wits Art Museum).

Library of Congress Cataloging-in-Publication Data

Names: Grogan, Bridget, author.
Title: Reading corporeality in Patrick White's fiction : an abject dictatorship of the flesh / by Bridget Grogan.
Description: Leiden ; Boston : Brill Rodopi, 2018. | Series: Cross/Cultures ; 204 | Includes bibliographical references and index.
Identifiers: LCCN 2018003557 (print) | LCCN 2018007089 (ebook) | ISBN 9789004365698 (E-Book) | ISBN 9789004365681 (hardback : acid-free paper)
Subjects: LCSH: White, Patrick, 1912-1990--Criticism and interpretation. | Human body in literature. | Body and soul in literature.
Classification: LCC PR9619.3.W5 (ebook) | LCC PR9619.3.W5 Z666 2018 (print) | DDC 823/.912--dc23
LC record available at https://lccn.loc.gov/2018003557

Typeface for the Latin, Greek, and Cyrillic scripts: "Brill". See and download: brill.com/brill-typeface.

ISSN 0924-1426
ISBN 978-90-04-36568-1 (hardback)
ISBN 978-90-04-36569-8 (e-book)

Copyright 2018 by Koninklijke Brill NV, Leiden, The Netherlands.
Koninklijke Brill NV incorporates the imprints Brill, Brill Hes & De Graaf, Brill Nijhoff, Brill Rodopi, Brill Sense and Hotei Publishing.
All rights reserved. No part of this publication may be reproduced, translated, stored in a retrieval system, or transmitted in any form or by any means, electronic, mechanical, photocopying, recording or otherwise, without prior written permission from the publisher.
Authorization to photocopy items for internal or personal use is granted by Koninklijke Brill NV provided that the appropriate fees are paid directly to The Copyright Clearance Center, 222 Rosewood Drive, Suite 910, Danvers, MA 01923, USA. Fees are subject to change.

This book is printed on acid-free paper and produced in a sustainable manner.

Contents

Acknowledgements VII

Introduction 1

1 **Abjection, Compassion, and White's Recuperation of Affective Corporeality** 18

2 **Mind/Body Dualism**
   History, Modernity, Criticism 50

3 **Pulsating Prose** 100

4 **The Body Imprisoned**
   Social Control and Corporeal Subversion 128

5 **Ladies and Gentleman?**
   The Corporeal Subversion of Identity in The Aunt's Story *and* The Twyborn Affair 162

6 **White's Somatic Spirituality** 181

7 **Abject Corporeality and Somatic Spirituality**
   Voss *and* The Eye of the Storm 212

Conclusion: Unifying the Fragments 244

Works Cited 259
Index 270

Acknowledgements

This monograph began as a doctoral dissertation completed in the Department of English at Rhodes University. I am indebted to many excellent teachers and colleagues from Grahamstown, South Africa, who contributed in many ways to my studies and to the final product that is this book. Malvern Van Wyk Smith introduced me to Patrick White's fiction and to the delight and finesse of sensitive and intelligent literary analysis. Dan Wylie, my supervisor, was unflaggingly enthusiastic, generous, and kind. Mike Marais modelled new approaches to reading and provided invaluable mentorship and guidance. Thanks also to Deborah Seddon, Margot Beard, Jamie McGregor, Wendy Jacobson, Sue Marais, Minesh Dass, Thando Njovane, Paul Walters, Gareth Cornwell, and Dirk Klopper.

I am also grateful to my colleagues in the English Department at the University of Johannesburg—Karen Scherzinger, Sikhumbuzo Mngadi, Jane Starfield, Dalene Labuschagne, Thabo Tsehloane, Nicole Moore, and Nora-Lee Wales. Thank you for the support you have provided as I have completed this work. Karen, Dalene, and Nora-Lee: thanks in particular for the very necessary lunches (and glasses of wine). My gratitude, also, to friends from Johannesburg and Grahamstown who have provided conversation, laughter, support, analysis, kindness, and advice as I have finished this project. Gerald Gaylard, Lauren Creese, Laura Alfers, Louella Sullivan, Jayne Euvrard, Claire Haggard, Karen McCarthy, Andy Carolin, Sam Vice, Lucy Allais, and Thad Metz: thank you.

Australian Literary Studies (ALS), *Journal of Literary Studies* (JLS), and the *Journal of the Association for the Study of Australian Literature* (JASAL) have kindly granted me permission to reprint versions of previously published work. Thank you also to Cambridge Scholars Publishing, who have allowed me to reprint a section previously published in *Patrick White Centenary: The Legacy of a Prodigal Son*, edited by Cynthia vanden Driesen and Bill Ashcroft.

Many thanks, too, to the Wits Art Museum and its senior curator, Julia Charlton, for granting me permission to use Robert Hodgins' lithograph *The Governess* (wonderfully reminiscent of Theodora Goodman and her associated colour imagery in *The Aunt's Story*) as the cover image for this book.

My gratitude is also due to Gordon Collier at Brill | Rodopi, co-editor of the Cross/Cultures series and an exceptional scholar of Patrick White. Gordon, it has been an honor to produce this book under your guidance. Thanks, too, to the anonymous reviewers who helped to make this book much better than it would otherwise have been. In addition, thanks to the wonderful scholars of Australian literature who have provided advice along the way: Cynthia vanden

Driesen, Bill Ashcroft, Lyn McCredden, Nicholas Birns, Russell West-Pavlov, Leigh Dale, and Brigitta Olubas. This work is based on the research supported in part by the National Research Foundation of South Africa (Grant Number 109070).

To my parents—John and Felicity—who have always welcomed me home, and to my siblings—Sean, Kathleen, and Patrick—thank you for your constancy. And, finally, I am indebted to Posy, Bob, and Boris, who at different stages in this project, in their wild corporeal joy and abandonment, have taken me out of my headspace and affirmed White's statement that "dog is God turned round."

Introduction

Patrick White's fiction returns repeatedly to the theme of corporeality. To select one example out of many: an episode from *The Vivisector* reveals its pervasive, ironic, and cumulative treatment of the corporeal. The novel's protagonist, the artist Hurtle Duffield, and his lover, Hero Pavloussis, travel to the Greek island of Perialos, where Hero hopes to atone for adultery. For Hero, the return to Perialos is a spiritual odyssey and an attempt, moreover, to flee the demands of the body and, in her view, the sins of the flesh. Yet her experience and the text's corresponding focus on corporeality disallow such escape. "Sounds of vomiting" punctuate the ferry trip to the island; "baskets of used paper" litter the lavatories; and when Hero and Hurtle finally arrive at Perialos, they are "weak at the knees, like discharged hospital cases."[1] At the inn, "the smell of urine" (380) pervades the corridor and, at their first meal, Hurtle attempts to "disguise the gristle collected between his teeth" (381). A funeral procession engulfs the couple as they make their way to the Convent of the Assumption and the mourners implore Hero to "kiss the corpse" (381). Meanwhile, on a terrace of a monastery overlooking the village, an old man "piss[es] in the wrong quarter; the wind [blowing] it back at him" (381). Goats on the mountain scamper "out of their caves and off amongst the olives, scattering dung" (382). At the convent, the abbess pours ouzo and sits with "eyelids lowered, smiling at something, probably not of a spiritual nature, but a concrete object in the world she had left" (385). Nearby, two convent orphans snigger, the pimples on "their glowing skins" shining "with a virulence of chicken-pox" (387). A little later, at the chapel of Theodosius, the saintly hermit, Hurtle and Hero find nothing but a "subsiding mound of human excrement beside the altar" (389).

    This episode, like many in White, is preoccupied with what is described in the early novel *The Living and the Dead* as the "abject dictatorship of the flesh."[2] The accumulation of corporeal imagery contributes to the narrative excess and energy of White's often lengthy, detailed fictions and, in this instance, creates the ironic bathos that Hero experiences on a trip she intended to be a spiritual journey. The more she tries to atone for the flesh, it seems, the more she is confronted with and tormented by reminders of her physicality. While this may simply suggest White's grotesque, deflating humor and the novel's attempt to cut a spiritually ambitious character down to size, a greater significance is

---

1   Patrick White, *The Vivisector* (1970; Harmondsworth: Penguin, 1985): 379. Further page references are in the main text.
2   Patrick White, *The Living and the Dead* (1941; Harmondsworth: Penguin, 1977): 263.

evident. The implication of the proliferation of bodily detail in the description of Hero's religious quest is that she has misunderstood spirituality as incorporeal. Ironically, the body arises to punish her for this, becoming an ambiguous symbol of both spirituality and horror. It returns to her, its resurgence allegorized in the image of the old man's urine blowing back at him as he pisses into the wind. Later, when Hero swallows the dregs of a cup of coffee, her disgusted expression—"the black lips spluttering and gasping; the terrible tunnel of her black mouth" (392)—becomes Hurtle's primary image of their travels. Choking not only on the coffee but also on the incrementally increasing corporeal insults she has suffered on her journey, Hero phrases one of White's fundamental imperatives: "*Dreck! Dreck!* The Germans express it best. Well, I will learn to live with such *Dreck* as I am: to find a reason and purpose in this *Dreck*" (392).

Like Hero, White's fiction engages in an extended attempt to locate meaning in the physical world. This has resulted in its tendency to foreground corporeality, which has led critics to comment on the solid presence of the body in the texts, with their emphasis on "gristle and sinews, veins in eyeballs, tufts of hair, the texture and pores of skin, nostrils, knuckles and goitres."[3] White's semantics are indeed often somatic. His emphasis upon the corporeal maps itself onto his narrative excess, which presents an "endless multiplication of palpable detail."[4] Deploying a mode of presentation and narrative "conducted through choking thickets of imagery,"[5] White equates language with the physical. His interest in the "*dreck*" of existence, meticulously contributing to the narrative detail of his fiction, exemplifies a linguistic sensitivity to bodily sensation, affect, and experience that has inspired one critic to comment on his writing as an "orchestra of responses" as though "the self were raw flesh stroked by a feather."[6]

Yet critics have identified White's interest in the body as a sign of radical disgust and thus of a defining dualism that posits the 'purity' of the disembodied spirit in relation to the 'pollution' of the material world. A.P. Riemer, for example, stands for many of White's readers in his claim that the writing is "dedicated to the notion that the body, the flesh and the senses are utterly

---

[3] Peter Beatson, *The Eye in the Mandala: Patrick White: A Vision of Man and God* (London: Paul Elek, 1976): 104.
[4] William Walsh, "Fiction as Metaphor: The Novels of Patrick White," *Sewanee Review* 82.2 (Spring 1974): 205.
[5] Walsh, "Fiction as Metaphor," 210.
[6] Cecil Hadgraft, "The Theme of Revelation in Patrick White's Novels," *Southerly* 37 (1977): 37.

worthless."[7] White's fiction, however, appears to emphasize dualism in order to subvert it. In particular, it questions the construction and maintenance of subjectivity according to a psychically defensive repudiation of the body that Julia Kristeva, subsequent to most of White's creative output, terms "abjection."[8] According to Kristeva, disgust or abjection ensures that aspects of the self, particularly corporeality and bodily products, are rejected and maintained as 'other'. White's writing consistently explores the construction of rational subjectivity according to the abjection of corporeality. His characters often "recoil" from the "helpless and unreliable body,"[9] imagining that they can "dispense with flesh."[10]

It is via the process of abjection that incorporeal concepts such as 'spirit' or 'mind' have arisen historically. White, however, presents such disembodied notions of subjectivity as symptoms of a damagingly narcissistic and inwardly orientated ontology which rejects the "flesh of relationships."[11] Moreover, he perceives the conceptual rejection of the material world as a consequence of modernity. His writing therefore seeks to undermine the distinction between mind and body that has developed into the concept of the self-enclosed, superior 'mind' fundamental to post-Enlightenment thought. Although White acknowledges the necessary repudiation of corporeality in the consolidation of modern subjectivity, his fiction strives for fleeting moments of redemptive unification in which 'disembodied' reason is subverted and subjectivity dissolves as it comes into accepting contact with its abjects. Such moments are significant in White's fiction: his characters are defined by "a prolonged waiting for some moment of revelation or fulfilment,"[12] some "ultimate in experience,"[13] which is eventually granted to them in the acknowledgement of corporeality. Like Stan Parker of *The Tree of Man*, they are "prisoner[s] in [the] human mind" aware that the "touch of hands, the lifting of a silence, the sudden shape of a tree or presence of a first star, hint[s] at eventual release."[14] The necessity of the acknowledgement of, or engulfment in, sensory experience appears to

---

7   A.P. Riemer, "Eddie and the Bogomils—Some Observations on *The Twyborn Affair*," *Southerly* 34.2 (March 1980): 26.
8   Julia Kristeva, *Powers of Horror: An Essay on Abjection*, tr. Leon S. Roudiez (*Pouvoirs de l'horreur: Essai sur l'abjection*, 1980; New York: Columbia UP, 1982).
9   Patrick White, *The Tree of Man* (London: Eyre & Spottiswoode, 1956): 114.
10 Patrick White, *Voss* (1957; London: Vintage, 1994): 34.
11 White, *The Tree of Man*, 124; White, *Voss*, 112.
12 Patrick White, "A Woman's Hand," in White, *The Cockatoos* (1974; Harmondsworth: Penguin, 1979): 10.
13 Patrick White, *A Fringe of Leaves* (1976; London: Vintage, 1997): 21.
14 White, *The Tree of Man*, 46.

shape White's fictions: submission to the flesh promotes the sought-after "state of pure living bliss"[15] experienced in the dissolution of self and other. Thus, for example, the narrative trajectory of *Voss* follows the eponymous protagonist's physical journey through the Australian desert and the simultaneous metaphysical journey toward accepting the body, an acceptance dramatized in the imagery of communion. In *The Eye of the Storm*, Elizabeth Hunter's aged, dying body is revered by her nurses and is the site of her own revelatory experiences. Ellen Roxburgh in *A Fringe of Leaves* literally re-incorporates the body when she ingests human flesh after stumbling upon an Aboriginal rite. And Stan Parker, at the conclusion of *The Tree of Man*, famously expresses his eventual celebration of corporeality when he points to a gobbet of his saliva and announces, "That is God."[16] The body in White's fiction does not remain other, but is constantly depicted as a redemptive aspect of the self.

In White's writing, corporeality is not simply a thematic concern. While the fiction undermines a subjectivity (or 'mind' or 'spirit') that arises due to the abjection of materiality, it also contests the assumption that language, traditionally associated with the processes of the mind, is rational, reasoned, and distinct from the body. Accordingly, it posits two contrasting forms of language: the "code language of human intercourse"[17] and "another language"[18]— a "language of flesh"[19]—that goes unspoken by his characters but that is embodied in the texts themselves. The rational, prosaic language of the social order is a precise form of signification that transparently communicates its meaning, thereby disguising the arbitrary relation between signifier and signified. For White, however, "words, whether written or spoken," are "frail slat bridges over chasms."[20] The 'poetic' language of corporeality, and of White's fiction at its most resonant, is opaque, ambiguous, and seemingly characterized by the disruptions of a disordering physicality.[21] In the experiences of White's characters, it is often a grammar of silence and is related to an intense awareness of embodiment. Thus, Theodora Goodman "would like to write a poem" although she cannot "describe [the] immensity" of her urge to representation.[22] If she could, however, she would produce a poem in which she

---

15 Patrick White, *The Eye of the Storm* (1973; London: Penguin, 1987): 24.
16 White, *The Tree of Man*, 495.
17 Patrick White, *The Aunt's Story* (1948; London: Vintage, 1994): 178.
18 White, "Five-Twenty," in White, *The Cockatoos*, 174.
19 White, *The Tree of Man*, 25.
20 White, *The Aunt's Story*, 128.
21 I term this physicality 'disordering' not to diminish it, but because it undermines and exceeds the ordering capacity of rational, symbolic consciousness.
22 White, *The Aunt's Story*, 53.

would "take, and touch, and join together all these sensations and make them palpable and whole."²³ This is what White's "language of flesh" attempts to do. It is, moreover, an expression of affect, of physically felt emotion that exceeds his characters' verbalization—for example:

> Himmelfarb realized he could never convey that sudden stampeding of the heart, sickening of the pulse, enmity of familiar streets, the sharp, glandular stench of unreasonable fear. For words are the tools of reason.²⁴

Nonetheless, White's concern with symbol, imagery, metaphor, paradox, and the affective pulse of language, in conjunction with descriptions of intense physicality, foregrounds a level of corporeal (and, in White's vision, sacred) experience that eludes ordinary expression: Himmelfarb may not be able to express his physical sensations, but White's description constructs and communicates them.

Extending from the contrast of a "code language of human intercourse" and a "language of flesh," White's fiction promotes corporeality as other to everyday language and thus also to traditional notions of subjectivity that are constructed discursively and that prompt the social restraint on and regimentation of the body. It therefore draws a distinction between socially constructed identity, associated with the image of the body, and a disordering, subversive corporeality linked to literary language, animality, and the natural world. Thus, it takes issue with the regulative discourses—of race, gender, and sexuality, for example—that construct identity, render the body docile, and repudiate the flux and disorder of a corporeality that nonetheless continues to "flower" and "flow," "as pervasive but evasive as experience."²⁵ Society is harsh on White's protagonists, who are often awkward outsiders failing to conform to social dictates in their appearances, performances of gender, and sexuality. They yearn to escape their subjectivity—to achieve the "ecstasy of complete, annihilating liberation."²⁶ Attempting to write characters beyond the symbolic order, however impossible a project this may be, White describes them as pushed to a point where "words finally shatter, or the envelope that protects human

---

23   *The Aunt's Story*, 53.
24   Patrick White, *Riders in the Chariot* (1961; New York: New York Review of Books, 2002): 192.
25   White, *The Aunt's Story*, 191.
26   White, *Riders in the Chariot*, 13.

personality."²⁷ His fiction persistently promotes the possibility that the "human being might still erupt, and assume fresh forms, or disintegrate."²⁸

This interest in the dissolution of subjectivity has been read as evidence of White's dismissal of the physical world. Yet the transcendence of identity is not the same as a removal from corporeality. In fact, White's characters appear to shed their subjectivity *as* corporeality rushes in on them, coinciding with the fragmentation of the body image. Thus, Theodora Goodman, of *The Aunt's Story*, dissolving into madness after her restrictive mother has died, feels "divorced from her own hands" as the "blood [begins] to flow."²⁹ Later in the novel, Holstius voices White's prevailing dismissal of the mirror image: "We are too inclined to consider the shapes of flesh that loom up at us out of mirrors"³⁰—too inclined, indeed, to consider the *image* of the body, but not the experience of the flesh itself. As Lacan's theory of the mirror phase posits, corporeality cannot be subjugated to the body image, which remains a spurious reflection of the self, and will inevitably return to overwhelm it. Thus, Laura Trevelyan, walking in the garden with Rose Portion, the servant who has represented for her a repulsive and subject-confirming physicality, suddenly feels "the woman's pulse ticking in her own body" and is overwhelmed by the sunlit acceptance of "common flesh."³¹ Similarly, Mary de Santis, pouring seed into a bird-feeder at the conclusion of *The Eye of the Storm*, experiences the intensity of her physicality as a "prism of dew and light," a "tumult of wings and her unmanageable joy."³² In such moments of corporeal engulfment, White presents the loss of identity as redemptive, reducing his characters to the "last shreds of personality"³³ as sensory experience and the physical world rush in to overwhelm them.

Such moments of unification with physicality constitute what Bill Ashcroft and Lyn McCredden have identified as White's concern with the sacred. Ashcroft argues that the sacred is manifested in White's interest in the "'unpresentability' of the sublime" evident in the "simple proximate reality of material things, and the persistent inability of language to fully apprehend it."³⁴ While

---

27   White, *The Aunt's Story*, 245.
28   White, *The Tree of Man*, 234.
29   White, *The Aunt's Story*, 11.
30   *The Aunt's Story*, 284.
31   White, *Voss*, 160.
32   White, *The Eye of the Storm*, 589.
33   White, *The Aunt's Story*, 139.
34   Bill Ashcroft, "The Presence of the Sacred in Patrick White," in *Remembering Patrick White: Contemporary Critical Essays*, ed. Elizabeth McMahon & Brigitta Olubas (Cross/Cultures 128; Amsterdam: Rodopi, 2010): 96.

he refers here to the significant presence of inanimate objects, the human body in White also challenges language's ability fully to capture it. White's concern with the uncapturable sublime occurs in conjunction with his presentation of the physical. As Lyn McCredden argues, a "hunger for both physical and sacred significance is communicated" in the writing and we therefore find in White an "earthed sacredness, a writerly seeking of ways to embrace both flesh and spirit"[35]—simultaneously. As this study argues, the loss of subjectivity, occurring simultaneously with the overwhelming nature of physicality, enacts the "somatic sacred" in White's writing. Corporeality in White is thus treated with greater complexity than most critics have suggested. While identity, associated with the body image or the socially constructed 'docile' body, is questioned in the writing via the emphasis on an apparent transcendence (which may be more productively viewed as what I term a 'somatic spiritualism'), corporeality and the intensity of lived embodiment remain vitally important aspects of White's writing, infusing his texts with the fine physical awareness and visceral affect for which they are known. This physicality of the text results in the reader's continuous attunement to the physicality of existence, thereby emphasizing reading, like all experience, as inherently embodied.

This book consists of seven chapters, each dealing with one of the following dimensions of White's writing: abjection and affect; engagement with the dualistic history of Western epistemology; corporeality and language; the distinction between the social and the natural; and somatic spirituality.

Chapter 1, "Abjection, Compassion, and White's Recuperation of Corporeal Affect," elucidates the primary theoretical underpinnings of my argument. It provides an outline of Julia Kristeva's theory of abjection and an account of how this theory illuminates White's early and under-theorized novel, *The Living and the Dead*, the novel that provides the phrase, "the abject dictatorship of the flesh," from which the title of this book is taken. The purpose of the chapter is twofold: to present the way in which a psychoanalytic and affective interpretation of White's depiction of corporeality may inform an understanding of his characterization and approach to narrative; and to demonstrate a reading, informing the study's analysis from this point onwards, that illustrates the significance of abjection, corporeality, and affect in White's writing. Specifically, the chapter identifies, via a focus on Lacan's theory of the mirror stage, the necessary abjection of corporeality inherent in the consolidation of identity. According to Lacan, in an idea taken up by Kristeva, the infant first attains

---

35   Lyn McCredden, "*Voss*: Earthed and Transformative Sacredness," in *Remembering Patrick White: Contemporary Critical Essays*, ed. Elizabeth McMahon & Brigitta Olubas (Cross/Cultures 128; Amsterdam & New York: Rodopi, 2010): 115.

subjectivity via its projective identification with its body image. This identification occurs at the expense of the lived experience of an inchoate embodiment fluidly unified in oceanic intimacy with the (m)other. In distinguishing between the body image (associated with socialized subjectivity) and corporeality, the chapter argues that it is in experiencing their constituting physicality that characters paradoxically appear to lose their bodies in the moments of mystical communion or transcendence for which White's writing is renowned. These moments of 'transcendence' often occur when characters confront death and experience a consuming sense of mortality inherent in abjection. Lacan names the overwhelming experience of the body *"jouissance,"* a term I employ to describe the engulfment of the self within corporeality that is so often fundamental to key passages in White and is frequently figured as mystical or sacred. This experience may be brought about as much by the affect of compassion as by that of abjection. For White, compassion frees the subject from the enclosure of narcissism and is rooted in a physical response to others. With reference to theories of affect, the chapter explores the bodily nature of emotion.

Building on the theory of abjection thus elucidated, Chapter 2, "Mind/ Body Dualism: History, Modernity, Criticism," provides a brief historical overview of Western thought that has subscribed to and promoted the conceptual denigration of the body. It accordingly reveals the historical Western imperative of denying or abjecting the flesh in the consolidation of particular notions of subjectivity, referred to, for example, as the 'soul' or the 'mind'—concepts of 'purity' elevated above the 'corruption' and mortality of the flesh. The chapter thus focuses in particular on a tendency in dualist philosophy extending from Plato through early Christian thought and into modernity. Descartes' notion of the *cogito* and Kant's positing of the transcendental ego are emphasized as significantly shaping the modern notion of the incorporeal self, a concept with which White's writing takes issue. Bakhtin's observations in *Rabelais and His World* are harnessed, moreover, to develop the theory that White contrasts the 'classical' notion of a sealed-off, 'disembodied' self—a notion that both Bakhtin and White identify as shaping Western modernity—with the concept of the 'grotesque body', a body that extends into and opens up and out to the external world. I argue that White's endorsement of the grotesque body, evident in his validation of the compassionate Arthur Brown of *The Solid Mandala*, forms part of his critique of modernity. This critique is identified in White's presentation of the moral corrosion associated with disembodied reason, a rationalism resulting, first, in the spiritual emptiness of the twentieth century and, second, in what White, following others, observes as the fascist Western concern with normativity. Despite White's fiction's critique of disembodied reason, similar in many ways to that of Horkheimer and Adorno, some of his critics implicitly support Western dualism by insisting upon its unproblematic presentation in White's fiction. The chapter concludes, therefore, by arguing that White in fact takes issue with the "metaphysics of presence," Derrida's label for the seeming stability of hierarchically structured binary oppositions. White's fiction subverts this stability by positing a philosophy of 'becoming' that is strongly associated with the flux and vicissitudes of corporeality.

In the third chapter, "Pulsating Prose," building upon my observations on the concept of 'becoming' important in White's writing and associated with the themes of fluidity and flux, I turn my focus to the stylistic significance of corporeality in White. White's fiction often thematizes the materiality of representation, drawing attention to the idea that corporeal energy invests the dynamics of literary language. In elucidating this aspect of White's writing, the chapter develops my focus on psychoanalysis in general and Kristeva in particular by discussing Kristeva's concepts of the "symbolic" and the "semiotic," as outlined in *Revolution in Poetic Language*. These terms denote the dual components of the signifying process, referring respectively to grammar and meaning-making (the socialized component of signification, or the *symbolic*) and the disordering corporeal energies that underpin yet threaten it (the pre-symbolic element of signification, or the *semiotic*, existing as a trace within the dynamics of representation). These dual elements of signification often seem evident, even emphasized, in White's fiction, contributing to its focus on the prosaic social order and the sense-deforming 'music' of poetic expression so often enacted by White's performative prose.

Chapter 4, "The Body Imprisoned: Social Control and Corporeal Subversion," builds on the Kristevan theory, introduced in Chapter 3, to argue that White's fiction not only undermines the stable, meaning-making capacity of language by emphasizing a 'language of flesh' but also undermines static, socially controlled identity (shaped by the symbolic order) via the fluid and shifting corporeality of its characters. The chapter thus elaborates on Chapter 3's focus on Kristeva's symbolic and semiotic to emphasize White's interest in the borderline between socialized subjectivity, constructed discursively, and the disordering realm of the corporeal pre-symbolic with its archaic roots in the infant's corporeal confusion and relation to the maternal body. Kristeva's concept of the semiotic *chora* is referred to in order to elucidate the suggestion in White's fiction of the easy slippage between identity and fragmentation, and the attention paid in that fiction to the imagery of infancy and the maternal. Thereafter, the chapter summarizes a number of theories attesting to the uncomfortable interrelation between the social order and the 'natural' body: the writings of Mary Douglas, Pierre Bourdieu, Michel Foucault, and Judith

Butler variously inform the argument, providing a theoretical framework for a reading of White's interest in the constitutive power of the social gaze and its influence on embodied identity.

Extending Chapter 4's observations, Chapter 5 provides a close reading of *The Aunt's Story* and *The Twyborn Affair*, focusing on how these novels, an early and late text in White's oeuvre respectively, question discursive identity and emphasize its subversion by corporeality. In particular, the novels interrogate gender constructions and the norms dictating colonial subjectivity, frequent targets of White's disapproval, undermining these via protagonists who resist normative confinement and embody a fluid corporeality.

In many ways, the argument of this study culminates in the final two chapters. In Chapter 6, "White's Somatic Spirituality," I argue that the dissolution of socialized subjectivity, corresponding to the subject's engulfment in corporeality, engenders the moments of somatic spirituality that pervade White's fiction. Kristeva and Élisabeth Roudinesco's writings support the argument that contact with the abject is fundamental to mystical experience, in which the dualisms of self and other, spirit and body, are dissolved. White's focus on corporeal mysticism manifests itself in a number of themes and interests taken up as areas of discussion in this chapter. The preoccupation of White's fiction with the subversion of 'disembodied' reason is evident in the treatment of physical objects and animality. The chapter begins with a discussion of the "mysticism of objects"[36] and the significance of dogs, both of which often function in White's writing as objective correlatives of human corporeality. The statement that dog is "God turned round"[37] reveals, first, the conflation of the sacred and the abject in White's fiction and, second, language's inherent capacity to undermine itself and thus the radical instability of seemingly discrete dualist concepts. Also discussed in the chapter is White's deployment of the imagery of Christ and the Eucharist, which further contributes to the theme of the abject sacred and the necessity of incorporating it into our notions of subjectivity.

Chapter 7 provides close readings of *Voss* and *The Eye of the Storm*, remaining focused on the interrelation of bodily acceptance and the somatic sacred. In *Voss*, the theme of the need to accept the body is linked particularly to the character of Laura Trevelyan, who becomes increasingly tinged with the redemption and compassion White associates with corporeal acceptance. The chapter also provides a detailed interpretation of *The Eye of the Storm*, dwelling

---

36   White, *The Tree of Man*, 398.
37   Patrick White, "A Cheery Soul," in White, *The Burnt Ones* (1964; Harmondsworth: Penguin, 1977): 189.

on the literal and metaphoric centrality of the abject body to the novel and the significance of its characters' relations to corporeality.

It is not my intention to impose a theoretical framework on White's fiction, which, of course, presents its own philosophies. The prose, moreover, is notoriously slippery: it oscillates between advocating dualism and unity and revels in the ambivalence of free indirect discourse, paradox, irony, oxymoron, and ambiguity. White's focus on the "grotesque mannerisms"[38] of his characters and the abject, sometimes carnivalesque, nature of his descriptions also render his writing resistant to interpretation. While I have not wished to subordinate the fiction to theory—in any case, it resists such confinement—theory has certainly shed light on White's difficulty. This book therefore foregrounds the areas of White's writing that troubled me upon first reading, areas that appeared resistant to interpretation and for which I sought explanation. I could see, for example, why White's critics would highlight his dualist impulses and read his treatment of the body as a symptom of disgust or dismissal. His characters occasionally claim the "incorporeal" as the "more significant part."[39] Yet such statements are undermined within the dynamics of the texts, an element of White's fiction I have therefore decided to explore.

Kristeva's theory of abjection and her interest in what she terms "poetic language"[40] have been particularly useful for the study of the theme of corporeality in White's writing. Like White, Kristeva explores conceptual oppositions, suggesting that each undermines the self-sufficiency of the other. Corporeality, then, invades the notion of 'mind', 'soul', or subjectivity, which is premised upon the repudiation of it in the first instance, a dynamic that is evident in White's fiction. Moreover, Kristeva questions the prevailing epistemological notion that language arises purely from the rational 'mind', a question with which White's writing, with its emphasis on intuition and the unconscious, and its critique of reason, appears also to grapple. My approach to White is therefore for the most part psychoanalytic. Because of White's interest in the elusive nature of human subjectivity and the murky hinterlands of the self, his sometimes baffling recourse to maternal imagery, and the darkly libidinal impulses of his prose, this seems appropriate. In addition to Julia Kristeva's *Powers of Horror* and *Revolution in Poetic Language*, the writing of Peter Brooks, Daniel Punday, Anthony Synnott, Judith Butler, Michel Foucault,

---

38   White, *The Eye of the Storm*, 265.
39   White, *Riders in the Chariot*, 76.
40   Julia Kristeva, *Revolution in Poetic Language*. tr. Margaret Waller (*La Révolution du langage poétique: L'Avant-garde à la fin du XIXe siècle*, 1974; New York: Columbia UP, 1984).

Mary Douglas, Mikhail Bakhtin, Elizabeth Grosz, and Élisabeth Roudinesco has proved invaluable.

White's oeuvre is large, and the task of selecting the texts on which to focus and how to do so has therefore not been entirely simple. Many full studies of White's oeuvre exist that read his texts one by one in chronological order. Carolyn Bliss's *Patrick White's Fiction: The Paradox of Fortunate Failure*,[41] Brian Kiernan's *Patrick White*,[42] Peter Wolfe's *Laden Choirs: The Fiction of Patrick White*,[43] John Colmer's *Patrick White*,[44] William Walsh's *Patrick White's Fiction*,[45] and Mark Williams' *Patrick White*[46] spring to mind. Moreover, a vast body of critical articles on White has been published. Much of this material provides summarizing accounts of the fiction. Bliss, Kiernan, Wolfe, and Walsh, for example, admirably compress White's plots into chapter-length accounts of the novels. Yet his plots are not exactly amenable to summary. As White himself admitted, "Characters interest me more than situations. I don't think any of my books have what you call plots."[47] White's narratives are indeed loosely organized, bent on elucidating character experiences rather than the fascination of story; they are thus better described as episodic than as plot-driven. I have accordingly decided to devote attention for the most part to specific episodes, characters, and the general theme of corporeality rather than to the unified narrative. Reading White's writing in order to elucidate the cohesion of the text may, after all, impose on the works a unity that does not altogether exist. Moreover, my intention is to reveal that White's fiction, from its outset, has remained stable in its approaches to subjectivity and corporeality, notwithstanding an increase in scatological intensity from *The Solid Mandala* onward. I have therefore picked examples to construct and support my argument, without adhering to the chronological progression of the oeuvre.

In this book, I aim in particular to build on the work of Michael Giffin and Veronica Brady, who have written salient accounts of White's 'excremental vision' and interest in psychoanalysis. In its concern with abjection, moreover, this study owes much to Andrew McCann's "The Ethics of Abjection: Patrick White's *Riders in the Chariot*," an excellent study which explores

---

41   Carolyn Bliss, *Patrick White's Fiction: The Paradox of Fortunate Failure* (London: Macmillan, 1986).
42   Brian Kiernan, *Patrick White* (London: Macmillan, 1980).
43   Peter Wolfe, *Laden Choirs: The Fiction of Patrick White* (Lexington: UP of Kentucky, 1983).
44   John Colmer, *Patrick White* (London: Methuen, 1984).
45   William Walsh, *Patrick White's Fiction* (Hornsby, NSW: Allen & Unwin, 1977).
46   Mark Williams, *Patrick White* (London: Macmillan, 1993).
47   Patrick White, "In the Making" (1969), in *Patrick White Speaks*, ed. Paul Brennan & Christine Flynn (1989; London: Penguin, 1992): 21.

White's "obsession with abjection" as informing an "ethical radicality" running throughout his fiction.⁴⁸ McCann argues that White strives to elucidate and undermine "the very oppositions that structure what we might call a fiction of the normal" (146). Dealing in particular with White's suburbia as a system of "social hygiene" (146), a "world of paranoid domesticity constantly threatened by forms of literal and metaphorical defilement" (146), he argues that the abject is "both sign of marginalisation and of redemption" (148) within this fictional space. McCann limits his reading to *Riders in the Chariot* and focuses predominantly on White's derogation of normative society and attention to the abject individuals that it casts aside. I want to extend McCann's ideas to a more general consideration of subjectivity and the body in White's oeuvre and to the theme of abjection as found throughout. Why does White focus on corporeality to such an extent? What does this say about his vision of Western modernity? How does his writing emphasize the body? How does this contribute to whatever theory of subjectivity and characterization may be implicit in White's praxis? How might a corporeal reading of White's fiction operate? Is there a relationship between the interest in the corporeal displayed in White's fiction and narrative itself?

To begin to answer the last of the aforementioned questions, most of White's novels conclude with the death of the protagonist. David Myers accordingly notes the corporeal obsession of the conclusions of White's texts, arguing that they are inclined toward "sombre, grotesque representations of insanity, old age, disease, physical hideousness, and death."⁴⁹ Catherine Standish, Stan Parker, Voss, three of the four protagonists of *Riders in the Chariot*, Waldo Brown, Hurtle Duffield, Elizabeth Hunter, Eddie Twyborn, and Alex Gray die at the close of their respective novels. Such endings strongly suggest that White's fictions are narratives of the body. For White, in a statement that represents his narrative concerns, the "presence of death [...] is also the present, all else has been past and future, stories and anticipation, by comparison."⁵⁰ In *Reading for the Plot*,⁵¹ Peter Brooks, like White, describes narrative as shaped by *thanatos*—reliant on a dynamic tension between the drive toward conclusion and the narrative detail impeding yet anticipating this ending. Story is therefore

---

48   Andrew McCann, "The Ethics of Abjection: Patrick White's *Riders in the Chariot*," *Australian Literary Studies* 18.2 (October 1997): 145.
49   David Myers, *The Peacocks and the Bourgeoisie: Ironic Vision in Patrick White's Shorter Fiction* (Adelaide, SA: Adelaide UP, 1978): 108.
50   White, *The Tree of Man*, 420.
51   Peter Brooks, *Reading for the Plot: Design and Intention in Narrative* (Cambridge MA: Harvard UP, 1992).

comparable to the living body moving inexorably toward death—White's oeuvre, indeed, "glitter[s] in its life" with "all the colours of decomposition."[52] Viewing narrative through the lens of Freud's *Beyond the Pleasure Principle*, Brooks explains it as the product of a tension between the delay that masters the death instinct and the drive toward conclusion that dramatizes it:

> Beyond and under the domination of the pleasure principle is this baseline of plot, its basic 'pulsation', sensible or audible through the repetitions that take us back in the text. Yet repetition also retards the pleasure principle's search for the gratification of discharge, which is another forward-moving drive of the text. We have a curious situation in which two principles of forward movement operate upon one another to create retard, a dilatory space in which pleasure can come from postponement in the knowledge that this [...] is a necessary approach to the true end.[53]

White's fiction productively harnesses this tension, suggesting that the body represents the text itself. Frequently, it foregrounds corporeality's excess—the "minutiae of flesh and blood"[54]—and hence its opposition to the forward propulsion of narrative. As it is expressed in *The Twyborn Affair*,

> it is so important to concentrate on the minutiae: the mauve-to-silver trail of the snail unaware that he's going to be crushed, the scrapings from the carrot which hasn't yet been sliced, the lovely long peeling from the white flesh of the unconscious turnip.[55]

White's often prolix fictions reveal a compulsive desire to return to and elaborate on corporeality: characters and readers are repeatedly driven to confront existence as embodied in texts that defer endings associated with death. These endings, nonetheless, are constantly alluded to via the accumulation of corporeal detail—the "bursts of kaleidoscopic imagery [...] filtered sensuously through [the] blood."[56] White's writing thus strongly enacts a corporeal dynamic that Daniel Punday identifies in narrative:

---

52 White, *Voss*, 47.
53 Brooks, *Reading for the Plot*, 102–103.
54 Patrick White, *The Solid Mandala* (London: Eyre & Spottiswoode, 1966): 160.
55 Patrick White, *The Twyborn Affair* (1979; London: Vintage, 1995): 77.
56 White, *The Vivisector*, 188.

> On the one hand, the body represents all of those brute physical events that work against overarching pattern; on the other, the body provides the order that the narrative gives to events.[57]

His writing presents what Punday has named "the unruly body": an "object that resists larger narrative patterns" (13). This concept is important because the body remains a "fundamental trope in our ways of thinking about order and narrative's ability to represent challenges to it" (13). As I will argue, White's treatment of corporeality opposes classical notions such as order, rationality, balance, and harmony—high-latinate linguistic concepts that oppose corporeality and that, as Bakhtin has argued, have shaped the rationality associated with modernity.[58] Indeed, White's bodies blur the boundaries necessary to maintaining fixed—in White's view, dangerously rigid—identities, overturning, moreover, the modern denial of the body that incorporates the hypocritical politeness of British colonialism. Even the image of the body as a unified entity is unsustainable in White. Associated with identity, as Lacan's mirror stage reveals, the body image gives way to the merging of flesh and landscape, to the empathy for corporeal suffering between otherwise separate individuals, to an acknowledgement of the spirituality of brute materiality, and to a corporeal excess taken up within the poetics of the texts themselves.

We need to look, then, beyond the concerns (and disgust) of critics like Ann Hulbert:

> Patrick White is a novelist who degrades his characters and disconcerts his readers. He mercilessly probes, picks, peers, sniffs at his creations, who ignominiously writhe while we squirm. [...] Imprisoned in flesh, White's characters voraciously seek a spirit of love in the world to lighten their lives, but they never find it. [...] Unsavory displays of [...] bodily functions [...] crammed into large books also do little to encourage readers, even hardy ones.[59]

White's fiction ultimately suggests that his characters are liberated by the flesh, rather than imprisoned within it; it is in their immersion in physicality and hence in their recuperation of 'otherness' that they discover a "spirit of love."

---

57   Daniel Punday, *Narrative Bodies: Toward a Corporeal Narratology* (New York: Palgrave Macmillan, 2003): 13.
58   Mikhail Bakhtin, *Rabelais and His World*, tr. Hélène Iswolsky (*Tvorchestvo Fransua Rable*, 1965; tr. 1968; Bloomington: Indiana UP, 2nd ed. 1984).
59   Ann Hulbert, "*The Twyborn Affair* by Patrick White," *New Republic* (3 May 1980): 37.

White's descriptions of corporeality may not make for easy reading, but it is in the physical details of his novels that the reader may encounter the liberating impulse of the writing. His fiction thus dwells on "that borderline where the hideous and depraved can become aesthetically acceptable."[60] This study therefore aims to reveal the energy of corporeality in White's aesthetics, to draw attention to the ways in which the theme of corporeality informs and enhances his texts, and to suggest that engaging with the body in literature plays a fundamental part in the reading experience and in textual interpretation, however 'disembodied' an experience the reader's immersion in a fictional world may appear to be.

To return briefly to our tourists on the island of Perialos, Hero has dismissed the world as "*dreck*" (392). Hurtle, however, as an artist, presumably shares the corporeal aesthetic of White's fiction and thus recognizes the sublime potential of *dreck* or the abject. Artistic vision, in White's writing, is a kind of alchemy. However, it is not a transformative vision but, rather, one that locates a golden value in physicality. To locate redemption in the seemingly unredeemed requires a linguistic engagement with a paradox that appears to elude the limits of representation. Yet Hurtle is a painter, an artist necessarily engaging with imagery and symbolism. White is similarly interested in the power of symbol to express the seemingly inexpressible. Thus, while Hero at the chapel bewails human degradation, White, through Hurtle, who is unable to express the significance of the material world in language, seeks a symbol that will do so. Hurtle tries to "point out the scaly sea, like a huge live fish, rejoicing in its evening play" (392), and later, when Hero is overcome by "*dreck*," he wants to draw her attention to a golden hen pecking under their café table:

> The warm scallops of her golden feathers were of that same inspiration as the scales of the great silver-blue sea creature they—or he, at least—had watched from John of the Apocalypse, ritually coiling and uncoiling before dissolving in the last light.
>
> *The Vivisector* 392

The hen is radiant in her attachment to the physical world, flashing her wings, "not in flight; she remained consecrated to this earth even while scurrying through illuminated dust" (393).

By inviting us, like the individual in the funeral procession, to "kiss the corpse" (382)—to accept the body—White's fiction illuminates the dust. Accordingly, this book, in its disregard for White's dismissal of the "tittuping

---

60   White, *The Vivisector*, 361.

archivist pick[ing] up a scent on a scholarly ramble [...] to enliven scholarship with muck" (484), explores and re-evaluates the author's treatment of corporeality. Perhaps we might re-interpret White's derogation of academia: his "muck" enlivens his writing, and attention to it indeed revitalizes what has, until of late, become a scholarship sometimes too polite to pay it heed, and often too concerned with the metaphysics of presence to notice it.

CHAPTER 1

Abjection, Compassion, and White's Recuperation of Affective Corporeality

'I am a man, and you are a man,' said Theodora.
'That is emotionalism.'
'It is flesh and blood.'
　　—*The Aunt's Story* 165

∴

In White's early novel *The Living and the Dead*, two statements regarding the body are significant to an understanding of his treatment of corporeality: at one point Eden Standish realizes that "compassion is oddly physical";[1] at another, human existence is described as governed by the "abject dictatorship of the flesh."[2] These quotations point up a productive literary tension running through White's oeuvre. The first statement assumes that it is by virtue of our physicality that we conceive of the positions and experiences of others; it implies that our bodies are fundamental to our ability to empathetically imagine —that physicality is significant in any active engagement with 'otherness'. The second statement, however, presumes that our perception of the body is fraught and uncomfortable. The body's exigencies, it states, intrude upon our lives, demanding and unwanted. As Elizabeth Hunter realizes in *The Eye of the Storm*, every moment is "roaring rushing you towards incurable illness old age death corruption,"[3] and, indeed, White's fiction emphasizes corporeality and the body's inexorable progression towards death. The functions of the body and its inevitable degeneration, both beyond the control of human consciousness, may leave one disempowered and psychologically severed from somatic experience. Unsurprisingly, then, the phrase "the abject dictatorship of the flesh" *personifies* physicality, thus distancing it from subjectivity and emphasizing the conceptual division between mind and body.

1　Patrick White, *The Living and the Dead*, 146.
2　White, *The Living and the Dead*, 263.
3　Patrick White, *The Eye of the Storm*, 528.

Further, its diction presciently, if unwittingly, gestures towards Julia Kristeva's theory of abjection as developed in her seminal *Powers of Horror*. In positing the construction of the seemingly self-sufficient subject in opposition to corporeality, Kristeva's writing has much in common with White's fiction, which, despite the distancing of the subject from the body that the aforementioned phrase implies, constantly interrogates the arbitrary boundary that separates subjectivity from the corporeal, simultaneously postulating the construction of the self upon the subject's shifting relation to corporeality.

As indicated earlier, Kristeva's theory of abjection informs this book, which focuses throughout on White's exploration and subversion of the dualism of self and flesh. This chapter thus sets the terms of the study by outlining Kristeva's theory and then elaborating on abjection as an affective dimension in White's writing. It therefore provides a primary theoretical focus while indicating, mostly through a reading of *The Living and the Dead*, the mode of interpretation I undertake throughout. The chapter both tightens and widens its focus on abjection by comparing it to the seemingly contrasting urge towards compassion also frequently expressed in White's fiction. I argue that both affects relate to the significance White ascribes to the dissolution of identity and thus to the transcendental or mystical focus of his work. Abjection involves the subject's rejection of corporeality in the consolidation of the image of the self, a disavowal White's writing associates with narcissism and prejudice. Compassion, by contrast, requires the subject's acceptance of the shared corporeality of self and other, an acknowledgement opening the self to communal pathways of affective interaction. Specific characters in White's oeuvre are required to accept the body at moments in which their inclination towards abjection is strongly evident. This imperative is extended to the reader, who is simultaneously called upon to engage with White's poetics of corporeality.

The 'Dictatorship' of Abjection

Kristeva's term 'abjection' describes the primitive psychogenic process which initiates and maintains the construction of subjectivity. Her theory outlines the phase of development in which the child acquires language and begins to take its place as a speaking subject within the symbolic order. For Kristeva, this involves the consolidation of a "clean and proper"[4] self upon the tenuous repudiation of those corporeal aspects (or abjects) considered disorderly, unacceptable, and anti-social. This process occurs when the child begins to

---
4 Julia Kristeva, *Powers of Horror*, 8.

distinguish between the inside and the outside of the body and to differentiate the self from the other, the subject from the object—oppositions necessary to the conception of the body as a unified whole and the linking of subjectivity to the body's form and limits. According to Kristeva, subjectivity is based on the exclusion of the disorderly elements of corporeal existence, elements she terms "abject." The condition or process of abjection requires a response of violent disgust, separating the self from abject physicality.

Kristeva's categories of the abject include bodily products, abhorred foodstuffs, the corpse, and, for the infant (although the negative association, according to Kristeva, remains throughout life), the maternal body. These examples disturbingly and ambiguously cross the symbolic border of the body separating the internal from the external, thus troubling the image of a sealed-off, self-enclosed subjectivity deeply implicated in the image of the body. The state of abjection, a condition of horror in response to physicality, is defined by ambiguity: as Kristeva explains, the abject is that which does not "respect borders, positions, rules," and that which "disturbs identity, system, order" (4). It must be defined as "radically separate [and] loathsome" (2), not because it is necessarily unclean in and of itself but because it threatens the constructed and arbitrary borders maintaining neat, enclosed subjectivity. As Elizabeth Grosz explains, "the subject must have a certain, if incomplete, mastery of the abject; it must keep it in check and at a distance in order to define itself as a subject."[5] The abject cannot finally be disposed of: abjection thus exposes the subject's control over the disorderly elements of corporeality as provisional and threatened. It therefore involves a horrifying confrontation with that which the subject has jettisoned in order to consolidate a stable sense of self within the symbolic order, a confrontation with that aspect of the self which therefore threatens to undo the very notion of 'self'. It is, as Grosz maintains, the "unspoken of a stable speaking position, an abyss at the very borders of the subject's identity, a hole into which the subject may fall."[6] The abject is "opposed to I":[7] it is "radically excluded and draws me toward the place where meaning collapses" (2), where subjectivity dissolves.

According to Kristeva, then, the borders of the body symbolically function as the borders of the self. Yet, as the theory of abjection contends, these boundaries cannot be definitively maintained. Instead, they remain porous, opening the inside of the body to the outside world. At the borders of the self, the

---

5   Elizabeth Grosz, "The Body of Signification," in *Abjection, Melancholia and Love: The Work of Julia Kristeva*, ed. John Fletcher & Andrew Benjamin (London: Routledge, 1990): 87.
6   Grosz, "The Body of Signification," 87.
7   Kristeva, *Powers of Horror*, 1.

abject, despite being something that the subject attempts to disavow, remains fundamentally part of it. Excrement, for example, is discharged from the inside of the body to the outside, becoming 'other' in the process, an otherness cemented by our understanding of waste as an object of revulsion—as abject (or, by etymology, 'cast/thrown off'). The problem inherent in such othering is that excrement is a part of the body that can never be finally expelled. It crosses the boundaries of the body, from the inside to the outside, but also defies such boundaries because it exists both internally and externally:

> It is something rejected from which one does not part, from which one does not protect oneself as from an object. Imaginary uncanniness and real threat, it beckons to us and ends up engulfing us.
> *Powers of Horror* 4

The abject incites a paradoxically horrifying desire because there is something compelling about loosening the shackles of the self. This remains terrifying, however, and so abjection is a state of ambiguity, beckoning yet repellent. As Kristeva argues, it "beseeches, worries and fascinates desire, which, nevertheless, does not let itself be seduced. Apprehensive, desire turns aside; sickened, it rejects" (1). The violent-disgust response whereby an aspect of the self becomes other to the self corresponds, as the example of excrement illustrates, to the notion of rigidly defined bodily boundaries separating the 'inside' from the 'outside'.

Subjectivity is thus implicated in an image of an ideally discrete and orderly body, its thresholds symbolizing the tentative borders of identity. However, the image of the body is merely an abstraction, a construction emptied of the affect, viscerality, sensations, consumptions, and excretions of the corporeal. Significantly, as Michael Bernstein observes, abjection is a process thus dependent upon "a fissure in the relationship between consciousness and corporality that arises at the most elemental levels of human response to the facts of physical existence itself."[8] Such a fissure is first evident during the mirror stage in infancy, famously theorized by Jacques Lacan. Lacan posits an interim phase between the infant's primitive, chaotic, and engulfing experience of bodiliness and its eventual acquisition of a social identity founded in language. It is during the mirror stage, when the infant first imaginatively identifies with its own reflection, that the Imaginary arises—one of Lacan's three "orders" or dimensions of the psyche, along with the Symbolic and the Real. The Imaginary is

---

8   Michael Bernstein, *Bitter Carnival: Ressentiment and the Abject Hero* (Princeton NJ: Princeton UP, 1992): 28.

the order of ego-formation, and, as the infant's experience of its mirror image attests, it emerges from the human fascination with form.⁹ In his explication of the development of the Imaginary, Lacan expands on Freud's theory that "the ego is first and foremost a bodily ego: it is not merely a surface entity, but is itself the projection of a surface"; in other words, it may be regarded as a "mental projection of the surface of the body" and is thus a reflection of the body as seen from without.¹⁰ Lacan contends that when the infant first perceives itself in the mirror, it is enraptured by the vision of a unified self—its body as others see it. This becomes its first conception of its identity: an image of the body in totality. The image, however, is discordant with the infant's experience of a diffuse self, consisting of a series of disjointed body parts and movements. Lacan explains:

> The *mirror stage* is a drama whose internal thrust is precipitated from insufficiency to anticipation—and which manufactures for the subject, caught up in the lure of spatial identification, the succession of phantasies that extends from a fragmented body-image to a form of its totality that I shall call orthopaedic—and, lastly, to the assumption of the armour of an alienating identity, which will mark with its rigid structure the subject's entire mental development.¹¹

Through the mirror image, the child's sensation of a fragmented body becomes whole through specular identification, and the ego is accordingly consolidated. As Elizabeth Grosz makes clear,

> through the fantasy of a cohesive, stable identity, facilitated by its specular identification with its own image, [the child] is able to position itself as a subject within the space of its body.¹²

---

9   The Symbolic refers to the register of psychic experience associated with the symbolic order: language, socialization, subjectivity, and the rules governing all. The Real, on the other hand, refers to the order (or disorder) of reality that cannot be captured within symbolic understanding. Hence the mirror phase is based on the misrecognition of the Real within a substitutive specular identity. This "Imaginary" misrecognition constitutes an intermediary phase between the pre-symbolic Real and the Symbolic. In its concern with positing experience beyond the limits of language, White's writing gestures towards the Lacanian Real.

10 Sigmund Freud, "The Ego and the Id" ("Das Ich und das Es," 1923), in *The Standard Edition of the Complete Psychological Works of Sigmund Freud*, vol. 19: *The Ego and the Id and Other Works (1923–1925)*, gen. ed. James Strachey (London: Hogarth, 1961): 26.

11 Jacques Lacan, *Écrits: A Selection*, tr. Alan Sheridan (New York: W.W. Norton, 1977): 4.

12 Grosz, "The Body of Signification," 82.

Identity thus comes into being via the *misrecognition* of a fictive, external 'self' that represents a coherence that the subject can never attain; this is the "distortion of the human body which is the human ego."[13] Because of the child's misrecognition of its image as itself, and hence the development of an "alienating identity,"[14] self and ego can never be unified, the ego remaining a merely imaginary identity prone to slippage and the threat of incoherence. However, via the specular identity of the Imaginary, the infant's first instance of symbolization, the child is prepared for the acquisition of language, and the concurrent establishment of a social identity. Simultaneously, it replaces its sense of itself as a series of corporeal sensations with an image of the body that is severed from the experience of physicality. This *image* of the body—unified, external, and for the first time categorized according to sex—cannot express the *sensations* of the body with their associations of internal fragmentation, disorder, and desire. As Grosz argues, "the illusion of a corporeal coherence" belies "the child's own lived experience."[15] According to Lacan, our first example of symbolization, then, involves a misrecognition of a reflected image of the body as the self, a reflection that does not cohere with experience and sensation, suggesting, therefore, the difficulties inherent in representing the body as it is felt and experienced. The subject will remain "incapable of adequately integrating the fragmented source of its corporeality provided by its senses with the completion, cohesion and totalization of the visual image of the body."[16] The physical, lived body thus remains 'other' to symbolization, eventually seeming even "to resist powerfully textual representation."[17] As I will go on to argue, White's favored characters frequently experience redemptive, visionary moments wherein their social identity—their sense of their reflected self—is subject to dissolution. In these moments, as the image of the body dissolves, the specificities of corporeality (as far as they can be represented, and White's writing points up the difficulties of such representation) are increasingly emphasized. White's fiction posits the sublimity of corporeality, which foregrounds fragmentation and strains the representational capacity of language.

Kristeva's theory, growing out of Lacan's, recognizes that subjectivity is threatened by the incoherence of corporeal experience. However, it also concedes that subjectivity emerges in response to a corporeality that therefore necessarily constitutes it. The violent response of abjection is the defensive

---

13   Norman O. Brown, "The Excremental Vision" (1959), in *20th Century Literary Criticism: A Reader*, ed. David Lodge (London: Longman, 1986): 518.
14   Lacan, *Écrits*, 4.
15   Grosz, "The Body of Signification," 82.
16   Grosz, "The Body of Signification," 83.
17   Daniel Punday, *Narrative Bodies*, viii.

attempt of subjectivity to maintain itself in the face of disorderly corporeality, but the conditions of its dissolution remain central to its existence. The subject's disgusted reaction to the "abject dictatorship of the flesh"[18]—the perception of a corporeal threat to the notion of seemingly "clean and proper" consciousness—requires that it "disavow part of itself in order to gain a stable self."[19] This paradox of rejecting aspects of the self to cement a static notion of subjectivity means, as Kristeva argues, that that which is expelled when the subject takes its place in the symbolic order is never fully jettisoned: it is "something rejected from which one does not part."[20] Indeed, it is an aspect of the self from which one *cannot* part. Accordingly, it "hovers at the border of the subject's identity, threatening apparent unities and stabilities with disruption and possible dissolution."[21] The abject is expelled yet remains consistently central to identity. Abjection, then, is a "reaction to the recognition of the impossible but necessary transcendence of the subject's corporeality,"[22] rendering corporeality an ambiguous horror that threatens the limits of identity. Hence Kristeva's observation:

> The more or less beautiful image in which I behold or recognize myself rests upon an abjection that sunders it as soon as repression, the constant watchman, is relaxed.
>
> *Powers of Horror* 13

The Constant Watchman: Elyot Standish and the Horror of Corporeality

From the outset of *The Living and the Dead*, the earliest of White's novels that he personally allowed to remain in print, abjection and the "constant watchman" of repression are emphasized in the male protagonist's horror of corporeality and mortality. Critics have called the novel "White's flattest and most trivial work,"[23] but it exhibits thematic concerns essential to his oeuvre. The novel therefore provides a good starting point for a study of abjection in White. The protagonist, Elyot Standish, rejects corporeality and is thus governed

---

18 White, *The Living and the Dead*, 263.
19 Grosz, "The Body of Signification," 86.
20 Kristeva, *Powers of Horror*, 4.
21 Grosz, "The Body of Signification," 87.
22 "The Body of Signification," 87.
23 Peter Wolfe, *Laden Choirs: The Fiction of Patrick White* (Lexington: UP of Kentucky, 1983): 50.

by abjection; by contrast, his sister Eden, in her engagement with the body, exemplifies compassion. These two characters, taken together, thus represent deliberately distinct approaches to embodiment in White's writing: rejection (associated with a kind of death-in-life) and acceptance (associated with living).

Elyot Standish embodies the self-denial—in effect, the misrecognition of the self—that White associates with the repudiation of physicality. Life is bodily, and Elyot cannot endure this:

> Contact with the living moment, that you watched in your shirt-sleeves from an upper window, the vague formless moments in the street, made you recoil inside your shirt too conscious of your own confused flesh.[24]

Elyot's vigilance in relation to corporeality is emphasized: he is himself a watchman, protecting himself from the confusion and disorder associated with the material body. While physicality is repulsive to him, he nonetheless unconsciously finds it enthralling.

This aspect of his character is emphasized throughout the novel. Near its beginning, Elyot witnesses a bus crashing into an oblivious drunkard. The episode is an important moment in his characterization: it emphasizes his tendency to hover between rigidly defensive hermetic alienation and the compelling desire to merge empathically with others. Prior to the accident, for example, Elyot has felt an odd sense of identification with this stranger, imagining that he

> might have merged with the drunk, fumbling now in his pocket for the bus fare or else the price of another drink, wondering feebly at the back of those yellow eyeballs if he was really going to vomit, or fall, just fall into a receptive gutter.
> *The Living and the Dead* 9

This transient identification quickly subsides into Elyot's characteristic sense of "remoteness" (10), yet when the shocked bus driver assesses the cause of the accident—"Walkin' with his eyes shut" (11)—the observation again elicits "some connexion" (12). Elyot has indeed shut his eyes—first to the degraded corporeality of the drunkard, and, secondly, to the onset of death. Both disturb him because these are aspects of life that he cannot escape. In particular, the sight of the stranger's blood distresses him: "It trickled out thin and private.

---

24   White, *The Living and the Dead*, 174. Unless otherwise indicated, further page references are in the main text.

No one had any business looking at this stream of blood. But there it was" (11). The exposed bodily fluid, compromising the division between the inside and the outside of the body, and also breaching the conceptual division between himself and the stranger, horrifies Elyot. The sight of blood weakens his sense of himself as a discrete subject gazing upon another individual: aware that his corporeality unites him with the dying man, he is beset with abjection.

Elyot's dread of abject bodiliness is suggested not only descriptively but also stylistically. The narration shifts rapidly and discomfortingly from third to first and second person as he observes the man's mouth, disturbingly magnified in his perception:

> The lips of the man blew in and out. On the blood a glitter of whitish froth. And I am standing here for what, you asked, for the buried moment, for that second of connexion on the kerb that broke too easily.
> *The Living and the Dead* 11

This rapid transition indicates Elyot's disturbance and hasty attempt to distance himself from his own discomfiture—a seeming quirk in White's style therefore dramatizes the character's divided responses. Second, it erodes the division between the narrator and the reader: Elyot's awareness of the unifying inevitability of death is shared with the reader, who is implicated in the abrupt appearance of the pronoun *I* and directly addressed with the pronoun *you*. Lastly, it dramatizes the crisis of identity evoked by a sudden and horrifying confrontation with death.

Such apparent idiosyncrasies of style as free indirect discourse and the second person voice thus relate to the importance of abjection. Implicit in this prose on the borderline between self and other is Elyot's very real concern with repudiating what is disturbing to him. As he walks away from the accident, his fear of death threatens to surface and overwhelm him:

> Try as his conscience might to raise the dead, the dead continued to lie with folded hands. It was quite remote. But he continued to feel sick. Something had lodged itself in his stomach, forced downwards by the mind. And it was a struggle to keep it there.
> *The Living and the Dead* 12

The thought of the accident victim will continue to haunt Elyot throughout the novel, and the dying drunkard becomes the literal embodiment of the corporeality and mortality he must face. Elyot cannot dissociate himself from the apparent stranger; instead, he feels himself uncannily splitting as he contemplates his own vulnerability: "the face [of the drunkard] drifted behind his own, its lips blowing outward on unshaped words, trying to resist the shapelessness" (17). This is what Kristeva describes as a "weight of meaninglessness": Elyot is on the "edge of non-existence and hallucination, of a reality that, if [he] acknowledge[s] it, annihilates [him]"[25]

Death Invading Life: The Impossibility of Binary Thinking

Abjection, emphasizing the "edge of non-existence," is not only a reaction to and unconscious rejection of disorderly corporeality but, more fundamentally, an affective awareness, however unconscious, of mortality and death, of the inevitability of non-being. Contrary to critical opinion, *The Living and the Dead* is an important novel in White's oeuvre because, as its title suggests, it engages with the symbolic importance of the body in the text and evinces, early on, White's prevailing concern with dualities (including, most obviously, the duality of life and death). More importantly, however, it illustrates the inevitable dissolution of dualities. A concern with death pervades the novel, most obviously as an analogue for Elyot's mode of living: a grim, enclosed, primly intellectual "devotion to dust." Elyot is the first of White's maligned intellectuals, a character overtly privileging mind over body. This is evident, for example, in a description of his long-running scholarly project, a book on Françoise–Louise de Warens, Jean–Jacques Rousseau's benefactress and mistress:

> There was the monograph he was doing on Mme de Warens. In the searching light of afternoon it seemed sadly irrelevant, one more word from Elyot Standish, its opposition to the solid fact of Mme de Warens, a case of lives and the shadows of lives. There was a warmth and fullness about the life of Mme de Warens, that a Standish, even a Rousseau didn't destroy. There came back vividly, if unattached to any context, the sunlight on bare arms, the frosted road that the feet trod beneath spring trees, somewhere, he felt, the sea.
> *The Living and the Dead* 221

While Elyot finds the body repulsive, he nonetheless yearns for the corporeal dimension of life symbolized by the warm, feminine, and embodied presence of de Warens, a figure resisting the cold stultification of a life in words. She

---

25   Kristeva, *Powers of Horror*, 2.

exists, even in Elyot's mind, as an instance of sunlit physical solidity, a representative of the body exceeding his rationalism.

The notion of the intellect as disembodied—as severed from the living flesh—equates rationalist existence with death. Repeatedly in White's fiction, moreover, reason and rationalism emerge at the expense of wakeful intuition, the latter a gift frequently bestowed upon his most excessively embodied characters. In a letter of 1940, White discusses the title of his forthcoming book:

> I'm thinking of calling the novel *The Living and the Dead*. I'm more and more conscious [...] of people being divided into two categories—the people who are aware and the people who are—well—just dead.[26]

In not recognizing the lives of others, linked as they are to the body and mortality, and in resisting his own physicality, Elyot is himself spiritually 'dead'. Those in the novel who are 'living', however, are those who immerse themselves in the materiality of existence, not only in a celebratory manner, as emphasized by the warm physicality of Mme de Warens, but also in a manner that accepts, along with physicality, the inevitability of its dissolution and decay. These are the characters the novel describes as "positive": Eden (Elyot's sister), Julia Fallon, and Joe Barnett, whose capacity to accept the body, emotion, and the uncertain flux of existence opens them up to compassion.

The novel thus reveals the beginning of a strong tension underpinning most of White's writing: the apparently discrete oppositions constituting dualisms—like the "living" and the "dead," respective metaphors for the emotionally and spiritually alive and moribund—are too thin to support the excesses that undermine them: characters associated with life accept literal death, while characters associated with death are living, albeit insipidly. Moreover, characters may shift between their associations with life or death. Life, White repeatedly suggests, cannot be divided into the static binaries upon which language apparently insists. Nor is identity so easily severed from the flux of the material world. Indeed, the inability of apparently univocal language and discrete identity to sever themselves from a flux of meaning exceeding them is comparable to the image of Elyot's face superimposed upon the face of the drunkard and attempting to resist the shapelessness of words and existence.

The excesses of both words and identity are thus emphasized in White's fiction, driving the texts beyond the strictures that dualism appears to impose upon them and finding their most obvious outlet in the concern with and presentation of corporeality. *The Living and the Dead* exemplifies White's

---

26 Patrick White, *Letters*, ed. David Marr (London: Jonathan Cape, 1994): 29.

understanding of the body as a site of excess coterminous with a kind of textual surfeit that defines his oeuvre. The obsessive concern with and provisionality of identity-construction, which relies on a series of oppositions including self/other and mind/body, characterizes this early novel, as it does White's writing in general. In the pages of *The Living and the Dead*, White works out many of the psychological dynamics and themes that will continue to constitute his fictions.

Importantly, death is not merely a trope for existential torpor in the novel. Literal death is a theme to which the text returns; thus, the body in its own right, in its materiality and not merely existing in White's fiction as symbol or trope of an emotional or philosophical condition, takes on significance. Sudden reminders of mortality arise to shake characters' complacency—for example, the bus accident described above, or the corpse of a dog from which Eden and Joe later recoil. The description of the latter evokes corporeal horror in the attention that it draws to the obdurate materiality of death: "The guts hung out through the belly fur. The nose was wrinkled in a last shudder of pain" (272). Joe's response to the carcass recalls Elyot's earlier reaction to the dying drunkard:

> Done for. The festoon of helpless guts torn out like the last existing privacy. The dog disgusted him, but he had to look, as if it had a bearing on himself, the sickness in his own stomach. He made himself look [...]. Man was born to this, no other dignity [...]. But there was a dignity he was jealous of, his own body, his privacy of thought. This was what made him tremble when he [...] saw the body of the dead dog.
> *The Living and the Dead* 270

This, of course, is another instance of abjection: Joe's disgust and nausea arise from the "bearing" that the corpse of the dog has "on himself." Indeed, its mirroring of his mortal condition bears down upon him relentlessly, the finality of death figured in the certainty of the phrase "Done for." Joe steps back in horror, associating his body image and his sense of self in his desire to protect his "own body, his privacy of thought," but the dog confronts him with the notion of the fallibility of the border between self and other, inner and outer, human and animal. As Elizabeth Grosz observes, the abject is an "insistence on the subject's necessary relation to death, to animality, and to materiality, being the subject's recognition and refusal of its corporeality."[27] Joe's response here, moreover, reveals an important aspect of the theme of abjection in White's

---

27 Grosz, "The Body of Signification," 89.

writing—a compassionate ethic revealing the equivalence of all (human) beings in relation to death: "Man was born to this, no other dignity."

Later in the novel, other deaths occur, including those of significant characters such as Catherine Standish and Joe Barnett. These deaths force others into further recognition of mortality, acts of horrified acknowledgement that open an abyss at the centre of existence, swallowing subjectivity and exposing the meaninglessness at the heart of symbolization. This is evident when Elyot scrutinizes the face of his mother Catherine's corpse toward the end of the novel:

> It had the simplicity that was still impossible to grasp, the immensity or simplicity, it was all one, in front of which man wavered, did not completely understand. Soon people would begin to say the kind of things they say about death, to wallow in their own sympathy, or shudder at their own repulsion. But death was a silence best left intact. Dying and death, he said. Dying. It did not fit the mouth.
> *The Living and the Dead* 335–336

Again, dichotomies and borders are emphasized as eroding. Elyot experiences "immensity" and "simplicity" simultaneously. Further, meaning eludes him in his inability to "completely understand," just as the uncertainty of subjectivity is foregrounded in the description of "man waver[ing]." Language, moreover, cannot contain or represent this experience: dying, indeed, does not "fit the mouth" (a double play on materiality: his mother's mouth/lips do not look as though she is dead; the very word 'dying' cannot be formed by Elyot's own mouth/lips). *The Living and the Dead*, then, foregrounds the impossibility of denying the body along with the denial of death, ironically suggesting that such repudiation is in fact the rejection of life in its totality.

White's characters, always on the edge of an abyss of meaninglessness paradoxically linked to a plethora of sublime, inarticulable meaning, are frequently reminded of the limits of their body and identity in relation to death, which intrudes as a horror not simply limited to the future but perpetually underlining the present. In *Voss*, for example, Laura discovers her servant Rose Portion's corpse at a moment in which the vigor and excitement of her youthful energy are replaced by her sudden realization of its inevitable decline:

> the girl who had arrived breathless, blooming with expectation and the roses she had pinned at her throat, was herself turned yellow by the hot wind of death. She was chafing her arms for some time beside the bed.

> She was gulping uglily, and touching the poor, living hair of the dead woman, her friend and servant.
>
> *Voss* 234

Such examples of death invading life underscore White's interest in relating death to the living subject. For the most part, his descriptions of death are focalized through the consciousness of a living character confronted with a sense of abjection that is sometimes related to a sense of sacred sublimity, a merging of self and other that White identifies not only with horror but also with love. At Rose Portion's funeral, Laura's proximity to the "terrible body of the dead woman, with its steady nostrils and its curved hands" (235), allows her to experience a temporary dissolution of the self:

> it had been exhilarating to know that terrestrial safety is not assured, and that solid earth does eventually swirl beneath the feet. Then when the wind had cut the last shred of flesh from the girl's bones, and was whistling in the little cage that remained, she began even to experience a shrill happiness, to sing the wounds her flesh would never suffer. Yet such was their weakness, her bones continued to crave earthly love, to hold his skull against the hollow where her heart had been. It appeared that pure happiness must await the final crumbling, when love would enter into love, becoming an endlessness, blowing at last, indivisible, indistinguishable, over the brown earth.
>
> *Voss* 235

The shattering awareness of death involves the temporary relinquishment of the provisional self. From such a state, Laura must "resume [...] her body" (235), or at least her socialized self, which defends against the dissolution that the above passage describes.

Ironically, in confronting the body, Laura apparently loses her body: the inevitability of death that Rose's corpse presents to her encourages her experience of transcendence precisely because it ruptures her sense of identity—the *image* of the body protected from corporeality. Moreover, as Laura's experience suggests, subjectivity is defined by a feeling of overwhelming lack. The circumscription of the self, which involves the erection of protective defences against the omnipresence of death and corporeality, isolates and disconnects it. Consequently, she longs to be permanently unified with the world and with others, a desire common to many of White's characters. Her yearning renders her "hollow," longing not only for an "earthly" relationship with Voss, which would allow her to lose herself in her relation to another person, but also for the dissolution that will render her "indivisible" and "indistinguishable" from the external world at large. This "final crumbling" is the experience of "love" as "endlessness."

Yet, while White's characters may strain toward such moments of revelation, they also resolutely resist them. Many, for example, shore themselves up against the ever-present threat of mortality, and thus erect a tenuous conceptual shield between their living selves and death. Kristeva, as we have seen, argues that abjection is the violent attempt to repudiate that which disturbs boundaries. She posits bodily waste—in particular the utmost form thereof, the corpse—as exemplifying the blurring of the boundary between interior and exterior, being and non-being. The corpse is "death infecting life"[28] and therefore the horrifying reminder of the inevitable outcome of our corporeality. It confronts us with the ultimately futile struggle to maintain ourselves as neat entities unsullied by the bodily waste that we expel and from which we turn away. As Kristeva observes, the corpse "does not *signify* death," but *is* death. It swallows up the safe distance created by the distinction between signifier and referent. In its meaningless materiality, it is utterly excessive, devouring the fragile speaking subject and its flimsy signification:

> In the presence of signified death—a flat encephalograph, for instance—I would understand, react, or accept. No, as in true theatre, without makeup or masks, refuse and corpses *show me* what I permanently thrust aside in order to live. These body fluids, this defilement, this shit are what life withstands, hardly and with difficulty, on the part of death. There I am at the border of my condition as a living being. My body extricates itself, as being alive, from that border. Such wastes drop so that I might live, until, from loss to loss, nothing remains in me and my entire body falls beyond the limit—*cadere*, cadaver [...] the corpse, the most sickening of wastes, is a border that has encroached upon everything.
>
> *Powers of Horror* 3

White's fiction thematizes encroaching borders, showing, however, that in confronting the abject, its characters and readers may experience a sense of redemptive integration. This involves the temporary forfeiture of subjectivity and a corresponding dissolution of conceptual structures. Form gives way to formlessness: death reveals that the "solidity of things" is "not assured."[29] While

---

28   Kristeva, *Powers of Horror*, 4.
29   White, *The Tree of Man*, 71.

many of White's characters resist dissolution, like Elyot Standish, who is determined to defend his notion of self against the doubt and flux that threaten to dismantle it, White's "positive"[30] characters differ because they acknowledge the disturbing aspects of existence—most notably death. Like many of White's questing, philosophical protagonists, Elyot, towards the end of the novel, recognizes that he has the "choice of the two ways, of the living or the dead" (305) and, like other denying characters in the novel and in White's oeuvre in general, gravitates toward the latter:

> You wanted instinctively to close the eyes, like Adelaide and Gerald, like Muriel, or the ranks of the red suburban houses, smothered in a plush complacency. Because the alternative, to recognise the pulse beyond the membrane, the sick heartbeat, or the gangrenous growth, this was too much, even at the risk of sacrificing awareness, and the other moments, the drunken, disorderly passions of existence, that created but at the same time consumed.
> *The Living and the Dead* 305

Here, abject bodily imagery—the "sick heartbeat," the "gangrenous growth"—stands in for a wordless horror present beyond a border of protection that characters erect between themselves and this omnipresent threat. The boundary between Elyot's stable self and those objects that threaten it is imaged as a "membrane," soft tissue both permeable and fragile. Thus, even the border that Elyot sets in place to consolidate and stabilize his sense of self bespeaks mortality and fallibility, an awareness that is simply "too much" to fathom or accept. Equally threatening, however, are the "drunken, disorderly passions of existence" (which retrospectively ascribe a symbolic function to the drunkard of the opening episode)—creative yet importantly and simultaneously *consuming* psychosexual drives. Elyot sees what is for him the fundamental challenge of life: "To recognise the sickness and accept the ecstasy" (305), and to yield to devourment and dissolution in the process.

Recognizing the Sickness and Accepting the Ecstasy: Perversity, *Jouissance*, and Sublimity

In its drive toward this recognition and acceptance, White's writing flouts the "Prohibition and Law" Kristeva views as "necessary if that perverse interspace

---

30   White, *The Living and the Dead*, 12.

of abjection is to be hemmed in and thrust aside."[31] In this respect, it is a literature of perversity that "acknowledges the impossibility of Religion, Morality, and Law," that "takes advantage of them, gets round them, and makes sport of them" (16). White, like the modern authors of Kristeva's focus in *Powers of Horror* (Dostoevsky, Lautréamont, Proust, Artaud, Kafka, and Céline), is "fascinated by the abject, imagines its logic, projects himself into it, introjects it, and as a consequence perverts language—style and content" (16). Moreover, in its articulation of the sacred, White's fiction engages with another aspect of modern literature that Kristeva identifies when she writes of literature as a mode of "secular religion" (17):

> The various means of *purifying* the abject—the various catharses—make up the history of religions, and end up with that catharsis par excellence called art, both on the far and near side of religion. Seen from that standpoint, the artistic experience, which is rooted in the abject it utters and by the same token purifies, appears as the essential component of religiosity.
> *Powers of Horror* 17

Literature is a means of safely confronting the abject, and, in this confrontation, provides a way of purifying it. The engagement of White's fiction with abjection constitutes the 'religious' or 'sacred' dimension of his writing, contributing to his characters' fleeting transcendence of their identity. In White, "recognis[ing] the pulse beyond the membrane"[32] indeed imparts to his characters and, by extension, his readers a prevailing sense of liberation, redemption, and ecstasy achieved by confronting the unspeakable. This is evident, for example, in the passage from *Voss* describing Laura's experience at Rose's funeral and quoted in the previous section. For Kristeva, it is from "straying on excluded ground"—in yielding to the compulsive pull of the abject—that one may experience "jouissance."[33] A Lacanian term notoriously difficult to translate from French into English, *jouissance* may be understood as the combination of "orgasm," "enjoyment," and "lust."[34] However, the term is ambiguous and does not necessarily connote pleasure. Lacan makes this clear in his 1966 lecture "Psychoanalysis and Medicine," quoted in Braunstein:

---

31 Kristeva, *Powers of Horror*, 16.
32 White, *The Living and the Dead*, 305.
33 Kristeva, *Powers of Horror*, 8.
34 Nestor Braunstein, "Desire and Jouissance in the Teachings of Lacan," in *The Cambridge Companion to Lacan*, ed. Jean-Michel Rabaté (Cambridge: Cambridge UP, 2003): 103.

> What I call jouissance—in the sense in which the body experiences itself—is always in the nature of tension, in the nature of a forcing, of a spending, even of an exploit. Unquestionably, there is jouissance at the level at which pain begins to appear, and as we know it is only at this level of pain that a whole level of the organism, which could otherwise remain veiled, can be experienced.[35]

Jouissance, then, is the engulfing of the subject by the body, an experience comparable to sublimity or psychosis. As Kristeva writes, it is a time of "oblivion and thunder, of veiled infinity and the moment when revelation bursts forth."[36] It occurs when the "ego gives up its image in order to contemplate itself in the Other" (9), Lacan's term for radical alterity beyond the illusory otherness of the Imaginary, which traps the subject in the reflected image of a socialized identity. The borders of subjectivity erode, and a sublime ecstasy results. According to Kristeva, both the sublime and the abject dissolve the binary of subject and object: the sublime "has no object either" (12). Instead, it is an overwhelming experience of excess beyond rational comprehension:

> When the starry sky, a vista of open seas or a stained glass window shedding purple beams fascinate me, there is a cluster of meaning, of colors, of words, of caresses, there are light touches, scents, sighs, cadences that arise, shroud me, carry me away, and sweep me beyond the things that I see, hear or think. The 'sublime' object dissolves in the raptures of a bottomless memory. It is such a memory, which from stopping point to stopping point, remembrance to remembrance, love to love, transfers that object to the refulgent point of the dazzlement in which I stray in order to be [...]. I find myself removed to a secondary universe, set off from the one where 'I' am—delight and loss.
>
> *Powers of Horror* 12

The abject and the sublime both yield potentially mystical, self-expanding or self-forfeiting experiences; indeed, the abject *is* sublime, a contention evident in White's representations of corporeality as sacred. We might think, for example, of Theodora Goodman attending church as a schoolgirl, where she sits beneath a stained-glass window depicting St. George and the slain dragon. Flooded by the sunlight filtering through the body of the eviscerated monster, she feels her "soul open[...] and flame[...] with the light that burst[s]

---

35 Braunstein, "Desire and Jouissance," 103.
36 Kristeva, *Powers of Horror*, 9.

through the dragon's wounds."[37] The illumination of corporeality depicted in the "stained glass window shedding purple beams"[38] upon Theodora constitutes one example of her sublime *jouissance*—the engulfment of her rational subjectivity within her corporeality forms one of the novel's persistent themes.

Oddly Physical: Compassion

At the beginning of this chapter, I mentioned that two phrases from *The Living and the Dead* contribute to an understanding of White's treatment of corporeality. The first—the "abject dictatorship of the flesh"[39]—contributes to the argument above. The second—"compassion is oddly physical" (146)—provides one possible explanation for White's emphasis on abjection: the two affects function together as opposing responses to corporeality. Abjection—a response of violent disgust—keeps the threat of physical existence and corruption at bay, while compassion submits to it, dramatizing, moreover, the ethical significance of acknowledging the body, however disturbing to the rational subject this acknowledgement may be. In *The Living and the Dead* (and elsewhere in White's fiction), compassion is represented as a feeling engendering the movement from the 'form' of identity to the *shapelessness* of its dispersal, a noun I have borrowed from the description of Elyot's dread regarding the face of the drunkard drifting behind his own (17). For White, compassion occurs when the subject succumbs to the supposed dictatorship of the flesh—thereby intuiting the body as a fundamental aspect of the self—and simultaneously experiences, via shared corporeality, the essential sameness of 'self' and 'other'.

This is evident throughout White's fiction, but perhaps most notably in *Riders in the Chariot*, in which the novel's four "seeker[s]"[40]—besides their obvious unification in their varying visions of the metaphysical image of the Chariot—are connected in their compassion for each other as physical beings. Recalling Elyot's horror of the blood of the dying drunkard in *The Living and the Dead*, a fascination with blood links two of White's visionaries, Mordecai Himmelfarb the Jew and Alf Dubbo the Aboriginal, characters united, moreover, in their shared compassion and understanding. Himmelfarb cuts his hand:

---

37 White, *The Aunt's Story*, 57.
38 Kristeva, *Powers of Horror*, 12.
39 White, *The Living and the Dead*, 263.
40 White, *Riders in the Chariot*, 103.

> The blood ran out of the wound in long vanishing veils. At moments the effect was strangely, fascinatingly beautiful. [...] So it seemed to appear also to the blackfellow.
> *Riders in the Chariot* 281

Arguably, the moment's beauty inheres in the compassionate understanding of shared embodiment, a beauty underscored by how the "long vanishing veils of blood" in the aesthetic of the body become, via the transformative effects of metaphor, the poetic language of the text.

Critics have not always noted White's emphasis on an aesthetic of corporeal compassion: Brian McFarlane, for example, argues as follows:

> movement towards pity in White is almost always subverted by his obsessive need to underline the physical horror of the flesh—greening, yellowing, purpling, greying, wrinkling, sagging, scarred and rotting.[41]

For White, however, compassion is indeed oddly physical; the focus on the flesh that McFarlane observes is in fact integral to the novel's emphasis on this affect. This emphasis is supported by the imagery of physical integration that foregrounds characters' understandings of each other. At one point the ugly, stunted Mary Hare, as she is described in the novel, encounters the Aboriginal Alf Dubbo:

> Once she had entered through his eyes, and at first glance recognized familiar furniture, and once again she had entered in, and their souls had stroked each other with reassuring feathers, but very briefly, for each had suddenly taken fright.
> *Riders in the Chariot* 79

Mary is able temporarily and metaphorically to 'enter' Dubbo's body because the two are similarly ostracized as a result of their 'unacceptable' physicality. Their shared experience of exclusion allows them to attain visionary empathy. For White, 'entry' into another's subjectivity is premised upon compassion, when characters feel in their own bodies the pain and suffering of another; it is the "catalyst of sympathy" that seems to "destroy the envelopes of personality, leaving the two essential beings free to merge and float."[42] Both

---

41　Brian McFarlane, "Inhumanity in the Australian Novel: *Riders in the Chariot*," *Critical Review* (Melbourne) 19 (1977): 37.
42　Patrick White, *Riders in the Chariot*, 94.

Hare and Dubbo, moreover, are aware of the importance of the body—Hare through her physical immersion in landscape and Dubbo through his understanding of the "bleeding" of corporeality into art. This recognition differentiates White's favored characters (such as Hare and Dubbo) from characters like Elyot Standish, who deny the body and are for the most part consequently associated with a kind of death-in-life. In both *The Living and the Dead* and *Riders in the Chariot*, and in White's fiction as a whole, the compassionate recognition of the constitutive importance of the body is comparable to what results for Kristeva from the relaxation of abjection or repression: the forfeiture of identity. Indeed, the "more or less beautiful image" of the self that Kristeva describes is repeatedly sundered in White's fiction, often to redemptive effect.

The significance of the forfeiture of identity in White has frequently been linked to his interest in a transcendentalism or spirituality that seems to require the severing of soul from body. I want to shift this understanding, however, to suggest that the moments in which White's characters transcend their identities, and seemingly the material world, are in fact deeply imbricated in his close attention to corporeality. In White, examples of the "beautiful image" that characters create of themselves possess significance. Narcissism is one of his primary concerns, figured in his writing as the ego's defence against, first, the corporeality that subjectivity abjects and, secondly, the selflessness associated with compassion. As Kristeva writes, abjection "*is a precondition of narcissism.* It is coexistent with it and causes it to be permanently brittle."[43] Further, she describes it as a "*narcissistic crisis*": abjection is "witness to the ephemeral aspect of the state called 'narcissism,'"[44] precisely because the borders of the self are threatened. White's understanding of the narcissistic crisis of abjection is evident in the ego-driven painter Hurtle Duffield's compulsion to spread excrement over his self-portrait in *The Vivisector*, "smear[ing] all that he repudiated in himself."[45] Here, Hurtle's self-image—and what may be read as either its defilement or, in White's recuperation of the repudiated body, its augmentation—emphasizes the inextricable linking of the subject to its undermining abjects. Narcissism defends against the abject, but it also, as White emphasizes, resists the selfless experience of compassion. As Satendra Nandan observes of White's fiction, moreover, it is only when the "disintegration of the shell of [the] ego" is achieved that the "reach for the infinite begins."[46]

---

43   Kristeva, *Powers of Horror*, 13, emphasis in original.
44   *Powers of Horror*, 13, emphasis in original.
45   Patrick White, *The Vivisector*, 249.
46   Satendra Nandan, "Patrick White: The Quest of the Artist," in *Patrick White Centenary: The Legacy of a Prodigal Son*, ed. Bill Ashcroft & Cynthia vanden Driesen (Newcastle upon Tyne: Cambridge Scholars, 2014): 121.

In *The Eye of the Storm*, Elizabeth Hunter dwells upon the threats to her overweening ego. Existing for the most part in a miasma of self, she lives according to a practical and defensive ethic: "*one can drown in compassion if one answers every call it's another way of suicide.*"[47] Nonetheless, she is eventually drawn into the selfless experience of "love," represented as relational and transcendental in White's fiction, and premised upon the acknowledgement of the constitutive significance of corporeality.[48] Indeed, "love," for White, is a form of "suicide," associated as it is with a merging with 'otherness' that his texts continuously work towards and promote. In this respect, it is comparable to confronting the abject—in fact, as Dorothy de Lascabanes thinks to herself in *The Eye of the Storm*: "Love and disgust are one […] the same shooting pain in both mind and body. Love: she must learn love."[49] Dorothy realizes that love and disgust both bring about a sense of one's potentially uncomfortable interrelation with the external world. Love, however, is the positive acceptance of one's relation to otherness; in vowing to "learn love," Dorothy suggests the preferability of the loss of a "monstrous egotism"[50] to the disgust-response that maintains it. The closing sentences of White's last-published work before his death, *Three Uneasy Pieces*, provide his final words on the subject of love, and on the importance of replacing the narcissistic 'I' with a compassionate 'we', thereby proclaiming a manifesto of sorts:

> I who was once the reason for the world's existence am no longer this sterile end-all. As the world darkens, the evil in me is dying. I understand. Along with the prisoners, sufferers, survivors. It is no longer I it is we
> It is we who hold the secret of existence
> we who control the world
> WE.[51]

White favors an open-ended, loving plurality of experience over the solipsism of the individual will. His fiction, then, is not primarily concerned with "the

---

47 White, *The Eye of the Storm*, 476, emphasis in original.
48 Although I use the term 'transcendental', I would like to temper its connotations of "rising above" the phenomenal world to suggest from this point onward White's focus on a *bodily* transcendentalism or *somatic* spirituality.
49 White, *The Eye of the Storm*, 391.
50 White, *The Aunt's Story*, 229.
51 Patrick White, "The Age of a Wart," in White, *Three Uneasy Pieces* (London: Jonathan Cape, 1988): 58–59.

incurable loneliness of the soul,"⁵² as G.A. Wilkes has argued. While his characters are often isolated and frustrated by their seeming inability to express themselves to others, White's writing, as Bill Ashcroft observes, works towards a "synthesis of self and other."⁵³ This merging of the self with the external world or with other individuals constitutes what Ashcroft and Lyn McCredden have recently identified as the theme of "sacredness" in his work, which may be linked to the prevalence of the theme of love. White does not limit his definition of love, precisely because the word, in his conception, gestures towards a merging of self and other and a dissolution of articulable meaning. As George Core observes, indicating the plenitude of significance associated with the term, the emotion

> in all its manifestations and guises—primitive, civilized, banal, sacramental, narcissistic, familial, mundane, romantic, carnal, platonic, natural, unnatural—is the encompassing theme of White's fiction.⁵⁴

Indeed, White is consistently interested in dissolving the ego to exceed the limits of subjectivity and representation, a striving towards 'otherness' that may best be encapsulated by the term 'love'. This fascination inheres in his many descriptions of the dissolution of identity, a dissolution occurring in moments of imagination and compassion whereby 'self' and 'other' converge and corporeality engulfs the subject. In *The Aunt's Story*, Theodora Goodman, "warmed"⁵⁵ by a letter from her much-loved niece, Lou, walks the streets at night, opened to others and described in a language of intense bodiliness:

> In the streets in which Theodora walked at dusk the sky was restless. Its fever fluctuated. The violet welts and crimson wounds showed. The trams gushed sparks. All along the streets the hour was fusing even the fragments of unrelated lives, almost of Theodora Goodman. The faces clotting at corners were not so very obscure in this light. The veins were throbbing with the same purple.
> *The Aunt's Story* 124

---

52   G.A. Wilkes, "Patrick White's *The Tree of Man*," in *Ten Essays on Patrick White*, ed. G.A. Wilkes (Sydney: Angus & Robertson, 1970): 33.
53   Bill Ashcroft, "More than One Horizon," in *Patrick White: A Critical Symposium*, ed. Ron Shepherd & Kirpal Singh (Adelaide, SA: Centre for Research in the New Literatures in English, 1978): 132.
54   George Core, "Poetically the Most Accurate Man Alive," *Virginia Quarterly Review* 53.4 (Autumn 1977): 766–767.
55   White, *The Aunt's Story*, 124.

The forfeiture of the self is productive in White's writing, particularly when it is linked to a compassionate understanding associated with spiritual illumination. Characters may merge empathetically in moments of loving understanding wherein the physical experience of another informs a mirroring physical response in the self. The episode from *The Living and the Dead* in which Elyot Standish attempts to distance himself from the bodiliness of the drunken stranger may be productively compared to a later episode in the novel, during which his sister, Eden Standish, discovers that "compassion is oddly physical."[56] Her experience vouches for the corporeal basis of empathy and enables her to shed her self-enclosed identity. Eden's experience is entirely contrary to Elyot's—her development from the despised enclosure of her subjectivity to the ecstatic identification with another is evident in the following passage, wherein her experience of this identification involves the acceptance, indeed the metaphorical incorporation, of a seemingly distasteful physicality:

> It made you sick, the business of being Eden Standish [...]. And then against the iron fence, the man in the macintosh, the voice half frozen, half liquid with the words of the Welsh singing, that she heard, not so much her ear, as right inside her, she was listening to it with her whole body, that became the contorted body of the man, sick inside the greenish macintosh. Feeling a scurry of grit on her face, she told herself she was sentimental. She was listening to the singing of a Welsh cripple. She was moved by the sick pallor of the face, the bones of a singing face, and the red inflamed boss that grew from the side of the nose. She could walk, was already walking away[...]. And it went on inside her, the singing, the voices of faces in the street, that flowed past her, melting with her own face. She had seen something for the first time. Her legs trembled when she closed the door, afraid to move from this discovery, a singing and revulsion in her own body.
>
> *The Living and the Dead* 146

Initially sickened by her enclosure within her identity—the "business of being Eden Standish"—Eden feels her body becoming that of the crippled man, and finds herself incorporating his wordless song of anguish and despair. Despite the disgust that she experiences, she feels united with all humanity, to the extent that she imagines her body transforming into his before her face melts into the faces of the crowd through which she is making her way. Eden is thus associated with formlessness: the limits of her body blur with another's, she merges with the crowd, and she 'melts' into humanity. Moreover, she has

---

56   White, *The Living and the Dead*, 146.

"seen something for the first time," suggesting that this unification with others constitutes an epiphanic experience—one of White's moments of visionary illumination. As it is with Eden, White's characters may find the borders of the self dissolving during such instances of compassionate understanding, but they may also deliquesce into the landscape, into music, into death, into what I have termed a "somatic spirituality": subjectivity frequently dissolves into an undefined formlessness or fluidity—the "immensity of shapelessness."[57] In such moments of forfeiture, the inevitable corporeality of existence is emphasized. For White, formlessness is an analogue for flux, incomprehension, death, obliteration, the dissolution of the fragile boundaries of the self, and the ongoing subliminal pulses and processes of the body. It allows, moreover, for the amorphous, conjoining experience of empathy. As Himmelfarb of *Riders in the Chariot* understands, in order to realize "lovingkindness"[58] he must incorporate the experiences of others:

> as all rivers must finally mingle with the shapeless sea, so he might receive into his own formlessness the blind souls of men, which lunged and twisted in their efforts to arrive at some unspecified end.
> *Riders in the Chariot* 204

Such formlessness involves the forfeiture of the ego, the yielding of the bounded body-image, and the empathetic absorption of suffering, a process that is neither comfortable nor pleasurable. Certain characters (such as Elyot Standish), as a result, adhere to the solidity of any sharply delineated, bounded form, which keeps at bay the horror associated with formlessness. However, a preoccupation with form—in particular the defined form of 'self'—also excludes the experience of love or compassion. White's treatment of corporeality incorporates these seemingly incommensurable feelings: the body, while it may horrify, is also a site of redemption.

As Eden's experience attests, it is via the body that White promotes the ethic of empathy existing between self and other. This emphasis upon compassion as physical highlights the affective aspect of his writing. Moira Gatens argues that affect causes us to "question commonsense notions of the privacy or 'integrity' of bodies through exposing the breaches in the borders between self and other evidenced by the contagiousness of 'collective' affects."[59] Indeed,

---

57   White, *The Aunt's Story*, 30.
58   White, *Riders in the Chariot*, 204.
59   Moira Gatens, "Privacy and the Body: The Publicity of Affect," in *Privacies: Philosophical Evaluations*, ed. B. Roessler (Stanford CA: Stanford UP, 2004): 115.

compassion is an excellent example of a feeling that passes between bodies. Eden's experience of the singing crippled man specifically emphasizes the "contagion" of affect: the "contorted body [...] sick inside the greenish macintosh," the "sick pallor of the face," the "bones," and the "red, inflamed boss" suggest that her feeling of empathy—during which she imaginatively transforms into this body—is comparable to the contraction of disease of a kind.

The conceptual connection between emotion and the body has had a long history in Western culture. The 'humoral model', which argued for an excess of one of the body's four fluid 'humors'—black bile, yellow bile, blood, and phlegm—producing the expression of personality traits and a propensity to certain emotions, extended from ancient times into the eighteenth century. In early modern times, it was believed, too, that "love and hate could be transmitted through bodily orifices, either by their emission by route of bodily fluids or via ingestion."[60] These conceptions of personality and emotion attest to the importance of the body to explanations of affect and to affect's 'contagious' movement between embodied individuals. Indeed, they suggest affect's 'fluidity', hence its ability to seep through the borders of the defended self.

The word 'compassion', derived from the term for 'fellow suffering' in the original Latin (*com* and *pati*), itself suggests the contagion of shared feeling. Sophie Ratcliffe notes that *compassion* (so important to the significance White ascribes to the body) is one of a number of cognate terms for *sympathy*, existing alongside *empathy* and *pity*.[61] Yet these terms are not entirely interchangeable. Pity, writes Martha Nussbaum, while initially serving as a synonym for sympathy or compassion, has "recently come to have nuances of condescension and superiority to the sufferer."[62] Perhaps this is why Brian McFarlane, quoted earlier, cannot reconcile "pity" in White with his simultaneous emphasis on the "physical horror of the flesh":[63] White seeks parity between 'self' and 'other' and continuously invokes the body as a 'great leveler' inciting empathy between characters (and reader) rather than the unequal response of pity. Suzanne Keen distinguishes between "the spontaneous, responsive sharing of an appropriate feeling as *empathy*" and "the more complex, differentiated feeling for another as *sympathy*."[64] The spontaneous, visceral response of empathy may give rise to the more complex, cerebral response of sympathy.

---

60   Deborah Lupton, *The Emotional Self* (Thousand Oaks CA & London: Sage, 1998): 74.
61   Sophie Ratcliffe, *On Sympathy* (Oxford: Oxford UP, 2008): 8–9.
62   Martha Nussbaum, *Upheavals of Thought: The Intelligence of Emotions* (Cambridge: Cambridge UP, 2001): 301.
63   McFarlane, "Inhumanity in the Australian Novel," 37.
64   Suzanne Keen, *Empathy and the Novel* (Oxford: Oxford UP, 2007): 4.

Thus, Ratcliffe suggests that a complex sympathy, originating in somatic identification, is required in the construction of social morality. She quotes Isobel Armstrong, who, in turn, cites Adam Smith:

> For Smith our moral sense is derived from being the attentive spectator of the action of others and from the resulting development of judgements which we then apply to our own conduct. But we cannot test the moral validity of anything except 'by changing places in fancy' with the person we are judging: 'we enter as it were into his body, and become in some measure the same person with him, and thence form some idea of his sensations, and even feel something which, though weaker in degree, is not altogether unlike them.' The morality of a society will be created by a series of delicately reciprocal acts of the imagination in which each person is able to call up an 'analogous emotion' in response to the feeling of another and is therefore able to check both his companion's conduct and his own.[65]

According to Smith, the compassion of "entering into another's body" is initially required in the construction of a moral sensibility, a sensibility which is nonetheless quite rational. For White, however, the leap from visceral compassion to sympathetic morality requiring the cognitive checking of one's behavior against another is not really at issue. His characters are arrested by their bodily responses to their environment and to others, reactions which they seldom rationalize, as the example of Eden Standish attests. Indeed, rationality is not exactly sanctioned in White's fiction. Arguably, then, sympathetic understanding and moral response are left to the reader's discretion. If there is a moral message in White's fiction, however, it is the injunction to acknowledge corporeality, for it is in bodily signs and sensations, and in the acceptance of the importance of the body to consciousness, that White's ethics and spiritual philosophy reside.

White's Affective Dimension

So far I have highlighted two affective dimensions of White's writing as they appear in his early novel *The Living and the Dead*: disgust or abjection—which Kristeva describes as a "twisted braid of affects"[66]—and compassion, both

---

65   Ratcliffe, *On Sympathy*, 9.
66   Kristeva, *Powers of Horror*, 1.

experienced as somatic sensations associated in one way or another with the dissolution of the "sterile end-all" or "evil" of enclosed subjectivity.[67] White is an author of affect par excellence. This is due, first, to his emphasis on what he viewed as the necessary transcendence of solipsism and the merging of self and other in moments of shared or celebratory corporeality, and, secondly, to the high pitches of emotional intensity he attains through physical description. In their introduction to *The Affect Theory Reader*, Melissa Gregg and Gregory Seigworth argue that affect is

> found in those intensities that pass body to body (human, non-human, part-body, and otherwise), in those resonances that circulate about, between, and sometimes stick to bodies and worlds, *and* in the very passages or variations between these intensities and resonances themselves.[68]

This is a 'rhizomatic', Deleuzian formulation: indeed, Deleuze notes that the dynamic affective interactions between bodies is fundamental to a definition of the body itself: "A body affects other bodies, or is affected by other bodies; it is this capacity for affecting and being affected that also defines a body in its individuality."[69] Accordingly, Seigworth and Gregg describe affect as an *"in-between-ness,"*[70] defining it thus:

> a palimpsest of force-encounters traversing the ebbs and swells of intensities that pass between 'bodies' (bodies defined not by an outer skin-envelope or other surface boundary but by their potential to reciprocate or co-participate in the passages of affect).[71]

The "force-encounters" and "intensities" passing between bodies are often evident in White's writing. In *Riders in the Chariot*, to cite merely one example, the intensity of hatred between Mary Hare, who resents her father's withholding of love, and Norbert Hare, who despises his daughter's irredeemable ugliness, is described as follows:

---

67   White, "The Age of a Wart," in White, *The Uneasy Pieces*, 58.
68   Gregory J. Seigworth & Melissa Gregg, "An Inventory of Shimmers," in *The Affect Theory Reader*, ed. Gregory J. Seigworth & Melissa Gregg (Durham NC & London: Duke UP, 2010): 1.
69   Gilles Deleuze, "Ethology, Spinoza and Us," in *Incorporations*, ed. Jonathan Crary & Sanford Kwinter (New York: Zone, 1992): 625.
70   Seigworth & Gregg, "An Inventory of Shimmers," 1.
71   "An Inventory of Shimmers," 2.

> their emotions were whirling, the spokes of whitest light smashing, the hooks grappling together, hatefully.
>
> The sweat was running down her body, she could feel, in molten streams. She caught sight of his tightening mouth, and his throat strung with gristle.
>
> *Riders in the Chariot* 71

White is indeed interested in the "ebbs and swells" of corporeal intensities and resonances, consistently relying on the premise that affect is physical. The implication of roiling feeling is important in his depictions of characters often "dehydrated by an excess of emotion both concentrated and suppressed."[72] White's writing seldom describes emotion without homing in on the body itself. In *Riders in the Chariot*, we are told that "intense conviction will sometimes best express itself through the ungainliness of spontaneity."[73] Character affect is for the most part suggested via corporeal signs, sometimes minute and sometimes expressionistically distorted. Harry Heseltine observes that we come to "the inner lives of [White's] characters as much through their hands, their skin, their breathing, as through anything else."[74] Indeed, emotion in White is often concentrated at the surface of the body, and thus, for many of his characters, "only a membrane is stretched between [...] feelings and exposure."[75] Brigid Rooney elegantly articulates the metonymic facility that the skin exhibits in White's writing:

> It is White's habit—consonant with his theatrical modes of representation—to attend to discomforts of the skin, to focus on the bodily surface of characters—their mannerisms, style, prudishness, habits. Tongues and teeth, awkwardly set or clashing, recur in asides, reminding us of characters' physical limits, and ratcheting up the grating tensions of sociability.[76]

What Rooney calls White's "epidermal preoccupation" ensures that "surfaces paradoxically become sites of intensity of feeling."[77] A description of Eadie

---

72   White, *The Twyborn Affair*, 68.
73   White, *Riders in the Chariot*, 14.
74   Harry Heseltine, "Patrick White 1912–1990," *Contemporary Literary Criticism* 69 (1992): 393.
75   White, *Riders in the Chariot*, 371.
76   Brigid Rooney, "Public Recluse: Patrick White's Literary-Political Returns," in *Remembering Patrick White: Contemporary Critical Essays*, ed. Elizabeth McMahon & Brigitta Olubas (Cross/ Cultures 128; Amsterdam & New York: Rodopi, 2010): 15.
77   Rooney, "Public Recluse," 15.

Twyborn with "blotched and raddled, leathery skin constantly boiling over in the past with emotion, resentment, frustration, curdled passion"[78] is one example attesting to the importance of bodily surfaces in White's writing. A description of Ruth Godbold is another: "She blushed red, all over her thick, creamy skin. It could have been blotting paper."[79] I want to add to Rooney's observations by proposing that, in his inscription of emotion on the skin, White suggests the importance of *reading* in the process of gaining empathetic understanding. The body itself becomes a text via which affect is communicated and gleaned. Mary Hare, for example, indicating the importance of a corporeal hermeneutics, notes the "extraordinary, revealing faces of men and women."[80] As a communicant with nature, moreover, she learns to oblige her horse by "studying the quiver of a nostril, the flicker of a muscle, and the varying assertions of silence."[81] Bodily scrutiny is frequently endorsed in White's fiction.

Dirk Klopper's argument for the importance of the body in biography may be extended to the importance of the body in literature generally. Where subjectivity is depicted, what is required is

> a mode of representation that simultaneously internalises the external fact, inscribing it as part of the psychic experience of the subject, and externalises the inner psychic experience, making it discernable and interpretable to the reader. Because it is the body that mediates the relation between external event and inner apprehension, what is required, then, is a way of figuring the body [...].[82]

This description attests to the importance of the body in the communication and sharing of affect. It also postulates an erosion of the dichotomies of inner/outer and mind/body. As Elizabeth Grosz contends,

> Only if the body's psychical interior is projected outwards and its material externality is introjected as necessary conditions of subjectivity, can the dualism of our Cartesian heritage be challenged.[83]

---

78 White, *The Twyborn Affair*, 393.
79 White, *Riders in the Chariot*, 283.
80 *Riders in the Chariot*, 36.
81 *Riders in the Chariot*, 27.
82 Dirk Klopper, "The Body in Biography," *Social Dynamics: A Journal of African Studies* 30.1 (June 2004): 84.
83 Grosz, "The Body of Signification," 82.

Literature reveals this projection and introjection as fundamental conditions of characterization, hence of subjectivity. White's fiction, for example, emphasizes the body's mediating role between 'external' events and environments and 'inner' psychic realities and has, accordingly, adopted a way of figuring the body premised, in particular, on the externalization of internal dynamics. Corporeal descriptions of White's characters are often more psychologically than physically descriptive. Despite the minute physical detailing accorded them, the reader ultimately gathers fragmented impressions of characters' bodies. Rather than describing a consolidated overall body image, White focuses his attention on physical minutiae and corporeal contortions, which correspond at the time to the character's psychological state. For example, Voss's initial warming to Laura Trevelyan, occurring when he recognizes a consonance between her character and his own, is registered via the narrative focus on his hands. He is described as opening up to Laura by "unlocking his bony hands, because the niece [Laura] was also, then, something of a stranger."[84] In *The Tree of Man*, Amy Parker's eyelids emblematize the chasm between herself and her husband: "She was closed, he saw. He was perpetually looking at her eyelids, as she walked or sat with these drawn down, in a dream."[85] In *Riders in the Chariot*, Mrs Jolley, representative of the banality of evil White's fiction associates with the materialistic sprawl of suburbia, reveals her frustration physically: "Mrs Jolley's white teeth—certainly no whiter had ever been seen—were growing visibly impatient. Her dimple came and went in flickers."[86] We are consistently presented, moreover, with such imagery as the "hot, rubbery lumps of […] exasperated lips"[87]—hands, eyelids, pores, throats, teeth, lips, and hair figure the internal realities of White's characters, encouraging the reader to notice the body as the locus of emotional and psychological responses. The implication, therefore, is that these responses are experienced as visceral, as somatic—by the character described, but also by the reader, who, faced with corporeal description, must respond with an awareness of physicality, which is itself an increased physical awareness. Moreover, White's representations of physical minutiae in moments of emotional intensity highlight the experience of embodiment as one of disorder and fragmentation, thereby subverting the choate, unified, and ultimately spurious notion of identity associated with the complete and coherent body image.

---

84 White, *Voss*, 12.
85 White, *The Tree of Man*, 303.
86 White, *Riders in the Chariot*, 51.
87 *Riders in the Chariot*, 393.

Seigworth and Gregg refer to affect as those "visceral forces beneath, alongside, or generally *other than* conscious knowing," the "vital forces" offering "persistent proof of a body's never less than ongoing immersion in and among the world's obstinacies and rhythms, its refusals as much as its invitations."[88] White's fiction deliberately evades "conscious knowing," seeking instead a language of intuition, poetry, suggestion, and bodiliness. Here, rational consciousness relies on the suppression of corporeal instinct and is therefore a symptom of psychic fragmentation. White's fiction bemuses Kristeva's "constant watchman" of repression and recuperates those aspects of existence denied by modern consciousness. Abjection is thus an important focus, along with the contrasting affect of compassion, both emphasized in White's fiction as "oddly physical."

---

88   Seigworth & Gregg, "An Inventory of Shimmers," 1, emphasis in original.

CHAPTER 2

Mind/Body Dualism
History, Modernity, Criticism

> The body is the tomb of the soul.[1]
> if I consider man's body as being a machine...[2]
> Purification is something only the Logos is capable of. But is that to be done in the manner of the *Phaedo*, stoically separating oneself from a body whose substance and passions are sources of impurity?[3]

⁂

The previous chapter discussed Kristeva's theory of abjection, which posits that subjective consciousness emerges in the rejection of corporeality but that subjectivity nonetheless remains provisional and threatened by the body (necessarily part of the self). Abjection (and affect more broadly) thus strongly undermines the dualistic notion that mind and body are separate and distinct, while simultaneously revealing the primitive psychic process that has led to this ongoing dualistic assumption, not only in lived experience but also across the historical trajectory of Western philosophy. This chapter explores the ways in which White's fiction represents, explores, and interrogates this long-running central tenet of Classical and modern philosophy: the ineradicable distinction between mind and body, which it attributes to a humanist egoism constructed as transcendent and superior in relation to the flux of the material world. Frequently, White's writing engages with Western metaphysics' prevailing notion that the mind or soul and body are separate, only to subvert the supposed opposition by emphasizing its antinomies as indissolubly linked.[4] In particular, frequent references to the "soul" or the "spirit" appear

---

1 Plato, *Phaedo*, tr. & ed. David Gallop (Oxford: Clarendon, 1975): 104.
2 René Descartes, *Discourse on Method and The Meditations*, tr. F.E. Sutcliffe (*Discours de la méthode*, 1637; Harmondsworth: Penguin, 1968): 163.
3 Julia Kristeva, *Powers of Horror: An Essay on Abjection*, tr. Leon S. Roudiez (*Pouvoirs de l'horreur: Essai sur l'abjection*, 1980; New York: Columbia UP, 1982): 27.
4 Here I conflate 'mind' and 'soul' not to suggest that the two concepts are necessarily interchangeable, but to argue that Western thought has separated either the 'mind' or the 'soul' from the body, depending on historical context or religious interest. Modern philosophy

to highlight the division, seemingly allowing the subjective 'soul' of White's characters separate status from the objective nature of their body. In *The Eye of the Storm*, for example, human experience is described as comprising the "dichotomy of earthbound flesh and aspiring spirit."[5] Similarly, in *Riders in the Chariot*, characters "struggle and sway inside the column of [the] body,"[6] striving to break free of what they perceive as the "prison of flesh."[7] In *The Tree of Man*, Stan Parker, touching his body, runs his fingers over "what was almost a cage of bones,"[8] and Willie Pringle of *Voss* exemplifies White's spiritually aspiring characters when he desires "escape from the prison of his own skull" and struggles "like an epileptic of the spirit to break out."[9] Yet ultimately such moments of dualism are subverted: "subtract one from two and the answer [will] be nought."[10] White, this chapter argues, emphasizes mind/body dualism because of its radical effect not only upon subjectivity specifically but also upon Western consciousness in general. His fiction reveals this dualism as based on the abjection of corporeality and, in response, elaborates an ethic of compassion and the possibility of somatic spirituality, whereby physicality is accepted to redemptive effect. White thus diagnoses dualism and narcissistic repudiation as deepset problems inherent in Western modernity. His writing responds to this defining psychosocial dynamic, providing a literary working-out of its potential dissolution.

History's Beheadings: Severing the 'Mind' from the 'Body'

The mind/body dualism emphasized yet subverted in White has formed the bedrock of Classical and post-Enlightenment Western thought. Not only has Western philosophy for the most part severed the mind from the body, it has succeeded in creating a hierarchy that has elevated the former at the expense of the latter. Late-twentieth-century and twenty-first-century thinking, including poststructuralism, feminism, postcolonialism, and queer theory, has sought to overturn established binary logic and to reveal the ideological

---

subsequent to Descartes, for example, is more likely to separate 'mind' from body, whereas Classical and Christian thought has been largely interested in the autonomy of the 'soul'.

5   Patrick White, *The Eye of the Storm*, 209.
6   Patrick White, *Riders in the Chariot*, 176.
7   White, *Riders in the Chariot*, 374.
8   Patrick White, *The Tree of Man*, 111.
9   Patrick White, *Voss*, 60.
10 Patrick White, *The Aunt's Story*, 146.

imbalances and inequalities arising from it, as well as its inherent contradictions. Despite these movements, dualism is persistently embedded in Western culture and the aforementioned schools of thought continue in accord with this embeddedness.

The most intractable binary within our philosophical history is that of mind and body, wherein the mind is constructed as superior to its apparent antithesis. As Elizabeth Grosz maintains, this established dualism has resulted in the ongoing perception of the body as "an intrusion on or interference with the operation of mind, a brute givenness which requires overcoming, a connection with animality and nature that needs transcendence."[11] The hierarchical structuring of mind/body dualism is mapped onto other binaries in such a way that 'mind' becomes associated with one pole of the linguistic structure and 'body' with the other. For example, the binaries of male/female and European/Other are inflected with the original dualism of mind/body so that 'male' and 'European' become associated with 'mind' and rationality, and 'woman' and 'Other' are metonymically linked to corporeality with its associations of unreason and disorder. Dichotomous thinking is inherently political: it "necessarily hierarchizes and ranks the two polarized terms so that one becomes the privileged term and the other its suppressed, subordinated, negative counterpart."[12] The negative associations of 'body'—Grosz describes these as "intrusion," "interference," "brute animality," and "nature"—suggest the associations and metaphors used to support prejudices such as sexism and racism. Moreover, they reveal that the complex psychosocial process of abjection is fundamental to Western civilization's elevation of itself, an elevation extended into discourses of oppression. White himself associates narcissism and abjection with power. As Lieselotte informs her lover Wetherby, "you love your power. I can feel it in your mouth in your moments of greatest revulsion."[13] Moreover, Voss's abjection requires that he is "forced to many measures of brutality in defence of himself."[14]

The Western celebration of the mind and denigration of the body can be traced back to the Ancient Greeks. From this point in history, dualistic thinking extended via Christianity into Enlightenment (and post-Enlightenment) modernity, the latter arguably beginning with the influential philosophy of René Descartes. Descartes is reputedly responsible for the modern detachment

---

11   Elizabeth Grosz, *Volatile Bodies: Toward a Corporeal Feminism* (Bloomington: Indiana UP, 1994): 3–4.
12   Grosz, *Volatile Bodies*, 3.
13   White, *The Aunt's Story*, 197.
14   White, *Voss*, 14.

of mind from matter, hence for the proliferation of modern prejudices based on binary logic. His philosophical legacy, however, appears to have originated in Classical times with Plato, who is generally considered to be the founding father of mind/body dualism. Plato viewed the body as the earthbound and insignificant receptacle of the 'incorporeal', 'permanent', and thus 'superior' soul. His *Phaedo* denounces the body as the soul's inescapable prison:

> as long as we possess the body, and our soul is contaminated by such an evil, we'll surely never adequately gain what we desire—and that, we say, is truth. Because the body affords us countless distractions, owing to the nurture it must have, and again, if any illnesses befall it, they hamper our pursuit of that which is. Besides, it fills us up with lusts and desires, with fears and fantasies of every kind, and with any amount of trash, so that really and truly we are, as the saying goes, never able to think of anything at all because of it [...]. [I]f we're ever going to know anything purely, we must be rid of it [...] it's then, apparently, that the thing we desire and whose lovers we claim to be, wisdom, will be ours—when we have died, as the argument indicates, though not while we live. Because, if we can know nothing purely in the body's company, then one of two things must be true: either knowledge is nowhere to be gained, or else it is for the dead; since then, but no sooner, will the soul be alone by itself apart from the body.[15]

Evil, distraction, impediment, disturbance, horror, pollutant, enemy of thought, muddler of knowledge, and opponent of truth—each of these bodily associations is evident in Plato's transcription of Socrates' argument for existence after death. Viewed as the final transcendence of the bodily prison, death gains positive associations; it is only beyond the physical world, in the realm of ideal Forms, that truth is located and reason is pure. Hence Plato's famous comparison of philosophy to the happy condition of death: "the philosopher's occupation," he explains, "consists precisely in the freeing and separation of soul and body."[16] A neo-Platonic impulse, which espouses the same "*soma-sema* (body = tomb) philosophy,"[17] has been ascribed to White, most notably in the critical argument for his dismissal of the body. However, White by no means

---

15   Plato, *Phaedo*, tr. & ed. David Gallop (Oxford: Clarendon, 1975): 11–12.
16   Plato, *The Collected Dialogues*, ed. Edith Hamilton & Huntington Cairns (Princeton NJ: Princeton UP, 1963): 50.
17   Anthony Synnott, "Tomb, Temple, Machine and Self: The Social Construction of the Body," *British Journal of Sociology* 43.1 (March 1992): 82.

denounces the material world, although there may be moments when he appears to do so. Elyot Standish, for example, in his pursuit of a disembodied rationality, is linked to the *unhappy* condition of 'death-in-life' that separates him from the 'positive', body-affirming characters of *The Living and the Dead*. Moreover, White's lack of interest in Platonic forms is frequently evident: as Bill Ashcroft rightly argues, alluding to Himmelfarb's oft-quoted statement, "God is in this table"[18]—"it is [in] *this* table, not any table, not the Platonic idea of table, but the present 'thisness' of material being" that White locates a sense of the sacred.[19] Stan Parker's famous expression of spiritual insight at the conclusion of *The Tree of Man* reflects this faith in the particular:

> I believe in this leaf, he laughed, stabbing at it with his stick. The winter dog's dusty plume of a tail dragged after the old man, who walked slowly, looking at the incredible objects of the earth [...].
> *The Tree of Man* 496–497

> I believe, he said, in the cracks in the path. On which ants were massing, struggling up over an escarpment. But struggling. Like the painful sun in the icy sky. Whirling and whirling. But struggling. But joyful. So much so, he was trembling.
> *The Tree of Man* 497

The specificity of *thisness* is characteristic of embodied existence, which existence cannot definitively be reduced to conceptual categories; indeed, just prior to Stan's enunciations above, he has pointed at his saliva and pronounced it "God," thus implicating corporeality and a sense of the unknowable sacred. As the discussion regarding Lacan's mirror phase in the previous chapter has shown, the lived body and the singularity of physical experience are elided by the body as a concept or an image. Bodily specificity, physical sensation, and corporeal abjects constitute vital components of White's interest in materiality and sacred experience.

For the early Christians, much as for Plato, it was imperative to resist the physical temptations preventing the self from attaining incorporeal spirituality. Frank Bottomley argues that from the outset of Christianity theologians reviled the body as "a sinful mass of flesh, a reminder of the Fallen nature of Man, and a hindrance to the achievement of spiritual purity."[20] Although Saint

---

18   White, *Riders in the Chariot*, 183.
19   Bill Ashcroft, "The Presence of the Sacred in Patrick White," 97, emphasis in original.
20   Frank Bottomley, *Attitudes to the Body in Western Christendom* (London: Lepus, 1979): 3.

Paul may have described the body as a temple, he was also wary of corporeality, which he associated with corruption:

> My inner being delights in the law of God. But I see a different law at work in my body—a law that fights against the law which my mind approves of. It makes me a prisoner to the law of sin which is at work in my body. What an unhappy man I am! Who will rescue me from this body that is taking me to my death?
>
> romans 7: 21–24

Saint Augustine, representing physical desire as the moral impediment to spiritual apotheosis, also conceptualized the body as an enemy. The body, understood by Augustine and others as a hindrance to spiritual purity and Christian morality, became, over time, an object of discipline and control. Ideals of martyrdom, virginity, celibacy, and even self-flagellation were expressed in Christian asceticism, for, as Saint Basil the Great, the founder of Eastern monasticism (and also an historical figure alluded to in *The Twyborn Affair*), expressed it, "The soul is as far superior to the body as heaven is above the earth and heavenly things above those of the earth."[21] In medieval times, Francis of Assisi, somewhat ironically, given his love for animals, would call "his body Brother Ass for he felt it should be subjected to heavy labour, beaten frequently with whips, and fed with the poorest food."[22] "We must hate our bodies with their vices and sins," he wrote,[23] suggesting that his loathing of corporeality was based on his belief in the body's inherent corruption. According to the German theologian and mystic Meister Eckhart (1260–c.1328)—who provides one of the epigraphs to *The Vivisector*—there is "no physical or fleshly pleasure without some spiritual harm."[24]

The Christian ascetics sought spiritual transcendence by confronting the body at its most abject and thereby controlling physical aversion. As if to invert Meister Eckhart's thesis that there can be no physical enjoyment without spiritual injury, Saint Teresa of Avila sought spiritual pleasure within the assault of the senses. She advised the sisters of her order to rid themselves "of love for this

---

21 Synnott, "Tomb, Temple, Machine and Self," 87.
22 Saint Bonaventure, *The Life of Saint Francis* (New York: Paulist Press, 1978): 222.
23 Bonaventure, *Saint Francis*, 70.
24 Meister Eckhart, "About Disinterest," in *Meister Eckhart: A Modern Translation*, tr. & intro. Raymond Bernard Blakney (New York: Harper & Row, 1941): 90, quoted in Charles Davis, *Body as Spirit: The Nature of Religious Feeling* (New York: Seabury, 1976): 35.

body of ours."[25] For Teresa, it was imperative that with "the grace of the Lord we shall gain dominion over the body," for to "conquer such an enemy is a great achievement in the battle of life."[26] Anthony Synnott observes that such mortification of the body required "going against one's 'natural' emotional desires and needs" because this is "necessary for the 'overcoming of self'" required by ascetic worshippers seeking spiritual transcendence.[27] His words recall Kristeva's argument that abjection dissolves subjectivity and is therefore tinged with mystical or sublime experience. Synnott provides two examples of this kind of self-punishing ascetic behavior: Saint Margaret–Mary Alacoque, who cleaned up vomit and diarrhoea with her tongue, and Saint Angela of Fuligno, who described the joy she attained from drinking the water in which she had washed the hands and feet of lepers:

> The beverage flooded us with such sweetness that the joy followed us home. Never had I drunk with such pleasure. In my throat was lodged a piece of scaly skin from the lepers' sores. Instead of getting rid of it, I made a great effort to swallow it and I succeeded. I shall never be able to express the delight that inundated me.[28]

As Synnott argues, "for these ascetics the body is not an instrument of pleasure: the body and the emotions are for the Lord, and both must be controlled."[29] Yet Saint Angela describes her experience of abjection as one of pleasure and delight: in confronting the body and in mastering her disgust, she attains the "overcoming of self" that Synnott suggests is fundamental to spiritual illumination. According to her testimony, there is thus a paradoxical joy to be found in the body at its most repellent. This, as observed in the previous chapter, is what Lacan and Kristeva term *jouissance*, an irrational physical joy and forfeiture of the self that corresponds to the engulfing of the subject by the body. White's fiction repeatedly harnesses this sacred dissolution of the 'self' into corporeality.

Despite the importance of the binary logic of Classical and Christian thought, mind/body dualism is generally thought to have become most potently influential with the rise of modernity. Changes from the sixteenth century

---

25 Teresa of Avila, *The Way of Perfection*, tr. E. Allison Peers (*El camino de perfección*, 1583; Garden City NY: Doubleday Image, 1964): 90.
26 Teresa of Avila, *Perfection*, 97.
27 Synnott, "Tomb, Temple, Machine and Self," 91.
28 In Synnott, "Tomb, Temple, Machine and Self," 91.
29 Synnott, "Tomb, Temple, Machine and Self," 91.

onwards, coinciding with the emergence of modernity, profoundly altered the ways in which the body was viewed. Bakhtin explores these changes in *Rabelais and His World*, arguing for modernity's distancing of itself from the joyful, grotesque, and carnivalesque corporeality defining the Middle Ages and particularly evident in medieval festivals. In Western cultures there was a growing immersion in self-consciousness about the body and its products, along with stricter social regulation of the body. Correspondingly, the self was associated with interiority, an 'inside' set up in binary opposition to the 'outside' world of society and materiality. As Francis Barker, Norbert Elias, and Michel Foucault have shown, this resulted in the subject's gradual "self-censoring":[30] voluntary self-control and bodily restraint became the norm. In his influential study of the emergence of modernity, *The Civilizing Process*, Norbert Elias argues that modernity coincided with the body's increasing privatization and invisibility. He analyzes the emergence of shame and embarrassment that began in the sixteenth century in relation to bodily functions. Focusing on the notion of *civilité*, or public bodily propriety, he posits that modes of civilized behavior were acts of self-control and that personal control largely involved regulation of corporeality. Restraining bodily functions, moderating one's facial expressions, observing strict table manners, and wearing 'appropriate' dress (this latter, in its broadest manifestation, taking the form of sumptuary laws) all became increasingly important. The body was now no longer simply a vessel of temptation and corruption 'containing' the more important soul, but was also potentially responsible for 'betraying' its owner and causing public shame and embarrassment. Yet again, albeit apparently for different reasons, it needed to be brought to order.

With the advent of the 'civilized self' and the attendant need on the part of the individual to quash his or her association with the excesses of corporeality, it is appropriate that the theory of the radical division between mind and body, although evident in Classical and Christian thought, should reach its apex during the seventeenth century in René Descartes' philosophy. Descartes distinguished the *res extensa* (material substance, or the body in space and time) from the *res cogitans* (the thinking substance, or the enclosed and self-sufficient mind). A scientist and mathematician, he revered mathematical reasoning as a method that could yield irrefutable proofs. His philosophy,

---

30   See Francis Barker, *The Tremulous Private Body: Essays on Subjection* (London: Methuen, 1984); Norbert Elias, *The Civilizing Process*, tr. Edmund Jephcott (*Über den Prozeß der Zivilisation*, 1939; tr. 1984; Oxford: Blackwell, 1994); Michel Foucault, *Discipline and Punish: The Birth of the Prison,* tr. Alan Sheridan (*Surveiller et punir: Naissance de la prison*, 1975; Harmondsworth: Penguin, 1991).

accordingly, was based on his desire to attain unassailable certainty through a dualism derived from a philosophical project that subjected humankind's apparent certainties to doubt in the hope that only the indubitable would remain. Through doubting bodily sensations and perceptions, Descartes concluded that they were indeed unreliable: while he could imagine himself without a body, he could not imagine himself without consciousness, by virtue of the fact *that he imagined*:

> I had persuaded myself that there was nothing at all in the world: no sky, no earth, no minds or bodies; was I not, therefore, also persuaded that I did not exist? No indeed; I existed without doubt, by the fact that I was persuaded, or indeed by the mere fact that I thought at all.[31]

According to Descartes, then, the certainty and self-sufficiency of thought reveal the mind and body as two distinct entities:

> from the mere fact that I know with certainty that I exist, and that I do not observe that any other thing belongs necessarily to my nature or essence except that I am a thinking thing, I rightly conclude that my essence consists in this alone, that I am a thinking thing, or a substance whose whole essence or nature consists in thinking. And although [...] I have a body to which I am very closely united, nevertheless, because, on the other hand, I have a clear and distinct idea of myself in so far as I am only a thinking and unextended thing, and because, on the other hand, I have a distinct idea of the body in so far as it is only an extended thing but which does not think, it is certain that I, that is to say my mind, by which I am what I am, is entirely and truly distinct from my body, and may exist without it.[32]

Of interest in the above passage is Descartes' emphasis on the thrice-repeated word "distinct." Quite obviously, the separation of mind from body requires the construction of concepts that must remain sequestered from each other. White's fiction repeatedly interrogates the binaries of discrete categories, including that of the "distinct" and the "amorphous," binary oppositions that are often figured as images of form and flux, correlating respectively with images of ego and corporeality. Form in White implies the solidity and distinction of

---

31   René Descartes, *Discourse on Method and The Meditations*, tr. F.E. Sutcliffe (*Discours de la méthode*, 1637; Harmondsworth: Penguin, 1968): 103.
32   Descartes, *Discourse on Method*, 156.

entities, but it is perpetually threatened by dissolution owing to the greater prevalence of flux and excess. It is worth recalling, for example, Chapter 1's discussion of Elyot Standish: his fear (common to body-denying characters in White) of "vague formless moments,"[33] and his constant desire to shore up his sense of self by ineffectually "resist[ing] the shapelessness" (17) that besets him in his encounters with abject corporeality. Indeed, the separation of subjectivity into a mind *distinct* from the body and remaining a *distinct* entity in itself becomes the focus of White's strident criticism throughout his fiction, but particularly in *Voss*, where the eponymous protagonist is characterized by, and critiqued for, his identification with the *cogito* and its attendant associations of disembodiment. Voss's love-interest and feminine mirror-image, Laura, is similarly initially associated with the rationalism and mathematical logic of Cartesian consciousness:

> She did believe [...] most palpably, in wood, with the reflections in it, and in clear daylight, and in water. She would work fanatically at some problem [...] just for the excitement of it, to solve and know [...]. [H]er mind seemed complete.
> *Voss* 9

Despite their belief in the completion and self-sufficiency of the mind, both Voss and Laura, through a series of trials associated with Voss's physical journey through the Australian outback, are confronted with the need to acknowledge the body's significance to subjectivity, and hence the impossibility of maintaining the limits of an 'incorporeal' rational subjectivity when faced with the exigencies of corporeality, a theme that dominates in White's oeuvre.

Descartes' philosophy inaugurated a tradition of thought premised on the notion of the *cogito*, or rational consciousness, and its separation from the physical world: his writings influenced rationalist philosophy and the emergence of Enlightenment thought. The Enlightenment, which instituted changes in philosophy beginning in the late-seventeenth century and continuing into the eighteenth, has in retrospect become synonymous with the advent of modernity. Immanuel Kant, the giant of Enlightenment philosophy, proclaimed in his *Critique of Pure Reason* that various mental forms or categories must exist within the perceiving subject in order to make sense of the external world. These categories constitute the "unity of [...] apperception I likewise entitle the transcendental unity of self-consciousness, in order to indicate the

---

33   White, *The Living and the Dead*, 174.

possibility of *a priori knowledge* arising from it."³⁴ A-priori knowledge, constituting the "transcendental ego," brings the world into being in consciousness via rational concepts. Thus, according to Kant's transcendental idealism,

> if I remove the thinking subject, the whole corporeal world must at once vanish because it is nothing but a phenomenal appearance in the sensibility of ourselves as a subject and a mode of its representations.³⁵

According to Kant's philosophy, we can never directly know "'things-in-themselves', because we process sensory data through pre-existing mental categories."³⁶ For Kant, there is therefore an unbridgeable gap between the physical world and reason. Reason, moreover, equates to freedom in his philosophy and is entirely liberated from immersion in the physical world, a world that simply cannot exist (to us) without it. Such thought is patently dismissed in White, where the specificity of the material world and a "mysticism of objects"³⁷ exceeding human consciousness are foregrounded. Indeed, as Cecil Hadgraft argues, White deploys "at its fullest his capacity to snare, as far as words may do, *das Ding an sich*, the thing in itself."³⁸

Enlightenment thought not only obliterated the body and the material world in favor of a-priori mental concepts and reasoning, but, as Deborah Lupton observes, it "built on the concerns of the Protestant Reformation in turning away from tradition, 'irrationality' and 'superstition' and towards 'scientific' and 'reasoned' thought in the quest for human progress."³⁹ From the Enlightenment perspective, the body was associated with 'irrationality' and viewed as an enemy of reason that required discipline and control. Moreover, the Enlightenment movement away from religion relegated spiritual thinking to the realm of the 'superstitious'. White's fiction, in its critique of modernity, is concerned with two related interests: bringing significance back to the body and recuperating the sense of metaphysical meaning lost to the secular world of twentieth-century modernity. Most rebellious in the face of modern philosophy is his location of metaphysical value *within* the physical world

---

34 Immanuel Kant, *The Critique of Pure Reason*, tr. Norman Kemp Smith, intro. Howard Caygill (*Kritik der reinen Vernunft*, 1781, 2nd ed. 1787; New York: St Martin's, 1965): 153.
35 Kant, *Critique of Pure Reason*, 383.
36 Vincent B. Leitch, *The Norton Anthology of Theory and Criticism* (New York: W.W. Norton, 2001): 500.
37 White, *The Tree of Man*, 398.
38 Cecil Hadgraft, "The Theme of Revelation in Patrick White's Novels," *Southerly* 37 (1977): 36.
39 Deborah Lupton, *The Emotional Self* (Thousand Oaks CA & London: Sage, 1988): 78.

itself. His writing is therefore also a 'critique of pure reason'; unlike Kant's, however, it critiques reason itself rather than employing reason in its critique.

In the nineteenth century, the Cartesian distinctions between mind and body, human and animal were radically challenged by such thinkers as Darwin, Nietzsche, Marx, and Freud. In *The Descent of Man*, for instance, Darwin shocked Victorian society with his statement that "man is descended from a hairy quadruped, furnished with a tail and pointed ears, probably arboreal in its habits."[40] With his theory of evolution, he revealed that the "human animal,"[41] to use White's phrase, is merely a body in process, evolved from other animals and still evolving. This "capsized Victorian values," Synnott explains,

> for now mind was dependent on body, as with other animals, and humans were not 'lords of creation' over animals but descended from these animals, and bearing their animal origins in their bodies for all to see.[42]

The demotion of the humanist transcendental ego is evident in *Voss*, and the imagery of evolution (or, perhaps, devolution) is figured as a threat to Voss's notion of the self:

> Blank faces, like so many paper kites, themselves earth-bound, or at most twitching in the warm shallows of atmosphere, dangling a vertebral tail, could prevent him soaring towards the apotheosis for which he was reserved. To what extent others had entangled him in the string of human limitations, he had grown desperate in wondering.
> *Voss* 178

The "string of human limitations" that is the "vertebral tail" images the mind's dependence on the animal body, as Darwin argued in a theory that had radical repercussions for the human conception of the body:

> The ancient dichotomies of mind/body, human/animal, superior/ inferior, asserted from Plato to Descartes were here not only denied, but in some senses reversed.[43]

---

40   Charles Darwin, *The Descent of Man, and Selection in Relation to Sex*, intro. John Tyler Bonner & Robert M. May (1871; Princeton NJ: Princeton UP, 1981): 389.
41   White, *Voss*, 250.
42   Synnott, "Tomb, Temple, Machine and Self," 94.
43   Synnott, "Tomb, Temple, Machine and Self," 94.

Despite the anti-humanism of such thinkers, mind/body dualism has resulted for the most part in the predominant Western assumption that identity, associated with the mind, is incorporeal. White's writing, however, suggests that it is "no longer possible to distinguish the cries of men from the lowing or bleating of animals";[44] abjection is provisional and corporeality and animality are ever-present factors of existence.

In the title of this section ("History's Beheadings"), I invoke the metaphor of decapitation not only because it graphically images the severing of 'mind' from 'body' fundamental to the history of Western thought, but also because it is an ironic metaphor that White's fiction itself uses to critique this dualism. In its damaging or lopping-off of heads, either via metaphoric description or via narrative action, it suggests the importance of a bodily consciousness unhindered by a supposedly superior rationality, while simultaneously enacting the deathliness of the rational affirmation of mind over body. Blue in *Riders in the Chariot*, one of White's foot-soldiers of suburban evil, represents a possible extreme of Western consciousness predicated on transcendental rationality. He is rational consciousness divested of affect, to the extent that he is emptied of it, a vacancy. Metonymic of European civilization's failures, his individual body represents and constitutes the social body. This is Classical reason utterly deformed:

> Blue had always been primarily a torso, an Antinoüs of the suburbs, breasts emphatically divided on unfeeling marble, or Roman sandstone. Somebody had battered the head, or else the sculptor had recoiled before giving precise form to a vision of which he was ashamed. Whether damaged, or unfinished, the head was infallibly suggestive. Out of the impervious eyes, which should have conveyed at most the finite beauty of stone, filtered glimpses of an infinite squalor: slops of the saloon, the dissolving cigarette butts, reflections of the grey monotonies, the greenish lusts. The mouth was a means of devouring. If ever it opened on words—for it was sometimes necessary to communicate—these issued bound with the brass of beer, from between rotting stumps of teeth.
> *Riders in the Chariot* 530

White's imagery reflects the corruption of modernity, figured in the images of squalor and the deformation of Classicism. Blue's "infallibly suggestive" head hints at modernity's distortion of the Classical values of balance, harmony, proportion, and order. Moreover, it gestures at modernity's reliance on the

---

44   White, *The Tree of Man*, 69.

model of Classical reason, which has resulted in a corrupt culture of "unfeeling marble," of anaesthetized affect. White is fond of images of battered or truncated reason. Voss's decapitation is another example dramatizing his violent blow to disembodied, Cartesian consciousness. Ultimately, Voss is forced to sever himself entirely from the head or mind; his actual decapitation at the hands of his Aboriginal captors, moreover, images the unsustainability of the notion of disembodied consciousness, ultimately revealing it, in both real and symbolic violence, as the "self-murder" of which he is so afraid.[45] Laura, too, is described as a Medusa-head, as rationality gives way to the mythic, Gothic horror of her "brain fever."[46] As she lies ill and hallucinating, Mrs Bonner, present at her sick-bed, is "petrified, both by words that she did not understand, and by the medusa-head that uttered them."[47] Mrs Bonner's own rational subjectivity is frozen in the face of Laura's disfigured reason. Such imagery suggests White's dread of a world that has promoted 'mind' over the affective, compassionate, and indeed spiritual realm of embodiment, subverting mind/body dualism by literalizing its defining division in the often Gothic imagery of decapitation.

Decapitation in White's fiction may be associated with his interest in imagery of fragmentation, related to what is described as the "fragmentation of modernity" in the epigraph from Henry Miller to Part Two of *The Aunt's Story*. Linda Nochlin's monograph on modern art, *The Body in Pieces*, takes as its subject-matter the importance of metaphors of fragmentation in the artistic and philosophical construction of the modern age. With reference to Henry Fuseli's *Artist Overwhelmed by the Grandeur of Antique Ruins*, in a description that correlates intriguingly with psychoanalytic accounts of the child's entry into the symbolic order as the experience of loss, Nochlin argues that modernity, mourning the bygone days of Classicism, is "figured as irrevocable loss, poignant regret for lost totality, a vanished wholeness."[48] Despite this sense of nostalgic longing, however, Nochlin notes that bodily fragmentation has also emerged in Western thought—in *modernism*—as "a positive rather than a negative trope."[49] Indeed, rather than merely "symbolizing nostalgia for the past [it] enacts the deliberate destruction of that past, or, at least a pulverization

---

45 White, *Voss*, 89.
46 The serpent-haired Medusa, with her petrifying gaze of stone, is, according to Greek myth, decapitated by Perseus. See White, *Voss*, 353.
47 White, *Voss*, 386.
48 Linda Nochlin, *The Body in Pieces: The Fragment as a Metaphor for Modernity* (London: Thames & Hudson, 1994): 7.
49 Nochlin, *The Body in Pieces*, 8.

of what were perceived to be its repressive traditions."[50] Indeed, White's modernism embraces the fragment as a metaphor of modernity, severing the head from the body in a particularly graphic image of the age, while simultaneously destroying the image of Classicism and its notions of order and reason as informing modernity.

The Divided Self: *The Solid Mandala*

Mind/body dualism is perhaps most emphatically dramatized in *The Solid Mandala*, where, at their most schematic, Waldo Brown represents the intellect and his brother, Arthur, corporeality. Like many of the characters White animates to explore the problematic notion of disembodied consciousness, Waldo is a cynical narcissist entrapped in his arid literary ambitions and inability to respond emotionally and physically to others. He has cultivated a "religion [...] of personal detachment, of complete transparency—he was not prepared to think emptiness—of mind."[51] This enclosing "religion" separates him from the external world and imprisons him in the empty condition of his narcissism. In his self-enclosure, Waldo is obsessed with the "penetrating voyage into the glass of the dressing table" (120). He likes to "refuse himself any awareness of escape from that intellectual ruthlessness he knew himself to possess. (He had once described the geography of his face in seven foolscap pages)" (120). Waldo refuses to respond to and receive from others, and therefore rejects the sustaining encounter with otherness that White associates with love. Instead, he is defined by what Arthur belatedly sees as the hatred he has "always directed, at all living things" (294), a distaste associating him with abjection and repression.

Arthur is Waldo's "half-wit" brother, an adjective suggested not only by his seeming intellectual incapacity but by the 'twinning' of the characters and the structure of the novel, which grants to each a lengthy, focalized section. Arthur's open and affective responses nonetheless emphasize his superior wisdom. Unlike his twin, he is "not impressed by reason" (31) and affirms life in all its physicality, messiness, suffering, and joy. Indeed, it is through Arthur that *The Solid Mandala* offers, as Lyn McCredden observes, a "hymn to the abject world."[52] While Waldo imprisons himself in his dry, inward-looking

---

50   *The Body in Pieces*, 8.
51   Patrick White, *The Solid Mandala*, 177.
52   Lyn McCredden, "'Splintering and Coalescing': Language and the Sacred in Patrick White's Novels," in *Patrick White Centenary: The Legacy of a Prodigal Son*, ed. Bill Ashcroft & Cynthia vanden Driesen (Newcastle upon Tyne: Cambridge Scholars, 2014): 48.

consciousness, Arthur is open to the healing force of the environment and the redemption of embodied empathy. He is therefore associated with love, which is beyond the limits of rational consciousness and effectively "too big a subject [...] to altogether understand" (208). Thus White employs the device of twinship to emphasize opposing relations to embodiment: the closed, controlling intellect that asserts its supposed superiority over the physical world and is incapable of love, and the animal, embodied, childlike consciousness that revels in an ecological, abject, and empathetic merging with the physical landscape and the bodies of others.

The dual focus of the novel, which Manfred Mackenzie terms "the consciousness of 'twin consciousness',"[53] is necessary in White's dramatization of the narcissistic danger of the rejection of the body; as William Walsh contends, White's "double theme" foregrounds the "tragedy of human incompleteness."[54] Mackenzie argues that White has always "told one story twice in the same book," proffering two (perhaps more) central viewpoints fixated on the "same events only to give them responses that are of a very different quality."[55] This "twin consciousness" is evident in the characterization of *The Living and the Dead*, where Elyot and Eden Standish exhibit opposing responses to the flux of existence. Gordon Collier, in the most complete study of the narrative structure of *The Solid Mandala*, cautions that "not all of the events in which Waldo and Arthur are involved are explicitly twice-told" and that differences and gaps in narration in the two sections therefore account for profoundly different interests.[56] Such a contrast in perspectives allows White to present a literary argument in favor of abjected aspects of experience—to foreground Arthur's way of being as a valuable and more integrated mode of existence, for example. In *The Solid Mandala* this perspectival difference is structurally enacted: the name of each twin provides the title of the two central and longest sections of the novel. Some events are twice, although differently, narrated through these contrasting perspectives, and each section is presented in diction and phrasing appropriate to the character that provides its focalization.

---

53   Manfred Mackenzie, "The Consciousness of 'Twin Consciousness': Patrick White's *The Solid Mandala*," *Novel: A Forum on Fiction* 2.3 (Spring 1969): 241–254.

54   William Walsh, "Patrick White's Vision of Human Incompleteness: *The Solid Mandala* and *The Vivisector*," in *Readings in Commonwealth Literature*, ed. William Walsh (Oxford: Clarendon, 1973): 421.

55   Mackenzie, "The Consciousness of 'Twin Consciousness'," 241.

56   Gordon Collier, *The Rocks and Sticks of Words: Style, Discourse and Narrative Structure in the Fiction of Patrick White* (Cross/Cultures 5; Amsterdam & Atlanta GA: Rodopi, 1992): 43.

Waldo's section begins, for example, in the narrative present, situating the reader within the adult consciousness of the character and revealing, moreover, Waldo's assertion of control over his brother's body:

> 'Put on your coat and we'll go for a walk,' he decided at last. 'Otherwise you'll sit here brooding.'
> 'Yes,' Arthur said. 'Brooding.'
> *The Solid Mandala* 23

The beginning of Arthur's section, by contrast, presents his childlike, primordial consciousness, or unconscious, in which sleep, animality, and the prelinguistic bodily union of the twins are emphasized:

> In the beginning there was the sea of sleep of such blue in which they lay together with iced cakes and the fragments of glass nesting in each other's arms the furry waves of sleep nuzzling at them like animals.
> *The Solid Mandala* 215

Oneiric imagery and the breakdown of syntax enact Arthur's imprecise and irrational consciousness and bind it to a linguistic expression that privileges the signifier over the signified: the precise meaning of words is not a priority for this character, who is not aligned with Enlightenment rationality. Arthur does not exert his mind over his physicality; rather, his 'mind' comprises the hazy, presymbolic fragmentation of the corporeal.

Unlike Arthur, Waldo, aligned with rationality, is the archetypal Enlightenment subject ardently believing in "human progress" (59), boasting that he has "seen the light" (153) and that he knows "in which direction enlightenment [lies]" (56). In accordance with his association with rational humanism, he finds Arthur's shambling physicality and animal intuition an embarrassment. From Waldo's perspective, Arthur is "good with animals," because it is "perhaps natural for them to accept someone who [is] only half a human being" (75). Yet, although he is disgusted with Arthur's physicality and animality, Waldo cannot repudiate his brother, try as he might—not least because he represents half of *himself*. Within the symbolic logic of the novel, the twins are an inseparable dyad, their link to each other imaged in their clasped hands during the long walks they take—walks that Waldo hopes will cause his sickly brother a heart attack. Arthur's persistent presence in his brother's life, however, dramatizes the impossibility of denying the body and, in fact, the imperative of accepting it:

> There was no escaping Arthur. At best he became the sound of your own breathing, his silences sometimes consoled [...]. [L]ife, as [Waldo] began in time to realise, is the twin consciousness, jostling you, hindering you, but with which, at unexpected moments, it is possible to communicate in ways both animal and delicate.
>
> *The Solid Mandala* 77

In this passage, Waldo acknowledges a "twin consciousness" in which abjected elements of experience "jostle" and "hinder" in their troubling of the boundaries of awareness. It is clear that Waldo and Arthur are two halves of a divided self and that Arthur's corporeality is indeed the sound of Waldo's "own breathing" which he cannot accept, although he longs to do so. Arthur's corporeality troubles Waldo because his concern with a supposedly incorporeal, rational consciousness does not allow him to accept his own body; his "sense of order, cleanliness and decorum,"[57] moreover, suggests his strong association with abjection. However, despite the threat to Waldo that Arthur represents, the latter's corporeality also opens the way to communication between self and other that is "both animal and delicate," defying the confining logic of reason. It is this potential enlargement of the self that Waldo rejects when he refuses to accept the importance of the body. And yet, for Waldo, Arthur's animality and corporeality are just as compelling as they are repulsive. During childhood, Waldo has delighted in his brother's body:

> Arthur's skin, ruddy where it ought to be, dwindled where protected to a mysterious, bluish white. Almost edible. Sometimes Waldo buried his face in the crook of Arthur's neck, just to smell, and then Arthur would punch, they would start to punch each other to ward off shame, as well as for the pleasure of it.
>
> *The Solid Mandala* 32

This buried memory with its incestuous associations reveals that Waldo is in fact compelled by physical communication and proximity and that his efforts to distance himself from the body are therefore attempts to sever an inherent and archaic aspect of himself and his experience. At some level, Waldo continues to desire the dissolution of his rigidly defended ego, which allows him to "get nothing out but a mumbling 'I I I'" (151). However, to protect his

---

57 Collier, *The Rocks and Sticks of Words*, 229.

fragile, apparently disembodied consciousness, he "must withdraw himself from his mind's mirror"—Arthur—whose corporeality, animality, and spirituality reflect Waldo's disavowals (63). This withdrawal represents Waldo's removal of himself not only from his specific other, Arthur, but also from all others (not to mention the corporeality that he conceives as other to his notion of the incorporeal self). Indeed, Waldo believes that to "submit himself to the ephemeral, the superficial relationships might damage the crystal core holding itself in reserve for some imminent moment of higher idealism," and Waldo, in a formulation indicating White's ironic treatment of the notions of essence and rationality, thus avoids "fleshly love—while understanding its algebra, of course—the better to convey eventually its essence" (183). Waldo, then, is defined by abjection, and throughout his life he rejects others, repudiating Arthur in particular when he discovers him in the library reading the "Grand Inquisitor" section of *The Brothers Karamazov*. Waldo, who works in the library, is shocked by Arthur's interpretation of Dostoevsky. This interpretation sheds light on the twins' rationalist, atheist father, George, who once carried the same novel "to the bonfire with a pair of tongs," causing Waldo at the time to shiver in his unconscious recognition of his father's abjection, "as though some unmentionable gobbet of his own flesh had lain reeking on the embers" (199). Waldo takes after his father, continuing to reject his "unmentionable" flesh, as well as the sacred spirituality with which White associates it. Arthur explains Dostoevsky's relevance to this aspect of his character:

> that is why our father was afraid. It wasn't so much because of the blood, however awful, pouring out where the nails went in. *He was afraid to worship some thing. Or body.* Which is what I take it this Dostoevski is partly going on about.
>
>   *The Solid Mandala* 200 (my emphasis)

For Waldo, taking after his father, the worship of the body is the denial of the mind. Arthur's reading therefore confronts him with the "unmentionable gobbet of his own flesh," threatening the disintegration of his rational identity. Thus Waldo orders Arthur out of the reading-room, addressing him as "sir" to indicate that "he, Arthur, his brother, his flesh, his breath, was a total stranger" (279).

However, Waldo's desperate attempts to cast aside and escape his brother are dramatized as dangerous: Arthur eventually kills Waldo (or accuses himself of killing Waldo—the description is unclear) and the twins' pet dogs defile the corpse, ripping open the throat and mutilating the genitals (303). The twins are throughout not only presented as 'mind' and 'body' but also respectively as 'masculine' and 'feminine'; they represent the impossibility of one gender existing without the other. While Waldo on one occasion dresses up in his dead mother's ball-gown, his arid and fleeting transgendered identity does not embody the androgynous unity that Arthur represents. In his reading at the library, Arthur encounters a passage that represents his "hermaphroditic" ability to resolve or dissolve opposites:

> *As the sun continually follows the body of the one who walks in the sun, so our hermaphroditic Adam, though he appears in the form of a male, nevertheless always carries about with him Eve, or his wife, hidden in his body.*
> The Solid Mandala 281 (italics in original)

Waldo's refusal to acknowledge and integrate his 'feminine' aspects—White represents as feminine those aspects of the self that are not associated with 'mind' and reason—eventually results in the ironic castration, hence emasculation, that the dogs perform upon his corpse. If Waldo represents Enlightenment reason's disavowal of embodiment, then his eventual fate emphasizes White's consistent interest in showing that the repression of the body and the abjection of animality result in their overmastering return. Indeed, Arthur drags Waldo "back repeatedly behind the line where knowledge [doesn't] protect" (46).

As I stressed at the beginning of this chapter, modernity, characterized by dichotomous thinking, is in White's conception frail and defensive, and his novels should be read as a critique of modern consciousness. The Enlightenment 'mind' in fact relies on the 'body' it rejects to define itself, a paradox that White's fiction rehearses. Waldo Brown's intellectualism, like Elyot Standish's in *The Living and the Dead*, is presented as a defensive and narcissistic abjection that cannot be maintained. Nonetheless, the rationality with which Waldo is associated is important *in relation to* Arthur's corporeality. Arthur relies on Waldo for his own oppositional identity. Moreover, the delicately balanced mingling of reason and corporeality functions to create an integrated self. As Arthur states after Waldo's death, "I don't think [...] I could live without my brother. He was more than half of me" (311). Quite literally, Waldo's section makes up more than half of the text. More important, however, is White's suggestion that reason is not worthless: subjectivity and signification would be impossible without it, but at its most ethical, redemptive, and honest, it must incorporate corporeality and open itself to the irrationality of the sacred.

The 'Classical' and the 'Grotesque'

One of the ways in which White's fiction emphasizes the history of Western dualism and its impact on modernity is by setting up a contrast between the 'classical' and the 'grotesque'. As I have argued, White frequently images the deformation or dismantling of Classical reason—for example, in the way in which the racist Blue of *Riders in the Chariot* is described as a sculpture of "unfeeling marble or Roman sandstone" that has been irrecoverably damaged.[58] Bakhtin notes that modernity, arising from "Descartes' rationalist philosophy," is based on the "aesthetics of classicism"—a concern with reason, seriousness, and univocal meaning and identity that rejects the grotesque and carnivalesque elements of embodiment.[59] White would agree: Classical aesthetics and modern reason, also imbricated in his fiction, reject corporeality in creating a stony and "unfeeling" image of rationalist identity that he associates with intolerance and oppression.

How does Bakhtin elaborate on the distinction between the Classical and the Grotesque or, more specifically, between the "closed body" and the "open body" with which he associates each respectively? In *Rabelais and His World*, Bakhtin demonstrates modernity's increasing movement away from the legitimated celebration of the body that characterized medieval festivals, during which people enacted a joyful, grotesque, and carnivalesque corporeality, liberating themselves momentarily from feudal oppression. Since the seventeenth century, the body in Western culture—particularly its lower strata—has become increasingly hidden, part of a private rather than a public domain. Bakhtin contends that, in contrast to the "open body" of the medieval carnival (a body open to the world and to others, revelling in its physicality and celebrating its orifices as sites of communication between 'inside' and 'outside'), the body in modern Western societies is entirely and prevailingly "closed." Morever, he foregrounds the body as a metaphor, in both instances, for an historicized understanding of subjectivity. In modern Western societies, the self is perceived as autonomous and individual, moving between a yearning to 'connect' with others and the need to maintain its individuality. As Deborah Lupton argues,

> Contemporary notions of embodiment similarly privilege self-discipline and autonomy, maintaining oneself as distinct from other bodies, keeping

---

58   White, *Riders in the Chariot*, 530.
59   Bakhtin, *Rabelais and His World*, 101.

one's bodily boundaries tightly regulated, shut off and distinct from others' bodies.[60]

This historical notion of the self and the body, she explains, has resulted from social and cultural changes since the Middle Ages: the transition from feudalism to capitalism, the Renaissance, the rise of the modern European state, the Enlightenment, the Industrial Revolution, and the emergence of capitalism.[61] These historical changes led to an intensified focus on the individual, an increased distinction between private and public space, and a widening gap between the notions of the self and the collective that led to the diminution of the significance of shared physicality as a leveler of hierarchies. Further, the rise of modernity coincided with the radical division of 'mind' (associated with the self) and 'body' (conceptualized as supplementary).

Rabelais' writing, a celebration of the carnival, employs language and imagery that run counter to the official discourse of the church and feudal culture characterizing his time, and therefore emphasizes the subversive (although conditionally sanctioned) capacity of the carnivalesque. The body and its functions were joyfully asserted during carnival celebrations and social hierarchies fell away in a collective and legitimated catharsis wherein social frustrations were relieved via the "therapeutic power of laughter."[62] According to Bakhtin, the medieval feast or carnival allowed people to indulge subversively in the excesses of their bodies, their passions, the negligible boundary between the 'inside' and the 'outside', and the engulfing of the mind by the body. These were features of what he termed the "grotesque body," defined by its "open, unfinished nature, its interaction with the world."[63] Rabelais' imagery, Bakhtin argues, depended in particular on his depiction of this "grotesque body," which, characterized by its orifices and protuberances, is "open," both extending into and incorporating the world and the collective.

In White, the bodies of certain characters extend into the world perceptually, physically, and affectively, responding to other bodies and the world in general. To some extent, then, his fiction admires the Rabelaisian "open body," on occasion deliberately harnessing a Gothic, medieval aesthetic of the grotesque in its implicit critique of modernity. In *The Eye of the Storm*, for example, Lotte Lippmann, one of White's most emphatically physical characters, is described as "grotesque: the stiffened lips in the stone face might have been

---

60 Lupton, *The Emotional Self*, 71.
61 *The Emotional Self*, 71.
62 Bakhtin, *Rabelais and His World*, 67.
63 *Rabelais and His World*, 281.

designed as an escape in times of downpour."⁶⁴ Imaged as a gargoyle, Lotte represents the Gothic realm of the uncontainable abject in White's fiction, a notable aspect of his writing undermining rationality; Voss's Romantic vision similarly incorporates the "Gothic splendours of death."⁶⁵ Accordingly, William Scheick identifies White's emphasis on the "grotesque nature of existence," a "subversive element [which] asserts its presence through the all too apparent distortions which disrupt the restrained harmony of social order."⁶⁶ White's contorted bodies, grotesque characters, and interest in the corporeal abject prompt this statement.

Just as Bakhtin noted a shift in modernity from the "open body" to the "closed body," White observed in twentieth-century Australia a "puritan strain" which he claimed to be "one of the great flaws of the Australian character," influencing its attitudes to corporeality: an inability "to distinguish between porn and bawdy—the sludge of today and the lusty tradition of world literature, as found in Chaucer, Shakespeare, Rabelais, to name a few exponents."⁶⁷ Everything to do with the body, he suggested (his opinion in accord with Bakhtin's understanding), had since the Renaissance become sordid in the eyes of the increasingly hypocritical and prurient West. Bakhtin maintains that by the seventeenth century, when bodies were "shut off" from the world as society became concerned with separating the public from the private, an aesthetic of classicism arose, defined by proportion, clarity of outline, formal design, and harmony. Accordingly, the excess and ambivalence of the grotesque body disappeared:

> A relatively progressive 'universally historic form' was created and was expressed in Descartes' rationalist philosophy and in the aesthetics of classicism. Rationalism and classicism clearly reflect the fundamental traits of the new official culture; it differed from the ecclesiastical feudal culture but was also authoritarian and serious […]. In the new official culture there prevails a tendency towards the stability and completion of being, toward one single meaning, one single tone of seriousness. The ambivalence of the grotesque can no longer be admitted. The exalted

---

64   White, *The Eye of the Storm*, 20.
65   White, *Voss*, 264.
66   William J. Scheick, "The Gothic Grace and Rainbow Aesthetic of Patrick White's Fiction: An Introduction," *Texas Studies in Literature and Language* 21.2 (Summer 1979): 132–133.
67   Patrick White, "The Reading Sickness" (1980), in *Patrick White Speaks*, ed. Paul Brennan & Christine Flynn (1989; London: Penguin, 1991): 75.

genres of classicism are freed from the influence of the grotesque tradition of laughter.[68]

As Ian Burkitt summarizes, "The person of rationalism and classicism is firmly encased in his or her closed bodily shell, alone with his or her doubt, uncertainty and fear."[69] Such a description may effectively be applied to many of White's body-denying characters. White's fiction emphasizes existential angst and despair, arising from a sense of self-entrapment, as a chronic condition of modernity. Moreover, it relates this despair to the rationalist, Classicist notion of the self. Scheick confirms that this notion is premised on abjection or repression:

> Order or proportion, the Classical ideal of fixed rational design, represents one side of the human will, the underside of which is the Gothic reality of an unfinished, irrational asymmetry.[70]

In its subversion of the rationalism of twentieth-century Western culture, White's fiction attempts to recuperate a subversive and transgressive bodiliness.

The Solid Mandala, for example, explicitly juxtaposes the classicism of modernity, with its emphasis on the "closed body," with the grotesque excesses of a body flaunting its animality and ambivalence. Waldo Brown, a staunch upholder of the disembodied, Classical, or Enlightenment mind, worries about the "gothic arches of dead grass [...] taking over from the classical" façade of the Browns' house.[71] Mistakenly, he assumes that he can preserve "the Classical which Dad called 'sacrosanct'" (223). Classical imagery enters the novel via the figure of George, Waldo's father, who has insisted on attaching "a pediment in the Classical style" to the family's suburban Australian house (37). Upon the stage of this "Classical" veranda, Waldo imagines that he will stage a play—a "Greek tragedy" (38)—which he has yet to write. When he refuses to allow Arthur to participate in this permanently embryonic masterpiece, his twin decides to put on his own show. Arthur's "play," which, unlike Waldo's, actually comes to fruition, grotesquely spotlights the aspects of existence that Waldo has abjected. As the grotesque antithesis of rationalism and Classicism, it problematizes the seeming stability of binary oppositions. The performance,

---

68   Bakhtin, *Rabelais and His World*, 101.
69   Ian Burkitt, *Bodies of Thought: Embodiment, Identity and Modernity* (Thousand Oaks CA & London: Sage, 1999): 49.
70   Scheick, "The Gothic Grace and Rainbow Aesthetic of Patrick White's Fiction," 132–133.
71   White, *The Solid Mandala*, 127. Further page references are in the main text.

taking place at the centre of the Classical veranda, reveals that rationalist identity is in fact brought into being via its defensive rejection of the animality and corporeality Arthur represents and that its inherent, constituting abjects therefore return to haunt it. Arthur's insistence that his play, too, is a Greek tragedy emphasizes the reliance of Waldo's defensive identity on what Arthur represents. The Classical stage must incorporate Arthur as much as it does Waldo, and Arthur's display of dumb animality and corporeality therefore enters and threatens the classical paradigm, while revealing its constituting relation to the latter.

In his play, Arthur enacts the tragedy of a cow that has lost her calf. Because the events of the novel are sometimes twice narrated, once through the focalization of Waldo and later through the consciousness of Arthur, it is worth quoting extensively from the text to analyze the importance of this "double telling."[72] In the following passage, from the section entitled "Waldo," the horror of Arthur's performance to the rigidly defended, body-denying consciousness is realized:

> 'And what will your play be about, Arthur?' Mother asked.
> 'A cow,' Arthur blurted out.
> 'But a Greek tragedy!'
> 'A cow's as Greek, I suppose,' said Dad, 'as anything else.' Then he added, in the voice of somebody whose opinion is sometimes asked: 'Whether she's a figure of tragedy is a matter for consideration.'
> Arthur was grappling with his problem.
> 'This is a big, *yellow* cow,' he told them. 'She's all blown out, see, with her calf. Then she has this calf. It's dead. See?'
> There was Arthur pawing at the boards of the veranda. At the shiny parcel of dead calf.
> Everyone was looking at the ground by now, from shame, or Waldo began to feel, terror.
> 'You can see she's upset, can't you?' Arthur lowed. 'Couldn't help feeling upset.'
> It was suddenly so grotesquely awful in the dwindling light and evening silence.
> 'Couldn't help it,' Arthur bellowed.
> Thundering up and down the veranda he raised his curved, yellow horns, his thick, fleshy, awful muzzle. The whole framework of their stage shook.

---

72 Collier, *The Rocks and Sticks of Words*, 79.

> 'That's enough, I think,' said Dad.
> 'Oh, Arthur!' Mother was daring herself to speak, 'we understand enough without your telling us any more.'
>
> *The Solid Mandala* 40

In this passage, Arthur's play meets his family's criticism, in particular his father's intellectual scorn asserted to him "in the voice of somebody whose opinion is sometimes asked." George's assessment of the play as an enigma to which reason must be applied—a problem of definition (can a cow be a figure of tragedy?[73])—is ironically cast against Arthur's embodied attempt to "grappl[e] with *his* problem"—the experience of suffering through empathy and, moreover, the attempt to express this. Arthur's play rapidly invades and overruns his family's mood of mildly amused superiority. His performance of animality arouses their shame and terror. Moreover, the language of the passage poetically foregrounds the awareness of death suffusing the scene. The rapid leap from the description of Arthur's performing a cow to the seemingly literal materialization of the dead calf suggests the shocking spur to imagination that his play becomes. Through his performance, death invades the scene of suburban, family existence. Simultaneously, his powers of empathy are emphasized to the extent that he seemingly *becomes* the cow: he lows, bellows, and raises "his curved, yellow horns, his thick, fleshy, awful muzzle." Occurring in Waldo's section of the novel, Waldo focalizes the passage. As Gordon Collier argues, "Waldo's narration struggles to avoid conceding that Arthur's playlet has touched the audience" and Waldo thus "endors[es] the validity and force of the theme."[74] Indeed, Arthur's performance has resulted in his metamorphosis, in engaging Waldo's imagination, thus forcing Waldo to empathize momentarily with the scene of animality and mortality he depicts. Nonetheless, Waldo is horrified by Arthur's transformation into what he has in fact constantly represented within the family structure: animal sentience and the perennial threat of death, both of which, like Arthur himself, are given transgressive feminine associations. In Waldo's view, Arthur is "grotesquely awful in the dwindling light and evening silence." This abject threat to the Brown family's sense of themselves rattles the "whole framework of their stage"; their entire conception of themselves and their lives—the way in which they frame their existence—is troubled.

---

73   There is, of course, an 'animal' aspect to the origins of tragedy, which term itself has been said to derive from Greek *trágos* 'goat'.

74   Collier, *The Rocks and Sticks of Words*, 83.

This episode receives further elucidation in Arthur's section of the novel. Here, the tragedy enacted is emphasized as, in fact, a dramatization of *the family's* tragedy. The inescapability of human frailty and mortality is further developed:

> All the members of his family were frail. As he went down to milk, there they were, sitting on the classical veranda. Mother who knew better than anyone how things ought to be done had sliced her finger doing the beans; Waldo who knew how to think was screwed up tighter than his own thoughts; and poor Dad, very little made him sweat under his celluloid collar.
>
> [...] when he returned along the path of trampled grass, he would have liked to cry. If they wouldn't have seen it. For there they were. Still. With Waldo going to write some old tragedy of a play.
>
> Arthur had by some means to distract.
>
> So he stood the bucket, and said more or less: 'I'll act you my tragedy of a cow.'
>
> For nobody would accuse him of not fully understanding a cow. And they sat looking at him, almost crying for his tragedy. As he stamped up and down, pawing and lowing, for the tragedy of all interminably bleeding breeding cows. By that time his belly was swollen with it. He could feel the head twisting in his guts.
>
> Everybody had begun to share his agony, but that, surely, was what tragedy is for.
>
> When Mother suddenly tried to throw the expression off her face, and said, 'Oh Arthur, we understand your tragedy without your showing us any more'.
>
> *The Solid Mandala* 230

Again, Arthur's capacity for compassion is underscored, but this time not merely in his ability to empathize with a dying animal and her sufferings. His compassion is extended to his family, who provide the creative impetus for a symbolic play dealing only ostensibly with the suffering of a cow in labor. Arthur is initially concerned with his recognition that "all the members of his family were frail," leading to his attempt to produce a performance that might "distract" them from this frailty on one level, but that may also thematize it. Arthur's capacity for empathy and association with animality are evident in his correct assumption that "nobody would accuse him of not understanding a cow." In his own experience, he more than understands—he merges with— the suffering animal that he imagines, realizing her experience of pain within his own corporeality: "his belly was swollen with it" and he "could feel the head twisting in his guts." Arthur's corporeal empathy, moreover, is shared with his family as affect is communicated via the signs of the body: "Everybody had begun to share his agony." Thus Arthur comes to an intuitive understanding of the term 'tragedy', one that is not intellectually influenced by notions of Classicism or a knowledge of Aristotle. Tragedy, in Arthur's conception of the genre, involves the communication of affect via the suffering body. However, this body—grotesque and animal—is upsetting to a twentieth-century family whose associations with rationality and logic lead them to dismiss it, even as they may inherently and viscerally identify with it: "'Oh Arthur, we understand your tragedy without your showing us any more.'"

White's Critique of Modernity

Arthur's grotesquely animal performance on the "Classical" stage of the Browns' veranda literalizes the staging of abject corporeality as a focal point of White's writing. Throughout his oeuvre, White rejects the body-denial he views as coextensive with Western civilization: Waldo's association with Enlightenment thought suggests that his narcissism and repudiation of the body may be extended to the historical context of the novel—postwar suburban Australia, a product of Western modernity—and related to the atrocities of the twentieth century, to which the novel briefly alludes. Indeed, if White has "concentrated on the destructive effects of the uncontrolled ego, his age, with its two world wars, has given him plenty of justification."[75] The historical derogation of the body arguably informs the brutality of modernity. As Michael Giffin notes,

> the myths which see the person as a duality of matter and spirit, or as an exiled soul trapped in a material body and waiting for release to some ideal transcendent realm are myths which some think to be the source of Western decline and decay.[76]

If the material world has no perceived sacred value, then it may indeed be cheapened and exploited. Further, belief in the body's insignificance may favor the bigoted oppression and objectification of those unfairly associated with

---

75   Geoffrey Dutton, *Patrick White* (Melbourne: Oxford UP, 1971): 28.
76   Michael Giffin, *Patrick White and the Religious Imagination: Arthur's Dream* (Lewiston NY: Edwin Mellen, 1999): 68.

embodiment and thus encourage the dismissal of any violence enacted upon them.

This shrugged-off brutality is evident in *Riders in the Chariot* in the mock-crucifixion of Himmelfarb by the agents of suburban normativity, the "Lucky Seven," who have just won the Lotto, among them Mrs Flack's putative nephew, Blue. In an alcoholic stupor of celebration that loosens their inhibitions on sexuality and violence, Himmelfarb's co-workers at Brighta Bicycle Lamps exact mob vengeance against him, his Jewishness and foreignness inciting their hostility and rage. Mrs Flack's constant discourse of hatred—curiously prescient of reactions to the contemporary global refugee crisis, post-Brexit, Trump-era Western xenophobia and nationalism, and the Australian scandal of Manus Island—speaks Blue into action:

> The voice of Sarsaparilla [...] took for granted its right to pass judgment on a soul, and indulge in a fretfulness of condemnation.
>
> 'I would not of thought it would of come to this,' Mrs Flack repeated, 'a stream of foreign migrants pouring into the country [...]. Who will feed us, I would like to know, when we are so many mouths over, and foreign mouths, how many of them I did read, but forget the figure.'[77]

The Lucky Seven's "joke" crucifixion of Himmelfarb occurs when this discourse of hatred galvanizes Blue into action, suggesting that prejudice insinuates itself discursively into the modern world, resulting in material suffering. Andrew McCann therefore argues that certain characters in White's fiction symbolize the ills of Western modernity:

> characters like Mrs Jolley and Mrs Flack in *Riders in the Chariot* do embody both the banality and the evil which seem to imply the triumph of forms of social hygiene and order.[78]

White's fiction, however, undermines such order through its concern with and imagery of physicality, a physicality which may thus acquire ethical and political associations. In a number of key images and passages centering on defiled physicality and the return of the traumatized body, it dramatizes modernity's brutality as returning to haunt it. The carcass of a dog in *The Living and the Dead*, for example, with its "guts [hanging] out through the belly fur,"[79]

---

77   White, *Riders in the Chariot*, 273.
78   Andrew McCann, "Decomposing Suburbia: Patrick White's Perversity," *Australian Literary Studies* 18.4 (November 1998): 64.
79   Patrick White, *The Living and the Dead*, 272.

is related to the "sad, sick, stinking world,"[80] an image that returns in *The Vivisector* as a metaphor for human cruelty (providing the novel with its title) just before a description of World War I. In a display window, Hurtle and his adoptive mother and sister observe

> a little, brown, stuffed dog clamped to a kind of operating table. The dog's exposed teeth were gnashing in a permanent and most realistic agony. Its guts, exposed too, [...] were more realistic still.[81]

Maman cries out, "'That is what I should never forget! But did. The vivisectionists! [...] There's nothing so inhuman as a human being'."[82]

In later life, White protested against inhumanity in the form of nuclear armament, and Hiroshima appears in *Three Uneasy Pieces* as an unrepresentable horror existing on the margins of the text. A clergyman and former chaplain in the navy recalls to the narrator, Paddy, a writer with clear autobiographical associations, his experience of visiting Japan after the dropping of the atomic bombs. His comment highlights the writer's difficulty in representing twentieth-century horror: "For all your creative brilliance, you couldn't imagine those days of brilliant hell."[83] Paddy agrees that the clergyman's assumption of "the distance between life and literature"[84] is correct. Nonetheless, the following passage, in which Paddy's privileged and utopian literary vision is interrupted by the clergyman's reminiscence, reveals White's attempt to access in his writing the horrors that exist on its margins:

> To be truthful, I would have preferred to evoke the exquisitely formal Japanese scroll of Hiroshima in its nest of mountains beside the Inland Sea, its pines and maples, its bathing huts, and booths where the idle seduced themselves with crinkled oysters and coral sculpture of prawns before reality ripped the scroll apart revealing the tatters of humanity.
>
> '...grey rags of skin, flesh in which the flies bred maggots in unprotected wounds, deformed limbs, inflated scars. I only talk about the living, mind you. Many had vanished into the air and were never seen again.'[85]

---

80   White, *The Living and the Dead*, 270.
81   Patrick White, *The Vivisector*, 135.
82   White, *The Vivisector*, 135.
83   Patrick White, "The Age of a Wart," in White, *Three Uneasy Pieces*, 47.
84   White, "The Age of a Wart," 47.
85   "The Age of a Wart," 47–48.

In the final section of *The Solid Mandala*, entitled "Mrs Poulter and the Zeitgeist," Waldo's dead body is central to White's critique of the spirit of Western modernity. When the Browns' neighbor, Mrs Poulter, discovers the corpse, the news episodes—the "*real* programmes"[86] that she watches avidly on television—take on a reality that they never had for her before:

> the clouds were building up, from beyond and over Sarsaparilla, for the Armageddon of which Mrs Poulter had read and heard. She knew now. All the films, all the telly, all the black-and-white of the papers was turning real, as the great clouds, the great tanks, ground up groaning over Sarsaparilla. To lock together. Men burning in their steel prisons [...]. The flat faces of all those Chinese guerrillas or Indonesians, it was the same thing, dragged out across the dreadful screen. All those Jews in ovens, that was long ago, but still burning, lying in heaps. Lone women bashed up in Mosman, Marouba, Randwick, places you went only in your sleep. Little girls held to the ground. The bleeding wombs of almost all women.
> *The Solid Mandala* 303

For Mrs Poulter, "Armageddon" represents the engulfing return of history's abjections. This is figured via a continuum of corporeal imagery, ranging from the specific details of war and the Holocaust to the more universal experience of menstruation in womanhood, all suddenly present in the banal suburban setting of Sarsaparilla. While it may seem gratuitous to associate the "bleeding wombs of almost all women" with "Jews in ovens [...] still burning, lying in heaps," the passage, via metonymic association, brings to the fore the unspoken, abjected elements of human experience and suggests, moreover, that the past comprises private and specific experiences of suffering and pain—the embodied anguish of individuals largely absent from the grand discourse of History. This is a suffering to which Mrs Poulter, through her own embodiment, suddenly relates. Moreover, it recalls Arthur's poem, the "disgusting *blood myth*" (214; emphasis in original), Waldo calls it, which has led him in his envy to destroy his own comparatively pallid and insufficient writing and which has engendered the moment of hatred between the brothers resulting in Waldo's death:

> my heart is bleeding for the Viviseckshunist
> Cordelia is bleeding for her father's life
> all Marys in the end bleed

---

86   White, *The Solid Mandala*, 299, emphasis in the original.

> but do not complane because they know
> they cannot have it any other way.
> *The Solid Mandala* 212

Compassion, White informs us, is indeed oddly physical. Moreover, the excessive horror at all forms of suffering—in the instance of Mrs Poulter's realization of the *Zeitgeist*, historical suffering inflicted on the individual—causes it to exist indefinitely, reasserting itself in the traumatic repetition of the imagery of corporeal defilement. For White, history is located in the violated body, an abject of the social order that cannot be definitively jettisoned, and which, owing to its ubiquitous presence, brings every specific historical suffering back into being.

This return of the suffering body in relation to the forces of history is perhaps most evident in *Riders in the Chariot*, in which White presents the Holocaust via the specificity of a single, agonized body: the Lady of Czernowitz. In his focus on the corporeal plight of the Jews, a profound sense of mourning and outrage enters White's writing. His description of Himmelfarb's train journey to and arrival at Friedensdorf ('village of peace'), a fictional concentration camp, is one of his most shocking and moving narrative sequences. Here, White is concerned with the collective sufferings and persecutions of history. Awaiting transportation among hundreds of others in a darkened shed, Himmelfarb is aware of a "solid mass, and that a mass soul suffered and recoiled."[87] Voices rise up in a single cry "out of the depths of history" (223): the Jews are one unified, timeless, suffering body. By the journey's end, they are once again incorporated into a single symbolic body. Marched naked into the gas chambers (Himmelfarb is spared by the guards), they are swallowed by the ravenous maw of Nazi evil. However,

> the door of the woman's bath-house burst open, by terrible misadventure, and there, forever to haunt, staggered the Lady from Czernowitz.
>
> How the hands of the old, helpless and furthermore, intellectual Jew, her friend, went out to her.
>
> 'God show us!' shrieked the Lady from Czernowitz. 'Just this once! At least!'
>
> In that long leathern voice.
>
> She stood there for an instant in the doorway, and might have fallen if allowed to remain longer. Her scalp was grey stubble where the reddish hair had been. Her one dug hung down beside the ancient scar which

---

87   White, *Riders in the Chariot*, 222.

represented the second. Her belly sloped away from the hillock of her navel. Her thighs were particularly poor. But it was her voice that lingered. Stripped. Calling to him from out of the dark of history, ageless, ageless, and interminable.
> *Riders in the Chariot* 237

The words the Lady of Czernowitz screams—"God show us!"—may be interpreted as the plea to be shown mercy, or as an injunction to the text itself to reveal human suffering, an instruction it immediately follows by detailing, in a discourse of degradation, a list of degraded physical features. The "leathern voice" is again the collective voice of suffering—"show *us*," she shrieks, in a voice that will linger for as long as individual bodies feel pain and oppression, and empathetically share this fundamentally equalizing experience. This is a voice from which Himmelfarb's intellectualism cannot protect him. White's fiction strips its characters and its modern context of the layers of narcissistic pretension that diminish the call to compassion, presenting the disfiguration of the body of suffering. Embedded in his fiction is the persistent throbbing of our shared embodiment; "stripped" and constant, it is "ageless, ageless, and interminable," constituting the groundrock of an ethic of equality.

White therefore relates the repudiation of the body to the atrocities of the twentieth century and the historical diminishment of individual suffering constituting historical violence. Moreover, his writing engages with and critiques the modern elimination of metaphysical value from secular, capitalist culture. In this respect, his thinking resembles that of Max Horkheimer and Theodor Adorno in *Dialectic of Enlightenment*. Horkheimer and Adorno consider the reasons for the rise of National Socialism in twentieth-century Germany. Writing during one of the darkest eras of European history, they attempted to answer the question of how this movement could have arisen at what had seemed the height of Western Enlightenment—how the "reversion of enlightened civilization to barbarism in reality" could have happened.[88] Their answer is that Enlightenment reason rids itself of religious and metaphysical sources of value, replacing these with the drive for power:

> In the face of the unity of such reason the distinction between God and man is reduced to an irrelevance [...]. In their mastery of nature, the

---

88 Max Horkheimer & Theodor W. Adorno, *Dialectic of Enlightenment: Philosophical Fragments*, ed. Schmid Noerr Gunzelin, tr. Edmund Jephcott (*Dialektik der Aufklärung*, 1944, rev. 1947; Stanford CA: Stanford UP, 2002): xix.

creative God and the ordering mind are alike. Man's likeness to God consists in sovereignty over existence, in the lordly gaze, in the command.[89]

White tackles the deification of Enlightenment consciousness in *Voss*, wherein the title character, who indeed assumes his "sovereignty over existence" and hence his "mastery of nature" and the body, unwittingly proclaims his atheism by asserting himself to be God-like:

> 'Atheists are atheists usually for mean reasons,' Voss was saying. 'The meanest of these is that they themselves are so lacking in magnificence they cannot conceive the idea of a Divine Power.'
> *Voss* 88–89

Horkheimer and Adorno see mass culture and fascism as eventually characterizing the self-interest of Enlightenment reason:

> The increase in economic productivity which creates the conditions for a more just world also affords the technical apparatus and the social groups controlling it a disproportionate advantage over the rest of the population. The individual is entirely nullified in the face of the economic powers. These powers are taking society's domination over nature to unimagined heights.[90]

For Horkheimer and Adorno, the increasing rationalization of modern Western culture has a double-edged consequence: it leads to social freedom, but also inevitably results in totalitarianism. Reason, in a sense, destroys itself through its association with overweening power.

White's disparagement of reason and rationalism in *Riders in the Chariot* reflects this: "Reason finally holds a gun at its head—and does not always miss";[91] so, too, does Himmelfarb's realization, subsequent to his experiences in Nazi Germany, that "the intellect has failed us."[92] In *Riders in the Chariot* in particular, the efficient manner in which the Holocaust was executed as the product of a deformed and corroded collective reason haunts White's writing. Here, the sanitized, body-denying space of Australian suburbia is likened to the horrifyingly clinical, body-destroying space of Nazi Germany, encapsulated in the

---

89 Horkheimer & Adorno, *Dialectic of Enlightenment*, 5–6.
90 Horkheimer & Adorno, *Dialectic of Enlightenment*, xvii.
91 White, *Riders in the Chariot*, 47.
92 *Riders in the Chariot*, 257.

experiences of the Jewish intellectual and immigrant protagonist, Himmelfarb. Many have criticized this correlation as excessive. Michael Wilding, for example, attacks White's symbolism yet refuses to read his work symbolically:

> The paralleling of his eccentric and grotesque episode of Himmelfarb's crucifixion with the historically attested killing of six million Jews cannot but suggest that the Australian working class shared a complicity in the holocaust. Yet there is no known historical evidence to support such a case. The portrayal of the proletariat as murderously and destructively anti-Semitic owes little to reality.[93]

However, the novel correctly recognizes both Nazi Germany and Australian suburbia as products of European rationalism. It suggests that Australia, like Germany, is potentially self-destructive in its denial of 'otherness'. Mrs Jolley, one of White's representatives of suburban evil, thinks of herself as "rational at every pore."[94] She is, in White's view, a vile product of the trajectory of the Enlightenment, itself symbolized by the mass-production of the Australian factory in which Himmelfarb works: Brighta Bicycle Lamps, its associations of light and capitalist banality suggestive of Enlightenment values. "Between Bach and Hitler," says Konrad Stauffer, Himmelfarb's German acquaintance, "something went wrong with Germany."[95] White's suggestion, however, is that something has failed during and after these years of modern transformation—within the Western world at large. Horkheimer and Adorno would agree:

> Enlightenment, understood in the wider sense as the advance of thought, has always aimed at liberating human beings from fear and installing them as masters. Yet the wholly enlightened earth is radiant with triumphant calamity. Enlightenment's program was the disenchantment of the world.[96]

Yet White's quaternity in *Riders in the Chariot*—Hare, Himmelfarb, Dubbo, and Godbold—are able in their various ways to envision the world's enchantment. Initially a Jewish academic, Himmelfarb becomes increasingly religious as his association with the intellect and Enlightenment thought shrinks. His

---

93   Michael Wilding, "Patrick White: The Politics of Modernism," in Wilding, *Studies in Classic Australian Fiction* (Sydney: Sydney Studies/Shoestring, 1997): 228.
94   White, *Riders in the Chariot*, 66.
95   *Riders in the Chariot*, 209.
96   Horkheimer & Adorno, *Dialectic of Enlightenment*, 1.

religious associations, moreover, become more pronounced during his years as an immigrant in Australia, when he is immersed in the context of the narrow-minded suburban secularism White's fiction deplores. Himmelfarb's growing mysticism is in stark contrast to the shallow materialism of colonial suburbia, which is implicitly compared to Europe by dint of the cruelty and exclusion that he experiences in both contexts.

During Himmelfarb's years in Germany, prior to the advent of Hitler, his father, an apostate Jew, ironically informed him of his proud belief that "the age of enlightenment and universal brotherhood [has] dawned at last in Western Europe."[97] Himmelfarb, however, learns bitterly through his experience of the Holocaust that this is not the case—the "age of enlightenment" certainly cannot be associated with brotherhood. Nor can it be associated with moral or metaphysical value. Nonetheless, Himmelfarb is one of the four visionary "riders" representing the possibility of a redemptive spiritual vision despite the secularism and materialism of postwar Australian existence. First, however, he must learn to attain the "degree of humility which always had eluded him" (256), the lack of which defines those characters White associates with rational thought. Himmelfarb must rid himself of corrupting reason and its hierarchical, narcissistic, and prejudiced associations. Part of his attainment of humility inheres in his acknowledgement, once he has rediscovered his religion, of a somatic spirituality. This is evident in a significant episode wherein he recognizes his spiritual 'mateship' with Alf Dubbo, a compassion based on shared vision and the awareness of shared corporeality. The episode describes Himmelfarb's realization that Dubbo is interested in Ezekiel's vision of the Chariot. He has left the Bible lying open in the washroom and Himmelfarb re-reads the passage. No longer does he hear "his own voice" narrating, however, but rather a mythic voice, "the voice of all voices, thick, and too throaty, and desolating in its sense of continuity" (404). For Himmelfarb, it provides a moment of lasting epiphany, drawing together a feeling of intense spirituality and a focus on embodiment:

> the voice no longer attempted to clothe the creatures themselves in allegorical splendour, of Babylonian gold. They were dressed in the flesh of men: the pug of human gargoyles, the rather soapy skin, the pores of which had been enlarged by sweat, the mouth thinned by trial and error, the dead hair of the living human creatures blowing in the wind of circumstance.
>
> *Riders in the Chariot* 404

---

97   White, *Riders in the Chariot*, 125.

Himmelfarb's transformation from rationalist to spiritualist, hence his identification of metaphysical meaning in the context of the secular world, reflects White's writing, which attempts to relocate metaphysical value in the brutal twentieth-century Western context and simultaneously to attest to its location in somatic experience. White's sensitivity to the somatic undermines Enlightenment thinking, with its goal of "domination over nature."[98] His metaphysics of the physical coincides with his derogation of capitalist materialism and his critique of the Western dismissal of the body. White's fiction blames modernity's obsession with rationalist gain for society's spiritual bankruptcy, and takes issue in particular with the bourgeois suburban values of materialism and heteronormativity. These values, according to White, have "sanitized" society, which has turned a blind eye to corporeality and constructed a dulled and defensive mind immune to the splendor and horror of existence.

Endorsing History's Decapitation? What Some of the Critics Say

Despite the evidence for and political significance of White's critique of Western dualisms, many of White's critics appear to have read his work according to their own dualistic assumptions of the knowable, disembodied self. Much of the writing concerning White's fiction responded to his work contemporaneously. The formalist theoretical framework of the New-Critical approach to literature, at its height in the mid-twentieth century, is thus common in the bulk of White criticism, which coincided with the moment of his writing, and many of his critics accordingly respond to his novels, as they would to the post-Enlightenment mind, as coherent and knowable. A number of critics have therefore described White as impatient with and dismissive of corporeality, perceiving it to be of secondary importance.[99] Brian Kiernan exemplifies this critical approach when he reads White's writing as presenting "the soul imprisoned in the corrupting flesh."[100] Like Kiernan, many critics justify their readings of White by privileging his concern with spirituality over his

---

98 Horkheimer & Adorno, *Dialectic of Enlightenment*, xvii.
99 It should be emphasized that critics' comments on White's treatment of the body rarely focus sustainedly on the corporeal aspect of his fiction. Ann McCulloch, in her book *A Tragic Vision: The Novels of Patrick White*, unwittingly provides an appropriate image for the absence of critical interest in White's take on corporeality when she relegates her comments on the significance of the body to an endnote.
100 Brian Kiernan, "The Novels of Patrick White," in *The Literature of Australia*, ed. Geoffrey Dutton (Harmondsworth: Penguin, 1976): 462.

representations of the phenomenal world. Ron Shepherd, for example, argues that White's fiction centres on

> the apparent dualism between mind and body, spirit and matter. The physical world and bodily existence is a façade which must be pierced by the deeper mind in order to arrive at a better understanding.[101]

Laurence Steven similarly observes that White's fiction

> forces a split between the transcendent realm of significance to which his visionaries gain occasional access, and the banal quotidian actuality in which we live our alienated lives.

This "gap," he continues, "leads to the dualities which are everywhere apparent in White: mind/body, spirit/flesh [...] and so on."[102] Peter Beatson, moreover, identifies the influence of Gnosticism on White's fiction. He consequently argues that White's characters fall from grace to nadir before ascending to a re-established zenith. As the soul approaches its apotheosis, he writes, "the body is seen at its most clumsy, afflicted, or dilapidated."[103] Thus, "more emphasis is placed on the incongruity of the flesh as the soul swims closest to its surface."[104] Beatson's summary eventually dismisses the body entirely: "Every book ends with the implication that the shell has, or will split apart, having outlived its protective and gestative functions."[105]

These observations exemplify a common reading of the body in White criticism. However, an alternative and more plausible interpretation is equally frequent. David Coad, for example, contends that it is "simplistic and inexact to say that White suffered from a Gnostic disgust of the flesh."[106] On the contrary: "The body, the physical, the actual sphere, the taking on of flesh is an essential part of White's double vision of man—a vision based on the idea of incarnation."[107] John Colmer agrees: "White's vision, like that of traditional

---

101 Ron Shepherd, "An Indian Story: 'The Twitching Colonel'," in *Patrick White: A Critical Symposium*, ed. Ron Shepherd & Kirpal Singh (Adelaide, SA: Centre for Research in the New Literatures in English, 1978): 29.
102 Laurence Steven, *Disassociation and Wholeness in Patrick White's Fiction* (Waterloo, Ontario: Wilfrid Laurier UP, 1989): 1–2.
103 Peter Beatson, *The Eye in the Mandala*, 109.
104 Beatson, *The Eye in the Mandala*, 109.
105 *The Eye in the Mandala*, 110.
106 David Coad, "Prophet in the Wilderness," *World Literature Today* 67.3 (Summer 1993): 511.
107 Coad, "Prophet in the Wilderness," 512.

Christianity, turns on the paradox that the spirit is incarnate in the flesh."[108] Similarly, Cynthia vanden Driesen regards White's treatment of the body as successful in establishing "a sense of the deep relevance and value of the actual physical world to the truly religious spirit."[109] Michael Giffin, perhaps most ardently, takes issue with the critical tendency to focus on White's transcendentalism, maintaining that "White questions any transcendental or spiritual signification that excludes the immanent material world."[110] A caveat is necessary here: the readings mentioned in this paragraph are not entirely similar. Coad argues for a "double vision of man" inherent in White, which appears to emphasize the author's dualistic tendencies. John Colmer, who, like Coad, references incarnation, posits a conception of "spirit" in "flesh"; without questioning the linguistic division of these categories, such commentary still maintains a neat binary. It is my contention, however, that dualism is subverted in White's fiction and that a "double vision" is promoted, only to be undermined or critiqued. This is because White does not appear to believe in constructing identity against an opposition or an 'other', and for this reason his writing displays a deep distrust of language, which is necessarily a system of differentiation and exclusion. Thus the "truly religious spirit"[111] bleeds into the material world, such that the two are, in fact, inseparable, constantly shifting and changing places to reveal eventually that the notion of an exclusionary, transcendental consciousness is questioned in White's writing.

The first group of critics mentioned above argues for the importance of transcendence in White's fiction; the second group emphasizes the value of immanence. White's writing appears to navigate between the seeming disavowal of corporeality and the celebration thereof, thus ensuring that both perspectives are, at different times, arguably correct.[112] Accordingly, critics have made what they will of the body in his fiction, choosing to privilege transcendence or immanence according to their own particular preferences. It should be noted, however, that this is more often the case with critics who note

---

108   John Colmer, "Duality in Patrick White," in *Patrick White: A Critical Symposium*, ed. Ron Shepherd & Kirpal Singh (Adelaide, SA: Centre for Research in the New Literatures in English, 1978): 73.
109   Cynthia vanden Driesen, "Patrick White and the 'Unprofessed Factor': The Challenge before the Contemporary Religious Novelist," in *Patrick White: A Critical Symposium*, ed. Ron Shepherd & Kirpal Singh (Adelaide, SA: Centre for Research in the New Literatures in English, 1978): 85.
110   Giffin, *Arthur's Dream*, 11.
111   vanden Driesen, "Patrick White and the 'Unprofessed Factor'," 85.
112   As I argue, however, the disavowal of the body often occurs in quite a specific manner in White's fiction, and is frequently attached to characters who exemplify a body-denial that the texts ultimately question.

a Judaeo-Christian emphasis in White's writing. Those who focus on his Indian religio-spiritual influence, however, such as Gursharan Aurora, emphasize his interest in both transcendence and immanence:

> White's works are affirmative assertions that after a journey through the cleansing fires of suffering, the soul rises again, renewed and regenerated. His characters seek to see the benign face of God in every animate and inanimate object of the world.[113]

Critical perspectives, however, usually rely on the assumption of dualism in White's work, in particular the division between the soul and the body. Critics' use of the terms 'physicality' and 'spirituality', which are largely inescapable in the interpretation of White's fiction, tend to promote the notion of White's interest in a metaphysics of dualism. Yet White, I would argue, invokes mind/body dualism with a view to critiquing it. The texts therefore posit the separation of mind and body *in order to* undermine this supposition. White's fiction, then, should be interpreted as critical of language itself, which necessarily promotes dualism due to its constant construction of identity in opposition to difference. Constantly seeking a way to undermine the exclusionary constructions of language, White thus presents a literature of 'doubleness', persistently emphasizing irony, ambiguity, paradox, and the possibility of multiple interpretations. Ultimately, White does not hold his antitheses "in polar tension," as Carolyn Bliss suggests.[114] Peter Wolfe's understanding of opposites in White is more apposite: they "interact, shift places, and lend mutual support."[115]

Elizabeth Grosz sees the image of the Möbius strip, the inverted three-dimensional figure-of-eight, as analogous to the interconnection of the body and the mind. Her description of the interplay of opposites may be applied to White's work:

> Bodies and minds are not two distinct substances or two kinds of attributes of a single substance but somewhere in between these two alternatives. The Möbius strip has the advantage of showing the inflection of mind into body and body into mind, the ways in which, through a kind of

---

113   Gursharan Aurora, "The Unity of Being—Synergies Between White's Mystic Vision and the Indian Religio-Spiritual Tradition," in *Patrick White Centenary: The Legacy of a Prodigal Son*, ed. Bill Ashcroft & Cynthia vanden Driesen (Newcastle upon Tyne: Cambridge Scholars, 2014): 336.

114   Carolyn Bliss, *Patrick White's Fiction: The Paradox of Fortunate Failure* (London: Macmillan, 1986): 22.

115   Peter Wolfe, *Laden Choirs: The Fiction of Patrick White* (Lexington: UP of Kentucky, 1983): 8.

twisting or inversion, one side becomes another. This model also provides a way of problematising and rethinking the relations between the inside and the outside of the subject, its psychical interior and its corporeal exterior, by showing not their fundamental identity or reducibility but the torsion of the one into the other, the passage, vector, or uncontrollable drift of the inside into the outside and the outside into the inside.[116]

Taking Fresh Shapes: Undermining a Metaphysics of Presence

How might we better understand and theorize White's interrogation of dualism? Is there a way of explaining how it is that White depicts the torsion of mind into body, the "passage, vector, or uncontrollable drift of the inside into the outside and the outside into the inside"?[117]

One possible way of understanding White's subversion of binaries is to interpret his emphasis on the corporeal as undermining what Derrida, in his interrogation of dualism, has termed the "metaphysics of presence."[118] According to Derrida, the history of philosophy centres on a metaphysics of presence, for all metaphysicians,

> from Plato to Rousseau, Descartes to Husserl, have proceeded in this way, conceiving good to be before evil, the positive before the negative, the pure before the impure, the simple before the complex, the essential before the accidental, the imitated before the imitation, etc. And this is not just *one* metaphysical gesture among others.[119]

Indeed, as Derrida argues, the notion of an originating identity, essence or presence in Western philosophy is "*the* metaphysical exigency, that which has been the most constant, most profound and most potent."[120] This originating identity appears to precede its opposition, creating the illusion of its independence and its hierarchical value. By this understanding, the 'mind' is originary, hence valued. What is considered to be secondary, according to Derrida, "is defined

---

116   Grosz, *Volatile Bodies*, xii.
117   *Volatile Bodies*, xii.
118   Jacques Derrida, *Of Grammatology*, tr. & intro. Gayatri Chakravorty Spivak (*De la Grammatologie*, 1967; Baltimore MD: Johns Hopkins UP, 1997): 22.
119   Jacques Derrida, *Limited Inc.*, ed. Gerald Graff, tr. Jeffrey Mehlman & Samuel Weber (Evanston IL: Northwestern UP, 1988): 93.
120   Derrida, *Limited Inc.*, 93.

in terms of *the lack of presence*";[121] thus, the 'body' is defined as the 'absence' of mind and therefore corresponds to Derrida's notion of the "supplement" (the term appearing as an addition to an apparently original term). However, no seemingly originary presence can be defined in and of itself without recourse to its opposition. The mind, therefore, cannot be present to itself in the absence of the body. Originary identities, then, rely on their constituting antitheses. Poststructuralist theory, then, critiques rational subjectivity, positing that the subject is vulnerable to, yet also constructed by, forces that are considered external to it. Derrida refuses the notion of disembodied, ahistorical reason: the Cartesian *cogito* is "not something that is naturally given."[122] Instead, he argues, "there *is* no identity, there is only identification or self-identification *as a process*."[123]

In its contestation of binary oppositions predicated upon the metaphysical notion of indisputable essence and in its refusal to articulate final meaning, White's writing anticipates these thoughts. In *The Aunt's Story*, for example, when Holstius comments to Theodora Goodman on the impossibility of reconciling "joy and sorrow," "flesh and marble," "illusion and reality," and "life and death," he notes the dynamic interplay at work between binary oppositions:

> one constantly deludes the other into taking fresh shapes, so that there is sometimes little to choose between the reality of illusion and the illusion of reality.
>
> *The Aunt's Story* 278

This observation of the inherent dynamism of binaries seems consonant with the poststructuralist notion that binary terms exist in an unsettled relationship of mutual dependence: while one term may be valorized over the other within a particular culture, it in fact depends for its meaning on the exclusion of this apparent other. As a result, the cultural privileging of one term over its 'other' is rendered unstable: the supplementary category of the dyad is central to the primary term, yet is simultaneously excluded from it. To return to Holstius's example, "reality," prized in Theodora's resolutely "reasonable," materialist, and colonial context, is in fact revealed as relying on "illusion," the 'other' it abjects. Evident in this example is White's critique of "classical metaphysics which has, according to modern and postmodern logic, distorted the western eye with

---

121 Niall Lucy, *A Derrida Dictionary* (Malden MA: Blackwell, 2004): 102, emphasis in original.
122 Jacques Derrida, "Following Theory," in *life.after.theory*. ed. Michael Payne & John Schad (London: Continuum, 2003): 25.
123 Derrida, "Following Theory," 25, emphasis added.

false conceptual language and exclusive philosophical categories."[124] Indeed, as White suggests through the mouthpiece of Mary Hare, language consists of "sad, bad word[s]," which "leave [...] out half."[125]

Critics influenced by the poststructuralist turn in theory have identified aspects of White's fiction that overturn the neat distinctions between mind and body suggested within his apparent language of dualities. Referring briefly to the importance of the body in White's writing, Michael Giffin argues that White's repetition of a "scatological and excremental motif" expresses a world vision "essentially bound up with the possibility of a real scatological presence, and the impossibility of any real presence in a disembodied Classical ideology."[126] Giffin's account focuses convincingly on White's contestation of "the problem of a Classical metaphysics" with its "dualistic language of exclusive philosophical categories."[127] Accordingly, he argues that White has

> a strong sense of how the Classical presumptions of the Enlightenment continue to undermine the twentieth-century [...] imagination, by shutting out non-linguistic and unconscious truths and by seeking refuge within the solipsism created by reason, by language and by the conscious mind.[128]

This solipsism of reason precludes the acknowledgement of the body's importance and the possibility of embodied compassion.

Veronica Brady supports Giffin's thesis. She argues, however, for the influence on White of Simone Weil's philosophy, in particular her assertion of a "primacy of physical necessity" over the "Cartesian premise that mind is the dominant factor."[129] Brady notes a similar philosophy in White which accounts for "the duality, the tension between body and mind so evident in his work,"

> in his insistence upon physical weakness, in particular upon an 'excremental vision' which many find so distasteful. Even his language insists upon

---

124 Michael Giffin, "Judaism between *Torah, Haskalah* and *Kabbalah*: The Revealed Imagination in the Novels of Patrick White," *Journal of Literature and Theology* 8.1 (March 1994): 66.
125 White, *Riders in the Chariot*, 383.
126 Giffin, *Arthur's Dream*, 15.
127 *Arthur's Dream*, 12.
128 *Arthur's Dream*, 12.
129 Veronica Brady, "The Novelist and the Reign of Necessity: Patrick White and Simone Weil," in *Patrick White: A Critical Symposium*, ed. Ron Shepherd & Kirpal Singh (Adelaide, SA: Centre for Research in the New Literatures in English, 1978): 108.

paradox as it reminds us of the bodily origins of experience, contesting the mind's longing for permanence and illusions of mastery, and showing how these origins precede the claims of grammatical propriety.[130]

Brady's argument develops earlier evaluations of White's work which, like John Colmer's, describe it as presenting what is "pre-eminently a dualistic universe," yet one which asserts "the unity of all things, and the possibility that his chosen elect may enjoy visions of such unity."[131] Although Colmer has argued that White's "vision of duality is more convincing than his vision of unity,"[132] his recognition of one of White's paradoxes begins to suggest that what fascinates White is in fact neither unity nor duality—nor transcendence nor immanence, for that matter—but perpetual dialectic. For White, dialectics are the inescapable bind of a human consciousness that must necessarily think in dualistic terms, but that perpetually experiences moments of ambiguity and illumination that gesture towards the indeterminacy between or even beyond binary oppositions.

The philosophical history of dialectics can be traced back to the Ancient Greeks, who compared opposing views in the belief that truth would emerge through their confrontation. Later, in modern philosophy, Hegel argued that a dialectical method would produce the underlying identity of contradictions, eventually resulting in a stable unification of opposites. Critics like John Colmer ascribe a Hegelian logic to White's fiction, arguing for the texts' stabilizing of contradictory elements. Indeed, a summary of Hegel's *Phenomenology of Spirit* reads much like traditional critical responses to White's writing. The *Phenomenology*, writes Sara Salih, follows "the progress of an increasingly self-conscious spirit towards absolute knowledge."[133] Hegel's great work, then, is comparable to a bildungsroman, or novel of development; indeed, Jonathan Rae has compared it to Homer's *Odyssey*, Dante's *Divine Comedy*, and Bunyan's *Pilgrim's Progress*.[134] Similarly, many critics have described the *raison d'être* of White's protagonists as a "spiritual odyssey,"[135] a phrase evoking both the Hegelian narrative and the genre of the bildungsroman or quest.[136] Laura Trevelyan

---

130   Brady, "The Novelist and the Reign of Necessity," 109.
131   John Colmer, *Patrick White* (London: Methuen, 1984): 21.
132   John Colmer, *Riders in the Chariot: Patrick White* (Melbourne: Edward Arnold, 1978): 2.
133   Sara Salih, *Judith Butler* (London: Routledge, 2002): 22.
134   Salih, *Judith Butler*, 22.
135   Steven, *Disassociation and Wholeness*, 15.
136   Douglas Loney, for example, describes *The Aunt's Story* as "an account of the odyssey of a woman's spirit; the story of Theodora Goodman's quest after true knowledge of her self

of *Voss* appears to advocate Hegel's notion of a journey toward absolute knowledge when she speaks of "True knowledge, which only comes of death by torture in the country of the mind."[137] However, while clearly courting Hegel's dialectical philosophy, White's writing defies the notion of eventual resolution and stable completion. As Alan Lawson notes, his narratives unsettle us "by appearing to offer a couple of very familiar narrative conventions [...] by offering, that is, *models of reading* in which we have been well-trained": namely, "the Hegelian Triad," "the journey of self-discovery," and "the quest for psychic or spiritual wholeness."[138] As Lawson argues, however, they are in fact narratives of fragmentation, concerned with the "repudiation of hierarchy, linearity, teleology, and singularity" and determined to illuminate "the irrational, the erratic, with multiplicity, with multi-faceted variants."[139] Indeed, Laura Trevelyan posits "true knowledge" as beyond conceptual understanding: "Knowledge was never a matter of geography. Quite the reverse, it overflows all maps that exist."[140] White's writing evades the static unification of opposites and exceeds the limits of a univocal representation. Moreover, in his impatience with the Enlightenment notion of the self-enclosed, self-knowing transcendental ego, his characters embark on narrative journeys wherein the self is dissolved rather than consolidated and wherein rational knowledge is inherently problematized.

White's Philosophy of Becoming

White's interest in dialectics and his articulation of a theory of productive motion which he terms "becoming" anticipate the poststructuralist attention to the philosophy of process. The attention he pays to flux and transfiguration, summarized in the term "becoming," is one of his primary thematic concerns, contributing to his representations of somatic spirituality, the human condition, and the narrative techniques through which he expresses these. For White, "motion [is] an expression of truth, the only true permanence";[141] in

---

and her world"; Loney, "Theodora Goodman and the Minds of Mortals: Patrick White's *The Aunt's Story*," *English Studies in Canada* 8.4 (December 1982): 483.
137   White, *Voss*, 446.
138   Alan Lawson, "Bound to Dis-integrate—Narrative and Interpretation in *The Aunt's Story*," *Antipodes* 6.1 (June 1992): 9.
139   Lawson, "Bound to Dis-integrate," 12.
140   White, *Voss*, 446.
141   White, *Riders in the Chariot*, 636.

other words, if there is any truth, it is that notions of truth and identity are unstable. Moreover, because of his strong association of "becoming" with human suffering, the term and its connotations furnish an important aspect of his philosophy of embodiment. An epigraph to his first novel, *Happy Valley*, asserts that "progress is to be measured by the amount of suffering undergone." In the novels that follow, the interest in becoming recurs, referring to the continuous evolution of embodied experience, which is often related to struggle and suffering. As Frank Le Mesurier of *Voss* explains, the "mystery of life is not solved by success, which is an end in itself, but in failure, in perpetual struggle, in becoming."[142]

Seigworth and Gregg's discussion of affect may provide a fruitful starting point for a re-assessment of how Le Mesurier's oft-quoted statement may be understood and extrapolated to White's fiction in general. They argue that "affect is integral to a body's perpetual becoming,"[143] and that the body,

> always becoming otherwise, however subtly, than what it already is, [is] pulled beyond its seeming surface-boundedness by way of its relation to, indeed its composition through, the forces of encounter. With affect, a body is as much outside itself as in itself—webbed in its relations—until ultimately such firm distinctions cease to matter.

White, it may be argued, is interested in what these theorists describe as "the affective bloom-space of an ever-processual materiality" (9), an observation which is particularly relevant to an author whose flower symbolism is always deeply imbricated with the "bloom-space" of corporeality and sexuality. In White, roses, like bodies, in one memorable example of "becoming," "sparkled drowsed brooded leaped flaunting their earthbound flesh in an honourably failed attempt to convey the ultimate."[144] Furthermore, roses are associated with the abject corporeality that threatens the notion of discrete subjectivity. In *The Solid Mandala*, as Waldo acknowledges: "Roseflesh on occasion had made him shiver."[145]

In its concern with dialectics and similar deployments of the term 'becoming', the writing of Gilles Deleuze seems appropriate to the interpretation of White's emphasis on process. Deleuze, as Claire Colebrook explains, argues "against a dialectic that would place contradictions together in order to

---

142 White, *Voss*, 267.
143 Gregory J. Seigworth & Melissa Gregg, "An Inventory of Shimmers," 3.
144 White, *The Eye of the Storm*, 205.
145 White, *The Solid Mandala*, 119.

reveal some final truth."[146] Instead, Deleuze conceptualizes a "superior dialectic" that allows "differences and contradictions to remain in tension." Rather than revealing "an underlying truth or identity," it discloses "difference and becoming."[147] As I mentioned earlier, we may be reminded of Grosz's image of the Möbius strip—the inverted figure-of-eight serving to illustrate the motion of a concept into its antithesis. This image suggests that the 'mind', for example, is not strictly unified with the 'body', but that binaries flow into each other so that it is ultimately impossible to locate where it is that one begins and the other ends. The two exist in a free-flowing relationship of difference and becoming. Being and becoming are philosophical concepts frequently contrasted in White's themes and imagery. Closed images of the body, predominantly via the imagery of Classicism and statuary, are unfavorably contrasted with the unstable, shifting imagery of flux and music. Such images respectively bespeak the enclosure of being and the open-endedness of becoming, and in their comparison suggest White's resistance to the former.

The history of Western thought has presupposed the notion of being, as Derrida's argument for the metaphysics of presence maintains. 'Being', or the concept of a stable, essential self that responds to flux or becoming, correlates with the idea of a self-enclosed mind. 'Becoming', by contrast, is contingent: it is related to the physical world, to the body, to that which is susceptible to change. Deleuze contends that experience does not happen to a fixed human subject with a stable point of view. Instead, he reformulates the human subject and its outside world (the seemingly stable subject/object divide) as fictions within the undifferentiated flux of experience: "the world (continuity and distinction) is an outright fiction of the imagination."[148] In the pantheistic vision expressed by Le Mesurier's description of his imagined death in *Voss*, White's similar concern with the construction of subjectivity is illustrated:

> O God, my God, I pray that you will take my spirit out of this my body's remains, and after you have scattered it, grant that it shall be everywhere, and in the rocks, and in the empty waterholes, and in true love of all men, and in you, O God, at last.
> *Voss* 297

---

146   Claire Colebrook, *Gilles Deleuze* (London: Routledge, 2002): 49.
147   Colebrook, *Gilles Deleuze*, 49.
148   Gilles Deleuze, *Empiricism and Subjectivity: An Essay on Hume's Theory of Human Nature*, tr. Constantin V. Boundas (*Empirisme et subjectivité*, 1953; New York: Columbia UP, 1991): 80.

Moreover, in the many descriptions of landscape that permeate White's fiction, the division between the enclosed subject, existing in a world of interiority, and the external world is broken down. Mary Hare of *Riders in the Chariot*, constantly merging with and dissolving into the landscape, exemplifies this. This aspect of her character is further emphasized by the metonymic facility of the house, "Xanadu," in which she lives. Xanadu is crumbling, its walls no longer setting up a barrier to the outside world. The "structure of Xanadu" is entering into a "conspiracy with nature":

> Creatures were admitted that had never been inside before, and what had hitherto appeared to be a curtain, loosely woven of light and leaves, was, in fact, seen to be a wall.
> *Riders in the Chariot* 377

This "wall," of course, is failing in its role as barrier between interior and exterior. Houses in White's fiction often symbolize subjectivity,[149] and once again we are presented with an image of the dissolution of the borders of the self: there is a free-flowing space of 'becoming' between what is 'inside' and the supposedly objective, 'outside' world.

Colebrook notes that Deleuze's philosophy reveals "the tendency for human life to form images of itself," a tendency most notably theorized by Lacan. It is, however, the ambition of the poststructuralists to explode the notions of being and essence that enclose us within the projections of our imagination. Deleuze's concept of becoming, which involves the dissolution of constructed, static images, is enacted stylistically in his work via language that draws attention to its instability and dynamism. For Deleuze, "the aim of writing should not be representation but invention."[150] Le Mesurier's notions of "perpetual struggle" and "becoming," conceived in relation to his writing endeavor, similarly posit writing as an act of invention that does away with the impossible project of an "accurate" representation premised on essence or truth:

> In the beginning I used to imagine that if I were to succeed in describing with any accuracy some thing, this little cone of light with the blurry

---

149   In this connection, see, for example, Gordon Collier, "Metonyms of Mood and Condition: The Semiosis of Habitation in Selected Australian Fiction Since Patrick White," in *The Cross-Cultural Legacy: Critical and Creative Writings in Memory of Hena Maes–Jelinek*, ed. Gordon Collier, Geoffrey V. Davis, Marc Delrez & Bénédicte Ledent (Cross/Cultures 193; Leiden & Boston MA: Brill | Rodopi, 2017): 255–293 (esp. 259–267).

150   Colebrook, *Gilles Deleuze*, 4.

edges, for instance, or this common pannikin, then I would be expressing all truth. But I could not. My whole life has been a failure, lived at a most humiliating level, always purposeless, frequently degrading. Until I became aware of my power. The mystery of life is not solved by success, which is an end in itself, but in failure, in perpetual struggle, in becoming.
Voss 271

The invention of art and language and its relation to 'becoming' is often emphasized in White's fiction. John Colmer perceptively identifies White's deployment of the artist-figure to "reconcile the duality of body and spirit in a manner impossible to ordinary people."[151] Yet this "reconciliation," more often than not, is a representation of motion in stasis: it is emphasized as the permanence of dialectical tension. Alf Dubbo's painting of the Riders in the Chariot exemplifies this paradox:

> From certain angles the canvas presented a reversal of the relationship between permanence and motion, as though the banks of a river were to begin to flow alongside its stationary waters.
> *Riders in the Chariot* 597–598

At the same time, the canvas depicts the physicality of the "riders" in a particular way:

> the souls of his Four Living Creatures were illuminating their bodies, in various colours. Their hands, which he painted open, had surrendered their sufferings, but not yet received beatitude. So they were carried on, along the oblique trajectory, towards the top left corner. And the painter signed his name, in the bottom right, in neat red, as Mrs Pask had taught him:
>   A.   DUBBO
> *Riders in the Chariot* 598–599

The Riders in the painting embody the motion of dialectic, representing the dynamic torsion of 'soul' into 'body' that 'illuminates' corporeality. Mary Hare is described a few pages earlier as "illuminated by the light of instinct" (594), revealing that corporeal instinct and the 'soul' are not irresolvably different concepts. That the Riders are "Living Creatures" is significant, suggesting the importance of the living body in White's writing. Further, the trajectory of the Riders sees them poised between Dubbo's signature—his identity—in the

---

[151] Colmer, *Riders in the Chariot*, 38.

bottom right corner of the canvas and the apparent beatitude represented by the space beyond the corner at the top left. This diagonal dynamism enacts White's concern with the loss of rational subjectivity—the movement from name to dissolution, *logos* to *jouissance*—inherent in the acceptance of the body. While it may be argued that the representation of 'souls' and 'bodies' maintains White's interest in dualism and thus in 'escaping' the flesh, Dubbo's experience as he finishes the painting precludes this interpretation:

> He sat down stiffly on the bed. The sharp pain poured in crimson tones into the limited space of the room, and overflowed. It poured and overflowed his hands. These were gilded, he was forced to observe, with his own gold.
> *Riders in the Chariot* 599

Despite this being the moment of his death, Dubbo's blood signifies his lifeforce and, moreover, in White's synaesthesia, suggests the illuminating artistry of physicality. It is the physical force of existence that engenders *Alf's* illumination—not merely the illumination of the painting—and provides the energy and narrative alchemy of the episode. This is a moment of poetic 'becoming' when the traditional associations of horror and disgust in relation to the body's incontinence are disallowed. Moreover, the body as a site of poetic excess is emphasized through the repetition of the words "poured" and "overflowed." Dubbo's art cannot be conceptually or linguistically contained, and neither can his body: his art is his blood and his blood his art. In this moment of *jouissance*, rationality is engulfed by the corporeal. Associations transform and expand to reveal White's poetic indeterminacy, linguistic suggestiveness, and ultimately his sense of the dynamic, embodied, and affective sacred. The purifying sublimation of art is revealed: first, via Dubbo's illuminated painting and, second, via the poetic elevation of corporeality. Indeed, as Kristeva notes in one of the epigraphs to the present chapter, the Logos is capable of purification. This, however, is emphatically not "in the manner of the *Phaedo*, stoically separating oneself from a body whose substance and passions are sources of impurity."[152] White's literature writes corporeality into its dynamics, the focus of the following chapter, confronting the reader with a liberating and sublime abjection.

---

152   Kristeva, *Powers of Horror*, 27.

CHAPTER 3

Pulsating Prose

This chapter explores the physicality of language and how this is thematized in White's writing. An interest in writing as physical manifests itself in White's fiction in two ways. First, it focuses on language's materiality, self-reflexively revealing it as composed of material signs and presenting imagery, metaphor, symbol, rhythm, and onomatopoeia, for example, as emphasizing this materiality. Second, it suggests that bodily processes and desire enter representation. The production of art, as White conceptualizes it, involves the externalization of internal ideas and affects. It is therefore compared to excretion and imagined as a process in which the body is turned inside-out. The workings of desire are also enacted in White's style—in the way in which signification operates to attest to the physical intensities within and between characters and thus between body and text. Moreover, White compares two contrasting modes of language: a poetic language attuned to the embodied experiences of his protagonists (performatively enacted in White's style itself), and a prosaic form of everyday expression. The latter communicates, but in a merely banal fashion, and cannot convey White's seemingly unrepresentable vision. The rational product of the 'disembodied' mind, it empties signification of corporeal impulse and affect. Poetic language, by contrast, points up the entry of corporeality into representation.

White often thematizes the materiality of language, thereby drawing the reader's attention to the fabric of his prose. Words may appear to gain shape and form for his characters, seemingly transmuting into physical objects, while simultaneously exceeding the narrow transmission of univocal meaning. Moreover, they proceed directly from the body: characters may "disgorge out of [the] throat chunks of words."[1] For White, poetic writing is dense, weighty, and inscrutable, in contrast to the apparently transparent language of rational, prosaic expression. This is evident when Laura Trevelyan, in the initial stages of realizing her affinity with Voss, experiences language as tangibly physical:

> She was too hot, of course, in the thick dress that she had put on for a colder day, with the result that all words became great round weights. She did not raise her head for those the German spoke, but heard them fall

---

1 Patrick White, *Voss*, 167.

and loved their shape. So far departed from that rational level to which she had determined to adhere, her own thoughts were grown obscure, even natural. She did not care. It was lovely. She would have liked to sit upon a rock and listen to words, not of a man, but detached, mysterious, poetic words that she alone would interpret through some sense inherited from sleep.

Voss 63

Laura links the tangible physicality of the "great round weights" of words to her departure "from [a] rational level," despite her initial determination to adhere to reason and logic. The passage suggests that language itself may depart from rationality, and therefore from its representative function, becoming "detached, mysterious, poetic." As she acknowledges the materiality of language and its affiliation with an unconscious dimension of experience—"some sense inherited from sleep"—Laura's thoughts grow "obscure, even natural." For this initially most rational of characters, not even her thoughts are sacrosanct: the mind, too, becomes "natural" or physical. Correspondingly, her awareness of the materiality of language is causally related to her physical experience: "She was too hot [...] *with the result* that all words became great round weights." Her bodily sensations ensure that she interprets Voss, her surroundings, and even language differently. Rationality thus disintegrates as physicality takes over, flooding not only Laura's awareness but also the dynamics of the text: the "great round weights" of Voss's words, stressed by the rhythm of the sentence, become the weighty signifiers of the narrative as well. The representation of Laura's body thus affects the rhythm of the text, contributing to its metaphors, interpretation, and indeed the physicality of Voss's "mysterious, poetic words." White's writing is often at its most linguistically and suggestively resonant when describing the material world in language that is presented as correspondingly material.

Such descriptions of language's opacity contribute to White's implication that representation is unable to capture experience completely. This failure of language indicates the limits of rational consciousness and is related to a prevailing sense of metaphysical questioning and mysticism. Arthur Brown, for example, recognizes that language is incapable of transparently expressing its meaning. However, as a chain of metonymically linked, material signifiers, it accumulates an increasing sense of significance:

he came up with something which was on his mind and spat it out, wet: "Tell Mrs Musto I'm concentrating on words. *The* Word. But also words

> that are just words. There's so many kinds. You could make necklaces. Big chunks of words, for instance, and the shiny polished ones. *God,* 'he said, and the spit spattered on Waldo's face,' is a kind of sort of *rock* crystal."
>
> *The Solid Mandala* 87 (emphases in original)

Arthur's discussion of language indeed makes a "necklace" of sorts, linking body, word, and material object and ascribing to each an enormous sense of spiritual significance. *God* is *word, rock crystal, spit,* and an overarching "kind of sort of" plenitude of inarticulable, indeterminate meaning. White's writing, too, accumulates a sense of uncapturable yet proliferating significance as it links words into webs of intimate connection.

For White, moreover, body and representation are so intimately associated that he conceptualizes writing, or the production of any art, for that matter, as a bodily process comparable to excretion. In fact, to illustrate the connection between the body and artistic production, he occasionally invoked metaphors of defecation to describe his literary output:

> I shocked some people the other night by saying writing is really like shitting; and then reading the letters of Pushkin a little later, I found he said exactly the same thing! It's something you have to get out of you.[2]

In the next sentence, he persists with the analogy: "I didn't write for a long time at one stage, and built up such an accumulation of shit that I wrote *The Tree of Man*."[3] In *The Vivisector*, Hurtle Duffield responds irritably to the question, "Painting anything lately?": "What could you reply? Am I breathing? Am I shitting?"[4] and Waldo in *The Solid Mandala* imagines literary creation as explosive excretion.[5] This focus on art as excretion has confounded critics, among them Lyndon Harries:

> The parallels between the workings of Hurtle's imagination and the movements of the lower bowel have a more artistic explanation, but even so, like so much else in White's novels, it may strike the average reader as very strange.[6]

---

2 Patrick White, "In the Making" (1969), in *Patrick White Speaks*, ed. Brennan & Flynn, 22.
3 White, "In the Making" (1969), in *Patrick White Speaks*, ed. Brennan & Flynn, 22.
4 Patrick White, *The Vivisector*, 413.
5 White, *The Solid Mandala*, 110.
6 Lyndon Harries, "The Peculiar Gifts of Patrick White," *Contemporary Literature* 19.4 (Autumn 1978): 467.

The Decorative Voice of Hidden, Secret Flesh: Barthes, Kristeva, and Locating Corporeality in Language

How do we make sense of the strangeness of the materiality—indeed, the often scatological physicality—of White's writing? According to Roland Barthes, modernist writing exemplifies a kind of bodiliness inherent in the dynamics of style:

> imagery, delivery, vocabulary spring from the body and the past of the writer and gradually become the very reflexes of his art. Thus under the name of style a self-sufficient language is evolved which has its roots only in the depths of the author's personal and secret mythology, that subnature of expression where the first coition of words and things takes place, where once and for all the great verbal themes of his existence come to be installed. Whatever its sophistication, style has always something crude about it [...]. Its frame of reference is biological or biographical, not historical: it is the writer's 'thing', his glory and his prison. [...] It is the decorative voice of hidden, secret flesh [...].[7]

Thus, Barthes draws attention to the primitive origins of a writer's style, which he locates within the writer's body and his or her psychic context. Style is emphasized as an unconscious "reflex" deriving from the pre-symbolic "subnature of expression"—the "decorative voice of hidden, secret flesh."

O.N. Burgess maintains that "to ask critics not to call White's style into question is to ask them to abdicate one of the tasks of criticism,"[8] and, indeed, corporeality appears to have much to do with White's style, which has been of great interest to many of his critics. John Colmer, for example, comments on White's "highly personal prose," which is "strikingly original in its rhythms and syntax, energetic in its movement, adventurously explorative in every way, full of shocks and surprises."[9] Veronica Brady identifies the "melodramatic pressures" that White places upon language via "lexical and syntactical distortions and violations as well as in the concreteness of description."[10] In the most

---

7   Roland Barthes, *Writing Degree Zero*, tr. Annette Lavers & Colin Smith (*Le degré zéro de l'écriture*, 1953/64; New York: Hill & Wang, 1968): 10–11.
8   O.N. Burgess, "Patrick White, His Critics and Laura Trevelyan," *Australian Quarterly* 33.4 (December 1961): 50.
9   John Colmer, *Riders in the Chariot: Patrick White* (Melbourne: Edward Arnold, 1978): 5.
10 Veronica Brady, "'Down at the Dump' and Lacan's Mirror Stage," *Australian Literary Studies* 11.2 (October 1983): 237.

comprehensive study of White's style to date, *The Rocks and Sticks of Words*, Gordon Collier notes the "almost palpable density" of White's writing, the "texture of language."[11] Most recently, J.M. Coetzee has attested to White's writing as an admixture of the "complex music of his prose and the mystical bent of his thought."[12] The rhythms, energies, pressures, concreteness, density, texture, music, and mysticism of White's prose may all be linked to his treatment of corporeality in language.

Roland Barthes's ideas strongly influenced the early writing of Julia Kristeva. In her first book, *Revolution in Poetic Language*, she likewise posited the entry of the body into symbolization. Her opening remarks decry previous theories of language in which the body has been dismissed: "Our philosophies of language [...] are nothing more than the thoughts of archivists, archaeologists, and necrophiliacs."[13] Kristeva maintains, then, that earlier language theories have killed off the body, objectifying corporeality rather than recognizing its constitutive importance in the dynamics of representation. In response, she proffers a theory that describes language as the *living* product of dynamic bodily investments:

> Instead of lamenting what is lost, absent, or impossible in language, Kristeva marvels at this other realm [bodily experience] that makes its way into language. The force of language is [a] living driving force transferred into language. Signification is like a transfusion of the living body into language.[14]

Kristeva is interested in the ways in which literary texts consolidate and undermine their own seemingly stable "subjectivity," much as the speaking subject acquires a tentative identity via the simultaneously formative and threatening process of abjection. This is an ongoing dialectical process: the "transcendental ego and the meaning posited by it are merely moments in 'the unfolding of' 'a signifying process' that exceeds them."[15] In both subjectivity and textuality, Kristeva maintains, conflicting tensions work to produce and destabilize rationality and coherence. The terms "symbolic" and "semiotic," which Kristeva

---

11   Collier, *The Rocks and Sticks of Words*, 1.
12   J.M. Coetzee, "Introduction" to Patrick White, *The Vivisector* (New York: Penguin, 2009): xiii.
13   Julia Kristeva, *Revolution in Poetic Language*, 13.
14   Kelly Oliver, "Conflicted Love," *Hypatia* 15.3 (Summer 2000): 8.
15   John Lechte & Maria Margaroni, *Julia Kristeva: Live Theory* (London & New York: Continuum, 2004): 12.

uses idiosyncratically, represent these tensions respectively, referring to the interlocking yet contradictory aspects of the signifying process. The semiotic (which should not be confused with Saussure's term for the study of the system of signs) refers to the various amorphous and unstable corporeal drives and impulses that traverse the infant's body prior to its induction into the symbolic order. Traces of this energy remain and return throughout life. The semiotic is therefore the *bodily* component of the signifying process, which bears traces of the infant's primordial relation to the mother's body prior to the development of the ego and the acquisition of language. Kristeva contends that the "music" of poetry and modern, avant-garde prose harnesses the "instinctual rhythm" of the semiotic, which disorders and punctuates meaning.[16] As John Lechte explains, the semiotic inheres in the "dynamic and unrepresentable poetic dimension of language: its rhymes, rhythms, intonations, alliterations—melody, the music of language."[17]

In contrast to the semiotic, Kristeva argues, the symbolic amounts to the socially constructed and rule-bound operations of signification. Unlike the libidinal, disordering (and therefore death-drive-associated) semiotic, the symbolic produces the laws of grammar and syntax, thereby promoting the unambiguous and rational expression of meaning and the coherence of the "speaking subject." As such, it generates the social order to which it accordingly conforms. Kristeva describes the symbolic as a "sacrificial order"[18] because it organizes and represses the corporeal impulses of the semiotic, holding the latter in check in order to produce coherent meaning and rational, unambiguous expression. Importantly, however, the symbolic is in a constant dialectical relationship with the semiotic, and its hierarchical dominance over the latter is by no means guaranteed.

Kristeva's distinction between the symbolic and the semiotic should therefore not be interpreted as a dichotomy equivalent to the hierarchical dualisms inherent in Classical and post-Enlightenment Western thought. Instead, her dialectical theory of the relationship between the symbolic and the semiotic dimensions of signification reveals that the semiotic aspect of the binary always invades its "opposition." White's fiction similarly explores the irruption of nature, body, the unconscious, and affect into the vulnerable constructs of culture, mind, consciousness, and reason. It shows that the boundaries we erect to keep ourselves within our seemingly stable modern constructs are in fact fluid,

---

16   Kristeva, *Revolution in Poetic Language*, 100.
17   John Lechte, *Julia Kristeva* (London: Routledge, 1990): 5.
18   Elizabeth Grosz, *Sexual Subversions: Three French Feminists* (Sydney: Allen & Unwin, 1989): 49.

slippery, and insubstantial, and it does so within "poetic language" that allows for the transgression of the symbolic and the promotion of the materiality of representation.

Kristeva's *Revolution in Poetic Language* emphasizes the bodily or semiotic component of language as an "abject" element of signification: like the abject, the semiotic cannot be definitively jettisoned; it continues to exist as a disruptive threat to coherence and meaning. It transgresses the limits of the symbolic in representations where the "relationships between words and concepts privileged by the symbolic are significantly disrupted,"[19] in signification that draws attention to its materiality rather than transparently evoking its referents. White's fiction favors "living words" over "dry communications which [do] not really convey."[20] It presents the semiotic, or the physical aspect and capacity of language, as ultimately more communicative than the bloodless, transparent transmission of meaning associated with the symbolic. Noel MacAinsh accordingly observes that White's prose "sways over the borderline between 'talk' and pre-verbal 'communication',"[21] attempting to access the affective, abject dimension of the latter within his literary language. Thus, it explores the "irruption of drives" into the "language which binds together the social unit."[22]

White's own descriptions of his writing and the writing process suggest that the abject, semiotic dimension of signification was of vital importance to him. In Freudian terms, he claimed that his fiction rose "up out of [his] unconscious":[23] "Practically everything I have done of any worth I feel I have done through my intuition, not my mind—which the intellectuals disapprove of."[24] Like his quasi-autobiographical character Alex Gray, White recognized the value of the "therapy of revolutionary violence,"[25] evinced in his favored theme of transgression and seemingly correlating with the release of psychic desire into language. In *Voss*, Frank Turner describes Le Mesurier's scribblings: "Mad things [...] to blow the world up, anyhow, the world that you and me knows. Poems and things."[26] In White's fiction, the unconscious processes invested in writing are destructive because they tear apart the rational assignment of

---

19   Ruth Robbins, *Literary Feminisms* (Basingstoke: Macmillan, 2000): 129.
20   White, *Voss*, 123.
21   Noel MacAinsh, "Voss and his Communications—A Structural Contrast," *Australian Literary Studies* 10.4 (October 1982): 439.
22   Kristeva, *Revolution in Poetic Language*, 62.
23   White, "In the Making" (1969), in *Patrick White Speaks*, ed. Brennan & Flynn, 21.
24   White, "In the Making," 21.
25   Patrick White, *Memoirs of Many in One* (London: Jonathan Cape, 1986): 72.
26   White, *Voss*, 255.

signified to signifier, disorder meaning, and enable the engulfment of reason by the corporeal.

In fact, White associated his creative impulse with destruction. As he explained in an interview, "everything I write has to be dredged up from the unconscious, which is what makes it such an exhausting and perhaps finally, destructive, process."[27] Moreover, as his letters attest, he linked his writing to his sexuality: "I feel more and more that creative activity in the arts is very closely connected with sexual activity";[28] "If I am anything of a writer it is through my homosexuality, which has given me additional insights, and through a *very strong vein of vulgarity.*"[29] Thus, not only are sexuality and abjection important to the working of White's fiction, but desire enters and helps direct the creative process. Moreover, it invests language with a rhythm and drive that threaten to disfigure logic and meaning. Such thoughts recall Elyot Standish's fear of the "drunken, disorderly passions of existence, that created but at the same time consumed."[30] The "drunken, disorderly passions" constitute the abject element of White's language, which White himself links to his scatological impulse—that "vein of vulgarity" pulsing strongly through his work.

Rationality and Corporeality: A Necessary Coupling

Kristeva's symbolic and semiotic modes exist in a relationship of interdependence. As she insists, "never the one without the other":[31]

> These two modalities [the symbolic and the semiotic] are inseparable within the *signifying process* that constitutes language, and the dialectic between them determines the type of discourse [...] involved [...]. [...] there are nonverbal signifying systems that are constructed exclusively on the basis of the semiotic (music, for example). But [...] this exclusivity is relative, precisely because of the necessary dialectic between the two modalities of the signifying process, which is constitutive of the subject. Because the subject is always *both* symbolic and semiotic, no signifying

---

27 Thelma Herring & G.A. Wilkes, "A Conversation with Patrick White," *Southerly* 33.2 (June 1973): 139.
28 Patrick White, *Letters*, ed. David Marr (London: Jonathan Cape, 1994): 339.
29 White, *Letters*, 537, emphasis in original.
30 Patrick White, *The Living and the Dead*, 305.
31 Toril Moi, *The Kristeva Reader* (Oxford: Basil Blackwell, 1986): 156.

system he produces can be either 'exclusively' semiotic or 'exclusively' symbolic, and is instead necessarily marked by an indebtedness to both.[32]

As it is with the speaking subject, so it is with the text. The subject emerges into symbolization out of the semiotic, against which it continues to build a sense of itself as rational and coherent, and with which it continues to be invested via the pulsations of drives and desire. Like Kristeva, White emphasizes the interconnection of rationality and bodiliness, never allowing the two to be radically separated. Despite his concern with the body, he is aware that the creative bodily component of language requires rational control in order to make sense; the two must be joined in a constant dialectic. Thus, White describes the significance of the relationship between sensuality and reason to his writing process: "What drives me is sensual, emotional, instinctive. At the same time I like to think creative reason reins me in as I reach the edge of disaster."[33]

In its characterization, White's fiction sometimes appears to embody the conflicting yet interrelated modalities of the symbolic and the semiotic. In *The Solid Mandala*, Arthur and Waldo Brown seem carefully depicted not only as interlocking, contrasting halves of a single self, but also as the antithetical forces contributing to a unified artwork. For Ann McCulloch, "Waldo is potentially the provider of Apollonian form; Arthur is the source, the wild, inebriated Dionysian force that requires form."[34] Thus, she points to the twins as personifying antithetical artistic or linguistic elements that together contribute to White's unified yet tensely dynamic style. Other critics have similarly noted that the twin brothers respectively embody humanity's "flesh and spirit, reason and will" and, together, the "interdependence [...] of these attributes."[35] It should be emphasized, however, that White's foregrounding of dualism is never quite this simplistic, and apparent antitheses are created in order ultimately to reveal the inherent slipperiness of conceptual oppositions. McCulloch's association of Waldo with Apollonian form and Arthur with the Dionysian force that requires it simplifies the concern in White's fiction with the dynamic between reason and corporeality; or, more accurately, its portrayal of abjection. Arthur does not require Waldo's body-denying "form" so much as Waldo requires the return of his repressions. As Gordon Collier meticulously argues:

---

32   Kristeva, *Revolution in Poetic Language*, 24, emphasis in the original.
33   Patrick White, *Flaws in the Glass: A Self-Portrait* (London: Jonathan Cape, 1981): 89.
34   Ann M. McCulloch, *A Tragic Vision: The Novels of Patrick White* (St Lucia: U of Queensland P, 1983): 28.
35   Patricia Morley, *The Mystery of Unity: Theme and Techniques in the Novels of Patrick White* (Montreal & Kingston, Ontario: McGill–Queen's UP, 1972): 185.

the surface movement of the narrative might easily tempt the reader to locate the Apollonian in Waldo and the Dionysiac in Arthur, if one were to take, say, the measuredly geometric 'artistic' strivings of Waldo and the unshackled, extravert, wordless dancing and histrionicism of Arthur at face value. But Arthur's mandala-dance describes (or *inscribes*, the body writing kinetically upon the earth) total, *geometric* form. He does not *need* words to give form to the instinctual—Dionysiac ecstasy (disorder) is under his Apollonian control. To identify Waldo as an Apollonian artist and Arthur as a Dionysiac force is to set up a false equation.[36]

Arthur, then, in his frequent embodiment of aesthetic form, is associated with the Apollonian, in contrast to Waldo, whose thin notion of "reason" abjects the corporeal and therefore, in White's vision, the aesthetic. As Collier argues, "what supervenes to thwart any narrow allegorical scheme [or, indeed, Waldo's repressions] is the central fact (central to all White's fiction) that our *physis* continually obtrudes to remind us of our humanity: nobody is exempt" (405).

Nonetheless, moments foregrounding the interconnection of "reason" (frequently emphasized as a misconception governed by abjection) and the body recur, ostensibly embodied in contrasting characters. These contrasts work at the "surface movement of the narrative," as Collier notes (404), alerting the reader to inseparable binary oppositions and setting up the dismantling of dualism worked out in the greater subtleties of White's characterization. One example is the image of the brothers Brown bound hand-in-hand as they wander the streets of Barranugli: "as they trudged, or tottered, they were holding each other by the hand. It was difficult to decide which was leading and which was led."[37] A similar relationship occurs in *The Twyborn Affair*. Here, Eudoxia Vatatzes (Eddie Twyborn's first feminine persona) strains against the entrapping masculinity of her "husband," Angelos, a character importantly (and ironically, given his love for the transgendered E.) obsessed with (religious) orthodoxy. The two enjoy playing piano duets together in performances that emphasize Angelos's identification with rule-bound law and Eudoxia's need for the fluid play of desire in music. It is helpful to recall Kristeva's description of music as a form of signification more reliant on the semiotic than the symbolic, but dependent, nonetheless, to some degree upon the latter. The music the couple perform is "reckless and at the same time controlled"; it is a "delirious collusion between two [...] united in their incongruity."[38] In her journal,

---

36 Collier, *The Rocks and Sticks of Words*, 404, emphasis in original.
37 White, *The Solid Mandala*, 19.
38 White, *The Twyborn Affair*, 17.

Eudoxia describes the frustration arising for her during their performances of Chabrier's waltzes:

> I would like to appear less tentative, less receptive of the ruler and the rules. I would like to *splash* music around me, while A. is determined to control my least impulse for extravagance [...]. Chabrier's oxydised streamers stream out behind us, in my case never freeing themselves because knotted to my wrists, and because the old bastard won't allow me the freedom of music.[39]

Thus, E. expresses her sense of confinement within the relationship. However, the passage also articulates a dialectic of freedom and restraint. Interestingly, E. perceives the "streamers" of Chabrier's waltz as tying her wrists like cords. Yet the metaphoric description of ribbons of sound knotted to her wrists—and, indeed, "streaming" from them—underscores the sense of music billowing forth from E.'s very body. The "freedom of music" is the essence of E.'s desire for liberation—from the restraints of social relationships, from her identity, and into a mode of signification that expresses her dissolution.

Despite the dialectic of liberation and restraint occurring in White's fiction, transgression—linked to freedom in/and corporeality—appears to prevail. Arthur, aligned with bodiliness, animality, holiness, and, because of his mental deficiencies, the haziness of pre-linguistic infancy, continuously outstrips his bookish, prosaic brother, Waldo, who, although associated with rationality and language, fails to produce anything of poetic worth despite his tortured attempts. It is Arthur who eventually produces a poem, about blood, which seemingly transforms, in White's language and in Waldo's focalization, *into* a drop of glittering blood. This emphasizes the interconnectedness of corporeality and poetry (and, indeed, Arthur's association with Apollonian form): "Arthur's drop of unnatural blood continued to glitter, like suspicion of an incurable disease."[40] White often describes characters' language or artistic modes of representation as bodily in nature. During a moment of high emotion, "it all came out of Waldo, not in vomit, but in words" (40). For Waldo, literature is characterized by the "daring of words, their sheer ejaculation" (122), and he wishes that he could conceive a poem that would "come shooting out with the urgency of shit and music" (110). In *Riders in the Chariot* and *The Vivisector*, "blood, or paint"[41] are indistinguishable. Moreover, Alf Dubbo's and Hurtle

---

39   White, *The Twyborn Affair*, 39, emphasis in original.
40   White, *The Solid Mandala*, 213.
41   White, *Riders in the Chariot*, 565.

Duffield's paintings are described as sexual releases. For Dubbo, art amounts to the expulsion of "the sensation in his stomach, the throbbing of his blood, in surge upon surge of thick, and ever-accumulating colour,"[42] and, for Hurtle, painting is a "drawn-out orgasm."[43] Desire can never be definitively resolved, and an ongoing process of painful (be)coming is emphasized as inherent in both corporeality and representation.

Repeatedly, then, White intimates that "the body [is] an instrument" of expression,[44] emptying itself into signification. Fascinated by the irrational, corporeal dimension of writing, he lashed out at his critics for their failure to step beyond the rational and the repressed: "For them the controlled monochrome of reason, for me the omnium gatherum of instinctual color which illuminates the more often than not irrational behavior of sensual man."[45]

Burning up the Guts: White's Linguistic Music

Julia Kristeva notes that "there are nonverbal signifying systems [seemingly] constructed exclusively on the basis of the semiotic (music, for example),"[46] and, interestingly, one way in which the semiotic dimension of White's writing seems emphasized is in its many descriptions of music. In his letters, White draws a link between literature and music:

> music has taught me a lot about writing. That may sound pretentious, and I would not know how to go into it *rationally*, but I feel that listening constantly to music helps one to develop a book more logically.[47]

Later, he alludes to the inspiration that he finds in music: "I get quite drunk with music, and play it a lot to lead me up to my work."[48] White seemed aware of a kind of pre-linguistic, irrational 'music' of language—Kristeva's semiotic— harnessed and shaped by the 'logic' of the symbolic and yet threatening the deformation of sense. Thus, Noel MacAinsh argues that the aesthetic principle of White's novels can be seen "as that of a complex interrelationship of parts in

---

42 *Riders in the Chariot*, 420.
43 White, *The Vivisector*, 204.
44 White, *The Vivisector*, 209.
45 White, *Flaws in the Glass*, 38.
46 Kristeva, *Revolution in Poetic Language*, 24.
47 White, *Letters*, 110.
48 *Letters*, 159.

the service of the destruction of meaning; it is a 'music' of destruction."[49] Not only does White acknowledge the inspiration of music; he also sees his writing as analogous to painting. His intention, for example, of imbuing *Voss* with the "textures of music, the sensuousness of paint,"[50] and his belief, as a writer, that more can be done "with paint and music; I am hobbled by words" are evinced in each of his novels.[51] His suggestion, moreover, that the "texture" and "sensuousness" of other arts may be transferred to literature indicates his emphasis on the rich materiality of language. Indeed, in White's writing we find the "music in letters" that Kristeva ascribes to James Joyce.[52] For White as for Kristeva, language and music harness corporeality in a movement toward signification that creates yet consumes. This is evident in the following reference to jazz in *The Living and the Dead*:

> There was nothing like the deep bass notes of the sax, or the higher, climbing, shining ones for burning up the guts. The nightly burning of the guts was the *raison d'être* of Wally Collins, a brief, orgasmic, almost death under the glare of chromium, more important this than sex, though appreciated too, the pursuit of skin through lingerie. But nightly the bowels rose in the sad surge of saxophones, the skin eroded by a white light, the mouth grown round and moist on a persistent note. He could feel his whole body shaped by a chord in music. His whole body writhed to burst its casing of black tailor's cloth. It drained the sockets of his eyes.
>
> *The Living and the Dead* 249

Music here is represented as a visceral emanation, a "burning of the guts." As a "brief, orgasmic, almost death," it is related to sex, death, and the loss of subjectivity that both entail. Moreover, it recalls the association of the subject-deforming semiotic with the death drive. Music sounds the entry of desire into signification, but also sings the tune of corporeal affect: Wally's "bowels [rise] in the sad surge of saxophones," indicating the transfusion of gut emotion into music and, simultaneously, into the language describing it. Alliteration, moreover, in conjunction with the stressed syllables *sad*, *surge*, and *sax*-ophone, attributes a rhythmic sensuality to the writing, emphasizing perhaps the beat of Wally's music but, more importantly, the sensuousness of the prose itself. Music and physicality are conflated, each determining the other, and Wally can

---

49   Noel MacAinsh, "Voss and his Communications," 441.
50   White, "The Prodigal Son," in *Patrick White Speaks*, ed. Brennan & Flynn, 16.
51   Herring & Wilkes, "Conversation," 138.
52   Kristeva, *Powers of Horror*, 23.

"feel his whole body shaped by a chord in music." As it rises up from inside him, he feels his "body writhe[...] to burst its casing of black tailor's cloth." Thus, in a description of music and the body that forcefully attests to the way in which corporeal desire (metaphorized as music) exceeds the bounds of subjectivity and pulsates in the rhythms of the text, Wally empties his body into music, which becomes the music of the prose itself.

Wally Collins's "burning of the guts" exemplifies White's concern with drawing non-verbal art into his writing. As Bill Ashcroft observes, White's fiction presents language as "inferior to art or music in capturing the inexpressible."[53] However, by harnessing a rhythmic, musical power within the workings of language itself, White articulates a sense of the uncapturable. In other words, a power of suggestion resides in the performative rhythms, images, excess, and sheer sensuality of the prose. This, of course, occurs not only during episodes in which music is thematized. Nonetheless, it is certainly emphasized in such descriptions, which may be interpreted as metatextual references to the poetic dimension of the prose itself.

In White's association of music with corporeality, expressed in many episodes throughout his oeuvre, the body "become[s] an instrument" expressing the inexpressible.[54] When Theodora Goodman attends a concert in which the pre-eminent 'cellist Moraïtis performs a concerto, music is presented as a complex embodied correspondence between the two:

> She watched him take the 'cello between his knees and wring from its body a more apparent, a thwarted, a passionate music. [...] The 'cello rocked, she saw. She could read the music underneath his flesh. She was close. He could breathe into her mouth. He filled her mouth with long, aching silences, between the deeper notes that reached down deep into her body. She felt the heavy eyelids on her eyes. The bones of her hands, folded like discreet fans on her dress, were no indication of exaltation or distress, as the music fought and struggled under a low roof, the air thick with cold ash, and sleep, and desolation.
>
> But in the last movement, Moraïtis rose again above the flesh. You were not untouched. There were moments of laceration, which made you dig your nails in your hands. The 'cello's voice was one barely subjugated cry under the savage lashes of the violins.
>
> *The Aunt's Story* 111

---

53   Bill Ashcroft, "The Presence of the Sacred in Patrick White," 96.
54   White, *The Vivisector*, 209.

In this moment of bodily empathy, identity disintegrates into music as corporeality, desire, and suffering are emphasized. For Theodora, "the music which Moraïtis played was more tactile than the hot words of lovers spoken on a wild nasturtium bed, the violins had arms" (112). After the concert, her body itself is imaged as an instrument: "Her hollow body vibrated still with all she had experienced. Now it was as empty as hollow wood" (16). The hollowness of the body, which has transformed in a moment of the protagonist's and therefore the reader's fleeting fancy *into* Moraïtis's 'cello, recalls another image in the text—the "hollow sphere" of the filigree ball (16). This is an object that Theodora's parents brought back from a trip to India during her childhood. The filigree ball has, in her imagination, the capacity to "fill [...] with a subtle fire" (131). Thus, it is compared to Theodora's body, which, although it is often presented as awkward and wooden, flares up throughout the novel with a rhythm of desire transferred to the narrative. Indeed, as the text concedes: "There were the people as empty as a filigree ball, though even these would fill at times with a sudden fire" (131). Both fire and music become associated with the "tactil[ity]" of White's "hot words,"[55] themselves associated with Theodora Goodman's roiling corporeality.

In *The Tree of Man*, Thelma Forsdyke also attends a concert. As the violin concerto begins, the "flesh of music" is increasingly emphasized.[56] Thelma imagines "opening her mouth" so that "music would enter in, and down the funnel of her throat"; she listens to the "lovemaking stage of music, when the tendrils creep around the breasts"; as the violinist plays, "the sweat pour[s] down his shoulderblades and down the backs of his knees" (488). His performance is emphasized as pain, struggle, and contortion: "he had begun to wrestle with the music, though the blood had not yet started to gush out of his yellow eyes" (488). For Thelma, the music becomes intensely personal. Its emotional strains loosen a corporeal affect evident in the text's irrational and metaphoric poeticism:

> She was brushed in sad gusts by the branches of the music. All the faces had ripened and were ready to fall from those branches. She was walking across the paddocks. Her stomach was thin and sloping. It was a personal sadness, or sickness, that had infected the music, and that she could not bear. [...] Nobody noticed any agony, because it is not visible in discreet people, even when whole ganglions of nerves are cut.
>
> *The Tree of Man* 489

---

55   *The Aunt's Story*, 112.
56   White, *The Tree of Man*, 488.

Even if Thelma does not visibly reveal her bodily anguish, the physicality of emotion is underlined as "whole ganglions of nerves" transmit her pain. Further, the concerto is conceptualized as the emotional "contagion" linking the body of the musician and the listener through a "personal sadness, or sickness, that had infected the music." Here, music crosses the boundary between individuals and alludes metonymically to the poetic musicality of White's writing, which takes up the difficulty and physical intensity of communicating the violence of corporeal affect.

Curiosity and Sensation: The Incentive and Pulse of the Text

While physical intensity is communicated in White's description of affect, it is also evident in the sexualization of White's writing, which dramatizes the body as both the source and the object of the expression of psychic dynamics. Desire is evident in White's texts in the general dynamics of the prose and, more specifically, in the frequent fetishization and sexualization of bodily imagery. The recurrent image of the male wrist, for example, often an object of libidinal fascination for White's characters, is undeniably phallic and an object of both desire and revulsion. Laura, dwelling on Voss's masculinity during the early stages of their acquaintance when she is uncertain whether she is attracted or repelled, fixates on his "wiry wrist with the little hairs."[57] Her reaction to her fascination confirms the sexualization of the image: she vows to "destroy these impressions"; Voss is "terribly repulsive to her."[58] Rather than Voss himself, Laura's desire, which impinges upon her self-sufficiency, is in fact the unconscious target of her disgust. It renders Voss's wrist phallic, shocking her "clean and proper" self into loathing. In *A Fringe of Leaves*, Ellen Roxburgh's illicit desire for her brother-in-law, Garnet, is similarly figured in her awareness of "his thick wrists and the hairs visible on them in the space between glove and cuff,"[59] a sight which elicits the "repulsion rising in her."[60] Later, she acknowledges that her adulterous liaison with Garnet is prompted by the fact that she is "physically incapable of resisting, most of all the hairy wrists and swollen veins."[61]

In a parallel example, White's often magnified distortions of women's lips appear to displace the female genitalia onto a more publicly acceptable facet

---

57 White, *Voss*, 72.
58 *Voss*, 72.
59 White, *A Fringe of Leaves*, 83.
60 White, *A Fringe of Leaves*, 101.
61 *A Fringe of Leaves*, 255.

of the body, nonetheless signifying the texts' sexualization. In *The Twyborn Affair*, the sexually voracious Marcia Lushington reminds Eddie Twyborn of

> a raw scallop, or heap of them, the smudged, ivory flesh, the lips of a pale coral. [...], her tongue suddenly flickered out and drew in a struggle of monkey fur, which she sucked for a second or two before rejecting.
> *The Twyborn Affair* 171

The female mouth, rather than functioning as an image of desire, is often the exaggerated focus of White's abjection. As David Coad observes,

> White uses the metaphor of the mouth seen as a trap, a sort of *vagina dentata* by means of which the 'mother' can carry out a castration threat.[62]

A horror of the maternal frequently enters White's writing, perhaps revealing misogynistic tendencies, but more importantly hinting at the threat of abjection to subjectivity. The mother's body appals because from this the infant must separate itself to attain autonomy. The fear and, indeed, the eventually subject-dissolving bliss, of being engulfed by the maternal pervade White's writing, occasionally contributing to his characters' self-preserving horror. Eddie Twyborn, for example, notices his mother Eadie in a "haphazard frock, exposing [...] the breasts which had suckled her child."[63] Loathing enters his focalization as he is confronted with the image of his mother's face: "she had tried to disguise [it] by smearing it with crimson and white which made him avert his own."[64] Moreover, her "gaping wound [is] smiling at him" as she tries "to sound like the girl she might never have been."[65] Eddie fears his mother's sexuality, which unconsciously reminds him of his amorphous, pre-symbolic origins within her flesh.

Yet bodies desire and are desired, thus invigorating the texts. Within this pattern, corporeality is imbricated with the desire for knowledge, the epistemological drive that often characterizes White's fiction. It thus emphasizes the body's role in inciting characters' curiosity concerning questions of existence and sexuality, and focuses the reader's attention on particular bodies that appear to raise such questions.

---

62   David Coad, "Patrick White's Castrated Country," *Commonwealth: Essays and Studies* 15.1 (1992): 88–95.
63   White, *The Twyborn Affair*, 151.
64   *The Twyborn Affair*, 151.
65   White, *The Twyborn Affair*, 151.

Peter Brooks identifies "epistemophilia" in literature that reveals a "curiosity about the body." This is writing that holds the "explicit or implicit postulation that the body—another's or one's own—holds the key not only to pleasure but as well to knowledge and power."66 In White, the body is frequently presented as the key to a mystery that characters attempt to solve. This enigma is most commonly bound up with the subjects of sex and death. In *The Aunt's Story*, Theodora Goodman's assertion during childhood that she "would like to know [...] would like to know everything" occurs in relation to the "great mystery that had taken place": the servant Pearl Brawne's pregnancy as a consequence of her relationship with her fellow worker, Tom Wilcocks.67 As Brooks observes, Freud's theories of the "birth of the epistemophilic urge from the child's curiosity about sexuality" suggest that there is an "inextricable link between erotic desire and the desire to know."68 Both, Brooks argues, "converge in writing, and where it concerns writing a body, creating a textual body, the interplay of eros and artistic creation is particularly clear."69 For Theodora and Fanny, prior to their puberty, Pearl is the "overflowing mystery of a big girl,"70 her body the focal point of their rapt attention. Characteristic of White's fiction, which so often adopts the indirect discourse of third-person focalizers, the narrative voice assumes the fascination of the child's perspective and focuses it firmly on the body:

> In Pearl the blood ran close to the surface and often flooded under the skin. But when she was undisturbed, Pearl was white, and especially her neck, in the opening of her blouse, Pearl swelled inside her blouse, and was white and big.
> *The Aunt's Story* 34

Pearl's body represents an epistemological bountifulness linked to the novel's focus on corporeal excess. Because she cannot be interpreted—"the face of Pearl that just could not be read" (36)—her body exceeds description: "There was no containing Pearl in common bounds. She was meant to swell, and ripen, and burst" (34–35). Pearl's sexual desire for Tom Wilcocks permeates the

---

66 Peter Brooks, *Body Work: Objects of Desire in Modern Narrative* (Cambridge MA: Harvard UP, 1993): xiii.
67 White, *The Aunt's Story*, 39.
68 Brooks, *Body Work*, 22.
69 *Body Work*, 22.
70 White, *The Aunt's Story*, 34.

narrative, ensuring that even the descriptions of objects and farmyard dogs surpass their everyday dimensions, to be transformed into the objective correlatives of her desolate desire:

> Her thick face swelled and cried. She chewed the corner of her handkerchief, on damp afternoons, when windows sweated and the dogs crouched in the yard, their thin tails tucked between their naked legs.
> *The Aunt's Story* 36

While the bodies of peripheral characters like Pearl may present epistemological dilemmas for White's protagonists, the bodies of his protagonists are similarly, and more significantly, figured as enigmas prompting other characters' and the reader's interpretation. Thus, Theodora Goodman herself signifies a mystery to be solved: her body is an opaque sign redolent with ungraspable meaning. "Her ugly mug," thinks Frank Parrott, poses a question "that you [cannot] answer" (15). Una Russell, at Spofforths' school, similarly senses in Theodora "something that she would not understand" and thus "something from which she must defend herself, or even hate" (49). She has failed to 'read' Theodora, whose face remains "half a brown shadow, the way the brim cut across" (49). For Una, she will remain "unexplained" (62), and for others, too, there is nothing "so remote as Theodora Goodman" (52), who sits "with her head bent, so that you [cannot] see" (113). According to Huntly Clarkson, who is a solicitor and thus represents law, rule, and social convention, Theodora sits "in shadow, and [draws] with her parasol on the floor characters that he [cannot] read" (100). Early in the novel, moreover, Violet Adams writes a letter to her erstwhile schoolfriend Theo, again emphasizing the latter's hermeneutic elusiveness: "very often you seemed to me a *closed book*!" (61; emphasis in original). White's socially conventional characters, like Fanny Parrott, prefer to "always ask the questions that have answers" (40), but Theodora's body remains a resolute question mark. The body in White's fictions is sometimes metonymic of the texts themselves: dense, difficult, ambiguous, transgressive, and, to a great extent, uncapturable.

If *The Aunt's Story* is uncapturable, this is partly because it focuses on the vicissitudes of Theodora's corporeality, which enter the narrative, investing it with a dynamic and disordering desire. Theodora may seem stiff and aloof to those who observe her—the archetypal spinsterish "aunt"—but her "story," wrapped up as it is in an irrational physicality, undermines this assumption. White's fiction seems invested with the libidinal energy of its characters: bodily desire often enters the narratives, shaping their rhythms and imagery. Much of Part One of *The Aunt's Story*, for example, is devoted to Theodora Goodman's burning adolescent desire. On her twelfth birthday, an age suggesting the onset of puberty, lightning strikes the oak tree at Meroë and she is thrown to the ground. Later, in a dream, she realizes that it is not the tree that has been charged with electricity, but her own body:

> There was the night [...] when she woke in bed and found that she was not beneath the tree. She had put out her hand to touch the face before the lightning struck, but not the tree. She was holding the faceless body that she had not yet recognised, and the lightning struck deep.
> *The Aunt's Story* 77

On the one hand, the faceless body may be read as Frank Parrott, the object of Theodora's desire, whom she has not yet recognized as such. On the other, the body could be her own and therefore interpretable as symbolic of the sexuality that she is unable to acknowledge. This second possibility is arguably countenanced by the fact that Theodora's corporeal energy invigorates the text and hammers at her consciousness, forcing her to 'recognize' her physicality as it asserts itself via the imperative of sexual desire. Her yearning for Frank, for example, reaches its apex on a night of overwhelming heat. The image of the moon is invested not only with the temperature of the evening but also with Theodora's burning physical longing: "It hung in the branches of the apricot tree, big, and swollen red, close, you could almost touch its veins" (79). This lunar imagery continues, endowed with corporeal associations taken up within the rhythm of the text itself:

> On hot evenings all the extremes of unlikelihood conspired, felt Theodora Goodman, and for that reason you waited, you waited for the red moon to crash like a thunderous gong through the leaves.
> *The Aunt's Story* 79

Amid this atmosphere of anticipation, emphasized by the repetition of "you waited, you waited" and rendered palpable by the onomatopoeic, dactylic rhythm of "crash like a thunderous gong through the leaves," Frank Parrott arrives, his horse thundering into Theodora's consciousness like the pulse of her own body:

> Then the drum beat down across the flat. You heard the horse's feet, beating the planks of the bridge. They beat deep, and more metallic, scattered and sauntered on the road, dropped and gathered, dropped and gathered, spurted as you heard the horse shy at a shadow. You could hear the fear protesting from his nose.
> *The Aunt's Story* 79

Metaphor, onomatopoeia, alliteration, repetition, and rhythm function together here to foreground not only the galloping rhythm of the horse's hooves but also the pulsation of Theodora's desire. This is an emphatically material language, emphasizing the Kristevan semiotic and underscoring the physicality of the moment described. Repeatedly stressed words of a single syllable—"drum beat down" and "beat deep"—mimic the very rhythm described. Again dactylic meter emphasizes the rhythm of a horse's galloping hooves in phrases like "beating the planks of the bridge." Moreover, the repetition of "dropped and gathered, dropped and gathered" introduces a cyclical rhythm performing the sound and movement described, but also investing the prose with the excitement that drives it forward. If a "subtle sort of onomatopoeia is constantly at work in language,"[71] then White's work harnesses and exaggerates this poetic mimesis of language, particularly when articulating the primal force of animal, bodily energy.

As the episode continues, this energy is pervasive: "the darkness in the neighbourhood of the tree was drenched with the smell of horse's sweat."[72] Here, Frank Parrott lies down with Theodora in a kind of fraternal matiness—he is after all, unbeknown to Theodora, about to propose to her sister, Fanny. This, however, does not decrease the intensity of Theodora's desire, nor the intensity of the narrative: "She had begun to suffocate. She could feel the pressure of the red moon" (81). Frank's feelings for her are a mystery to her, as they are to him, and this incites her desire:

> 'I could tell you,' Frank began.
> 'What could you tell?' she asked.
> 'Nothing,' he said.
> He stirred uneasily in the grass. And again the moon pressed through the branches of the old trees. He rolled over and looked at the house. [...] If she had touched him, touched his hands, the bones of her fingers would have wrestled with the bone in the palm of his hand.
> 'There will be such a downpour,' she said thickly, biting a blade of grass.
> He said that it was time the dam filled, looking still at the lighted house.
> Oh God, she would have said, go, go, or stay, let us throw aside words. Now she felt that only the hands tell. To take in her lap the palpitating moon.
> *The Aunt's Story* 82

---

71 David Abram, *The Spell of the Sensuous* (New York: Vintage, 1996): 145.
72 White, *The Aunt's Story*, 80.

In the above passage, a palpable tension between language and the body is realized. Frank has nothing to say, but his physical uneasiness conveys his potential desire. Moreover, his inability to speak draws Theodora on, perhaps to solve the mystery of his body, "and again" the narrative is thick with the imagery and dynamics of her yearning. The moon "presse[s] through the branches of the old trees," exerting the pressure of its corporeal associations. Touch overrides speech as the dominant image of communication and Theodora imagines bone wrestling with bone in her desire to conjoin with Frank. Still, despite the contrast drawn between touch and language, her speech is emphasized as "thick" with desire. Language, not necessarily in what it says but in how it communicates it, transmits corporeal affect. The "downpour" that Theodora predicts is clearly not a polite allusion to the weather but, rather, conveys the flooding of corporeal longing into her awareness and hence into the narrative. She may want to "throw aside words" as sexual desire overwhelms her rational subjectivity, but her desire is in fact evident in the words of the prose, in the palpably physical imagery of, for example, the "palpitating moon."

White's fiction strives to be a writing of sensation rather than of rationality, and this sensation is located within literary prose, rather than within the transparent communications of everyday language. Voss, riding through the bush, exemplifies the striving toward both sensory experience and its representation:

> He no longer rode consciously, but was carried onward by sensation. He was touching the bark of those trees that were closest to him (they were, in fact, very close; he could see the gummy scabs on healed wounds and ants faring through the fibre forests). He was singing, too, in his own language, some shining song [...].
> *Voss* 143

As the particularity of the physical world is magnified for Voss, emphasized via White's fascination with minutiae, and rational consciousness is replaced with physical sensation, he sings "*in his own language*," a language which is not specified as his mother-tongue German and which therefore invites the reader to entertain also the possibility that it is a "language" of attuned and subject-dissolving sensation—the "shining song" of White's prose itself. As the poetic dynamics of eroticism in *The Aunt's Story* suggest, this language of sensation, harnessing the semiotic, often comes to the fore when characters are forced to yield to the dominance of their bodies and hence to their physical sensations in their respective circumstances and contexts.

Her Mouth Exploded into a Purple Flower: Marking the Body with the Sign of Its Desire

As I argued above, male wrists and female lips often index sexuality, desire, and disgust in White's fiction. Taking this discussion further, the dynamics of affect and desire become evident in White through descriptions of bodily markings, in particular a sardonic focus on lurid make-up. Descriptions of the manner in which the body is marked link the sign-system of language to corporeal signs which may be physical symptoms of heightened emotion. The bodily sign described in language renders language corporeal, just as it emphasizes corporeality as a language in itself. White's short story "Five-Twenty" exemplifies his interest in what he terms "another language":[73] a language of materiality that seemingly discharges the physical drives and affects of his characters.

Peter Brooks argues that marks on the body in literature play a special role in emphasizing the connection between the body and the linguistic signifier:

> The sign imprints the body, making it part of the signifying process. Signing or marking the body signifies its passage into writing, its becoming a literary body, and generally also a narrative body, in that the inscription of the sign depends on and produces a story. The signing of the body is an allegory of the body become a subject for literary narrative—a body entered into writing.[74]

Garish and distorted lipstick often functions as a mark of physical desire, indicating the merging of sign and body (*sema* and *soma*) occurring so often in White's writing. In *Riders in the Chariot*, the young Ruth Godbold's mouth grows "distorted and fleshy" in her early encounters with her husband-to-be and her burgeoning lust has, quite literally, a marked effect upon her wealthy and flighty employer, Mrs Chalmers–Robinson:

> when her maid was all arrayed, the mistress appeared somewhat feverish, her eyes more brilliant than ever before. She had done her mouth. There it was, blooming like a big crimson flower, with a little, careful, mauve line, apparently to keep it within bounds.
> *Riders in the Chariot* 338

This image of excess and control, and its suggestion that the "little, careful, mauve line" will fail miserably in its attempts to restrain the blaring desire of

---

73   White, "Five-Twenty," in White, *The Cockatoos*, 174.
74   Brooks, *Body Work*, 3.

the "big crimson flower," is an effective metaphor for the inevitable entry of transgressive desire into White's signification. Moreover, Mrs Chalmers–Robinson's lipstick signs her body, marking it as the site of desire, but also indicating the spillage of this desire into the sign itself. Similarly, Elizabeth Hunter in *The Eye of the Storm* miscalculates "the explosive force of her lust, she had felt its first tremor that evening when misdrawing her mouth in lipstick."[75]

Lipstick is an important image in "Five-Twenty," wherein White's somatic semantics are strongly evinced. In this short story from *The Cockatoos*, Ella and Royal Natwick, living in misery in a house on the side of the Parramatta Road, set their transient moments of happiness according to the regular appearance of a pink Holden that drives past, identifiable in the stream of traffic, every evening at five-twenty. The story explores White's favored themes of confinement, repression, and the eventual liberation of corporeal desire, its expression initially trapped within a patriarchally controlled conjugality. The driver of the Holden becomes for Ella the object of her yearning for a life outside the entrapment of her unhappy marriage. To her delight, after Royal's death, the man appears in her garden, to become the target of her increasingly unrestrained desire. The garden is a setting that has previously been developed as the externalization of her repressed yet forceful lust:

> She had never seen such cinerarias: some of the spired ones reached almost as high as her chin, the solid heads of others waited in the tunnel of dark light to club you with their colours, of purple and drenching blue, and what they called 'wine'. She couldn't believe wine would have made her drunker.[76]

White's characters are often "made drunk by life,"[77] and sensory drunkenness is foregrounded in descriptions in which desire overtakes rationality, entering the prose via saturated color imagery or rhythmic effect. Synaesthesia, imagery, and metaphor remind the reader of the physical world and foreground its potentially overmastering effects upon rationality. In the passage above, Ella, combined with the reader via the second-person "you," is assaulted with the color of her cinerarias, "of purple and drenching blue." As rational perception yields to corporeal sensation, she and the prose are rendered "drunk." Simultaneously, White's writing turns psychedelic in its description of a vivid color correlating with his protagonist's sensuality. Flowers often symbolize corporeality in White: the rose recurs as an image of the flesh and Eudoxia

---

75   White, *The Eye of the Storm*, 93.
76   White, "Five-Twenty," 171.
77   White, *Voss*, 116.

Vatatzes' *carn*ation gown signals her *carn*ality in *The Twyborn Affair*. In "Five-Twenty," cinerarias display "the colours of flesh with blood pulsing beneath the skin."[78]

Ella Natwick's Holden-driving stranger stumbles into this setting of desire when he appears in the garden after his car has broken down on the Parramatta Road. Agreeing to his request to use the telephone, Ella realizes that "her voice sound[s] muzzy" and wonders if he will "think she [is] drunk."[79] Imagery associates drunkenness with the potent sensuality of the flowers, objective correlatives of Ella's sexuality. Gradually, her desire transforms the narrative. In the garden, she begins to describe her cinerarias to the stranger. The "muzzy" sensuality of her speech, enacting the disorder of her desire, becomes the drunkenness of the prose itself:

> As she was about to explain *she got switched to another language.* Her throat became a long palpitating funnel through which the words she expected to use were poured out in a stream of almost formless agonized sound.
> 'What is it?' he asked, touching her.[...]
> And for answer, *in the new language*, she was holding him. They were holding each other, his hard body against her eiderdowny one. As the silence closed round them again, inside the tunnel of light, his face, to which she was very close, seemed to be unlocking, the wound of his mouth, which should have been more horrible, struggling to open. She could see he had recognized her.
>
>   "Five-Twenty" 174 (my emphases)

Ella is "switched to another language." This is a "language" of physicality: empathy in touch, the channeling of raw emotion, and, beyond this, the language of a literary text interested in the performative representation of raw corporeal affect.

Ella invites the stranger back for coffee the following day and prepares for his visit with a trip to the cosmetics counter. After "investing in a lipstick" and rouge,[80] she is somewhat alarmed by the starkness of their color. Leaving the shop, she goes home to try out her new purchases. While David Myers describes

---

78 Rose Marie Beston, "More Burnt Ones: Patrick White's *The Cockatoos*," *World Literature Written in English* 14.2 (July 1975): 524.
79 White, "Five-Twenty," in White, *The Cockatoos*, 172.
80 White, "Five-Twenty," 176.

this scene as "silly farce,"[81] it in fact cements the link between the imagery of the garden and Ella's body, thereby indicating the importance of imagery to the depiction of a corporeal desire that eludes rational description. The effect of the make-up is startling, not only on Ella's face as she silently applies it, but also within the imagery of the text itself:

> She wasn't quiet, though, not a bit, booming and clanging in front of the toilet mirror. She tried to make a thin line, but her mouth exploded into a purple flower. She dabbed the dry-feeling pad on either cheek, and thick mauve-scented shadows fell. She could hear and feel her heart behaving like a squeezed, rubber ball as she stood looking. Then she got at the lipstick again, still unsheathed. Her mouth was becoming enormous, so thick with grease she could hardly close her own lips underneath. A visible dew was gathering round the purple shadows on her cheeks.
>
> She began to retch like, but dry, and rub, over the basin, scrubbing with the nailbrush. More than likely some would stay behind in the pores and be seen. Though you didn't have to see, to see.
>
> "Five-Twenty" 176–177

Again synaesthesia and onomatopoeia evoke Ella's overwhelming horror when confronted with the image of her body marked by the sign of its unspeakable, abject desire. This, again, is "another language"—a "body language" of physicality evident in her corporeality but also manifesting in the poetic sensuality of White's writing. The excess of desire is emphasized: a "thin line" of lipstick becomes an "explosion" of color. Moreover, her lips, in White's metaphoric language, transform into a cineraria, the story's dominant image of desire, as "her mouth explode[s] into a purple flower."

Abrams defines metaphor as occurring when a "word or expression that in literal usage denotes one kind of thing is applied to a distinctly different kind of thing, without asserting a comparison."[82] White's use of metaphor in the preceding example is distinctive because it describes a moment of transformation, rather than simply linking "flower" and "mouth" in a static image. No comparison is asserted; instead, we are presented with language *in its moment of comparison* as a commonplace signifier (mouth) transforms into the unexpected (flower). "Her mouth exploded into a purple flower" is thus

---

81   David Myers, *The Peacocks and the Bourgeouisie: Ironic Vision in Patrick White's Shorter Fiction* (Adelaide, SA: Adelaide UP, 1978): 120.

82   M.H. Abrams, with Geoffrey Galt Harpham, *A Glossary of Literary Terms* (Boston MA: Thomson Learning, 2005): 102.

an instance of the 'becoming' of White's language—the flux and flooding of desire into representation, and the performative depiction thereof occurring in the emphasis on a metaphor of blossoming, of becoming.

The affect and excess of Ella's experience are strongly emphasized in the above quotation. Corporeality becomes pronounced as she feels her heart constricting like a "squeezed, rubber ball" and as her mouth becomes "enormous, so thick with grease she could hardly close her own lips underneath." Although desire is not only present in the visible appearance of the body—"you didn't have to see to see"—White's hyperbolic imagery ensures that his readers do in fact envisage the visible manifestations of desire, hence register the body as a site of *marked* narrative importance. The body thus becomes a meaningful signifier when it is literally "signed" by the mark of its desire, one of the ways, as Ella's experience attests, in which White's bodies "enter[...] into writing,"[83] transforming it into "another language" of corporeality and sensation.

White's attunement to the physical has a pronounced effect on the reader, for whom the materiality of the text constructs the corporeality of the character. In *The Pleasure of the Text*, Roland Barthes discusses the role of the body in the text and in the reading thereof:

> Apparently Arab scholars, when speaking of the text, use this admirable expression: *the certain body*: What body? We have several of them; the body of anatomists and physiologists, the one science sees or discusses [...]. But we also have a body of bliss consisting solely of erotic relations, utterly distinct from the first body: it is another contour, another nomination; thus with the text: it is no more than the open list of the fires of language (those living fires, intermittent lights, wandering features strewn in the text like seeds [...]. Does the text have a human form, is it a figure, an anagram of the body? Yes, but of our erotic body. [...] The pleasure of the text is that moment when my body pursues its own ideas—for my body does not have the same ideas I do.[84]

Barthes distinguishes between the body as an object and the body as a source and site of pleasure and affect. The text maps itself onto this second notion of the body—the "body of bliss"—and the joy of both body and text are evident within the latter as "living fires, intermittent lights, wandering features." These are the specificities and plurality of the text—its imagery, rhythms, and

---

83 Brooks, *Body Work*, 3.
84 Roland Barthes, *The Pleasure of the Text*, tr. Richard Miller (*Le plaisir du texte*, 1973; New York: Hill & Wang, 1975): 16–17.

stylistic features—which replicate "our erotic body" with its multiple sites of pleasure, foregrounding the semiotic dimension of signification. The "pleasure of the text," of both its dynamics and its interpretation, exists beyond rationality and thus beyond conscious subjectivity—"for my body does not have the same ideas I do."

CHAPTER 4

The Body Imprisoned
Social Control and Corporeal Subversion

> bodies never quite comply with the norms by which their materialization is impelled.[1]

∴

Chapter 1's discussion of Kristeva and Lacan drew attention to the way in which identity is consolidated on the basis of the abjection of corporeality. The child's entry into the symbolic order is premised on the distinction that it makes between identity as recognized in the image of the body and the inchoate sensations of corporeality that it must disavow in order to identify with this image, with which it is nonetheless never fully unified. The image of the self, initially recognized during Lacan's mirror phase, is thus the first instance of symbolization, preparing the child for its induction into the symbolic order and thus to be shaped by the rules of language, socialization, and subjectivity. Identity and representation are therefore inextricably linked, both enabling the emergence of the symbolic or social order and being inescapably and simultaneously shaped by it.

These theoretical observations are of value in interpreting White's fiction, which distinguishes *socialized identity* or subjectivity (the socialized image of the body, relating, for example, to how it is gendered, raced, or similarly encoded socially) from *corporeality* (the material body). The movement of White's fiction towards the obliteration of identity thus also involves the rejection of the social order. When his characters seemingly transcend their bodies in fleeting moments of dissociation from the world of normative experience, they are actually exceeding their acquired, socialized, and, for White, inauthentic identity. Their subjectivity is engulfed by and dissolved in the flux of the corporeal. Although this 'experience', beyond language and outside of subjectivity, cannot be interpreted by White's characters, it is (ideally) perceived as valuable

---

[1] Judith Butler, *Bodies That Matter: On the Discursive Limits of "Sex"* (London: Routledge, 1993): 2.

and meaningful by White's readers, particularly because his protagonists are so often rejected as outsiders, their identities shaped as abject within a rigidly normative social order. Their shedding of subjectivity, therefore, which is also a rejection of society, often appears as redemptive or, at the very least, painfully necessary.

Contrary to Kirpal Singh's view of White's writing, then, his characters are not engaged in a "quest for selfhood"[2]—at least, not if selfhood is understood as identity shaped within the social order—but, rather, in the attempt, as with Theodora Goodman, to "destroy the great monster Self."[3] As William Walsh argues in contrast to Singh, White's writing is particularly concerned with the "release from the self and even indeed with [its] obliteration."[4] White's characters, A.L. McLeod concurs, set themselves the "goal of extinction of the self":[5] they transcend identities that are associated with the *body image*, which explains the contradictory moments of transcendence in which they appear to submit to a primordial, fragmentary bodiliness. This suggests an alternative reading to what Andrew Riemer describes as one of White's main preoccupations: "the sporadic flashes of insight when the spirit escapes momentarily from the bondage of habit and the flesh."[6] While Riemer's emblematic reading is taken directly from White, who undoubtedly foregrounds moments of transcendence, a close reading of these moments reveals that more is at stake. For example, Mary Hare longs to feel "her body slipping from her,"

> or elongated into such shapes of love and music as she had only noticed long ago in dancers, swaying and looking, no more governed by precept or reason, but by some other lesson which *the flesh might at any moment remember.*
> *Riders in the Chariot* 394 (my emphasis)

Hare's desire to transcend her body is really her yearning to dispose of the identity with which her body (or at least its image) is associated and to enter a state of bodiliness (a memory embedded in the flesh) that precedes discursive,

---

2 Kirpal Singh, "The Fiend of Motion: Theodora Goodman in Patrick White's *The Aunt's Story*," *Quadrant* 19.9 (December 1975): 90.
3 Patrick White, *The Aunt's Story*, 128.
4 William Walsh, "Fiction as Metaphor," 201.
5 A.L. McLeod, "Patrick White: Nobel Prize for Literature 1973," *Books Abroad* 48.3 (Summer 1974): 441.
6 Andrew Riemer, "Back to the Abyss: Patrick White's Early Novels," *Southerly* 47.4 (December 1987): 348.

rational, and representational consciousness. She desires, then, an escape from the "bondage of habit" but not, as Riemer observes, from the "bondage" of flesh.

Exploring White's engagement with and frequent rejection of the social order and the rules it places upon embodiment, this chapter begins with a discussion of Kristeva's concept of the semiotic *chora*, thus extending the focus of Chapter 3. As the mobile space between the symbolic and the semiotic, the *chora* disrupts subjectivity and symbolization and is linked to the maternal body. It serves as a useful concept for a discussion of White's interest in maternal imagery (often linked to death and/or the disintegration of subjectivity) and his harnessing of pre-symbolic and corporeal imagery as part of his rejection of the social forces that shape identity and modes of embodiment. Moreover, it provides a starting point for an analysis of the ways in which White associates a plenitude of inarticulable meaning with states of wordlessness. The chapter then reviews what it is that necessitates the striving beyond language as well as the loss of identity in White's fiction, focusing on the ways in which the body is shaped in and circumscribed by discourse and how White engages with and yet undermines this in his fiction.

An Escape-Route from Identity: The Semiotic *Chora*

Mary Hare, longing to "feel her body slipping from her"[7] yet yearning for a memory embedded in the flesh, is close to what Kristeva, following Plato's *Timaeus*, calls the *chora*. This is the sacred, sacralized space 'between' the symbolic and the semiotic through which body, emotion, imagination, intuition, and instinct enter and disorder subjective consciousness. Kristeva conceptualizes the *chora*

> both spatially (as the 'in-between' produced by the ambiguous relatedness of two always already socialized bodies: that is, the body of the not-yet-subject and that of its [m]other); and temporally (as the beginning before 'the Beginning,' the mobile origin 'before' the imposition of 'the Word').[8]

The function of the semiotic *chora* is to "displace the speaking subject,"

---

7   White, *Riders in the Chariot*, 394.
8   Maria Margaroni, "'The Lost Foundation': Kristeva's Semiotic *Chora* and Its Ambiguous Legacy," *Hypatia* 20.1 (Winter 2005): 79.

(re)tracing its emergence not only 'before' *logos* [language as the manifestation of reason] but also in returning it to the maternal body, beyond the phallus as the structuring principle of the symbolic order.[9]

The semiotic *chora*, then, remains as a trace of the pre-symbolic, preceding language, identity, gender, and socialization. Although associated with the maternal feminine, its existence prior to symbolic categorization renders it ambiguous and androgynous. Moreover, the *chora* is a "mobile and extremely provisional articulation"[10] between two bodies (between corporeality and the discursive order), the "infant's confused mass of body parts and the mother's already socialized body."[11] As such, it is a primal space of ordering where symbolism is first generated, providing the "raw material of signification."[12] However, it is also the space where order collapses under the pressure of the death drive and corporeal instinct and thus "the space where the subject is both generated and negated."[13]

White's writing, as I have argued, taps into the "maternal [...] creative entrails,"[14] explicitly referring to the maternal body to indicate his characters' yearning for the pre-symbolic and to emphasize occasions in which their subjectivity is seemingly derailed. The maternal body foregrounds the corporeal or semiotic component of his writing. Winfried Menninghaus observes that in the mother–child dyad

> there are no clear distinctions of subject and object, inner and outer, 'I' and others, but only fluid heterogeneities, rhythmic streaming of libidinal drives and matter.[15]

White's interest in the maternal body therefore contributes to his thematization of formlessness and flux and of infantile, pre-symbolic regression as equivalent to the 'transcendence' of identity and the symbolic order. His writing harnesses the abject and, according to Kristeva,

---

9   Margaroni, "'The Lost Foundation,'" 79.
10 Julia Kristeva, *Revolution in Poetic Language*, 25.
11 John Lechte & Maria Margaroni, *Julia Kristeva: Live Theory* (London & New York: Continuum, 2004): 14.
12 Kristeva, *Revolution in Poetic Language*, 93.
13 *Revolution in Poetic Language*, 28.
14 Patrick White, *The Vivisector*, 465.
15 Winfried Menninghaus, *Disgust: Theory and History of a Strong Sensation* (Albany: State U of New York P, 2003): 370.

> devotees of the abject [...] do not cease looking [...] for the desirable and terrifying, nourishing and murderous, fascinating and abject inside of the maternal body.[16]

Maternal imagery is significant throughout White's fiction: in *The Vivisector*, Hurtle Duffield is obsessed with "Mumma's hollow body,"[17] wondering "what Mumma felt with a red baby screwing its way out of her guts."[18] He imagines his art as "dragged out" in "torment and anguish, by a pair of forceps."[19] *The Eye of the Storm* is an extended study of the abject maternal, focusing in detail on the dying body of Elizabeth Hunter and her relation to her children, Basil and Dorothy. In *The Twyborn Affair*, E. Twyborn's numerous performances of identity play out in relation to his/her simultaneous yearning for and rejection of the maternal. For example, in the loss of rationality accompanying dreaming, Eadith Trist, E.'s third identity, envisions a "young woman, her face softened by the light to a blur in which her features [are] lost."[20] The woman bathes a recently born child. When the dreamer, envying the infant, attempts to help, the vision turns horrific:

> Dishwater, sewage, putrid blood were gushing out of the faceless mother from the level at which her mouth should have been. The intruder was desolated by a rejection she should have expected.
> *The Twyborn Affair* 352

One possible reason for E.'s rejection by the maternal ideal is that s/he is still firmly rooted in the symbolic, against which the semiotic is constructed as abject; hence the dishwater, sewage, and blood gushing from the realm of the maternal (it spews, moreover, replacing language, from the distorted mouth). At the novel's conclusion, however, E. is described as returning to "his mother's womb" in death (352), the dream finally realized as s/he escapes the bondage of language and the social order.

Imagery of infantile regression is common in White's writing. In *Voss*, Ralph Angus dies in the heart of the Australian continent while simultaneously returning to a state of infancy:

---

16   Julia Kristeva, *Powers of Horror*, 54.
17   White, *The Vivisector*, 76.
18   *The Vivisector*, 68.
19   *The Vivisector*, 259.
20   White, *The Twyborn Affair*, 352.

> So the great gong boomed in his ear and Ralph Angus died, as young ladies of his own class offered him tea out of Worcester cups. Deliciously their fingers of rose and lilac braided him up in their possessive hair. They smothered him, and mothered him, until, at the last, he was presented as a swaddled baby. In this, his beard could have caused doubts, but he had parted from it: there it was, sprouting from the sand, independently, like a plant.
>
> *Voss* 425–426

Colonial class privilege and masculinity, the markers of Angus's identity, inevitably disintegrate as his subjectivity is overwhelmed by the "smothering" and "mothering" linked to the semiotic *chora* that Kristeva associates with *thanatos* and the dissolution of the speaking subject. Simultaneously, then, *logos* and subjectivity disintegrate in the oceanic dispersion of death.

Death and the semiotic *chora* are similarly associated in *The Eye of the Storm*: Dorothy Hunter suspects that clear vision, occurring in conjunction with the disintegration of the ego, is "something you shed with childhood and do not regain unless death is a miracle of light."[21] The noun "infancy," derived from the Latin *infantia*, means 'inability to speak'. Once the child is inducted into the symbolic order and language, the oceanic maternal becomes abject:

> By virtue of its own mechanism, all signification requires the repudiation of the undivided maternal being—assuming (with Saussure) that language is the field of discrete and differentiated articulation, the incision into presignificative 'clouds' of sound and sense.[22]

White's interest in the maternal and in infantile regression therefore contributes to the tendency of his fiction to gesture beyond the differentiating limits of language. As Menninghaus observes of Kristeva's notion of the abject maternal, associated with the subject-deforming semiotic dimension of language,

> it is preobjectival; it forms no circumscribed subject; it is undifferentiated; it is nameless—indeed, *the* nameless and unnameable; it is given in an athematic and pre-reflective mode of perception; and it transcends the antithesis of conscious and unconscious.[23]

---

21   White, *The Eye of the Storm*, 288.
22   Winfried Menninghaus, *Disgust*, 371.
23   Menninghaus, *Disgust*, 370, emphasis in the original.

Frequently, then, White presents moments of helpless inarticulacy in which a general plenitude of meaning, associated with "the nameless and unnameable," is suggested. In *The Vivisector*, for example, Hurtle Duffield observes a young woman, Muriel Devereaux, thrown into the contortions of an epileptic fit:

> It was frightful; so much so, he couldn't look at it: the girl tossing and lowing, sometimes the colour of her own cerise taffeta, sometimes washed white, or drenched with a sickly plant-green.
> *The Vivisector* 299

In Hurtle's painterly vision, the girl appears to attempt to signify through her corporeality something that ultimately cannot be communicated. Her mother's panicked response suggests this failed message: "What is it? Baby? What is it you want? [...] Only tell me" (299). Her words act "like a blow," prompting her daughter to further disfiguration: "the girl gulped; then she threw back her head and stuck out her cerise tongue, before lolling forward again, rolling her china eyeballs" (299). Hurtle, however, understands the contortionist:

> For an instant the possessed one glanced at the only other of her kind, and they were swept up, and united by sheet lightning, as they could never have been on the accepted plane.
> *The Vivisector* 299

Muriel's epilepsy appears to embody the difficulties of White's prose, itself striving through the blurring of focalization and the image of the struggling body to reach the moment of mystical unity the characters appear to attain. Kristeva contends that corporeal affect may be located in the breakdown of language, the detachment of signifier from signified:

> Within the blanks that separate dislocated themes (like the limbs of a fragmented body), or through the shimmering of a signifier that, terrified, flees its signified, the analyst can perceive the imprint of [...] affect.[24]

Peter Brooks similarly argues that corporeality accompanies the dissolution of meaning, or a "fall from language":[25]

---

24   Kristeva, *Powers of Horror*, 49.
25   Peter Brooks, *Body Work*, 7.

If the sociocultural body clearly is a construct, an ideological product, nonetheless we tend to think of the physical body as precultural and prelinguistic: sensations of pleasure and especially of pain, for instance, are generally held to be experiences outside language; and the body's end, in death, is not simply a discursive construct. Mortality may be that against which all discourse defines itself, as protest, or as attempted recovery and preservation of the human spirit, but it puts a stark biological limit to human constructions. The body, I think, often presents us with a fall from language, a return to an infantile presymbolic space in which primal drives reassert their force.[26]

Throughout *Riders in the Chariot*, Mary Hare, who longs for a "lesson which the flesh might at any moment remember,"[27] is associated with the image of the foetus. As a child she "drift[s] through the pale waters of her mother's kindness like a little, wondering, transparent fish" (27), and she appals her father by throwing herself to the ground and hollowing out a "nest in the grass, with little feverish jerks of her body, and foolish grunts, curling round in the shape of a bean, or position of a foetus" (28). "Ugly as a foetus. Ripped out too soon" (71), is Norbert's assessment of his daughter. Verging on the animal, straying into the territory of the purely corporeal, and constantly associated with fragmentation, Hare is linked to the pre-symbolic. She seems able to attain it on occasion when, like Muriel Deveraux, she suffers fits and her "mind leav[es] her," its "filthy waves" floating "off the fragments of disintegrating flesh" (47). After one such seizure, claiming that she has "never been so far before," she recognizes that the possibility of the loss of self is embedded in the physical world and that "*lovingkindness*" exists "at the roots of trees and plants, not to mention *hair*" (609; italics in original). Mary yearns to attain completely the subject-dissolving condition of wordless, irrational corporeality, as is evident in her envy of the trance-like state of dancers who are somehow able to lose themselves in the "memory of flesh."

In its refusal of the sociocultural constraints placed upon the body (often related to social judgment, bigotry, and oppression), White's fiction strives to express a poetry of corporeality through a prevailing concern with imagery associated with the pre-symbolic and an intense interest in fleshly and physical existence. It posits human subjectivity, the *construction of identity*, as built upon the tenuous rejection of its archaic origins and its corporeality. In concentrating on textually recuperating both, however, it rejects the social norms

---

26   Brooks, *Body Work*, 7.
27   White, *Riders in the Chariot*, 394.

and pressures that shape and order bodies and identities, the focus of the remainder of this chapter.

The Social Body and the Natural Body: Discipline and Punishment

Foregrounding the loss of identity as liberating, White's fiction takes specific issue with normative discourses dictating compulsory and oppressive modes of embodiment and repressing primal corporeal drives. The idea that the body is shaped in discourse is evident in White and also fundamental to poststructuralist philosophy: "For writers as diverse as Lyotard, Irigaray, Deleuze, Derrida and Foucault, the body is conceived as a fundamentally historical and political object" and conceptualized as the central object "over and through which relations of power and resistance are played out."[28] It is "inscribed by those discourses and material practices that constitute its social environment."[29] Deborah Lupton elaborates:

> Bodies, within certain limits, are highly malleable. The ways in which we perceive our bodies, regulate them, decorate them, move them, evaluate them morally, and the ways in which we deal with matters such as birth, sexuality and death are all shaped via the sociocultural and historical context in which we live.[30]

Pierre Bourdieu theorized society's control over the body in his concept of *habitus*. According to Bourdieu, culture is "made body"[31] when apparently trivial and arbitrary practices become automatic and habitual activity. *Habitus*, he explains, is our "embodied history, internalized as a second nature and so forgotten as history."[32] In *Natural Symbols*, the anthropologist Mary Douglas also maintains that culture is made body. She identifies two distinct yet related conceptualizations of the body: the social body (society) and the physical

---

28 Elizabeth Grosz, "The Body of Signification," 81.
29 Anne Cranny-Francis, *The Body in the Text* (Melbourne: Melbourne UP, 1995): 2.
30 Deborah Lupton, *The Emotional Self* (Thousand Oaks CA & London: Sage, 1998): 32.
31 Pierre Bourdieu, *Outline of a Theory of Practice*, tr. Richard Nice (*Esquisse d'une théorie de la pratique*, 1972; Cambridge: Cambridge UP, 1977): 94.
32 Pierre Bourdieu, *The Logic of Practice*, tr. Richard Nice (*Le sens pratique*, 1980; Stanford CA: Stanford UP, 1990): 56–57.

body. Famously, she argues that the two form an intimate dyad, each influencing the other:

> The social body constrains the way the physical body is perceived. The physical experience of the body, always modified by the social categories through which it is known, sustains a particular view of society. There is a continual exchange of meanings between the two kinds of bodily experience so that each reinforces the categories of the other. As a result of this interaction the body itself is a highly restricted medium of expression. The forms it adopts in movement and repose express social pressures in manifold ways.[33]

Douglas maintains that the human body is "always treated as an image of society and that there can be no natural way of considering the body that does not involve at the same time a social dimension."[34] As Anthony Synnott explains, "the social body constrains the perception and the construction of the physical body";[35] hence, "natural bodies are marked, organized, and produced as cultural bodies."[36] Accordingly, "bodily control is an expression of social control."[37]

Theorists like Michel Foucault and Judith Butler argue against the notion of a self-enclosed consciousness (separate from the body) in their analyses of the discursive construction of subjectivity in society. They link the formation of the self to the ways in which the body is moulded and constructed. Foucault emphasizes how society exerts power over the body of the individual, rendering it "docile" and demanding that it conform to pre-ordained norms. He associates modernity's movement towards dualism with the emergence of "bio-power," his term for a discursive force exerted over the bodies of individuals, disciplining and regulating them, and turning them into cogs in the collective social machinery. As he argues in *Discipline and Punish*, Cartesian dualism coincides historically with the "body as object and target of power."[38] He identifies two registers of discourse constructing the category of "Man-the-Machine": "the anatomico-metaphysical register, of which Descartes wrote the first pages" and the "technico-political register, which was constituted by a

---

33 Mary Douglas, *Natural Symbols: Explorations in Cosmology* (London: Barrie & Rockliff, 1970): 65.
34 Douglas, *Natural Symbols*, 70.
35 Anthony Synnott, "Tomb, Temple, Machine and Self," 80.
36 Brooks, *Body Work*, xii.
37 Douglas, *Natural Symbols*, 70.
38 Michel Foucault, *Discipline and Punish*, 136.

whole set of regulations and by empirical and calculated methods [...] for controlling or correcting the operations of the body."[39] Foucault is primarily interested in this second register. The regulations and methods thereof, he argues, were developed in the penitentiary and came to install various controlling habits in individuals, shaping their subjectivity. They developed in conjunction with political subjugation and control, spreading beyond the penal system to all institutions managing groups of people and therefore bodies: the school, the army, the hospital, the factory, the family, and society at large. Eventually the subject appropriates the control that society exerts and is habituated into disciplining his or her body accordingly.

Foucault's interest in the history of the prison is of obvious relevance to Australian fiction, which so often responds to the nation's history as a penal colony. White's 'historical' novels, *Voss* and *A Fringe of Leaves*, present the penal system as a trope for punitive social Law. In *Voss*, the emancipated convict Judd's back is "laced with scars, of an ugly purple, and the shameful white of renewed skin,"[40] revealing the disciplinary measures inflicted upon his body by the social order. Judd understands that power is discursive and that "words were not the servants of life, but life, rather, was the slave of words."[41] In *A Fringe of Leaves*, Jack Chance's body is similarly inscribed: "The expanse of the man's back was covered with what appeared to be a patternless welter of healed wounds."[42] Like Foucault, White extends his focus on penality and its disciplinary control of individuals to all social 'disciplines' or techniques for managing people—to the symbolic order at large. The violence inflicted on the bodies of prisoners mirrors the force of social pressure exacted upon the body of Ellen Roxburgh in the tenuous shaping of her genteel, Victorian, and feminine identity. Her subjectivity is determined by words and naming, by the symbolic practices of the social order. Thus, Ellen's mother-in-law advises her to "keep a journal: *it will teach you to express yourself, a journal forms character besides by developing the habit of self-examination*."[43] The symbols or language of femininity, the novel maintains, are learnt through cultural induction. *A Fringe of Leaves* therefore follows the progress of Ellen from her humble beginnings as a working-class farmer's daughter, Ellen Gluyas, to her initiation into genteel femininity as Ellen Roxburgh, the wife of Austin, the gentleman. This transformation unfolds according to a process involving "*self-examination*" learnt and

---

39 Foucault, *Discipline and Punish*, 136.
40 White, *Voss*, 149.
41 *Voss*, 203.
42 White, *A Fringe of Leaves*, 279.
43 White, *A Fringe of Leaves*, 47, italics in the original.

internalized from society's discursive management. In becoming "Mrs Roxburgh," Ellen must adhere to a new grammar of corporeal control, suppressing the rougher ways of her Gluyas self:

> As for chapped hands and red cheeks, Ellen tried rubbing in milk as soon as she learned she ought to be ashamed. She smeared them with the pulp from cucumbers according to the old receipt [...] in *The Lady's Most Precious Possessions*. Ellen's cheeks stayed red until they toned down, seemingly of their own moving, to look by the best light what might have been considered a golden brown. (Not until herself became a lady was she properly blanched, by sitting in a drawing-room, and driving out in a closed carriage, and keeping such late hours the fits of yawning forced the blood out of her cheeks.)
> *A Fringe of Leaves* 48

This transformation of identity via the regulation of the body, however, is highly provisional. Always underlying Ellen's subjectivity is a repressed, wordless, and abject physicality that threatens to arise in moments of temptation—her submission to adultery with her brother-in-law, Garnet, and her sexual relationship with the escaped convict Jack Chance, for example—and in moments when the necessity of physical survival overwhelms unnecessary social mores. Increasingly, after she is shipwrecked and captured by an Aboriginal tribe, she loses herself in an engulfing corporeality. The unconscious prerogatives of the body are, for White, as for Joseph Conrad, always of greater exigency than the maintenance of spurious, socially constructed identities.

The Human Eye Takes Aim: The Social Gaze

The theme of the construction of the docile body in normative (middle-class, heterosexual, white, Australian) society appears to have been of strong personal importance to White. As a gay man writing in the twentieth-century, postwar, postcolonial Australian context, he felt keenly the constraints of the normative control of the body. According to his biographer, David Marr, White's homosexuality and childhood sickliness shaped his conflicted experience of his physicality: "When he was a child, asthma had brought out his jealousy and self-loathing and his sense of powerlessness in the face of a hostile world."[44] This "jumble of painful feelings was intensified as he came to grips

---

44   David Marr, *Patrick White: A Life* (London: Jonathan Cape, 1991): 75.

with homosexuality."[45] Marr observes that White felt "afflicted, set apart," and that a "strong vein of self-loathing marked him for life."[46] White himself admitted to such feelings: "As a homosexual I have always known what it means to be an outsider."[47]

Arguably because of White's troubled sense of his own embodiment, many of his characters are profoundly awkward physically. John Beston bases his assertion that there is a "general distaste for physicality" in White's fiction on the presence of characters who are "rarely comfortable within their bodies." They "stagger, or stumble, or skitter, especially when assailed by strong emotion; they totter and lurch and galumph."[48] While this does not necessarily exemplify White's "distaste" for physicality, it does reveal his intense fascination with it. In particular, it indicates his interest in the effects of the perceived gaze of others on the subject's experience of his or her physicality. Theodora Goodman's awkwardness, for example, stems from her suspicion of her socialite mother's disapproval:

> This is my daughter, Theodora, Mrs Goodman did not say, but looked, my daughter Theodora who is unlike me either in behaviour or in body, and who at best was an odd, sallow child in that yellow dress that was such a mistake.
> *The Aunt's Story* 92

Awkward embodiment also characterizes Voss, who is painfully aware that to some he is "uncouth," a "nasty man."[49] As this nastiness becomes increasingly "apparent to Voss himself," he experiences himself as the "victim of his body, to which other people had returned him. So he walked furiously. He was not lame, but could have been."[50] Voss despises society for "returning" him to his body by reminding him of his social insufficiencies. Significant, then, to his understanding of his mind's distinction from his body is his association of the latter with others' perceptions. When the social gaze reminds him of his awkwardness, he perceives himself as "lame." Moreover, White's ambiguous prose

---

45   Marr, *Patrick White*, 75.
46   *Patrick White*, 75.
47   Patrick White, "In This World of Hypocrisy and Cynicism" (1984), in *Patrick White Speaks*, ed. Brennan & Flynn, 156.
48   John B. Beston, "Patrick White, *The Twyborn Affair*," *World Literature Written in English* 14.2 (August 1980): 201.
49   White, *Voss*, 26.
50   *Voss*, 26.

blurs focalization to suggest the merging of Voss's sentiment with the external omniscient viewpoint that apparently produces it: "He was not lame, but could have been." He is aware of his body when it impinges problematically upon his consciousness, which occurs when he identifies with an external gaze. As Voss walks along the road, feeling himself the "victim of his body," he imagines the "human eye [...] taking aim through slits of shutters."[51]

Foucault compares modern society to Jeremy Bentham's panopticon design for prisons, in which a single guard can watch over many prisoners simultaneously while remaining unseen. Under this invisible gaze, the prisoner submits to and internalizes disciplinary social control. Such an objectifying gaze is emphasized in White's writing and internalized by his protagonists. Sometimes this is the gaze of a specific individual, but more often it is the gaze of society itself, a generalized, unidentifiable, and internalized eye associated with discursive control. White's many descriptions of awkward embodiment relate to the gaze. In a passage from *Riders in the Chariot* that is often cited as indicative of White's division of body from soul, the eccentric Mary Hare runs home from the post office, after which, in the proleptic *entrée* of the narrative, a local gossip attempts to embroil the postmistress in a discussion of Hare's visible physical "*differen[ce]*":[52]

> Where the road sloped down, she ran, disturbing stones, her body quite agitated as it accompanied her, but her inner self by now joyfully serene. The anomaly of that relationship never failed to mystify, and she stopped again to consider. For a variety of reasons, very little of her secret, actual nature *had been disclosed to other human beings.*
>
> *Riders in the Chariot* 12–13 (my emphasis)

While the reader's attention is drawn to the division between an inner and an outer self, this is not a simple example of an unambiguous schism between consciousness and corporeality. Although Hare's emotions are calm while her body is frenzied, she is more concerned with her body's seeming inability to express her 'inner' thoughts to others and thus with a duality springing from an ambiguity of the body, which is experienced simultaneously as subject and object, self and other. Mary Hare experiences her body as separate from her self because she identifies, at this point, with the observer to whom her emotions are untranslatable and undisclosed, or, more likely, for whom her emotions are immaterial. Other human beings, for Hare, are all akin to the gossips at

---

51   *Voss*, 26.
52   White, *Riders in the Chariot*, 7, emphasis in the original.

the post office, and gossip in White's writing represents a prevailing discourse of normative control. Hare's sense of the 'inner' self as distinct from a body prompting social censure will transform over the course of the novel as she comes into contact with three similarly ostracized individuals, for whom her emotional and physical states are important: Himmelfarb, Godbold, and Dubbo, the other three visionaries who similarly intuit the significance—spiritual, ethical, and constitutive—of corporeality.

Exceeding a Frozen Identity: The Metaphor of the Statue and the Excess of Corporeality

The preceding sections have outlined two contrasting aspects of the body in White's fiction: the fluidity of pre-symbolic corporeal energy arising from the materiality of the body itself, and the regulated body, coinciding with the construction of subjectivity, and brought into being according to the external imposition of the social order internalized by the self-regulating subject. White suggests that society has the power to shape, mould, and freeze the body into a static image. Occasionally, he deploys the symbol of the statue to point up the discrepancy between the cold stiffness of socially sanctioned subjectivity and the fluid force of corporeality associated with moments of liberation and 'transcendence' in his fiction. Arguably, an intermediary space comparable to Kristeva's *chora* exists between the deadness of the symbolic statue and the vitality of physical energy. Characters sometimes alternate between their static representation in the image of the statue and their liberation through the dynamics of corporeality. In *A Fringe of Leaves*, for example, Austin Roxburgh thinks of his wife, Ellen, as a sculpture of sorts. She could be

> the project which might ease the frustration gnawing at him: to create a beautiful, charming, not necessarily intellectual, but socially acceptable companion out of what was only superficially unpromising material.
> *A Fringe of Leaves* 61

Austin is Pygmalion to Ellen's Galatea, but, as Mr Merivale remarks early in the novel, "Mrs Roxburgh is a woman, not a marble statue,"[53] a proclamation to which the length of the text, obsessed with the demands of her corporeality, will attest. The metaphor of the statue occurs, moreover, in *The Aunt's Story* and *The Tree of Man*.

---

53   *A Fringe of Leaves*, 17.

In *The Aunt's Story*, Theodora Goodman "transcends" her body in a dance that paradoxically emphasizes her physicality, or, more specifically, her desire:

> the proud striped skirt of Theodora streamed with fire. Her body bent to the music. Her face was thin with music, down to the bone. She was both released from her own body and imprisoned in the molten gold of Frank Parrott.
>
> *The Aunt's Story* 76

This dance occurs during Theodora's adolescence at a ball organized by the Parrotts, where she has found herself torn between propriety and a physical excitement to which she eventually yields. The imagery of the episode emphasizes White's concern with the juxtaposition of social norms and their inscription upon the body and the corporeal transgression of these norms. Before Theodora erupts into her uninhibited dance, she is implicitly compared to a statue: "In one corner of one room there was a statue, holding her hands in a position of ugly and unnatural modesty, and this was all wrong" (72). Theodora wonders "where she could put her own hands, but she could not think. Wherever she put them, these too were ugly and unnatural" (72). Clearly the statue represents the fixity of normative feminine identity, as well as White's implicit judgment on social propriety with its rules of "ugly and unnatural modesty." The statue is Theodora's desire rendered immobile—fixed, cold, and dead. As Peter Brooks observes of the female nude,

> Beginning with the Hellenistic period (whose most influential works are the so-called Capitoline and Medici Venuses), the female nude assumes the form of the *Venus pudica*, caught in a gesture of modesty in which she partly covers her sex, and therefore may draw greater attention to it.[54]

The statue in *The Aunt's Story* covers her pubic area, drawing attention to sexuality, yet emphasizing it as trapped in an image and identity of cold, unyielding stone—a frozen, colonial femininity.

Making a connection between statuary and the living body, Slavoj Žižek comments on the "long ideological condition of conceiving a statue as a frozen, immobilized living body, a body whose movements are paralyzed (usually by a kind of evil spell)."[55] He continues:

---

54   Brooks, *Body Work*, 17.
55   Slavoj Žižek, *The Plague of Fantasies* (London: Verso, 1997): 87.

the statue's immobility thus involves infinite pain [...] engendered by the stiffness of the living body, its freezing into the form of a statue is usually a sign of pain miraculously filtered by the statue, from the trickle of blood on the garden statue in Gothic novels to the tears miraculously shed by every self-respecting statue of the Virgin Mary in Catholic countries.[56]

For Žižek, the statue is uncanny because it seems to exemplify a petrified living subject. Importantly, moreover, it indicates a split between the "'dead' symbolic order which mortifies the body and the non-symbolic Life-Substance of *jouissance*."[57] This description is useful for a reading of the image of the statue in White's fiction. Theodora identifies with the "infinite pain" of the statue related to the "stiffness of the living body."[58] However, for her, this stiffness melts into the joy of corporeality, the "non-symbolic Life-Substance of *jouissance*," which erupts into her experience. As her socialized identity, associated with the discursive realm of the symbolic order, dissolves, she does not care how she comports herself. Correspondingly, the text becomes increasingly physical and *jouissance* engulfs her in her dance with Frank. Trapped in the prohibitive bounds of socialized identity, others attending the ball are mesmerized by Theodora's transgressive dance, which is both "strange and wonderful," yet also, importantly, "shameful, because they [do] not understand."[59] For those trapped in convention, the body is moulded and sculpted to the dimensions of the social order. Abject bodies exceeding the normative imperatives of society are repulsive and compelling because they represent the potentially liberating corporeal possibilities that convention disallows.

In *The Tree of Man*, the image of the statue is again deployed to suggest the sanitized identity of an 'acceptable' femininity. The novel's protagonist, Stan Parker, works for a brief period for Mr Armstrong, who lives on a country estate called Glastonbury. Outside the establishment is a decorative "stone statue of a woman modestly disguising her nakedness with her hands."[60] Glastonbury is presented as an architectural example of the colonial attempt to efface Australian indigeneity and to replicate England in a foreign clime. The dishonesty and abjection of such an imperative is emphasized: the embellishments of colonial wealth sanitize and obscure nature, corporeality, and mortality, and obfuscate

---

56   Žižek, *The Plague of Fantasies*, 87.
57   *The Plague of Fantasies*, 89.
58   White, *The Aunt's Story*, 87.
59   *The Aunt's Story*, 76.
60   White, *The Tree of Man*, 65.

the colonial subject's perilous teetering on the brink of an indefinable abyss, whether this be the ever-present reality of death, the danger of the untapped unconscious, or the threat to a rigidly defended "clean and proper" identity. A character called Madeleine is engaged to one of the Armstrong sons. She flits briefly in and out of the narrative, appearing to Amy Parker in particular as a figure of romance and nobility removed from the quotidian reality of Amy's life. For Amy, Madeleine's existence resembles a "novelette" (184), and Madeleine's identity is indeed a fiction: initially, she is unattainable and beautiful, more sculpture or myth than embodied woman. Her sexuality, drives, and mortality are obscured by her performance of genteel, colonial femininity. Her sanitized identity, like the statue outside the house, disguises her nakedness—her corporeality.

Madeleine's narrative function becomes clear when a fire breaks out at Glastonbury and Stan must rescue her from the centre of the burning house. For White, imagery of fire often correlates with burning corporeal energy or desire, as it does in the characterization of Theodora Goodman. The impossibly remote and seemingly incorporeal Madeleine has abjected her physicality through her performance of femininity. It returns to her, however, during this episode, momentarily consuming and destroying her fragile subjectivity. White's description enacts Madeleine's 'descent' from incorporeal untouchability to animal degradation. When Stan eventually finds her in the upper storey of the burning building, he is at first overwhelmed by her mythic, incorporeal beauty: he has "never seen anything glowing and flowing like this woman in her shining dress" (181). However, when Madeleine points out the nearest exit, the servants' staircase, she opens "with her own hands the stuffy door that divided the classes" (182). This is an important symbolic transition in the sequence describing the fire: Madeleine is no longer "sitting somewhere in one of the rooms in the house, in silk and diamonds" (180), entirely removed from the working-class Stan. Instead,

> She had turned sallow, almost ugly, he was close enough to see, and it made him comfortable. On one side of her nose, that was very beautiful and fragile, there was a little mark, like a pockmark. And suddenly he wished he could sink his face in her flesh, to smell it, that he could part her breasts and put his face between.
>
> She saw this. They were burning together at the head of the smoking staircase. She had now to admit, without repugnance, that the sweat of his body was drugging her, and that she would have entered his eyes, if she could have, and not returned.
>
> *The Tree of Man* 183

Stan recognizes Madeleine's corporeality, as she herself becomes increasingly aware of it. As she loosens her grip on genteel identity, so her "repugnance"—the horror of abjection when confronting the corporeal—diminishes. In accepting the body, moreover, Madeleine loses her hold on rationality, feeling "the sweat of his body [...] drugging her." She longs to lose herself entirely by "entering" his eyes and "not returning."

Yet this is merely one step downwards in Madeleine's plunge from aristocracy, symbolically enacted by the couple's descent of the spiral staircase. At the half-landing,

> Madeleine's beauty had shrunk right away, and any desire that Stan Parker might have had was shrivelled up. He was small and alone in his body, dragging the sallow woman.
> *The Tree of Man* 183

Madeleine's loss of identity has surpassed Stan's for the moment, and he is unable to follow her into her submission to pure corporeality. Increasingly, she becomes a body yielding to inevitable suffering and mortality. In the last stage of the couple's hellish descent, Stan, too, surrenders to pain and the proximity of death, merging with Madeleine in compassionate understanding:

> It was not their flesh that touched but their final bones. Then they were writhing through the fire. They were not living. They had entered a phase of pain [...]. When her teeth fastened in his cheek it expressed their same agony.
> *The Tree of Man* 183

Social hierarchies dissolve as the body itself is reduced from flesh to bone in imagery foregrounding the inevitability of death. The "phase of pain" that the characters enter is the leveling awareness of their shared corporeality.

Finally, outside on the singed lawns of Glastonbury, Madeleine is utterly diminished socially. Befouled beside the fiancé she has snootily disregarded and who is contrastingly "handsome and clean," with "white cuffs" and "smelling of bay rum," Madeleine, her hair burned off, begins a "kind of dry retching, holding her head, and falling even to all fours," while around her animal body ring "loud explosions of laughter" (184). With this, Amy's "novelette [is] finished" (184). The "statue" of modest womanhood has disintegrated into the animality and corporeality from which it has been dissociated. Class is dissolved—so much so, that after the fire a bricklayer sticks his hat "on the statue of the naked woman" and performs a "lewd dance, of renunciation and possession" (187).

The dissolution of the form of identity into the flux of corporeality is a vital component of the treatment of the body in White's fiction. It emphasizes the pretentiousness of a superior notion of subjectivity based on the repudiation of the body and punishes those characters intent on denying their corporeality and hence their physical equality with all others. In these moments, the 'return' of corporeality is not redemptive; it is, however, necessary to White's dismantling of social hierarchies and spurious identities.

Constructing Subjectivity, Controlling the Body: "Dead Roses" and "Clay"

The short stories collected in *The Burnt Ones* and *The Cockatoos* are particularly effective examples of White's interest in the tension between social demands and corporeal imperatives. Relatively ignored in existing criticism, they strongly evince White's indictment of social norms and sanctioned subjectivity. Queerness and corporeal drives are consistently thematized in them, and White's critique of conjugality is at its strongest here. In two stories from *The Burnt Ones*, "Dead Roses" and "Clay," this tension is particularly evident.

"Dead Roses" focuses on the character of Anthea Mortlock, née Scudamore, whose younger years are dominated by her controlling mother. As a young woman, Anthea temporarily escapes her mother's clutches to holiday with family acquaintances. Always maintaining a strong hold on her propriety, she does not submit entirely to her attraction to a fellow guest, Barry Flegg, despite their fumblings on the beach on one occasion. However, this moment remains for her a strong memory of sexual potency, for shortly after she leaves for home she marries her father's obnoxious acquaintance, the elderly Mr Mortlock, and must suffer his financial control and desiccated impotence; she becomes 'locked' in a living death, as Mortlock's name suggests. By submitting to her mother's regulation of her desire and the stultifying institution of her marriage, Anthea denies her sexuality.

At the beginning of the story, the young Anthea Scudamore's body is marked by a "vaccination mark which glare[s] white from the girl's passive arm."[61] This mark is a metonym for the inscription of social rules upon the body, particularly those governing the repression of sexuality and thus 'immunizing' against the disorder of transgression. Anthea's dominating mother has inculcated in her an obsessive fear of physical contact, and she grows up terrified

---

61 Patrick White, "Dead Roses," in White, *The Burnt Ones*, 16.

of "becoming involved in any process of skin."[62] This results in her frustrated sexuality, symbolized by the "dead roses" of the title. After her marriage to the decrepit Mr Mortlock, an odd ritual she develops emphasizes the constraints placed upon her subjectivity and body by gender norms and conjugality. Mr Mortlock insists on wheeling manure up a hill in a barrow, a task of which he is physically incapable. Anthea, in response, hitches both ends of a cord to the front of the barrow, steps into the loop, winds the cord tightly around her body, and pulls as her husband ineffectually pushes. The act becomes symbolic:

> With Mrs Mortlock it was all seriousness, part of the necessary ritual she must evolve by inspiration to help her bear her chosen existence. So she bent and heaved. Her ribs strained. Her neck grew ugly. Sharp daggers of pain stabbed at times into her back. As she pulled, and bit her lips. To suffer thus enduringly was to ensure her continued happiness.
> "Dead Roses," in *The Burnt Ones* 57

This Sisyphean description satirizes the ties or constraints on Anthea's body as she 'suffers' in enduring what White sarcastically refers to as the "continued happiness" of marriage. In this hyperbolic enactment of social restraints, Anthea is subject to the "project of docility," which acts on the body by obtaining "holds upon it at the level of the mechanism itself—movements, gestures, attitudes."[63]

In another short story from *The Burnt Ones*, "Clay," the name of the eponymous protagonist is a metaphor for the malleability of identity according to the demands of society. Again, social rules are manifested in corporeal control. Clay's mother, another of White's matriarchs "associated with the futile world of social values,"[64] enforces and reifies gender norms by constantly insisting that her son have his hair cut. Her explanation as she leads him away from the barber's reveals White's satirical treatment of society's control of the body in defence against deviations from the socio-cultural norm:

> There Clay a person is sometimes driven to things in defence of what we know and love I would not of done this otherwise if not to protect you from yourself because love you will suffer in life if you start talking queer

---

62 White, "Dead Roses," 24.
63 Foucault, *Discipline and Punish*, 136.
64 John Barnes, "New Tracks to Travel: The Stories of White, Porter and Cowan," *Meanjin* 105/25.2 (Winter 1966): 157.

> remember it doesn't pay to be different and no one is different without they have something wrong with them.
> "Clay," in *The Burnt Ones* 118

Here Mrs Skerrit's torrential chatter represents the constant insertion of the dominant discourse of middle-class Australian society in Clay's consciousness. That Clay threatens his mother's heteronormative values by "talking queer" is evidenced in her attempt to render him starkly masculine. Clay's identity is imposed upon him from without, and small textual details suggest his interpellation into social convention: his name; his mother's *wedding* photograph, over which he obsesses; the influence on him of Mr Stutchbury, employee of the Department of *Education*; and his eventual job at the Department of *Customs* and Excise.

According to Judith Butler, gendered identity is learnt and reified via its continual re-enactment through bodily performance. The process of repetition is "at once a re-enactment and re-experiencing of a set of meanings already socially established; and it is the mundane and ritualized form of their legitimation."[65] White is aware of this dynamic, which Butler terms "performativity": "the reiterative and citational practice by which discourse produces the effects that it names."[66] Clay's wife is a pallid copy of Mrs Skerrit: "I think perhaps you are like my mother," he tells her.[67] Leading up to his marriage, moreover, Clay experiences himself as a passive object bobbing on the tide of repetitive social forces:

> 'Marj is so like you, Mum.'
> 'Eh?' Mrs Skerrit said.
> He could not explain that what was necessary for him, for what he had to do, was a continuum. He could not have explained what he had to do, because he did not know, as yet.
> "Clay," in *The Burnt Ones* 123

Mrs Skerrit's guttural grunt reflects her emptiness, just as Clay's inability to understand the imperative to enter into marriage reflects his lack of agency.

---

65   Judith Butler, *Gender Trouble: Feminism and the Subversion of Identity* (London: Routledge, 1999): 140.
66   Judith Butler, *Bodies That Matter: On the Discursive Limits of "Sex"* (London: Routledge, 1993): 2.
67   White, "Clay," in White, *The Burnt Ones*, 122.

In "Dead Roses," too, Anthea Scudamore is a facsimile of her mother Betsy and therefore of the performance of femininity. In the focalization of her father,

> She was so bright, so thoughtful, so damn pleasant. She had learnt it all. Squinting through the glare of the veranda Bill Scudamore thought to see Betsy, or at least the wax which still had to be worked up into the replica. Some men, he understood, allowed themselves to experience twinges of renewal or desire on recognizing the past in the present, but his was a disbelieving nature, and this, surprisingly, his child. The white wax which sense of duty was moulding into a smile. This greenish, girlish flesh under a large summer hat. It made him examine his own hands.
> "Dead Roses," in *The Burnt Ones* 14

Like Ellen Roxburgh and Clay, Anthea is the wax on which society in the form of her mother imprints its expectations. As Mrs Scudamore observes to a friend: "It is thrilling to watch the blossoming of a young girl, particularly when she happens to be one's daughter. One's very own act of creation."[68] Anthea's identity, in one of the images favored by White and discussed above, is associated with the "solid sculpture of her body,"[69] indicating the static subjectivity that the symbolic order prompts her to perform, an identity which indicates that "bodily control is an expression of social control."[70]

Like Clay, Anthea has no agency in the construction of her identity. Judith Butler's philosophy of the body, which precludes agency, is therefore of interest for a reading of this aspect of White's fiction. Ian Burkitt explains:

> the body acts not because of any essence of individuality contained within it—a soul, a mind or an identity—but because of the power invested in it by the symbolic order. [For Butler] the body and its powers of agency are constructed in the same stroke through discourses.[71]

As Burkitt argues, however, questions arise from such a philosophy:

> If the gendered, desiring body is a creation of the symbolic laws and discursive taboos, why did these form in the first place? What would law and

---

68 White, "Dead Roses," 14.
69 "Dead Roses," 65.
70 Douglas, *Natural Symbols*, 70.
71 Ian Burkitt, *Bodies of Thought*, 92.

taboo have to operate against or regulate if desire and the body are only ever constituted within its confines?[72]

Burkitt observes that law and taboo must arise as reactions to a material, desiring body that therefore precedes them, and rightly criticizes Butler for subordinating the "experience of being a body" to the "mechanism to which the body is constructed."[73] In literature, the experience of being a body cannot be elided and, for White, the experience of *being* a body is fundamental to his characters, whose bodies assert themselves against identities prescribed by the symbolic order.

In "Dead Roses," Anthea's desire is liberated when her husband dies, and is evident in the way in which she chooses to mark her body. Her mother observes: "I have never known you paint your nails. Do you think, Anthea, such a vivid red is in the best of taste?"[74] Anthea's "lovely dripping nails" (66) sign her body with the transgressive excess of her desire. The corporeal yearning to which she has never been able to give release is revealed when she encounters Barry Flegg, the object of her adolescent yearnings, and his family many years later in Greece. An old man walking past presents Mrs Flegg with a bunch of crimson roses which are soon "glowing and spilling from her stained lap" (73). The blooms provide a vivid contrast to the dead roses that have littered Anthea's marital home and indicate the surprising awakening not simply of a desire that she has not expected, but of a stirring lesbianism, perhaps oedipally inflected but, more importantly, undermining the story's prior themes of marriage and heterosexuality:

> at some point in that incalculable night, she awoke to her own face. The glass was overflowing with it. The grey face, emerging from the washes of sleep, had been mutilated unmercifully. Extinct terrors caked her lips, choked her long, dusty throat. But it was not the isolation of her own reflected and reflective face of which Mrs Mortlock was chiefly conscious. She began, with a slow distaste, to accept that she had been dreaming of Cherie Flegg, of her stained leopard-skin matador pants.
>
> It was only then that Mrs Mortlock's face forced itself on her, out of the glass, and the breath went *crrkk* in her throat, and she fell back, and switched the light off.
>
> "Dead Roses," in *The Burnt Ones* 76

---

72 *Bodies of Thought*, 94.
73 *Bodies of Thought*, 94.
74 White, "Dead Roses," 66.

Anthea's encounter with her mirror image stages a typically Whitean conflict between identity and corporeality. In her transgressive desire, she exceeds her defined identity, awakening to her own "overflowing" face and to an awareness of her sexuality similarly exceeding the limits of her body image. The experience is beyond the bounds of the symbolic—it is "incalculable." Moreover, her identity, imaged as a "grey face," is "mutilated unmercifully" and, in its confrontation with the threat of the abject, besieged by "extinct terrors" and a "slow distaste." Gradually, in defence of her normative identity, Anthea recognizes with anguish the polymorphous sexuality that threatens her selfhood. The story ends ambiguously. Whether the face that "force[s] itself" upon her is her identity struggling to consolidate itself again or the "overflowing" "face" of transgression is left open to interpretation. Nonetheless, such ambiguity ultimately reinforces the troubling of the borders of Anthea's identity. As the breath goes "*crrkk* in her throat," we are reminded of the fall from language that the body may represent as well as its disruption of subjectivity and transgression of social prohibition. In stories such as "Dead Roses," White explores alternative sexualities while critiquing the resilient strength of a compulsory heterosexuality and the discursive laws promoting its continuance.

The Body in Theory, The Body in Practice: Catherine Standish

For Anthea Scudamore, "the body [...] in theory" is very different from "the body [...] in practice,"[75] a distinction drawn in *The Living and the Dead* that recalls the contrast Ian Burkitt emphasizes between the "mechanism to which the body is constructed" and the "experience of being a body."[76] This is the case with many of White's characters, more often than not women, who appear to struggle between two or more opposing identities, sometimes indicated by different names. In his critique of marriage, White suggests that socially sanctioned practices are increasingly repressive of 'natural' corporeality. Ellen Roxburgh in *A Fringe of Leaves* reverts, at times, to her maiden name of Ellen Gluyas, a name associated with a more primitive, physical aspect of her character. The Princess de Lascabanes of *The Eye of the Storm* is also Dorothy Hunter, and the novel's reversion to her prior identity tends to coincide with descriptions of her seemingly more authentic physical awkwardness.

Such slippages of identity have been interpreted as evidence of White's misogyny. Simon During, for example, contends that

---

75   White, *The Living and the Dead*, 24.
76   Burkitt, *Bodies of Thought*, 94.

> for [White], women do not preserve boundaries and autonomy: they are enveloping, fluid, capable—like old witches—of myriad transformations, and all because they are not quite complete in themselves.[77]

Yet identity, in White's fiction, is never self-sufficient and is therefore prone to incoherence and disruption. Arguably, feminine identity better enacts the performance of civilized embodiment in White's imaginary, based as it is on notions of etiquette, politeness, and the denial of the lower body strata. To be 'ladylike' requires a marked distancing from corporeality. Thus, women "symbolize the trap of social and cultural repression."[78] According to Veronica Brady, moreover, White has

> a keen, if satiric eye for what he sees around him, for the women who allow themselves to become mere commodities, and his critique of them is even more radical than most feminists' since he finds them guilty of a kind of defilement [...]. These women betray the archaic claims of the self.[79]

Not always, however—White's female characters, divided so starkly between corporeality and social demands, draw attention to this fragmentation and may be set on the path towards discovering a regenerative or painful bodiliness: they may be required to "respond to their destiny, the 'call to go further' which, [...] in *Voss* especially, women [...] hear more easily than men."[80] This indeed means that women are more closely aligned with abjection in White's fiction, which may be taken as exemplifying its inherent sexism. For White, however, archaic versions of the 'self', more closely associated with an uninhibited corporeality, possess greater authenticity than those acquired later. Social identity, ever evolving, is thus presented as increasingly repressive of corporeality.

White's interest in the painful and ultimately impossible social repression of corporeality is evident even in his earliest fiction. In *The Living and the Dead*, the impetuous, naively charming Kitty Goose, born into a working-class family, becomes after marriage the refined and sophisticated Catherine Standish

---

77 Simon During, *Patrick White* (Oxford: Oxford UP, 1996): 46.
78 John Docker, "Patrick White and Romanticism: *The Vivisector*," *Southerly* 33.1 (March 1973): 44.
79 Veronica Brady, "Patrick White and the Question of Woman," in *Who Is She?*, ed. Shirley Walker (St Lucia: U of Queensland P, 1983): 181.
80 Brady, "Patrick White and the Question of Woman," 182.

(mother of Elyot and Eden). Kitty's physical spontaneity, eventually lost in the affected social performance of the spurious Catherine, suggests her more authentic character. She first appears in the novel, before her marriage, pulling "too hard at a hesitant door, almost jerking from its socket either knob or arm."[81] As the narration shifts to second person to emphasize her physical intensity, she can barely contain "the breath that was bursting in your lungs, the words that were waiting for expression in your mouth" (18). Although Kitty is not "one of those women who accept the body more in theory than in practice" (24), she is entirely "changed with her changed name" (36) after marriage. She becomes "conscious of her own impetus, entering a room" and is "less dumpy, lumpy anxious, in fact she [is] more Catherine Standish and less Kitty Goose" (37). The description of Kitty's transformation suggests that it is naming, hence language, that acts as a catalyst for change and constructs identity. Catherine Standish has, in a sense, been spoken into existence, and a new identity emerges from society's expectations of her as a married, middle-class woman. White is aware, then, of the performativity of identity evinced in his portrayal of Catherine, whose "clothes [...] more than fulfilled the primary function of being clothes" (37). Catherine dons a ready-made identity while abjecting her former self. She is one of White's docile female bodies, her character moulded into an amalgamation of "acquired conventional poses" (279). Involved in a reiterative performance of social expectation, she is merely the "mechanism of Catherine Standish" (288).

Despite her mechanized identity, however, she is perhaps the most embodied character in *The Living and the Dead*. Her embodiment relates, on one level, to her exemplification of the maternal in the novel. As the mother of Eden and Elyot Standish, she represents the abject maternal—the semiotic *chora*—that both forms and threatens their subjectivity. As a figure of abjection, moreover, she is often overwhelmed by her inability to manage her ageing body, a failing that corresponds to her lack of control over an inchoate, indifferent world where mortality is inevitability. An identity spoken into being, White suggests, cannot be sustained; the inexorability of bodily change ensures this. Like Madeleine's in *The Tree of Man*, Catherine's body asserts itself seemingly to taunt her constructed self and, by extension, the selves of her children, and to remind both character and reader that corporeality cannot be finally abjected. As she ages, Catherine is obsessed with her declining sexuality, contemplating with "sagging face" (315) the "contempt of the bodies of assured younger women" (217). Her ageing face derides her as she refuses to face up to her corporeality:

---

81   Patrick White, *The Living and the Dead*, 18.

> Because you couldn't yet accept, though it was still early in the morning, you said, the volcanic skin, the grease that lay in the valleys of the nose, that you had to own, the tousled accusation of a face, it was almost subhuman, or else an accentuation of the human, it was this perhaps that hurt [...]. There was the composite regret that rose up to confront the too concentrated human mess, to which time had reduced a face.
>
> *The Living and the Dead* 316

Catherine Standish seeks relief from the horrors of ageing through sex, a response, moreover, to her awareness that she has simply become a concatenation of "gestures continued from habit and convention" (287). Tired of having her body shaped according to the social expectations of femininity, she wants to "sink down into the easy, satisfying coma of the flesh" and thus transgresses social law by acceding to the "improper" demands of corporeality (241–242). As she ages, she increasingly experiences the "coma of the flesh." Toward the end of her life, for example, she disgraces herself at a party, where, drunk on desperation and gin, she collapses, her intoxication evident in the syntactical disfiguration of language that performatively replicates the engulfing of her subjectivity within her corporeality:

> You could have cried the gramophone it sank down and stroked the carpet it surged upward through the warm throat faces were bluish a gin bluish and the words the bubbles in gin [...] he had been waiting said to make your acquaintance without a chin to dance to push against a body she said a soul she said it was not a quiver of refusal you accepted a phrase you accepted anything after a point your own abject collapse.
>
> *The Living and the Dead* 322

Catherine, in this passage, struggles with the distinction between body and soul: "a body she said a soul she said it was not a quiver of refusal." This appears to be the drunken recollection of a conversation in which an individual is described in the slang of the time as a 'body' before the description is rejected (presumably by Catherine) in favor of the term 'soul'. The confused narration, however, states that this is *not* an interjection "of refusal you accepted a phrase you accepted anything after a point your own abject collapse." The refusal of corporeality is impossible when Catherine's body engulfs her experience—both in her confused awareness and in the drunken disorder of the description itself. Indeed, her final experiences usher in the "abject collapse" towards which many of White's fictions drive.

The impatient outburst of one of the young flappers at the event consolidates Catherine's association with the return of repressed corporeality, recalling her previous disorientated musings on the distinction of body and soul: "Throw out the body, someone do" (325). The body, however, remains obstinately present. Even in death, Catherine

> remain[s] tied to the body, to its final writhing, you felt the hand groping in the belly, the mouth gaped in an endless scream. There was no exaggeration in the engraving out of Dante that disturbed the childhood Sunday.
> *The Living and the Dead* 329

What looks like an 'art' image here is indeed consonant with indices elsewhere of the body inhabiting a liminal realm of diminishing physicality, though the Dante reference here is actually a flashing into terminal consciousness of Catherine's childhood memory of an engraving of the Gorgon or Medusa in *The Inferno* (Canto IX: 52–54), as is made clearer two pages later:[82]

> Out of an increasing pain flickered the engraving from the bookcase, the snakes she could remember, and the mouth prised open by an endless agony.
> *The Living and the Dead* 331

The association of death with an overwhelming sense of the agony, grotesquerie, and significance of corporeality is common in White's writing. Ultimately, death is not an escape from the body but, rather, provides the most intense experience of corporeality. As Brooks argues, "the primacy of the body may be most dramatically felt in its failure: the deathbed is a privileged literary space."[83] Catherine's final moments deny her the sense that the material world has become insubstantial:

> Too poignant or too irrelevant the physical world, reduced [...]. Mrs Standish opened her eyes. Her body drifted in the stream that was not herself, gentle or inevitable. Or it moved in jerks of pain, this was too close, too much the self, as if you were answerable for the act of living, the answer was the racked body.
> *The Living and the Dead* 335

---

82   This seems, however, to be a fiction, as the description accords less with Gustave Doré's engraving than with Caravaggio's tonda (as Perseus's mirror-shield) of 1595.
83   Brooks, *Body Work*, 5.

Although, like Catherine, White's characters may question the association of body and self, ultimately the self that is "answerable for the act of living" *is* the "racked body." Indeed, the body is often the answer in each of White's fictions, becoming increasingly significant in the lives of his characters until it pulsates in their experience and the text. The trajectory of the character of Catherine Standish attests to the fact that identity, a constructed mechanism, is simply insufficient to the task of holding corporeality at bay. The "body in theory" is certainly not "the body in practice" (24) and White's fiction persistently sets out to prove the inequality of this spurious equation.

Control and Otherness: Group Identity and Its Abjects

"Throw out the body, someone do": the bored words of the young woman at the party at which Catherine Standish disgraces herself resound throughout White's fiction. Bodies perceived as undisciplined and unruly are transgressive and 'other' in the smooth-running machinery of society, refusing to conform to the "mechanism" of identity that Catherine Standish, for example, initially embodies (288). Hence, they are subject to further discipline via ostracism and punishment. In *Riders in the Chariot*, Mordecai Himmelfarb, having escaped Europe during World War II and alighted in Australia, works in the Brighta Bicycle Lamps factory, where he is quickly incorporated into the "machinery of labour."[84] According to Karl Marx, two bodies are constantly in competition: "that which we may call the body of the factory, i.e. machinery organised into a system" and "the collective labourer, or social body of labour."[85] Ultimately, for Marx, in a philosophy presaging the theories of society and the body described earlier in this chapter, "it is not the workman that employs the instruments of labour, but the instruments of labour that employ the workmen."[86] Himmelfarb's role in the factory symbolizes the instruments of society exacting their toll upon his body and individuality.

However, White's focus is seldom on working bodies in a capitalist system. More importantly, bodies in White become 'docile' when they internalize society's discursive imperative of nationalist, middle-class, and gendered norms and subscribe to the institutions of marriage and the nuclear family. White's most visionary characters do not accede to these dictates, and often their very outsider status appears to constitute their vision. In the Brighta Bicycle Lamps

---

84   White, *Riders in the Chariot*, 590.
85   Karl Marx, *Capital* (Moscow: Progress, 1968): 372.
86   Marx, *Capital*, 398.

factory, heavy machinery, working its relentless rhythm, symbolizes the dead weight of the social machinery that constructs the Jewish Himmelfarb as an outsider. White's description of the factory's industry attains a heavy-handed emphasis: "the machinery continued to belt, to stamp, and to stammer with an even more hilarious blatancy, to hiss and piss with an increased virulence."[87] Personification and physical imagery—suggesting that machinery can "stamp" and "stammer" and "piss"—emphasize the common trope of the body as an image of society (the social body/body politic) and of normative political ideology. The bodies of White's outsiders do not conform to the structure of the social body which, accordingly, rejects them.

Indeed, group identity, like individual subjectivity, is maintained via abjection, the normative compulsion to "throw out the body" that does not conform.[88] Like subjectivity, strongly defined group identity is provisional, open to ambiguous threats from both within and without. Kristeva's notion of abjection in fact derives from Mary Douglas's theory of pollution and taboo developed in her seminal *Purity and Danger*. Douglas espouses the link between the social and the physical body by arguing that the boundaries of the physical body decided on in culture are taken up in discourse to represent necessary social limits:

> ideas about separating, purifying, demarcating and punishing transgressions have as their main function to impose system on an inherently untidy experience. It is only by exaggerating the difference between within and without, above and below, male and female, with and against, that a semblance of order is created.[89]

In Douglas, the boundaries of the body are those of the social order and vice versa. Thus, where the limits of the social order are strictly policed—within the paranoid and defensive topography of White's suburbia, for example—notions of pollution relating to the body arise: "pollution is a type of danger which is not likely to occur except where the lines of structure, cosmic or social, are clearly defined."[90] Pollution involves the transgression of such rigid lines of structure. Anyone defying the limits of society via the limits of the body is thus condemned:

---

87   White, *Riders in the Chariot*, 280.
88   White, *The Living and the Dead*, 325.
89   Mary Douglas, *Purity and Danger: An Analysis of Concepts of Pollution* (London: Routledge & Kegan Paul, 1966): 4.
90   Douglas, *Purity and Danger*, 113.

> A polluting person is always in the wrong. He has developed some wrong condition or simply crossed over some line which should not have been crossed and this displacement unleashes danger for someone.[91]

The archaic, subject-forming process of abjection thus extends to social governance, explaining the primitive and often nameless horror inherent in the maintenance of ideological boundaries. White understands the importance of othering to the construction of group identity: "To some it is always unendurable to watch the antithesis of themselves."[92] This is because group identity is threatened by whatever does not conform: "That which is marginal is always located as a site of danger and vulnerability."[93] White's suburbia, as Andrew McCann argues, is a topography of prohibition, law, and abjection.[94] Here, bodies are expected to adhere to rigid notions of normality or else are cast aside and maligned.

This abjection is strongly evident in the opening pages of *The Solid Mandala*. The first, short section of the novel, "In the Bus," focuses on a conversation between Mrs Poulter and Mrs Dun as they travel by bus through the suburb of Sarsaparilla. The two converse about their suburban existences—the pleasures of having a veranda, the convenience of new shops, and eventually, with a frisson of delight, the neighbors. Gossip, as I have argued, exemplifies White's concern with discursive normativity. Mrs Poulter, who muses during this prologue on how it is "so important to be decent,"[95] lives across the road from the Brown brothers. Decency, it seems, equates to the suburban mindset's rejection of disturbing corporeality—its compulsion to remain "clean and proper."[96] After the conversation has established itself within the comforting realm of suburban gossip that sets up the neighbors, Arthur and Waldo Brown, as 'other' to the normative Mrs Poulter and Mrs Dun, the actual sight of the retired brothers impinges disturbingly on the women as they stare through the window of the bus:

> 'Look!' Mrs Poulter almost shouted. [...]
> Then Mrs Dun did resentfully notice the two old men, stumping, trudging, you couldn't have said tottering—or if so, it was only caused

---

91 *Purity and Danger*, 113.
92 White, *Riders in the Chariot*, 525.
93 Elizabeth Grosz, *Volatile Bodies*, 195.
94 Andrew McCann, "The Ethics of Abjection," 145–155.
95 Patrick White, *The Solid Mandala*, 12.
96 Kristeva, *Powers of Horror*, 8.

by their age and infirmities—along what passed for pavement between Barranugli and Sarsaparilla. The strange part was the old gentlemen rose up, if only momentarily, blotting out the suburban landscape, filling the box of Mrs Dun's shuddering mind. She was still shocked, of course, by Mrs Poulter's thoughtless alarm. It could have been that. But she almost smelled those old men. The one in the stiff oilskin, the other in yellowed herring-bone, in each case almost to the ankle. [...] She sensed the scabs, the cracks which wet towels had opened in their old men's skin.[97]

The corporeality of the brothers Brown enters the discrete space of 'decency' symbolized by the enclosed bus and "the box of Mrs Dun's shuddering mind." In her horrified vision, the Browns eclipse the suburban landscape, disturbing her normative bearings and invading her subjectivity. Their invasion is presented as the infiltration of magnified corporeal detail: so vivid is Mrs Dun's imagining of "the scabs, the cracks which wet towels had opened in their old men's skin," an image recalling the openness of the grotesque body to the world, that the sight is almost olfactory. Imagery of the liminal or marginal is employed: the twins traverse the pavement "between Barranugli and Sarsaparilla" and the window of the bus is the permeable membrane that cannot protect the suburbanites from the sight and return of their abjects.

Mrs Dun is appalled by the sight of the brothers, not least because it troubles her heteronormative assumptions: she "never saw two grown men walkin' hand in hand."[98] Her response is the reaction of the outraged social body: "The breath was snoring between Mrs Dun's corrected teeth."[99] As one of White's sanitized suburbanites desperately concerned with denying corporeality—her refusal of the abject is evident in the "correction" of her dentures—Mrs Dun is deeply shaken by this unmitigated vision of "hideous, pitiable humanity."[100] Even when the bus is far beyond the scene, the vision returns to haunt her, prompting her renewed abjection: "The old men rose up again in Mrs Dun's mind, and she hated what she saw."[101] The memory will continue to disturb her:

---

97   White, *The Solid Mandala*, 19.
98   *The Solid Mandala*, 19.
99   *The Solid Mandala*, 19.
100 William Walsh, "Patrick White's Vision of Human Incompleteness: *The Solid Mandala* and *The Vivisector*," in *Readings in Commonwealth Literature*, ed. William Walsh (Oxford: Clarendon, 1973): 421.
101 White, *The Solid Mandala*, 20.

[she] could feel her own gooseflesh rise. As they waited to escape from the suffering bus the features of their familiar town began fluctuating strangely through the glass. Like that blood-pressure thing was on your arm.[102]

The Browns, then, threaten the self-presumption and complacency not only of the awful Mrs Dun but also of the suburban existence that she represents. The clear boundaries of middle-class group identity are troubled by these heavily embodied, senescent, and marginal presences. Throughout White's fiction, a strongly emphasized corporeality undermines the conjugal, familial, bourgeois, gendered, and sanitized associations of the suburban context.

---

102   White, *The Solid Mandala*, 21.

CHAPTER 5

Ladies and Gentlemen?
The Corporeal Subversion of Identity in The Aunt's Story *and* The Twyborn Affair

Extending Chapter 4's discussion of the way in which corporeality undermines socialized identity, this chapter focuses in detail on *The Aunt's Story* and *The Twyborn Affair*, revealing how these novels, one occurring early in White's oeuvre and the other towards the end of it, question discursive identity and foreground its subversion by corporeality. White wrote that these novels, along with *The Solid Mandala*, were his particular favorites.[1] Interested in why they should stand out, Gordon Collier observes that they represent "his most consistent, daring and unified essays into the nature of human identity (particularly the quest for psychical and sexual wholeness)";[2] they are, moreover, closely concerned with the arbitrary yet resilient nature of gender constructions and the norms dictating colonial subjectivity. As the previous chapter attests, White's fiction is consistently interested in socialization and in what he presumed to be the damage it inflicts on the psyche. His writing therefore gestures towards a utopian unity associated with a prelapsarian innocence and wholeness experienced in infancy, but lost thereafter due to the acquisition of language and, consequently, enculturation. As Norbert Hare proclaims in *Riders in the Chariot*, "All human beings are decadent [...]. The moment we are born, we start to degenerate. Only the unborn soul is whole, pure."[3] White connects this sense of wholeness with death, which promises relief from the demands of discourse. Death thus assumes maternal associations in the writing, recalling the merging of 'self' and 'other' characterizing the relationship between mother and infant.

In *The Twyborn Affair*, as Angelos and Eudoxia travel away from France by train, they observe a mother breastfeeding her child:

> At one point a young mother opened her blouse and offered an enormous breast to her two-year-old, who fastened on it, cheeks working as though he meant to get the whole thing down.

---

1 Patrick White, *Flaws in the Glass*, 145.
2 Gordon Collier, *The Rocks and Sticks of Words*, 5.
3 Patrick White, *Riders in the Chariot*, 45.

> The old man took his companion's hand. 'That is how it was in the beginning. [...] So it should be at the end too—in the after life—if we didn't know there isn't any.[4]

Like Angelos, White's favored characters seek to regain this sense of unity between self and other, while knowing that to regain it permanently and consciously is impossible. They strive for the synthesis characterizing the relationship of mother to child and the experience of death. Another way in which White aims to achieve synthesis is by challenging the binary assumptions of discourse via the ambiguous, excessive bodies of his transgressive characters: Theodora Goodman of *The Aunt's Story* is subtly androgynous, while E. of *The Twyborn Affair* oscillates via transgendered episodes between three personae: Eudoxia Vatatzes, Eddie Twyborn, and Eadith Trist. Both characters, moreover, embody the ambiguity of Australian Englishness.

As a colonial author who felt suspended between Australia and England, and whose homosexuality contributed to his disaffection in a normative and conservative colonial society, White was well suited to exploring the intersection of colonial and gendered identity. As Gregory Graham–Smith observes, he opposes the "monolithic knowledge of orthodox enculturation" with the "transgressive and resistant agency of sexual and social knowledges which hegemonic schools of thought would seek to efface."[5] The supplementary excesses of colonial hybridity and sexual ambiguity mark this realm of abjection and transgression. White's favoring of liminality is evinced in an oft-quoted statement from *Flaws in the Glass*, which pertains to his own subject-position as a writer and reveals his personal conception of his sexuality:

> Ambivalence has given me insights into human nature, denied I believe to those who are unequivocally male or female [...]. I would not trade my halfway house, frail though it be, for any of the entrenchments of those who like to think themselves unequivocal.[6]

White favors protagonists who embody this equivocation—often quite literally. The protagonists of *The Aunt's Story* and *The Twyborn Affair* resist the

---

4 Patrick White, *The Twyborn Affair*, 117.
5 Gregory Graham–Smith, "Against the Androgyne as Humanist He(te)ro: Patrick White's Queering of the Platonic Myth," in *Remembering Patrick White: Contemporary Critical Essays*, ed. Elizabeth McMahon & Brigitta Olubas (Cross/Cultures 128; Amsterdam & New York: Rodopi, 2010): 178.
6 White, *Flaws in the Glass*, 154.

categorization implicit in binary constructions, particularly with regard to gender, and their corporeality and desire infiltrate and suspend their identities. In these novels, White links society's inability to recognize sexuality outside heteronormative assumptions to language's failure to describe subjectivities exceeding strictly dualist gendered positions: as one of E. Twyborn's admirers writes in a letter, "Men and women are not the sole members of the human hierarchy to which you and I can also claim to belong."[7] Gender as an exclusionary system dictating behavior and sexuality is one of the binaries most offensive to White, who conceptualized his queerness as a "temperament" consisting of "man, woman, artist—or all in one."[8] Thus, the autobiographical *Flaws in the Glass* reveals that he associated homosexuality with a privileged intuition gained from sexual ambivalence. David Coad accordingly observes that White, a "believer in man's [sic] psychic androgyny," considered the "balance between the masculine and the feminine sides of the individual to be of vital importance."[9] For White, homosexuality is equivalent to androgyny, the possession of both male and female characteristics, and is potentially characterized by a visionary insight mythically associated with the hermaphrodite. According to Kari Weil, androgyny figures the "dialectical synthesis of what is objectively known (identified as the masculine) and the unknown Other (identified as feminine) who will make that knowledge complete."[10] In the Classical tradition, the androgyne is, "above all, a figure of primordial totality and oneness, created out of a union of opposed forces."[11] In psychological terms, moreover, it has often been considered to be "an archetype or a universal fantasy" associated with a "repressed desire to return to the imaginary wholeness and self-sufficiency associated with the pre-Oedipal phase before sexual difference."[12]

In *The Solid Mandala*, Arthur's thoughts regarding the difference between Tiresias, who oscillated between the sexes, and Adam Kadmon, an hermaphroditic figure embodying both sexes at once, suggests the difference between gendered identity and the unified condition of androgyny that induction into the symbolic order precludes:

---

7   White, *The Twyborn Affair*, 426.
8   White, *Flaws in the Glass*, 80.
9   David Coad, "Patrick White: Prophet in the Wilderness," 513.
10 Kari Weil, *Androgyny and the Denial of Difference* (Charlottesville: UP of Virginia, 1993): 2.
11 Weil, *Androgyny and the Denial of Difference*, 2.
12 Weil, *Androgyny and the Denial of Difference*, 3.

> 'If you want to know, I was thinking about Tiresias,' Arthur said to interest him. 'How he was changed into a woman for a short time. That sort of thing would be different, wouldn't it, from the hermaphroditic Adam who carries his wife about with him inside?'
>
> The Solid Mandala 283

Arthur's observation is a comment on his brother's moment of transvestism, when Waldo puts on one of his mother's dresses, an episode revealing his identity as profoundly fragmented. White's distinction between the unification of androgyny and the compulsory dualism of gender extends into *The Twyborn Affair*, which similarly posits its occasionally transgendered protagonist's performative identity as fragmentary and spurious. E. Twyborn is fragmented because of "his" compulsory subscription to the dualistic discourses of sex and gender, and therefore his necessary commitment to performing a fragmentary identity.[13] Enculturated into a socially sanctioned identity, E. feels that he embodies nothing but lack:

> Nothing is mine except for the coaxing I've put into it. For that matter, nothing of me is mine, not even the body I was given to inhabit, nor the disguises chosen for it [...]. The real E. has not yet been discovered, and perhaps never will be.
>
> The Twyborn Affair 79

White oscillates, then, between his conception of the androgyne as a figure of integration and the contrary impossibility of such wholeness in the symbolic order.

Neither protagonist, of *The Aunt's Story* or *The Twyborn Affair*, can be contained by society's expectations. Theodora Goodman of *The Aunt's Story* defies normative assumptions because of her inability to meet the standards of an 'acceptable' femininity. She is androgynous, as suggested by her slight moustache and the frequent shortening of her name to Theo. Moreover, the second half of her name, elided in the text yet made significantly present by its absence, may allude to Freud's famous case history, "Dora" (1905), in which he explained the psychogenic origins of hysteria, arguing that hysterical symptoms are both psychological and somatic. This is of relevance to *The Aunt's Story*,

---

13   The necessity of fixing on either a male or female pronoun when referring to E. reveals the compulsory subscription to the binary of gender inherent in language. Because he is biologically male, I refer to E. as masculine, unless referring specifically to one of his feminine personae, in full knowledge that this gendered specifity subverts his ambiguity.

wherein Theodora's narrative, itself concerned with its protagonist's growing insanity, is described as the tale of "her own blood,"[14] concerned with the "pulse of existence" (54).

That gender is produced by a compulsory system of bodily semiotics is obvious in *The Twyborn Affair*, but already evident in *The Aunt's Story*. Theodora grows up as an awkward teenager beside her conventionally pretty sister, Fanny, perpetually falling short of her mother Julia's expectations. Importantly, the novel associates Julia with discursive power; she fits into White's pattern of autocratic mothers through whom normative control is channeled. From the novel's opening, Julia is reductively referred to as "the voice" (11). She is defined by her sterile ability to "speak languages and read them" (65) and she flings "her grammar like a stone" (128). On the surface, this may appear to contradict the argument that White's writing evinces an interest in the wordless unity between mother and child. However, *The Aunt's Story* provides an alternative image of the maternal in its presentation of "roselight." Roses are a substitute for the maternal love that Julia withholds and also metonymic of the body. Theodora is compelled by the "smooth flesh of roses" (21). The blooms provide the warm, corporeal association that Julia's connections with the symbolic prevent her from embodying. As a child, like a foetus in the womb or floating in the sleepy, unformed consciousness of infancy, Theodora drifts in a state of diffuse identification with the roses and the "roselight" emanating from the garden (20):

> Theodora, lying in her bed, could sense the roses. [...] She stretched with her feet to touch the depths of the bed, which she did not yet fill. She felt very close to the roses the other side of the wall [...]. [S]he lay in the warm bed, remembering sleep, and drifted in the roselight that the garden shed.
> *The Aunt's Story* 20

> Altogether this was an epoch of roselight. Morning was bigger than the afternoon, and round, and veined like the skin inside an unhatched egg.
> *The Aunt's Story* 21

The images of rose and roselight find an effective comparison in Kristeva's concept of the semiotic, which, like the roses, constitutes the "other side" of identity. The similarity between the roselight and the semiotic dimension of signification is further reinforced in Part Two when Theodora, entering her

---

14 Patrick White, *The Aunt's Story*, 19.

bedroom at the Hôtel du Midi, is confronted with oppressive rose-patterned wallpaper:

> She began to turn in her small room. Maroon roses, the symbols of roses, shouted through megaphones at the brass bed. Remembering the flesh of roses, the roselight snoozing in the veins, she regretted the age of symbols [...].
> *The Aunt's Story* 138

The natural rose is associated with the semiotic as opposed to the symbolic, and becomes a metaphor for androgyny and hybridity, both of which elude the strict binaries created by the exclusionary precision of the symbolic. Interestingly, Julia's first directly quoted words cut into Theodora's sleepy union with the maternal, semiotic roselight, imposing upon her the symbolic rules of convention and language: "'Theodora, I forbid you to touch the roses,' said Mrs Goodman" (21).

Besides embodying discursive control, Julia is associated with the hard, "statuesque" outline of form, hence with the circumscription and construction of the body image. In her view, "things" exist in "hard shapes" (56) and "everything [has] a form, like bronze or marble" (65). Described as a "marble statue wearing silk" (65), White's favored image of discursively constructed identity, Julia is "perfect within her limits, but, like marble, she [does] not expand" (88). In contrast, Theodora frequently exceeds the supposed limits of the self: "Mother had not dissolved at dusk under the apple trees. But sometimes, and even in a straight pew, Theodora's own soul opened and flamed" (56). Theodora knows that the flux of corporeal affect has been subordinated to static identity—the "human body" has "disguised its actual mission of love and hate" (19). The novel works to retrieve corporeal feeling, emphasizing the bodiliness constantly underlying and threatening the supposedly stable subject. "'Thinkin' leads to all this perpendicular emotion. You must listen to your belly and the soles of your feet'" (90), a drunken stranger informs Theodora. This exhortation runs throughout the novel, which performatively endorses Theodora's advice to the coldly intellectual Wetherby to rediscover his "flesh and blood" (174). "Perhaps you should forget to think" (165), she tells him, thereby advocating what Veronica Brady identifies as a perpetual concern of White's writing—the return to the "primitive sensorium."[15]

---

15 Veronica Brady, "Patrick White and the Question of Woman," 186.

Like most of White's protagonists, Theodora desires escape from her identity, which she terms "the great monster Self";[16] she wants to defect from the symbolic order embodied by her mother and her mother's cruelty. Brady's reading of *Memoirs of Many in One* is equally applicable to *The Aunt's Story*:

> if most writing involves naming, the creation of images and illusions, these *Memoirs* represent a kind of unnaming, a return instead to its origins, to memory and desire, the secret language of the body.[17]

Arguably, the most notable stimulus for Theodora's yearning to escape her identity occurs during her childhood when her mother contrasts her unfavorably with her sister, Fanny, thereby lending approval to the latter's performance of gender while simultaneously casting Theodora into the realm of the abject. When the two little girls put on special dresses "for Mother's sake,"[18] Mrs Goodman's reaction has significant consequences for the thematic patterning of the novel as a whole. "My roses, my roses, you are very pretty," she exclaims, because Fanny is "as pink and white as roses in the new dress" (114). Theodora, however, is not quite as appealing: "And Theo," says her mother (implicitly suggesting with this name her daughter's failed femininity), "all dressed up. Well, well. But I don't think we'll let you wear yellow again, because it doesn't suit, even in a sash. It turns you sallow" (114). Julia Goodman's words directly influence Theodora's sense of identity. As a child, Theo knows that "sallow" means "too yellow," and yellow subsequently becomes a predominant color in the novel, indicating her disturbance regarding her supposed physical deficiencies and linking her to the indigenous Australian landscape as it is presented in the description of her family's farm—the yellow landscape of "Meroë."

Early in the novel, the materiality of the word "Meroë" is emphasized. The pragmatic pastoralists dwelling on exotically named properties speak in "flat and dusty local accents" (19) of the Goodman property. They have incorporated the label "Meroë" into everyday speech as the banal signifier of the apparently "unequivocal hills" without debating "why their flat daily prose burst[s] into *sudden dark verse* with Meroë in their mouths" (19; my emphasis). The equivocal poetry of the landscape corresponds to the equivocal poetry of Theodora's body: "Meroë was my bones and my breath" (87), Theodora writes in a letter after her father's death and the sale of the property. Indeed, a strong physical

---

16 White, *The Aunt's Story*, 128.
17 Veronica Brady, "Glabrous Shaman or Centennial Park's Very Own Saint? Patrick White's Apocalypse," *Westerly* 31.3 (September 1986): 77.
18 White, *The Aunt's Story*, 27.

relationship exists between the character and her childhood place, suggesting that the primitive energy informing her early years remains with her, and that the landscape is a physical extension of the body in White's fiction. This is signified in the novel to some extent by color. John and Rose Marie Beston observe that "White links the yellow house and grass and the black hills of Meroë with Theodora's yellow skin and black dress or hat."[19] Throughout the novel, both Theodora and Meroë are described as "yellow" and associated with the black ash of extinguished fire. The "yellow house" at Meroë is set against the hills, which have "heaved out their black volcanic rock, and closed."[20] Like the dry, scrubby landscape, with its "tussocks grey in winter, in summer yellow, that the black snakes threaded, twining and slippery" (20), Theodora is "yellow, scraggy, and unattractive" (18). "Black [has] yellowed her skin," and, as a middle-aged spinster, she is "dry, and leathery, and yellow" (12). Although burnt-out, she smoulders yet: her "eyes burned still, under the black hair, which she still frizzed above the forehead in little puffs" (12). Both black and yellow become repetitive signifiers of the physicality of landscape and character and are taken up as a rhythmic repetition in the novel's "dark verse" (19) of embodiment. Yellow evokes Theodora's sallow ugliness and thus her status as a social outsider. It renders her abject and suggests, by association, that the indigenous landscape, by settler standards, is abject as well. Corporeality and the physical world exceed and threaten settler subjectivity.

Altogether, then, Theodora defies the label "English rose" that her sister Fanny exemplifies. Julia's efforts to foist a normative gendered identity upon her daughter are related to her colonial subjectivity and run in parallel to her efforts to control the Australian landscape. The rose becomes a condensed symbol of both colonial settlement and normative colonial femininity. Imposing her "Englishness" on her surroundings, Julia commands, God-like, from her sofa, "let there be roses" (20)—on one level, a demand for a particular kind of settler landscaping; on another, insistence on a specific enactment of colonial femininity. Interestingly, this statement is a performative utterance: it is, as the philosopher and linguist J.L. Austin would name it, a "speech act," functioning to accomplish something verbally or to bring something new into existence.[21]

---

19   John Beston & Rose Marie Beston, "The Black Volcanic Hills of Meroë: Fire Imagery in Patrick White's *The Aunt's Story*," ARIEL: *A Review of International English Literature* 3.4 (October 1972): 35.

20   White, *The Aunt's Story*, 64.

21   Austin's notion of the performative influenced a number of poststructuralist theorists—among them Judith Butler, who appropriated and adapted Austin's definition to explain her theory of the discursive nature of gender construction. Butler proposes that language produces identity, that "performativity [should be understood] not as the act by which a

Discursive performativity is strongly evident in *The Aunt's Story*, as it is in White's fiction in general. Julia's statements are not only immediate commands: they also shape her daughters' identities as normative and abject respectively. The normative Fanny marries into a family called Parrott, implying her mimicry of her mother. She is Julia's *"pretty little parakeet,"*[22] 'parroting' Mrs Goodman and thus revealing her adherence to the "reiterative power of discourse"[23] that produces the re-enactment of gender. Fanny, like her mother, is associated with symbolic law. As a child, she "makes many rules" and Mrs Goodman is proud of "her daughter Fanny Parrott," who speaks "to her in words."[24] Fanny capitulates, then, to a variety of social codes producing a conventional, colonial femininity figured, in one example, in her performance of music "as it should have been played" (27). Because music is associated with the body in the novel, as elsewhere in White's fiction, Fanny's perfectly deciphered and entirely plastic Chopin, a "whole bright tight bunch of artificial flowers surrounded by a paper frill" (28), becomes a metaphor for the normative performance of gender. It juxtaposes Theodora's stiff-fingered, rule-breaking, expressive performance of an "agonizing angularity that Chopin had never meant to be" (27). Theodora plays her implicitly more authentic yet transgressive music to the disgust of a pinch-faced, rule-bound Mrs Goodman who "possesse[s] Chopin" (27). Her "thin dark, struggling arms" at the piano will be remembered by Julia "with distaste" (109).

Despite his focus on the dominance and rigidity of discursive identity, White postulates another possible performance of gendered and colonial subjectivity. The symbol of the rose embraces multiple and contradictory meanings. While Julia Goodman may bring a colonial rose garden into being, it rapidly transforms into a symbol of rebellion. Indeed, her "artificial rose garden" becomes "so untidy that it look[s] indigenous" (21). Her discursive and colonial imperatives are thus slowly undermined:

> it gave Mrs Goodman a feeling of power to put the roses there. But the roses remained as a power and influence in themselves long after Mrs Goodman's feeling had gone.
> *The Aunt's Story* 21

---

subject brings into being what she/he names, but, rather, as that reiterative power of discourse to produce the phenomena that it regulates and constrains" (*Bodies That Matter*, 2).

22   White, *The Aunt's Story*, 27, emphasis in original.
23   Judith Butler, *Bodies That Matter*, 2.
24   White, *The Aunt's Story*, 99.

The rose becomes a symbol of colonial hybridity, and, moreover, a symbol of androgyny. Theodora finds in a rose a "grub-thing stirring as she opened the petals to the light"; Fanny is horrified, but Theo cannot "condemn her pale and touching grub" (22). As many critics have noted, this element of the novel is an allusion to William Blake's poem "The Sick Rose." Pam Morris argues that Blake's rose with its invisible worm conveys a "barely disguised concern with sexual love, and, perhaps, with the female and male genitals."[25] The rose in *The Aunt's Story* suggests a sexual ambiguity correlating with this Freudian imagery. Theodora, according to others, is "some bloke in skirts"[26] and "should have been a boy" (32). Like her father, with whom she identifies, she enjoys hunting. Yet, for her mother, traipsing around the countryside with a phallic rifle is "wrong and unreasonable" (32). It is "unreasonable" because it does not fit Julia's binary understanding of discrete 'masculine' and 'feminine' identities, a binary framework of logic that the novel repeatedly undermines.

White's treatment of sexual indeterminacy, less overt in this early novel, reaches its apex in the later *Twyborn Affair*, his most comprehensive exploration of the topics of sex, gender, and sexuality. By means of the protean, transgender protagonist, E., who oscillates between performances of 'man' and 'woman', the novel posits the unreliability of the notion of fixed gendered identities. E.'s changing personae—correlating with his physical movements between Europe and Australia—see him appearing first as Eudoxia Vatatzes in France, the 'wife' of the aged Angelos; then as Eddie Twyborn, the returning Australian prodigal son; and, finally, as Eadith Trist, the eccentric madame of an exclusive bordello in London. As a writer who finds both gendered and national identity so dubious, it is unsurprising that White should eventually problematize both in a character who slips fluidly between genders and geographical locations. In *The Aunt's Story*, too, Theodora moves between continents: White embodies in the protagonists of both novels, then, the possibility of a liminal transculturalism.

More significantly, however, both novels sustainedly interrogate the construction of gendered identity. In *The Twyborn Affair*, E.'s gender shifts mean that identity in the novel is never quite what it seems: E. is consistently questionable as 'woman', dubious as 'man', and the novel's emphasis on cross-dressing signifies gender as a reel of potentially disjointed performances. For Judith Butler, gender is the repeated enactment or performance of embodied behavior:

---

25   Pam Morris, *Literature and Feminism: An Introduction* (Oxford: Blackwell, 1993): 99.
26   White, *The Aunt's Story*, 67.

> Such acts, gestures, enactments [...] are performative in the sense that the essence or identity that they otherwise purport to express are *fabrications* manufactured and sustained through corporeal signs and other discursive means.[27]

Because gender is a performance or "fabrication," the parodic nature of drag "enacts the very structure by which any gender is assumed" and makes explicit the "mundane way in which genders are appropriated, theatricalized, worn and done."[28] The theatricality of gender is a constant theme in *The Twyborn Affair*. It is not only the protagonist who is "something of a fake";[29] virtually every character in the novel is similarly bogus, and even normative gender is foregrounded as a dramatization. Consequently, fancy-dress and dressing-up are recurrent themes in the novel. In Part Two, Eddie, out of drag, attends a fancy-dress ball aboard the ship taking him home to Australia. In Part Three, Eadith Trist is invited to a society weekend at a country house called "Wardrobes." The novel's scathing satire of the mingling of upper-class society reinforces its focus on the pervasiveness of human dissemblance and posturing and emphasizes identity—in particular, gendered identity—as a masquerade, a function of clothing and theatrics.

That colonial Australian identity is imbricated with a specific performance of gender is even more strongly the focus of *The Twyborn Affair* than of *The Aunt's Story*, where again the suggestion of mimicry crops up via the reference to overtly feminine women as parrots. When Joan Golson, whose closeted bisexuality is a significant aspect of her characterization, arrives in her hotel rotunda with the strangely exotic Eudoxia, they are met with "the eyes of chattering female macaws and parakeets, their stare levelled at interlopers from beneath wrinkled mauve-to-azure lids."[30] Yet the "regrettably Australian" (67) Joanie, despite her polymorphous sexuality, is herself something of a parrot, both in her proneness to mimicry and in her Australian heritage. At the novel's beginning, she is on holiday in France, having sojourned briefly in England. Quite evidently, being a colonial abroad has filled her with anxiety. She believes that even the "English servants [are] given to taking liberties in the service of Colonials" (11) and has, accordingly, become the "less than confident Joan Golson of Golsons' Emporium, Sydney" (12)—a citizen of a lesser 'empire' of sorts. Indeed, Sydney is described as "home," "as opposed to Joanie's

---

27   Butler, *Gender Trouble*, 185, italics in the original.
28   Judith Butler, "Imitation and Gender Insubordination" (1990), in *The Judith Butler Reader*, ed. Sara Salih (Malden MA: Blackwell, 2004): 127.
29   White, *The Twyborn Affair*, 220.
30   White, *The Twyborn Affair*, 83.

'Home,' where the shops [are] the real, Bond Street ones, not Golson's Emporium" (59). White, amusing in his satire of the Australian colonial cringe, shows Joanie betrayed by an accent that "often teetered, or so she heard, however closely she managed it" (13). Joan's sense that she is "inferior" (11) and her fear of the "unflinching eyelids, the non-committal smiles of the English when faced with what is regrettably colonial" (13) dominate the opening episodes of the novel. With its initial emphasis on Joanie's "Australianness," *The Twyborn Affair*, which is for the most part devoted to the interrogation of seemingly fixed identities of gender and sexuality, suggests that national and colonial identities cannot be separated from gender, an implication humorously suggested by Joanie's colonial "manhandling of gender" in her attempts to speak French (83).

Joanie admires E. (as Eudoxia) sexually and is also, as it turns out, E.'s mother Eadie's former lover. Significantly, then, while Joanie anxiously maintains her spurious "Englishness," she is simultaneously secretly fascinated by Eudoxia Vatatzes, revealing her femininity and heterosexuality as equally provisional. As Eudoxia, E. is in drag, thus further problematizing Joanie's sexuality. However, Eudoxia's drag is evident not only in her performance of gender but also in her strangely unidentifiable nationality, which, like her transgender identity, makes her enigmatic. An exchange between Joan Golson and the snooty Miss Clitheroe of the "*English* Tea-room and Library" (81; my emphasis)—Joan's favorite haunt in St. Mayeul, which is never referred to without that important adjective of nationality—amusingly indicates the novel's deliberate blurring of nationality and gender:

> Mrs Golson asked, 'What is *she*? I mean, of course, her origins.'
> Miss Clitheroe hesitated. 'She could be English. She is very well-spoken. But one can't always tell, can one? in a world like this.'
> She looked at Mrs Golson, who feared that she was being lumped among the undesirables.
> *The Twyborn Affair* 47 (emphasis in the original)

Nonetheless, according to the transgressive Eudoxia, who hides her "Australianness" as much as her biologically male body (which is revealed to the reader only at the conclusion of Part One), "Englishness" is a deplorable condition. She addresses her lover, Angelos: "If I weren't emotional, you'd call me a cold fish—or worse still, an Anglo-Saxon" (37). For Eudoxia, to be Anglo-Saxon is to suppress one's emotions, and to do so is to engage in the measured performance of a false identity. Being English is as much of a performance as gender; Joanie Golson's mimicry of "Englishness" is thus a kind of transvestism, as much a copy of a copy as gender performativity.

English and Australian identities constitute an important binary contributing to Part One of *The Twyborn Affair*, predominantly expressed via Joanie Golson's colonial cringe. While Miss Clitheroe's *English* tearoom and library is an uncomfortable space of judgment for Joan Golson, the Hotel *Australia* arises in her memory as the important setting of her simultaneously shameful and triumphal moment of gender-bending with Eadie Twyborn. She recalls her father's dying words:

> *If what they tell me is true, Joanie ... and what strangers tell is usually true ... dancing at the Australia with a woman ... in a corked-on moustache ... then I've failed to...*
> The Twyborn Affair 172 (italics in the original)

What Joanie's father has failed to do is to impart to his daughter the symbolic law that insists on a woman's mandatory performance of femininity and heterosexuality, a symbolic law that White associates with the dominance of Britain over its potentially transgressive colony. Joan's father's incomplete statement suggests the failure of symbolic law, dependent on binary logic, and thus the opening of the text to the theme of revolutionary transgression associated with indigenous Australia and transgressive sexuality.

As I have argued, *The Aunt's Story* is an important novel in White's oeuvre because it reveals clearly, early on, his frustration with the socio-linguistic construction of binary oppositions. At the novel's conclusion, a character named Holstius appears to Theodora. He comments on the impossibility of reconciling "joy and sorrow," "illusion and reality," and "life and death."[31] "For this reason," he tells her,

> you must accept. And you have already found that one constantly deludes the other into taking fresh shapes, so that there is sometimes little to choose between the reality of illusion and the illusion of reality.
> The Aunt's Story 278

Although Holstius notes the intractability of binary thinking, instructing Theodora that it is imperative simply to accept it, he identifies the inherent dynamism of binary oppositions: the supplementary or marginal category of the dyad is central to, yet excluded from, the primary term. To return to Holstius's example, then, "reality," perceived by an apparently objective reason

---

31 White, *The Aunt's Story*, 278.

and prized in Theodora's resolutely materialist, colonial context, is in fact revealed as dependent on illusion, the antonym it abjects.

Another antonym of reality or reason is, of course, irrationality, and this term and its synonyms correspond increasingly in White's fiction to transgressive gender and sexuality (already we have seen Theodora's androgyny described by her mother as "unreasonable"). White is interested in the "irrational, not to say perverse."[32] In *The Twyborn Affair*, Eddie Twyborn wishes that his normative father, Judge Edward Twyborn, the novel's embodiment of social Law, "might have understood the greater seriousness of coming to terms with a largely irrational nature."[33] In Part Two, Eddie returns to Australia, having caused his parents concern and embarrassment by simply disappearing for a number of years (during which he conducted his relationship with Angelos as 'Eudoxia Vatatzes' and thereafter enlisted as a soldier during the First World War). The reason for Eddie's originally fleeing Australia may be traced to his impending marriage to Marian Dibden, the fear of which overwhelmed him and resulted in his flight from a game of lawn-tennis—that "frightfully colonial" diversion—to which the narrative repeatedly and fleetingly returns. Incidentally, the image of the sporty young man or woman is one to which White returns in his representations of the normative Australian, reminding us of the Foucauldian "docile body." In Australia, according to White, satirically and perhaps unkindly, this is the trained, muscular body of mindless conformity. One of the giggly young overtly heterosexual women who flirts with Eddie aboard the ship on which he returns to Australia is caustically described, for example, as having "sinewy tanned arms [...] permanently tensed as though for a volley at tennis" (140).

Eddie's inability to last the "reasonable" game of tennis—in effect, to last the game of marriage—haunts him throughout the narrative. He imagines, in relation to his father, that he has "perverted justice by his disappearance" (156). The narrator continues in ironic mode (repetition and the emphasis thereon underlining irony):

> Judge Twyborn did not intend to pursue the *reason* why; it might have been too *unreasonable* for one who put his faith in *reason* despite *repeated* proof that it will not stand up to human behaviour.
>
> *The Twyborn Affair* 156 (my emphases)

---

32   Patrick White, "A Cheery Soul," in White, *The Burnt Ones*, 169.
33   White, *The Twyborn Affair*, 160.

E.'s sense of suffering regarding "the unreason with which he was cursed, and worse than that, a rebellious body" (149–150) places him at odds with a society in which the docile body is heterosexual, overtly masculine or feminine, and comfortably performing a British colonial identity.

Normative society posits heterosexuality as an "originary" identity presiding over its "supplement," homosexuality—the latter a seeming addition to the "original," normative, and *"reasoned"* identity of the former. However, seemingly originary terms rely on their supplements, suggesting that abjection is at work in conceptual categorization.[34] Thus, Tamsin Spargo argues that "heterosexuality could be seen as a product of homosexuality, or rather of the same conceptual framework."[35] In *The Twyborn Affair*, presumably to question the framework of binaries, desire proliferates, unconstrained by socialized identity. Because E. cannot identify comfortably as masculine or feminine, he remains for the most part "in disguise," whether he wears drag or not. The desire he inspires in other characters thus interrogates the categories of 'heterosexuality' and 'homosexuality': in his role as a woman, the attraction that E. exerts for men cannot be considered heterosexual, nor, in the same guise, can his attractiveness to women be explained as lesbianism. Sexuality is far more complicated, presented as fluid and polymorphous.

The Twyborn Affair exemplifies Judith Butler's conviction that the ostensibly natural coherence of the categories of sex, gender, and sexuality—linking, for example, the male body, masculine gender, and heterosexual desire—is culturally constructed rather than ontologically given: "gender does not necessarily follow from sex, and desire, or sexuality generally, does not follow from gender."[36] The novel questions the cultural assumption that physical sex naturally produces a specific gender and sexuality: "Who's to decide […] what is natural and what isn't?"[37]

In *Bodies That Matter*, Butler argues that the construction of the normative, heterosexual subject involves disavowing a "domain of abjection," the simultaneous construction and repudiation of the category of sexuality.[38] Further,

> this disavowed abjection will threaten to expose the self-grounding presumptions of the sexed subject, grounded as that subject is in a repudiation whose consequence it cannot fully control.[39]

---

34 Eve Kosofsky Sedgwick, *Epistemology of the Closet* (Berkeley: U of California P, 1990): 10.
35 Tamsin Spargo, *Foucault and Queer Theory* (Cambridge: Icon, 1999): 46.
36 Judith Butler, *Gender Trouble*, 135–136.
37 White, *The Twyborn Affair*, 317.
38 Butler, *Bodies That Matter*, 3.
39 *Bodies That Matter*, 3.

Like Butler, White recognizes marginal sexuality as a "domain of abjection." In fact, he repeatedly compares sexual ambiguity or queerness to the physically abject, an impulse in the novel that has provoked negative criticism. John Beston's review, for example, defines *The Twyborn Affair* as a "repulsive novel on the whole," characterized by a "physical and sexual nausea that hurls itself at us."[40] Critics are generally baffled by the novel's interest in abjection, unwittingly exposing their homophobia:

> the narrative presents difficulties both in the style imposed on it and in the subject matter it relates. For some reason, its major character spends two-thirds of his adult life in women's clothing. And no one seems to notice. Its minor characters flatulate, masturbate, seduce members of their own sex, display gross eating habits, exult in depravity, suffer from squamous skin, decay, disease. And none of them seem to mind. But from such raw materials, such behaviour, such reactions, White constructs his novels.[41]

White constructs his novels from "such raw material" in a manner that confronts the reader with the "unreason" of the abject, having associated unreason with supplementary subject-positions cast aside as inferior and unclean. Thus, abject corporeality recurs throughout the novel. Eadith Trist, for example, suddenly recognizes her affiliation with Gravenor's queer nephew, Philip Thring:

> The tremulous mirror he was offering her must have reflected the sympathy she felt for this boy. More than that: they were shown standing together at the end of the long corridor or hall of mirrors, which memory becomes, and in which they were portrayed stereoscopically, refracted, duplicated, melted into the one image, and by moments shamefully distorted into lepers or Velasquez dwarfs.
> The tatters of diseased skin and hydrocephalic deformities were in the end what brought them closest.
> *The Twyborn Affair* 400

The juxtaposition of the mirror reflection and abject imagery recalls Lacan's and Kristeva's interest in the unrepresentable excess created by socially ratified identity. Moreover, it reveals the cruelty and distorting power of heteronormativity, relegating alternative sexualities to the disfigured and shameful category

---

40   John B. Beston, "Patrick White, *The Twyborn Affair*," 201.
41   Robert Ross, "Patrick White's *The Twyborn Affair*: A Portrait of the Artist," *Commonwealth Novel in English* 2 (1983): 94–95.

of the abject. Yet White's purpose in conflating marginal sexuality with the abject does not merely bespeak the power of normalizing discourses. The abject destabilizes categories, and *The Twyborn Affair* exposes the categories of 'masculine', 'feminine', and 'heterosexual' as shaky and duplicitous constructions. When Eddie dreams that he is seated beside "Helen of the Harelip" at the edge of a still, clear rock-pool, he is aware that they are "united by an understanding as remote from sexuality as the crystal water in the rock basin below."[42] Their mutual status as abject outsiders allows them to exceed the confinement of sex, thereby tingeing their interaction with the purity of love and compassion. This is the aspect of White's work that, Manly Johnson claims,

> disturbs some readers most: White's search through the underworld of experience for the radical human qualities of charity, toleration, and love—which appear often in his work, but always amidst the stench of life at its rankest.[43]

White's emphasis on shared corporeality, however, provides a basis for the philosophy Eadith Trist espouses, which undermines heteronormative prejudice: "All of us—even those you consider corrupt—I'd like to think of as human beings."[44]

White's fascination with abjection, then, should not be read as indicative of his belief that the body is "utterly worthless."[45] His tone is not so much repelled as "amused" when Eddie, jackerooing at Bogong, is drawn to the "daggier" sheep that require shearing:

> It was an aspect of his own condition he had always known about, but it amused him to recognise it afresh while snipping at the dags of shit, laying bare the urine-sodden wrinkles with their spoil of seething maggots, round a sheep's arse.[46]

Rather than adverting to White's manichaean tendencies, the novel's emphasis on bodiliness and perpetual fascination with the sordid and the repulsive rub the reader's nose in the effluent of existence, reminding us that identity is

---

42   White, *The Twyborn Affair*, 273.
43   Manly Johnson, "Twyborn: The Abbess, the Bulbul, and the Bawdy House," MFS: *Modern Fiction Studies* 27.1 (Spring 1981): 164.
44   White, *The Twyborn Affair*, 334.
45   A.P. Riemer, "Eddie and the Bogomils," 26.
46   White, *The Twyborn Affair*, 279.

predicated on abjection: human pretension abjects corporeality and heterosexual hegemony abjects sexual ambivalence. Both, White emphasizes, return to trouble our unstable notions of the self; it is part of the human predicament that reason, or any other seemingly fixed position or identity, "is the most unstable raft" and that any "refugee from life lashed to its frail structure [is] threatened with extinction by the seas of black unreason on which it float[s], sluiced and slewing."[47]

The Twyborn Affair concludes in a moment of "unreason" when E., dressed in masculine clothing but still wearing the excessive make-up of his last feminine persona, is blown up in the bombing of London during the Blitz, an episode that enacts the dissolution of the consolidated body image into the fragmentation of corporeality. Arguably, E.'s body is fragmented—symbolizing his fractured identity—because it is impossible to embody a liminal position between masculinity and femininity: language and our discursive constructions simply will not allow it. Thus, Susan Lever argues that E.'s body

> may be seen as participating in a binary language structure, which demands that it be male or female but which can never allow the expression of both elements at once.[48]

However, *The Twyborn Affair* offers a literary solution to the problem of rigid discursive binaries. The novel, like the ambivalently gendered E., ends ambiguously, exploding the body image as it blows apart categorization and the univocal meaning of the symbolic dimension of language. Before the bomb blast, E. is on his way to reunite with his mother, Eadie. When he imagines that he is on a "short and painful visit to his mother's womb,"[49] it is evident that he seeks the unification referred to earlier, lost, it would seem, due to language and socialization. Ultimately, Eadie may be in a London hotel room, her son Eddie dead before reaching her, but she imagines herself back in Australia, drying her hair in the sunlight while she awaits her *daughter* Eadith. The novel concludes with an image of warm maternal acceptance: Eadie, coextensive with E.'s Australian home, welcomes E. in both masculine and feminine personae, in androgynous form: "Eadith Eddie no matter which this fragment of my self which I lost is now returned where it belongs" (431–432). Eadie's imagination becomes her experience and the text shifts accordingly to accommodate this unreal reality.

---

47   White, *The Twyborn Affair*, 71.
48   Susan Lever, "*The Twyborn Affair*: Beyond the Human Hierarchy of Men and Women," *Australian Literary Studies* 16.3 (May 1994): 291.
49   White, *The Twyborn Affair*, 428.

The London setting, it seems, becomes an Australian garden as irrationality, and presumably the associations it has gained over the course of White's oeuvre take precedence. The novel closes as Eadie—impossibly—watches a bulbul at a birdbath shaking "his little velvet jester's cap, and rais[ing] his beak towards the sun" (432). *White's* jest is to merge Australia and England, masculinity and femininity, suggesting that the imagination may exceed the discursive limits of reality.

In conclusion, White's emphasis on the physical ambiguity and conceptual elusiveness of his characters implies that the body is in excess of the discourses supposedly constructing it. Neither E. Vatatzes/Twyborn nor Theodora Goodman is confined by the interrelated categories of national identity and gender of such importance to their society. Both, too, defy the unequivocal nature of prosaic language that White critiques throughout his oeuvre. White's bodies are not docile but unruly, represented in a language of ambiguity enacting their "poetry of rebellion" (129) and revealing that "desperate words, ordinarily dry, [may] grow [...] quite suddenly fleshy and ripe."[50] While his fiction emphasizes, then, the difficulty of maintaining liminal identities under the weight of heteronormative and colonial discourses, it nonetheless continually conveys the perpetual struggle of linguistic and narrative ambiguity as a valid literary means of resisting inadequate discursive constructions. Moreover, it posits a language of corporeality in which identity dissolves and the ambiguous merging of self and other is effected. In White's poetics of corporeality, rigid symbolic categories disintegrate as the "brittle body [...] trumpet[s] its own silver."[51]

50   White, *The Aunt's Story*, 273.
51   *The Aunt's Story*, 67.

CHAPTER 6

White's Somatic Spirituality

1. Man has no Body distinct from his Soul; for that call'd Body is a portion of Soul discern'd by the five Senses, the chief inlets of Soul in this age.
2. Energy is the only life, and is from the Body and Reason is the bound or outward circumference of Energy.[1]

∴

Two epigraphs to *The Solid Mandala* may be applied to White's oeuvre: Paul Éluard's "There is another world, but it is in this one"[2] and Meister Eckhart's "It is not outside, it is inside: wholly within."[3] These statements suggest that White is not concerned with a transcendence that denies the body; they posit instead his insistence on the importance of the physical world and the location of imaginative and mystical experience within it. Yet White's critics have not always observed his interest in the metaphysics of materiality. Accordingly, Hedda Ben-Bassat identifies an "explicit point of controversy" in the study of White.[4] Critics, she argues, oscillate between "radical materialistic" readings emphasizing "only the literal earthly layer" of the novels and "equally radical spiritual" readings attuned only to their "symbolic or allegorical level."[5] Such interpretations unfold from dualistic interpretations that propose White's interest in "*two* basic marvels of life, *two* basic mysteries: the mystery of the physical world, and the mystery of the spirit, the concrete and the abstract."[6]

---

1 William Blake, *The Marriage of Heaven and Hell* (1790–93; Oxford: Oxford UP, 1975): xvi.
2 Cf. Éluard, "Il y a assurément un autre monde, mais il est dans celui-ci," *Œuvres complètes* (Paris: Gallimard, 1968), vol. 1: 986.
3 Probably taken by White from C.G. Jung, "The Symbolism of the Mandala," in Jung, *Psychology and Alchemy*, tr. R.F.C. Hull (*Collected Works* 12; London: Routledge & Kegan Paul, 1953): 102, fn.5, taken by Jung from Franz Pfeiffer, *Meister Eckhart*, tr. C. De B. Evans (Leipzig, 1857; London: J.M. Watkins, 1924), vol. 1: 8.
4 Hedda Ben-Bassat, "To Gather the Sparks: Kabbalistic and Hasidic Elements in Patrick White's *Riders in the Chariot*," *Journal of Literature & Theology* 4.3 (November 1990): 327.
5 Ben-Bassat, "To Gather the Sparks," 327.
6 Dorothy Green, "*Voss*: Stubborn Music," in *The Australian Experience: Critical Essays on Australian Novels*, ed. W.S. Ramson (Canberra: Australian National University, 1976): 290–91, italics in the original.

Lyn McCredden has recently argued, however, for White's "incarnational understanding," which involves the "sacred and material in constant exchange";[7] White's fiction has "always been in excess of merely material and historical interpretations"[8] and "sacred possibilities" are held "in dramatic tension with earthed, bodily, and sexual realities."[9] Perhaps the argument could be taken further: in juxtaposing the mystical and the physical, White implies that the sacred and the material are finally inextricable. His placement of "human excrement beside the altar"[10] emphasizes the uncomfortable yet inescapable yoking of the body and the sacred, both of which are abjected from modern society's emphasis on a disembodied, rationalist subjectivity and both of which he attempts to recuperate—together.

This chapter discusses White's interest in a 'somatic spirituality' which intertwines two supposedly opposing concepts of an historically reified dualism, ultimately suggesting that 'spirit' and 'soma' inform each other to present mysticism as embedded in corporeality. White attaches sacred significance to a physicality that precedes consciousness and subjectivity. While his characters frequently experience a state of 'transcendence' that critics have associated with a dismissal of the physical world, they, in fact, appear to be liberated from subjectivity as corporeality engulfs them. These moments of liberation, occurring in conjunction with an emphasis on the physical, constitute what I term the 'somatic sacred' in White's writing. In this chapter, I explore this dimension of White's fiction. In particular, White's interest in the sacred potential of the physical world is evident in the treatment of objects and animality in his fiction. Moreover, the characters it identifies as "saints" are the most ordinary of human beings, defined nonetheless by an extraordinary compassion for physical suffering. In addition, this chapter addresses the compassionate and sanctifying acceptance of corporeality. White's deployment of the imagery of Christ and the Eucharist is analyzed to indicate, first, the sacredness of physicality and, second, the redemptive necessity of incorporating it into our notions of subjectivity; of 'ingesting' it, as it were.

The "Mysticism of Objects" and "Dog Turned Round"

Physical objects in White's fiction have curiously mystical associations. In *Voss*, for example, Willie Pringle looks at the "heartbreaking beauty and simplicity

---

7 Lyn McCredden, "*Voss*: Earthed and Transformative Sacredness," 110.
8 McCredden, "Earthed and Transformative Sacredness," 109.
9 "Earthed and Transformative Sacredness," 111.
10 Patrick White, *The Vivisector*, 389.

of a common table or kitchen chair" and realizes that "in some more important sense their entities would continue to elude him."[11] Bill Ashcroft suggests that White's interest in the physical world involves his locating the sublime

> in the proximate details of everyday life—objects observed beyond the possible entrapment of language, which resist interpretation, objects whose luminosity defies explanation, whose material being bodies forth a presence that lies outside structures of religious meaning.
> *Voss* 64

By drawing attention to the resistance of objects to meaning-making, White's fiction denies the objectifying aspect of the controlling consciousness. This is one of the ways in which he rejects Enlightenment reason, refusing, for example, Kant's theory that the transcendental ego contains "original pure *a priori* concepts, which represent objects prior to all experience."[12]

For White, material objects resist the foreclosure of interpretation, their specificity opposing the generalizing properties of language: "objects are indescribable,"[13] says Lieselotte in *The Aunt's Story*. For Theodora Goodman, there is "perhaps no more complete a reality than a chair and a table,"[14] although she does not attempt to explain what this reality could be. Later, when she is asked if she believes in God, her response roots the sacred in the material world: "I believe in this table"; "I believe in a pail of milk."[15] In *Voss*, Palfreyman is unable to formulate a prayer. However, upon catching sight of a battered quart pot and a swollen saddlebag, objects "of simple form and humble purpose,"[16] he is able to "proffer their images to God" and "know that his intention [is] acceptable."[17]

Rodney Edgecombe argues that White's objects are "made perfect by their subjection to the needs of man, and therefore earn their status as surrogate prayers."[18] Yet, far from their 'subjection to man', their significance resides in their resistance to human consciousness. Within the perceptual field, David Abram explains, objects must always elude consciousness:

---

11 Patrick White, *Voss*, 64.
12 Immanuel Kant, *The Critique of Pure Reason*, 315.
13 Patrick White, *The Aunt's Story*, 158.
14 White, *The Aunt's Story*, 135.
15 *The Aunt's Story*, 152.
16 White, *Voss*, 274.
17 *Voss*, 274.
18 Rodney Edgecombe, "Faith, Pride and Selfhood in Patrick White's *Voss*," *English Studies in Africa* 27.2 (1984): 137.

from the perspective of my bodily senses, there is no such thing that appears as a completely determinate or finished object. Each thing, each entity that my body sees, presents some face or facet of itself to my gaze while withholding other aspects from view.[19]

Language, moreover, shaping rational thought, can only approximate material reality while never containing it. Hence Willie Pringle's knowledge that "entities [will] continue to elude him";[20] the limits of perception and language ensure that this is the case. Objects therefore become associated with a sense of mystery and uncapturable, mystical significance. As it is summarized in *The Tree of Man*, there is a "mysticism of objects" in White's writing, in which "some people are initiates."[21] These are the people who recognize the sacred, unnameable aspect of the physical world. For them, objects form part of a materiality preceding reason; longing to release themselves from the shackles of subjectivity, they envy material objects. Theodora Goodman, taking off her clothes and lying down in the creek, imagines merging with her surroundings: "soon her thin brown body was the shallow, browner water. She would not think. She would drift. As still as a stick."[22] For Veronica Brady, White's commonplace objects "assume a new value, reminding us that 'the world is all that is the case'."[23]

To engage with the material world and the body as synonymous with the self is also to encounter and acknowledge one's animality, commensurate with the abjects of corporeality and nature against which human subjectivity defines itself. Descartes argued that the body is a machine, severed from the soul, and that animals, without rational consciousness, are similarly mechanistic. As Abram maintains, however,

> to acknowledge the life of the body, and to affirm our solidarity with this physical form, is to acknowledge our existence as one of the earth's animals, and so to remember and rejuvenate the organic basis of our thoughts and our intelligence.[24]

---

19   David Abram, *The Spell of the Sensuous*, 50.
20   White, *Voss*, 64.
21   White, *The Tree of Man*, 398.
22   White, *The Aunt's Story*, 38.
23   Veronica Brady, "The Novelist and the New World: Patrick White's *Voss*," *Texas Studies in Literature and Language* 21.2 (Summer 1979): 176.
24   Abram, *The Spell of the Sensuous*, 47.

For Julia Kristeva, abjection and animality are intimately related: "The abject confronts us with those fragile states where man strays on the territories of *animal*."[25] Abject animality, moreover, is "edged with the sublime."[26]

In his attention to corporeality, the sacred, and humankind's construction of a 'disembodied', hubristic, god-like consciousness, White often experiments with the signifier 'dog' as an anagram of 'God'. At the end of "A Cheery Soul," the awful Mrs Docker, a suburbanite so self-confident, cheery, and insufferable as to be loathsome, attempts to befriend a stray dog. The animal is quick to act on its discernment, "lift[ing] his leg on the supplicant, and walk[ing] stiffly off."[27] Mrs Docker recognizes with horror that "her sentence ha[s] been written by a dog" and, worse, that dog is "God turned round."[28] It is difficult to know exactly what this observation connotes. Is this Mrs Docker's recognition that there is no God? Is her sudden understanding of "God" one that reverses her former conceptions? Has God turned His back on her? Has her hubris been dismantled? Whatever one's interpretation may be, the implication is that 'God' and animality are entangled in White's fiction in ambivalent unity.

This implication of animality and the sacred relies on White's understanding that, according to Western philosophical tradition,

> human beings alone are possessed of an 'incorporeal' intellect, a rational soul or mind which, by virtue of its affinity with an eternal or divine dimension outside the bodily world, sets us radically apart from, or above, all other forms of life.[29]

This, in White's view, is an entirely incorrect understanding of 'God', erroneously relating the concept to the hubristic, 'superior' human ego. In contrast to the construction of this hierarchically superior consciousness, dogs are frequently featured in White's texts as symbols of corporeality and selfless love. For White, love is conceptualized as the dissolution of the self into the Other, hence the yielding of the self to *another* notion of God—beyond hubris, language, and subjectivity. In their abjection, dogs embody the sacred mysticism that defines White's fiction and the paradoxically redemptive threat that the abject poses to hermetic subjectivity:

---

25 Julia Kristeva, *Powers of Horror*, 12, italics in the original.
26 Kristeva, *Powers of Horror*, 11.
27 Patrick White, "A Cheery Soul," 188.
28 White, "A Cheery Soul," 189.
29 Abram, *The Spell of the Sensuous*, 47.

limited animal intelligence will look out suddenly from its limitations and close with the human consciousness on the verge of all manner of mystical understanding.
The Tree of Man 481

In *The Solid Mandala*, Arthur, himself the embodiment of abjection, adores the dogs, Scruffy and Runt. When Arthur first acquires Scruffy as a puppy, Waldo finds him "seated on the edge of the veranda grunting apparently with joy, kneading the formless lump of fat, gazing at it, snout against snout."[30] As the puppies get older, Arthur, in his own animality, is increasingly associated with his pets:

> The rangier, the more shameless they grew, lifting their legs on furniture when men weren't looking, or even when they were, the more often was Arthur driven to scrabble on the floor amongst them, to grab himself an armful of dog, to plant his nose in one or other of the moist-blackberry noses so that *he and dog were one*.
> *The Solid Mandala* 181 (my emphasis)

Dogs are transgressive, the antithesis of shame and propriety—as is Arthur. Moreover, dogs signal corporeality and mortality, reflecting the horrifying materiality of being that reasoned subjectivity abjects. As the twins age, the dogs reflect their senescence. On a walk, one of the dogs looks back at his masters: "His splather of tongue hung, palpitating suspiciously, against the yellow stumps and bleeding gums" (63). Simultaneously, "Arthur, as though in sympathy with the dog, held up his thick white muzzle and began to howl" (63). In Waldo's mind, the dogs mirror Arthur's animality and corporeality, aspects of himself that Waldo is incapable of accepting:

> when they got them, he hated Arthur's dogs—though technically one of them was his own. If anyone, thinking of his good, had been interested enough to accuse Waldo Brown of neglecting his responsibilities to his fellow man, nobody could have accused the dogs of neglecting theirs: in being, in reminding at least one of their owners of the exasperation, the frustration of life, in farting and shitting under his nose, in setting beneath his feet traps of elastic flesh and electric fur [...]. So the whole purpose of the dogs, together with Arthur, seemed to be to remind, constantly to remind.
> *The Solid Mandala* 187

---

30   Patrick White, *The Solid Mandala*, 178.

The "purpose of the dogs," and of Arthur, in Waldo's defensive opinion, is to recall him to the corporeality that he, as one of White's resolutely rationalist characters, cannot accept. Revealing the "frustration of life, [and] farting and shitting under his nose," they remind Waldo, disturbingly, of an aspect of himself that he rejects for shame. But the body in White's fiction, at its most abject, is a route to the sacred, if not the sacred itself. The submission to corporeality dissolves the ego, and so the body informs compassion and love. Arthur understands, therefore, that "dogs are less brutal than men, because they are less complicated" (217)—without ego, they inhabit their corporeality rather than protecting themselves from it by means of a hierarchically superior notion of subjectivity. Resiliently physical, they are associated in White's fiction with compassion.

Voss's dogs, for example, are "quick to sense [his] desire to express tenderness,"[31] however repressed this urge to compassion may be. They draw this dangerously rational character into the affective response of empathy and he "suffer[s] for them, when their pads split, when their sides [are] torn open in battle with kangaroos, or when, in the course of the journey, they simply [die] off" (265). He is, moreover, "morbidly grateful for the attentions of their hot tongues, although he would not have allowed himself to be caught returning their affection" (265). Despite Voss's clear need for the love and compassion that his dogs represent, a kindly comment from Judd, indicating his awareness of Voss's fondness for his bitch Gyp, results in a perverse act of cruelty figured in the text as self-inflicted harm. Voss shoots the dog, ostensibly because she is eating too much, but also to prove that he is in no way dependent on affection:

> the German called to his dog, and she followed him a short way. When he had spoken a few words to her, and was looking into the eyes of love, he pulled the trigger. He was cold with sweat. He could have shot off his own jaw.
> *Voss* 266

In shooting his dog, Voss has symbolically driven a bullet into his own corporeality. The hallucinatory Laura, embodying Voss's repudiations and traveling beside him, does "not accept," because she herself is "dog-eyed love" (267) and selfless compassion requires the recognition and acceptance of animality and bodiliness. When Voss describes the simpleton Harry Robarts as a dog, the latter is confused. "Licking the hands" (382), he ventures in response. Voss disagrees: "No, tearing at one's thoughts" (382). Again, the dog is figured as the antithesis of rational subjectivity. Harry's words reinforce the canine association with

---

31   White, *Voss*, 180.

love and the physicality of compassion, and Voss's refusal does not necessarily contradict this: corporeality and compassion both threaten the limits of defended, rational subjectivity. Exposing these limits as permeable, they provide possible avenues to the mystical loss of self that White associates with the experience of 'God'.

As already indicated, the word 'God' is implicit in the word 'dog' and vice versa. Hubris and the reaction of repudiation or abjection are therefore revealed as one and the same: the god-like self is an illusion, because it cannot be severed from its dog-like corporeality. However, the state of abjection is associated with 'God' as 'love'. Dogs, with their animal and corporeal associations, therefore open White's texts to a mysticism inherent in the acceptance of corporeality.

Humble Everyday Saints

As contended in the previous section, in White's concern with physicality and animality, his characters either choose or are forced to distance themselves from rationalism. They immerse themselves in the physical world, exhibiting ways of being that may open them to the experience of mystical dissolution when the 'mind' fragments into unbounded unity with materiality. Because White's fiction drives towards such moments, his characters appear to undergo a kind of sanctification resulting from their experience of physical suffering and their yielding to corporeality. For White, this accepting submission to bodiliness correlates with clarity and humility—the loss of ego equivalent to mystical experience. Accordingly, he acknowledges that "the state of simplicity and humility is the only desirable one for artist or for man. While to reach it may be impossible, to attempt to do so is imperative."[32] The sublime loss of self, we remember, is also the experience of abjection, one of the ways in which it may be possible, albeit momentarily, to reach a state of simplicity and humility. Kristeva writes that "the abject is edged with the sublime,"[33] and White's characters experience the sublimity of the abject as mysticism or sacred communion. For Kristeva, "mystical Christendom turned [the] abjection of self into the ultimate proof of humility before God."[34] Élisabeth Roudinesco also comments on the interrelationship of abjection and mysticism:

---

32 Patrick White, "The Prodigal Son" (1958), in *Patrick White Speaks*, ed. Brennan & Flynn, 16.
33 Kristeva, *Powers of Horror*, 11.
34 *Powers of Horror*, 5.

> If we look at the mystics who gave their bodies to God, or the flagellants who imitated the passion of Christ, [...] we find, in different guises, the alternation between the sublime and the abject that characterizes our dark side at its most heretical, but also at its most luminous: voluntary servitude seen as the greatest of freedoms.[35]

Many of White's most embodied characters exemplify this servitude and are committed to the care of others and to facing the abject unflinchingly. Judd is the patient and ultimately saintly figure of Voss's expedition who offers himself compassionately to others by "appoint[ing] himself nurse."[36] Palfreyman, having suffered a period of illness, recalls how

> the convict had brought him a shallow iron basin of water, and a lump of crude, yellow soap, and although this humble man had waited on him, they had gratefully sensed they were equal in each other's eyes.
> *Voss* 138

The self-enclosed and fatally hubristic Voss, hindered by his own physical aversions, is unable to "trap their shy secret" (138), despite his yearning to do so. What eludes him for most of the novel is the acknowledgement that the body is the fundamental basis of life, preceding rational consciousness, shared by all, flattening hierarchies, and promoting a compassionate ethic of equality and humanity. Characters who care for the body attain this significant knowledge.

By contrast, characters who resist identification with others experience the body as intensely private, their body image mirroring their enclosed and rigidly defined subjectivity. When Voss himself is kicked in the stomach by a mule, Judd attends to him and is struck by the fragility of his exposed embodiment, a poignant physical weakness that does not accord with the apparent strength of his self-image:

> Tinged by the mule's hoof with saffron and purple, this part of his anatomy must originally have been ivory in colour, very thin, moreover, and private, so that, as he worked, the convict had been forced continually to turn his head, and turn his head, to look out into the haze, and thus avoid violating further the privacy, that almost sacrosanctity of which he was aware.
> *Voss* 212

---

35 Élisabeth Roudinesco, *Our Dark Side: A History of Perversion* (Cambridge: Polity, 2009): 7.
36 White, *Voss*, 133.

For Voss, the experience is humiliating and exposing: he "despised all sickness; he despised physical strength; he despised, though secretly, even the compassion he had sensed in the ministrations of Judd" (212). In short, Voss loathes anything to do with the body, including the corporeal affect of compassion. He hierarchizes his rationalism over the body, rejecting the latter, but is nonetheless haunted by the knowledge of the need for compassion, which, as *The Living and the Dead* informs us, is "oddly physical":[37] "His own strength, he felt, could not decrease with physical debility. But, was Judd's power increased by compassion?"[38] The philosophy informing *Voss* is indeed that "voluntary servitude" to corporeality becomes, as Roudinesco argues of mystical experience, the "greatest of freedoms."[39] In compassion, and in the acknowledgement that the body in its weakness, vulnerability, and suffering is sacred, Judd's power is certainly increased. Precisely because of his attunement to the physical world and his corresponding ethic of compassion, he becomes Voss's greatest adversary.

White, then, demonstrates a profound respect for those who display compassion. In his "Credo," published in 1988 at the conclusion of his writing career and two years before his death, he offers his personal spiritual belief:

> I am coming to believe, not in God, but a Divine Presence, of which Jesus, the Jewish prophets, the Buddha, Mahatma Gandhi and Co. are the more comprehensible manifestations. This Presence controls us but only to a certain degree: life is what we, its components, make it. Hence the existence of megalomaniac politicians, dictators, mafia millionaires, greedy landlords, rapists, murderers, self-obsessed spouses within the same scheme which embraces the Teresas, St. John of the Cross, Thomas Merton, and others who continue to speak to us out of the historic waxwork-museum—all these along with the anonymous who lift us from the gutters, wiping the vomit from our lips, who comfort us as our limbs lie paralysed on the pavement, feed us within their limited means, and close our eyes—these humble everyday saints created for our consolation by the same mysterious universal Presence ignored, cursed, derided, or intermittently worshipped by the human race.[40]

---

37   White, *The Living and the Dead*, 146.
38   White, *Voss*, 212.
39   Roudinesco, *Our Dark Side*, 7.
40   White, "Credo" (1988), in *Patrick White Speaks*, ed. Brennan & Flynn, 197.

White indicates his belief in a divine power that manifests itself obliquely in spiritual leaders, but which is ultimately removed from the human world of dualities. Within our largely godless existence, there is hope, however: in addition to the records of the martyrs of the past and "created for our consolation" are the "everyday saints." These anonymous, humble, compassionate people tend to "our" corporeality, the collective personal pronoun emphasizing humanity's shared and equalizing bodiliness. White's heroes and heroines are themselves "humble everyday saints," individuals who accept the body and care for others who, like themselves, suffer physically. They embody a realm of sacred alterity, a world within this one, and enact his preoccupation with the redemptive dissolution of love. In *Riders in the Chariot*, for example, Ruth Godbold nurses the other three visionaries at various times in their lives. In her suburban context, she is an anonymous force of compassion:

> Mrs Godbold nursed Miss Hare the winter the latter had pneumonia. Many people remained unaware, because Mrs Godbold did not talk, and Godbolds were no-hopers of the worst kind, and who, anyway, ever saw or spoke with that old, dirty, mad Miss Hare? [...] For Miss Hare, Mrs Godbold had become and indeed remained, the most positive evidence of good.
>
> *Riders in the Chariot* 83

White's humble saints, although they may struggle with their own corporeality, and although, like the convict Judd, they are no strangers to suffering, do not shy away from confronting the body: "the sinless overlook the stains."[41] Throughout White's oeuvre, the spiritual experiences of his characters are contingent upon their unflinching recognition of their bodies, or their acceptance of corporeality in general, and often arise from a confrontation with the abject elements of the body of the self or the other. Thus, Elizabeth Hunter, nursing her husband through the final stages of cancer, loses herself "in a mystery so immense and so rarely experienced, she functioned, it could truthfully have been said, by reverence."[42] As she approaches death herself, surrounded by nurses similarly immersed in the sacred mystery of tending to a dying body, she acknowledges in a dream that "stench is sanctity,"[43] that abject physicality, as White's fiction presents it, is sacred.

41　Patrick White, *The Eye of the Storm*, 190.
42　White, *The Eye of the Storm*, 198.
43　*The Eye of the Storm*, 190.

Stench is Sanctity: Mysticism and Corporeality

Writing to Clement Semmler in 1970, White expressed belief in the conjunction of the spiritual and the "sordid":

> churches defeat their own aims, I feel, through the banality of their approach, and by rejecting so much that is sordid and shocking which can still be related to religious experience.[44]

Indeed, his fiction contends that the sordid and the shocking may *constitute* religious experience; mysticism depends on the "sordid and shocking" aspects of corporeality. It is a transgressive state relying on an identification with corporeality that social norms do not allow. White's transcendentalism thus harnesses abjection; the acceptance of the body is not merely an ethical imperative within his imaginary, but also a spiritual one.

Élisabeth Roudinesco defines mysticism thus:

> an ordeal involving the body, or [...] otherness in the form of the absolute: not only the other that exists within us, but the forgotten, repressed part on which religious institutions are built.[45]

In *The Eye of the Storm* "heresy mingled with the night scents and sickroom smells,"[46] and in *The Twyborn Affair* it is associated with socio-sexual transgression. Religious experience is repeatedly linked to the abject. In *The Vivisector*, Hurtle Duffield, after suffering a stroke, will seek "a god—a *god*—in every heap of rusty tins amongst the wormeaten furniture out the window in the dunny of brown blowflies and unfinished inscriptions."[47] Ellen Roxburgh's notorious moment of cannibalism in *A Fringe of Leaves* is presented as an instance of intense spirituality, of sacrament, nourishing "not only her animal body but some darker need of the hungry spirit."[48] Perhaps most famously, Stan Parker at the conclusion of *The Tree of Man* professes his faith by spitting on the ground and proclaiming his saliva "God." Although this is in response to the harassment of an intrepid traveling evangelist, the episode is not entirely ironic.

---

44   Patrick White, *Letters*, ed. David Marr (London: Jonathan Cape, 1994): 363.
45   Roudinesco, *Our Dark Side*, 12.
46   White, *The Eye of the Storm*, 150.
47   White, *The Vivisector*, 561, emphasis in original.
48   Patrick White, *A Fringe of Leaves*, 274.

As Stan stares at the "jewel of spit," he is possessed of a "great tenderness of understanding":[49] "God" in White's fiction resides in the body.

According to Michel de Certeau, we define as mystical

> that which departs from normal or ordinary paths, that which is not inscribed within the unity of a faith or a religious reference, and which is marginal to a society that is becoming secularized and to an emerging knowledge of scientific objects.[50]

White's mystics are indeed outsiders; they are abject within the realm of secular modernity and they defy scientific rationalism and Enlightenment dualism through their engagement with modes of being beyond classification. Moreover, as Roudinesco observes, Certeau compares mysticism to psychoanalysis: "Both criticize [...] the principle of the unity of the individual, the privilege accorded to consciousness, and the myth of progress."[51] Like abjection, mysticism decentres the subject; it is premised on abjection in the simultaneous transcendence of horror and recuperation of corporeality that it may entail. For the Christian martyrs of the Middle Ages, who were "excited by abnormality," the body, "either putrefied or tortured, or intact and without any stigmata," was an object of fascination.[52]

In *Memoirs of Many in One*, Alex Gray recalls the "French mystic demonstrating her piety and self-abnegation by picking up from the street a gobbet of beggar's spittle and forcing herself to swallow it."[53] She wonders whether she will be able to do the same:

> Could I come at swallowing my Mystic's spittle if I managed to assemble [others] to witness my self-mortification and acknowledge my sanctity?
> *Memoirs of Many in One* 94

Such moments of "self-mortification" for an audience are, however, contradictory and preclude mystical experience; humility cannot coincide with the desire for an audience. Voss thus emphasizes his entrapment in the ego when,

---

49 White, *The Tree of Man*, 496.
50 Michel de Certeau, "Mystique," in *Encyclopédie universalis* (Paris: Encyclopaedia Universalis, 1978), vol. 2: 522, tr. in Roudinesco, *Our Dark Side*, 12–13.
51 Roudinesco, *Our Dark Side*, 13.
52 *Our Dark Side*, 11.
53 Patrick White, *Memoirs of Many in One*, 94.

wanting to upstage Judd as healer, he forces himself to attend to the diarrhoea of Le Mesurier:

> Prospective saints, he decided, would have fought over such an opportunity, for green and brown, of mud, and slime, and uncontrolled faeces, and the bottomless stomach of nausea are the true colours of hell.
>
> *Voss* 270

Yet a "prospective saint" is not the same as an authentic one, and White's "humble, everyday saints" do not face the abject with revulsion. Abject corporeality is not the color of hell in White's fiction, but potentially the color of love. Hence, Voss's mystical preceptor Laura Trevelyan is associated with the color green, and Rose Portion, the character who finally draws Laura to corporeal acceptance, is linked to the color brown. Arthur Brown (whose surname also denotes the color of abjection) tells his brother Waldo, after the latter has suffered an access of diarrhoea, that he has "never jibbed at mopping up." Turning to the task with patience and compassion, he is "glad to perform the humblest act of all."[54] Sanctity, according to White, involves a selfless engagement with the abject, the dissolution of the ego, hence the attainment of compassionate mutuality.

Kristeva observes that fundamental to the experience of mysticism is the disintegration of the self into a state of corporeal joy or engulfment that corresponds to a union with others and with the uncapturable plenitude of materiality hovering on the margins of the symbolic order:

> The mystic's familiarity with abjection is a fount of infinite jouissance. [...] The Christian mystic, far from using [jouissance] to the benefit of a symbolic or institutional power, displaces it indefinitely (as happens with dreams, for instance) within a discourse where the subject is resorbed (is that grace?) into communication with the Other and with others.[55]

Such "discourse" defies the symbolic and thus transgresses the rules of the social order:

> Mystical discourse [...] requires inversions, conversions, marginality and abnormality. The way it perverts the body is an attempt to grasp something that is unspeakable, but also essential.[56]

---

54   White, *The Solid Mandala*, 292.
55   Kristeva, *Powers of Horror*, 127.
56   Roudinesco, *Our Dark Side*, 13.

Mysticism, then, is either a discursive or an embodied attempt to access an experience beyond signification and subjectivity, one that is simultaneously sublime and abject. As Maryvonne Nedeljkovic argues, in words recalling Kristeva's above, White's fiction strives for a "theism in which the ego is resorbed,"[57] evident in the last lines of Frank Le Mesurier's prose poem "Conclusion":

> O God, my God, I pray that you will take my spirit out of this my body's remains, and after you have scattered it, grant that it shall be everywhere and in the rocks, and in the empty waterholes, and in true love of all men, and in you, O God, at last.
> *Voss* 297

White emphasizes mysticism as the loss of self, a goal exceedingly difficult for his sometimes narcissistic characters to attain, but towards which they are inexorably pushed by virtue of their inescapable corporeality.

A Veritable State of Communion: The Significance of Accepting Corporeality

White's fiction foregrounds the necessity of accepting corporeality, the constituting philosophy informing its ambivalent emphasis on dualism and its subversion, and a necessity enacted thematically and stylistically. Because White does not accept that 'spirit' can exist without its binary opposite 'body', his narratives show that it is only *through* physicality that moments of spiritual illumination are attained. Thus, although White may claim that "the unsinkable condom and the smell of shit which precede the moment of illumination make it more rewarding when it happens,"[58] his fiction ultimately diminishes the apparent opposition of body and spirit to suggest the impossibility of illumination *without* the acknowledgement of such corporeal detritus. As Veronica Brady argues, "defilement is the prelude to a beatitude which does away with self-awareness, absorbing it into some ultimate maternal matrix."[59] Accepting the self as a body is linked to moments of spiritual illumination in White's work. In *The Living and the Dead*, "the mystic must return to his

---

57   Maryvonne Nedeljkovic, "Voss or the Uneasy Conscience," *Commonwealth: Essays and Studies* 9.2 (1987): 85.
58   Patrick White, *Flaws in the Glass*, 157.
59   Veronica Brady, "Patrick White and the Question of Woman," 180.

original structure of flesh and bone,"[60] yet whether the mystic ever leaves this structure is rendered doubtful.

Towards the conclusion of *Riders in the Chariot*, a description of Himmelfarb at prayer becomes increasingly concerned with the physical. The description exemplifies the corporeal mysticism pervading White's work, a concern with somatic spirituality also evident in White's favored symbol of the embodied Christ. *Riders in the Chariot* underscores the importance of corporeality to mystical illumination by intensifying the narrative focus on the body as Himmelfarb's experience becomes increasingly spiritual. The episode's trajectory towards a physical acceptance correlating with mystical experience exemplifies White's texts more broadly. Initially, as Himmelfarb offers up his words to God, the materiality and immanent potential of his language are emphasized: "the words that fell from his mouth were leaping crystals, each reflecting to infinity the words contained within the words."[61] Not only is the physicality of language emphasized, but the episode intimates a plenitude of meaning in language, emphasizing the mystical, unrepresentable significance White implies. Further, it correlates with an increasing focus on the corporeal, to the extent that Himmelfarb's prayer becomes his offering-up of flesh:

> The Jew prayed, and the statue which had been broken off the pediment of time, and set down on the edge of the morning, became a man. The rather chapped lips were forming words of their own flesh.
> *Riders in the Chariot* 521–522

Not only is the physicality of language emphasized, but the description increasingly engages Himmelfarb's corporeality. The light that descends upon him is soon no longer a sublime efflorescence with cold, mineral associations,

> a matter of crumbling gold, together with the gold slips of elusive feldspar, forming upon the deposits of porphyry and agate with which the solid firmament was streaked.
> *Riders in the Chariot* 522

Instead, light gains corporeal, blood associations, dissolving "at last into a sea of moving crimson":

---

60 White, *The Living and the Dead*, 143.
61 White, *Riders in the Chariot*, 521.

> The crimson sea lapped at the skin of the man as he stood at prayer, the tips of his ears and the hollows of his temples grew transparent, his cheeks were flushed with crimson.
> *Riders in the Chariot* 522

Whether the external light or the pulse of blood is being referred to is unclear, as the binary of exterior and interior dissolves. Finally, as Himmelfarb calls out for salvation, his experience of spiritual 'union' is emphatically physical:

> the shawl fell back from his shoulders in the moment of complete union, and the breeze from the window twitched at the corner of his old robe, showing him to be, indeed, a man, made to suffer the torments and indignities. The hair lay in thin, grizzled wisps in the hollow between his breasts; the thongs of veins which bound his scraggy legs, from the ankles to the knees, were most arbitrarily, if not viciously entangled.
> *Riders in the Chariot* 522

Himmelfarb experiences his condition of abjection as a "veritable state of communion"[62] during which interior and exterior, the self and the Other, merge. Simultaneously, he is brought into contact with the alterity of the sacred or the sublimity of the abject. This mystical moment recalls his discovery of Alf Dubbo's Bible, open at the first chapter of Ezekiel. As Himmelfarb reads the prophet's description of the Chariot, he recognizes that the "four living creatures" in it are fundamentally corporeal; thus "allegorical splendour" is transformed into flesh:

> The voice no longer attempted to clothe the creatures themselves in allegorical splendour, of Babylonian gold. They were dressed in the flesh of men; the pug of human gargoyles, the rather soapy skin, the pores of which had been enlarged by sweat, the mouth thinned by trial and error, the dead hair of the living human creatures blowing in the wind of circumstances.
> *Riders in the Chariot* 404

As *Riders in the Chariot* reveals, its "four living creatures"—Himmelfarb, Hare, Godbold, and Dubbo—are themselves "dressed" in the mortal "flesh of men,"

---

62   Kristeva, in Charles Penwarden, "Of Word and Flesh: An Interview with Julia Kristeva," in *Rites of Passage: Art for the End of the Twentieth Century*, ed. Stuart Morgan & Frances Morris (London: Tate Gallery, 1995): 23.

their bodies emphatically entering the imagery of the text so that spirit and soma are finally indivisible and the novel requires interpretation simultaneously on the material and symbolic levels.

According to Peter Wolfe, "White's characters exist as solid bodies before they pronounce wisdom or doom."[63] The description of Himmelfarb attests, however, to the fact that they also exist as solid bodies during and after their mystical experiences. White's fiction is interested in "the *physical advantages of mystical ecstasy*,"[64] and its spiritual impetus illuminates the flesh. Katherine Brisbane therefore observes that his novels are "full of stigmatic manifestations of the spiritual."[65] White's language, emphasizing physical imagery through such techniques as assonance and alliteration, enjoins the reader to accept the body in minute and painful detail: the "thin grizzled wisps of hair," the "thongs of veins viciously entangled." To read White is to engage with a language of physicality that replicates the specificity of corporeality.

For Himmelfarb, "the Word remain[s] as testimony of substance,"[66] to the extent that his lips form "words of their own flesh,"[67] another instance of the emphasis on the semiotic over the symbolic which here assumes mystical associations. Himmelfarb's observations on the "testimony of substance" recall John's verse describing Christ's incarnation, even if they seem to invert it: "the Word became flesh and dwelt among us" (John 1:14). Anthony Synnott interprets these words thus: "God became Man. Divinity was humanized, in all its fleshiness, was divinized."[68] Synnott's summary is comparable to Laura Trevelyan's articulation of the three-stage process of human 'becoming' in *Voss*: "How important it is to understand the three stages. Of God into man. Man. And man returning into God."[69] These sentences in *Voss* may be interpreted in a number of ways. First, they describes the incarnation and the passion of Christ. Second, they suggest that humanity itself is Christ-like, emerging from the spiritual and eventually returning to it. This interpretation, however, does not accord exactly with White's fiction of redemptive corporeality, for it implies that the second stage of "Man" correlates with the entrapment of the spirit, which must bide its time before it is once again liberated. Himmelfarb's moment of 'union', occurring when he is described at his most corporeal,

---

63 Peter Wolfe, *Laden Choirs: The Fiction of Patrick White* (Lexington: UP of Kentucky, 1983): 3.
64 White, *Riders in the Chariot*, 172. (My emphasis.).
65 Katherine Brisbane, "Australian Drama," in *The Literature of Australia*, ed. Geoffrey Dutton (Harmondsworth: Penguin, 1976): 269.
66 White, *Riders in the Chariot*, 257.
67 *Riders in the Chariot*, 522.
68 Anthony Synnott, "Tomb, Temple, Machine and Self," 85.
69 White, *Voss*, 386.

denies this reading. If White's characters are Christ-like, then they resemble the living Christ, embodied and suffering. Third, then, Laura's words suggest a three-stage process *within* life, whereby humanity, humbled into recognizing the significance of physical existence, becomes godlike by relinquishing the limits of the transcendental ego and merging with the physical world. In a final interpretation of Laura's statement: if God is *logos* (Word), then language itself becomes flesh, its transubstantiation bringing about its mystical illumination.

In White, God and corporeality cannot be separated, and many of his characters are Christ-like in their incarnation, a transformation according with their acceptance of embodiment and revealing White's concern with a poetics of the body. Crucial to his conception of corporeality is the fact that Christ had a body, hence was human, an emphasis on the spirituality of the flesh White shared with his Romantic predecessor William Blake. Jean Hagstrum identifies the significance of the corporeal Christ in Blake's work, which is often based on descriptions of the Bible:

> although the interpretations have varied enormously through the centuries, the language of the Bible proclaims loudly that Jesus possessed and possesses a body.[70]

This embodiment is similarly important for key scenes in White's oeuvre, where the significance of the prose is linked to the spiritual significance of Christ's body. When Arthur dances his "mandala" for Mrs Poulter, for example—in an episode suggesting that *The Solid Mandala*'s informing symbol, the Jungian mandala,[71] is in fact coextensive with the body—he is depicted as a Christ-figure:

> in the centre of their mandala he danced the passion of all their lives, the blood running out of the backs of his hands, water out of the hole in his ribs. His mouth was a silent hole, because no sound was needed to explain.[72]

The passion of Christ is compared here to both inevitable mortality and the physical passion of existence, entering the text through the description of Arthur's frenzied body. Arthur's dance reveals his own martyrdom by linking

---

70   Jean H. Hagstrum, "Christ's Body," in *William Blake: Essays in Honour of Sir Geoffrey Keynes*, ed. Morton D. Paley & Michael Philips (Oxford: Oxford UP, 1973): 130.

71   White read Jung's *Psychology and Alchemy* while writing *The Solid Mandala*. From this, he drew the novel's constituting symbol.

72   White, *The Solid Mandala*, 267.

him to the suffering of Christ. Corporeality's effect on signification is evident: the "silent hole" of his mouth represents a fall from language and thus a lapse into corporeal silence that coincides with the implication of a mystical significance eluding explanation. As the literal embodiment of corporeality in *The Solid Mandala*, Arthur is best able to communicate meaning in dance, even if that meaning is irrational, mystically incomprehensible, and defies symbolic capture. His body, like Christ's, represents the entanglement of physicality, abjection, and spirituality. As Ann McCulloch argues, moreover, Arthur's dance "can be understood to embody the meaning of the text"[73]—quite literally, it would seem. The meaning of the text and the meaning of Christ are often interlinked. When Amy Parker looks at Mr Gage's painting of the crucifixion in *The Tree of Man*,

> the flesh began to move her, its wincing verdigris and sweating tallow. She knew this, as if her sleep had told her of it. Great truths are only half-grasped this side of sleep.
> *The Tree of Man* 289

For Alf Dubbo, retouching the wounds of his painting of the "dead Christ with the love that he had never dared express in life," he finds the blood "gushing from his own mouth, the wounds in the canvas shining and palpitating with his own conviction."[74] The materiality of Christ reflects the bodiliness of White's prose. For White, artistic conviction is physical.

Because the body of Christ is abject in its mysticism, White's characters do not always comfortably assimilate it. When Palfreyman is woken by the dread sight of Voss sleepwalking, horrific because it implies the fallibility of the explorer's seemingly controlled and controlling consciousness, a lapse in his own rational perception presents Voss as a decapitated Christ-figure:

> Through some trick of moonlight or uncertainty of behaviour, the head became detached for a second and appeared to have been fixed upon a beam of the wooden wall. The mouth and the eyes were visible. Palfreyman shivered. Ah, Christ is an evil dream, he feared, and all my life I have been deceived.
> *Voss* 177

---

73 Ann M. McCulloch, *A Tragic Vision*, 52.
74 White, *Riders in the Chariot*, 592.

This passage suggests White's interest in adapting the Christ-image to his own philosophy. Christ becomes more than a metaphor of embodiment, symbolizing, moreover, the acceptance of corporeality, decay, and corruption as routes to, if not fundamental elements of, mystical illumination. The very materiality of Christ's body constitutes its significance, and Palfreyman has been unaware of this. He has in fact shied away from the indignities of the flesh throughout his life. As he tells Voss, he has been incapable of loving his deformed, humpbacked sister; her corporeality has appalled him. In particular, he recalls her misshapen body at the mirror: "She had outlined her lips completely in red ink, giving them the arch of a perfect, but horrifying mouth. I was very frightened" (262). As he recounts his tale of past failure—his "inability to return her love" (263)—his sister enters the imaginary, mythic space of the desert to appear before the two men as another hallucinatory female figure. Much like Laura, she represents the significance of the flesh:

> She was twisting a bunch of small flowers, violets they could have been, which were her offering, but from which the flesh was coming away in terrible jerks. Of all the blots and distortions of evening, the shadow of her hump upon the ground was the most awful.
> *Voss* 263

Awful flesh, terrible deformity, and the shadowing burden of sexuality: Palfreyman's error has been not to accept the abject body. His neat, disembodied, rational vision of Christ is thus perverted as he realizes his mistake in the distorted image of the sleep-walking Voss. In his horror at his failings, he perceives the new Christ-image as "evil" and after

> the bones of the naked Christ had been drawn through the foetid room, by sheets of moonlight, and out the doorway, the fully conscious witness continued to lie on his blanket face to face with his own shortcomings and his greatest error.
> *Voss* 177

When the moonlight "return[s] Voss to the room," his inevitable physical corruption is emphasized: "his bones were creaking and his skin had erupted in a greenish verdigris" (177). This is Palfreyman's recognition of what constitutes the relation between Christ and humanity—corporeality, decay, and suffering—and this is the path laid out for Voss, who places too much faith in his mind and too little in his body, the latter asserting itself in the 'weakness' of his somnambulism and the mind subverted in the pre-rational, prophetic image of the headless Christ, foreshadowing his eventual literal and figurative decapitation.

As R.P. Laidlaw argues, "Voss's view of fleshly life is dominated by his awareness of physical decay. Hence his rage against Jesus Christ, a god who chose to become flesh."[75] Voss initially believes that Christ is a "miserable fetish" and scorns Christ's association with the body. This is evident in his contemptuous taunting of Palfreyman when the latter is attending to the ailing Turner: "Mr Palfreyman in his capacity of Jesus Christ, lances the boils."[76] Yet Voss will himself become Christ-like when he accepts his physical weakness and casts aside his over-identification with reason, as symbolized in his eventual decapitation. As Judd, the sole white survivor of Voss's expedition, later observes,

> I am convinced that Voss had in him a little of Christ, like other men. If he was composed of evil along with the good, he struggled with that evil and failed.
> *Voss* 445

Laura, in one of her moments of paradoxically lucid irrationality during her "brain fever" (353), comments that "human truths are also divine. This is the true meaning of Christ" (371). Indeed, one such human truth is the facticity of the body, which White's characters are driven to acknowledge.

Communion Literalized: Eucharistic Imagery

The acceptance of the body in White is often suggested through the imagery of incorporation, not least in the trope of communion, the symbolic ingestion of the body of Christ, or, more generally, the acceptance of the notion of the somatic sacred. Thus, eucharistic imagery, prevalent in White's fiction, dramatizes the themes of incorporation, interiority, and somatic spirituality. For White, the symbol of Christ does not allude to an underlying structure of Christian dogma in his writing. Rather, it functions as an index of embodiment, of corporeality illuminated with significance, and simultaneously of language embodying meaning; in accordance with eucharistic symbolism, where bread is taken through the notion of transubstantiation to literally become the body of Christ and wine His blood, sign is inseparable from signification, body from spirit.[77]

---

75 R.P. Laidlaw, "The Complexity of *Voss*," *Southern Review* (Adelaide) 4.1 (1970): 7.
76 White, *Voss*, 242.
77 The *OED* defines transubstantiation, generally, as "the changing of one substance into another," and, specifically, as the "conversion in the Eucharist of the whole substance of

In White, the Eucharist emphasizes the sacred importance of accepting and internalizing the significance of the body. A communion scene in *The Tree of Man*, for example, dramatizes a congregation's collective striving for spiritual epiphany in an episode in which corporeality is strongly emphasized. Initially, the apparent degradation of the body is contrasted with an elusive spirituality:

> the priest of God, who was taking bread with the tips of his fingers and tasting wine with his fumbling mouth, was also trying desperately to transcend bread and wine. But the act in its sublimity was too difficult. His wretched cheeks continued to munch. A piece of dough had stuck to his gum.
> People had begun to go up, to kneel at the Communion rail. Their bodies were terrible. The soles of their shoes, exposed to the knave of the church, did a double penance.
> *The Tree of Man* 430

The awkwardness of the body is emphasized in this quotation: it is "fumbling," "desperate," and "wretched." At first, bread and wine are not enough for the "priest of God," who wishes to transcend the banality of substance but finds himself unable to do so. Doomed to the physicality of "munching," he is unable to divest himself of the material world, and the seemingly unredeemed dough of the bread sticks to his equally unredeemed gum. The body is "terrible" in its seemingly Godless materiality: not even the 'souls' of the worshippers are mentioned; instead, the "*soles* of their shoes" do comical "double penance," presumably out of shame for their stark physicality.

Yet the scene soon modulates: the munching priest, his abject physicality foregrounded by the insult of the adhesive dough, becomes a figure of somatic spirituality, of transcendence *in* physicality—of 'becoming':

> In spite of the weight of his strong boots, which tried to fix him to the carpet, the young man was mounting at last. But in the struggle had become elongated. He had increased in stature but was held. As he moved along the line a purple line of transcendent glass flowed through his marble robes. His head, at the extremity of his body, filled with the sonorities of

---

the bread into the body and of the wine into the blood of Christ, only the appearances (and other 'accidents') of bread and wine remaining: according to the doctrine of the Roman Catholic church." This notion implies an absolute transformation, in contrast to 'consubstantiation', in which the elements of bread and wine are held to *coexist* with the body and blood of Christ.

> his voice, was touching at last in its achievement. The substantial squares of bread were true by the very fact of their substance.
>
> *The Tree of Man* 430

This passage suggests that 'transcendence' occurs when it is ostensibly denied. Indeed, the *substance* of the body is necessary for attaining ecstasy. Communion imagery, moreover, emphasizes the unification of meaning and body after which the writing strives.

Receiving further attention in *Voss*, the Eucharist gains compound associations over the course of the novel as Voss is gradually brought to the point where he must internalize corporeality and shed his notion of the transcendental ego. The limits of the body are conceptualized as the limits of subjectivity and the literal act of ingestion becomes a metaphor for internalizing, hence accepting, otherness. The ingestion of the communion wafer also enacts the moment in which the body and spiritual significance coalesce, symbolizing the convergence of sign and meaning. Incorporated into the symbol of the Eucharist are White's concerns with corporeality, mortality, the abject sacred, the presentation of existence as irresolvably physical, language as substance, and compassion as involving both physical acceptance and 'communion' with both others and the Other.[78]

Towards the end of the novel, captured by Aboriginals, Voss is fed a witchetty grub:

> The white man was conscious of that pinch of soft white flesh, but rather more of its flavour, hot unlike that of the almond, which also is elliptical. He mumbled it on his tongue for a while before attempting to swallow it, and at once the soft thing became the struggling wafer of his boyhood, that absorbed the unworthiness in his hot mouth, and would not go down. As then, his fear was that his sinful wafer might be discovered, lying before him, half-digested on the floor.
>
> *The Tree of Man* 388

The witchetty grub is "soft white flesh," metonymic of the vulnerable corporeality of the captured European explorer. Associated with Voss's body, the "soft white flesh" tastes "hot," like his "hot mouth." Voss is required to ingest neither a grub nor the Eucharist per se, but his own symbolic body, a body in this instance associated with Indigenous Australia, another of Voss's abjects, because it does not conform to his subjective constructions. Because he is so averse to

---

78   Here the term 'the Other' is used in the Lacanian sense to indicate radical alterity.

his body (and that of Australia), swallowing the grub is a struggle, and it "will not go down." Voss's rationalist hubris makes him "unworthy" of corporeality and the physical world, which are linked to Christ in their associations with humility, redemption, and somatic spirituality.

Communion imagery is also significant in *A Fringe of Leaves*, which continues the exploration of the theme of the need to accept the body and the sacred significance White ascribes to doing so. Like Voss, Ellen Roxburgh must accept corporeality in her struggle for survival in the Australian landscape. Shipwrecked and captured by an Aboriginal tribe, she is forced to shed her feminine English identity and to come to terms with the corporeality that its attainment and maintenance repudiate. The novel's bodily emphasis has been overlooked by critics who insist on its interest in the 'soul'. Kay Schaffer argues that the novel "presents the solitary individual in search of an ultimate insight through his or her confrontation with the terrifying metaphysical geography of the mind, soul, and spirit";[79] A.J. Hassall maintains that White is "less interested in his heroine's physical journey than in her internal growth and development."[80] Yet metaphysics and physicality go together: acceptance of the body is figured quite literally as the ingestion of human flesh—Ellen's act of cannibalism when she stumbles upon a recently abandoned Aboriginal rite and "tast[es] flesh from the human thigh-bone in the stillness of a forest morning."[81] The episode begins as she trails behind the tribesmen who have left to conduct a funeral rite. Gradually, she casts off her socialized identity:

> She was the 'Ellen' of her youth, a name they had attached to her visible person at the font, but which had never rightfully belonged to her, any more than the greater part of what she had experienced in life. Now this label of a name was flapping and skirring ahead of her among the trunks of great moss-bound trees, as its less substantial echo unfurled from out of the past, from amongst fuchsia and geum and candy-tuft, then across the muck-spattered yard, the moor with its fuzz of golden furze and russet bracken, to expire in some gull's throat by isolated syllables.
>
> *A Fringe of Leaves* 270–271

---

79   Kay Schaffer, "Australian Mythologies: The Eliza Fraser Story and the Constructions of the Feminine in Patrick White's *A Fringe of Leaves* and Sidney Nolan's 'Eliza Fraser' Paintings," *Kunapipi* 11.2 (1989): 1.

80   A.J. Hassall, "The Making of a Colonial Myth: The Mrs Fraser Story in Patrick White's *A Fringe of Leaves* and André Brink's *An Instant in the Wind*," ARIEL: *A Review of International English Literature* 18.3 (1987): 18.

81   White, *A Fringe of Leaves*, 274.

Ellen's name "flaps" and "skirs" ahead of her as she sheds the associations of her identity, related here to the imagery of vegetation and place: the flowers of Cheltenham where she has lived during her marriage, the "muck-spattered yard" of her childhood farm and the surrounding moors, and the expiry of her socialized subjectivity in the raucous, meaningless, "elliptical," and language-deforming cry of the Australian seagull. The retrogression of her identity, figured in imagery that takes her back in time, suggests her eventual embodiment of a primal, animalistic 'self' preceding the repudiation of corporeality in the infantile subject-forming process of abjection. White thus draws a comparison between the primitive roots of identity and tribal 'primitivism', a racist identification that ironically reveals his own European abjections.

When Ellen approaches the scene, the ceremony is over and she senses in the group "something akin to the atmosphere surrounding communicants coming out of church looking bland and forgiven after the early service" (271). Ignoring Ellen, the party leaves her to engage in her own sacrament. This is perhaps the most excessive moment signalling the mystical acceptance of corporeality in White's fiction:

> As she went, she tried to disentangle her emotions, fear from amazement, disgust from a certain pity she felt for these starving and ignorant savages, her masters, when she looked down and caught sight of a thigh-bone which must have fallen from one of the overflowing dillis. Renewed disgust prepared her to kick the bone out of sight. Then, instead, she found herself stooping, to pick it up. There were one or two shreds of half-cooked flesh and gobbets of burnt fat still adhering to the monstrous object. Her stiffened body and almost audibly twangling nerves were warning her against what she was about to do, what she was, in fact, already doing. She had raised the bone, and was tearing at it with her teeth, spasmodically chewing, swallowing by great gulps which her throat threatened to return. But did not. She flung the bone away only after it was cleaned, and followed slowly in the wake of her cannibal mentors. She was less disgusted in retrospect by what she had done, then awed by the fact that she had been moved to do it. The exquisite innocence of this forest morning, its quiet broken by a single flute-note endlessly repeated, tempted her to believe that she had partaken of a sacrament. But there remained what amounted to an abomination of human behaviour, a headache, and the first signs of indigestion. In the light of Christian morality she must never think of the incident again.
>
> *A Fringe of Leaves* 272

This is the climactic episode of *A Fringe of Leaves*, and the tension that it reveals between disgust and hunger communicates the oscillation between subject-formation and dissolution, and the relation of this oscillation to corporeality. Ellen's disgust and racism protect the provisional European identity that she performs as Mrs Roxburgh. Her disgust is renewed when she notices the human thigh-bone. Her "stiffened body" and "audibly twangling nerves" signify the abjection that she experiences. Yet, while her rational self quails, her corporeal self begins to assimilate the "monstrous object," to take it in quite literally. In the process, her own corporeality and animality are emphasized as she "tears at it with her teeth," "spasmodically chewing" and "swallowing by great gulps." Disgust and the ravenous breaching of taboo, presumably eliciting the reader's revulsion, give way to a moment of sacramental "awe." By ingesting human flesh, Ellen experiences the mysticism and *jouissance* inherent in accepting corporeality. Like one of the Christian mystics, she swallows the abject to commune with the sacred. Losing herself in the moment of mystical illumination, she nonetheless quickly regains her identity when her disgust resurfaces and she realizes that she has committed an act that is an "abomination of human behaviour." Her realization coincides with one of White's favored indices of rationality on trial—her *headache*. Ellen's subject-affirming, body-denying reason is reinstated when she recalls that in the "light of Christian morality she must never think of the incident again." In her radical communion with corporeality, she has, however, experienced the "alternation between the sublime and the abject that characterizes our dark side at its most heretical."[82]

Ellen's cannibalism is prepared for earlier in the novel when her sickly and corporeally averse husband, Austin, tends to the sea boils of the repellent ship steward, Spurgeon. Encountering Spurgeon, Austin imagines a "white light threaten[ing] to expose the more protected corners of human personality" and experiences

> the trappings of wealth and station, the pride in ethical and intellectual aspirations, stripped from him with a ruthlessness reserved for those who accept their importance or who have remained unaware of their pretentiousness.
> *A Fringe of Leaves* 208

Similarly, the limits of identity are revealed as provisional when a confrontation with corporeality becomes inevitable. Prefiguring the thigh-bone as

---

82 Roudinesco, *Our Dark Side*, 7.

"monstrous object" (272), Austin views Spurgeon as a "thoroughly repulsive object" (209), who causes him to realize that, at the expense of his embodiment, he has led an enclosed and cerebral existence: "his experience of life, like his attitude to death, had been of a predominantly literary nature" (209). Tending to Spurgeon's boils allows Austin to experience sanctity in humility, during which his body "throbs" and "surges" back into his awareness:

> Mr Roxburgh who originally had no intention of touching the boil was now faced with doing so [...]. So he set to, gingerly at first, grimacing with a disgust his patient was fortunately unable to see, and rubbed with stiffened, bony fingers, till the activity itself began to soothe, not the patient necessarily, but without doubt the physician.
>
> For the first time since landing on this desert island Austin Roxburgh was conscious that the blood was flowing through his veins. To an almost reprehensible extent, he throbbed and surged with gratitude.
>
> *A Fringe of Leaves* 211

Throughout his life Austin has denied the body, and his ministrations to Spurgeon provide him with the means of engaging with his own corporeality. His "throbbing and surging" is "almost reprehensible" because of the extent to which he has repudiated the body in defence of his identity. After the steward dies and physical conditions become increasingly difficult, his need to accept the body becomes even more insistent. He is disgusted to realize that his need to re-incorporate his physicality into his notion of the self, merging with his hunger for human connection, is confused with physical hunger itself. His thoughts wander deliriously under the conditions of physical deprivation:

> As one who had hungered all his life after friendships which eluded him, Austin Roxburgh did luxuriate on losing a solitary allegiance. It stimulated his actual hunger until now dormant, and he fell to thinking how the steward, had he not been such an unappetising morsel, might have contributed appreciably to an exhausted larder. At once Mr Roxburgh's self-disgust knew no bounds.
>
> *A Fringe of Leaves* 231

This fantasized act of cannibalism, a breach of taboo rapidly defended against by the abjection that consolidates rational subjectivity, emerges again during a dream in which it is conflated with the communion ceremony:

> *This is the body of Spurgeon which I have reserved for thee, take eat, and give thanks for a boil which was spiritual matter...* Austin Roxburgh was

not only ravenous for the living flesh, but found himself anxiously licking the corners of his mouth to prevent any overflow of precious blood.

Upon suddenly waking, Mr Roxburgh discovered his mouth wide open. He would have set about ejecting anything inside it, from his stomach too, had they not been equally empty.

A Fringe of Leaves 231 (italics in the original)

Austin's oscillation between incorporation and ejection prefigures Ellen's moment of sacrament in the Australian forest. Both characters, then, are driven toward climactic moments involving the symbolic reincorporation of corporeality, figured in the imagery of the Eucharist.

Critics have made much of Ellen's cannibalism in the "heart of darkness,"[83] Australia, commenting for the most part on its implications for White as a postcolonial author. According to Schaffer,

> [White] portrays the possibility of white cannibalism as acceptable, when imagined in the dreams of a starving Austin Roxburgh at the time of the shipwreck and the steward Spurgeon's death. He also acknowledges that the practice of native cannibalism was not uncommon, as revealed through Delaney's reports to the Merivales of natives killing and eating white trespassers on Aboriginal territory at the start of the novel.[84]

As Hassall argues,

> White portrays the Aborigines in *A Fringe of Leaves*—from Ellen's point of view—as nasty, brutish and primitive. The view is external, and there is no attempt to explore their inner lives, or the ways in which they relate to their world.[85]

According to Cynthia vanden Driesen, however, White distinguishes between white and black cannibalism and is therefore sensitive to Aboriginal identity:

> The blacks are shown to practise a form of ritual cannibalism (such as has been referred to in the studies of anthropologists); it is the whites who

---

83   Karin Hansson, "The Indigenous and the Metropolitan in *A Fringe of Leaves*," *World Literature Written in English* 24.1 (April 1984): 182.
84   Schaffer, "Australian Mythologies," 171.
85   Hassall, "The Making of a Colonial Myth," 20.

are shown to indulge in a form that is more nearly the 'abomination of human behaviour'.[86]

The cannibalism of the whites, she continues, "underlines the bestiality of the act in comparison to the mystical purpose prompting indigene behaviour."[87] This appears a rather idealistic interpretation of a symbolic novel that to some extent—like *Voss*—subjugates the sensitive representation of Indigenous peoples to White's metaphysical vision of the dissolution of white identity. Moreover, as Hena Maes–Jelinek observes, the scene of Ellen's cannibalism "is obviously given a mystical significance."[88] Ellen's action may be bestial, but it is in its bestiality that its mysticism inheres. The "animality" of the Aboriginal tribe, as White presents it, allows Ellen to momentarily re-incorporate her own. Yet we may also interpret Ellen's anthropophagy as her ingestion of Indigenous Australia and therefore as her acceptance of it. White's fiction frequently presents the possibility of a white indigeneity in characters that merge with the landscape of Australia, becoming elemental to it. In this way, the novel may be considered an "enabling myth for [White's] postcolonial society."[89] Theodora Goodman, Voss, Laura Trevelyan, Rose Portion, Mary Hare, and Ellen Roxburgh all lose their European associations to become embedded, in one way or another, in the Australian landscape. Ellen's ingestion of Aboriginal flesh, like Voss's swallowing of the witchetty grub, may be read as a moment in which the boundary between the identities of settler and aborigine is eroded.

Nonetheless, White's treatment of indigenes remains highly ambivalent, characterized by the ambiguous desire for the unification of white identity and Aboriginal Australia and the diminishment of the latter. The subordination of Aboriginal society to white identity enables White's comparison of the archaic merging with otherness fundamental to psychoanalytic understandings of the basis of European subjectivity with racist associations linking Aboriginality to animality, pure corporeality, and primitivism. *A Fringe of Leaves* is one example in which the dissolution of subjectivity does not appear to correlate with White's ethic of compassion, at least not in its extension to Aboriginal people.

---

86   Cynthia vanden Driesen, *Writing the Nation: Patrick White and the Indigene* (Cross/Cultures 97; Amsterdam & New York: Rodopi, 2009): 95.
87   vanden Driesen, *Writing the Nation*, 97.
88   Hena Maes–Jelinek–Jelinek, Hena-->, "Fictional Breakthrough and the Unveiling of 'Unspeakable Rites' in Patrick White's *A Fringe of Leaves* and Wilson Harris's *Yurokon*," *Kunapipi* 2.2 (1980): 37.
89   Hassall, "The Making of a Colonial Myth," 4.

Voss, with its dense patterns of imagery and self-conscious symbolism, is perhaps a more successful novel in this respect.

Still, both novels reveal the threat to identity that constitutes the confrontation with the abject, and against which the subject is protected via the response of disgust or abjection. *A Fringe of Leaves*, however, more so than *Voss*, emphasizes the *jouissance* of the encounter with the abject as temporary: if we do not dissolve in death, like Voss, then we exist irrevocably within language, within a social order, and our moments of aspiration beyond it must necessarily be short-lived if we are to retain any sense of ourselves at all. Indeed, as Hassall observes, "the struggle of the individual woman or man against the prison-house of society endures."[90] Hence, Ellen Roxburgh, "returning voluntarily to the prison to which she had been sentenced,"[91] re-enters civilization; seemingly unchanged after her capture and ingestion of flesh and re-incorporated into the social order, she proves herself to have been a "lifer from birth."[92]

---

90 Hassall, "The Making of a Colonial Myth," 26.
91 White, *A Fringe of Leaves*, 359.
92 *A Fringe of Leaves*, 359.

CHAPTER 7

Abject Corporeality and Somatic Spirituality
Voss *and* The Eye of the Storm

> No Beast is there without glimmer of infinity,
> No Eye so vile nor abject that brushes not
> Against lightning from on high, now tender, now fierce.¹

∴

This chapter provides close readings of two novels in which the interrelated themes of abject corporeality and somatic spirituality are particularly significant. In *Voss*, the necessity of the acceptance of corporeality is dramatized in the depiction of Laura Trevelyan. Her relationship with the heavily embodied servant, Rose Portion, sets up her association with the body, extending into her role as Voss's mystical guide as he learns the need to accept corporeality during his harsh encounter with the Australian desert. Laura's hallucinatory appearances to Voss gradually lead him to the recognition of somatic spirituality and the necessary rejection of the narcissistic and fragile notion of consciousness as disembodied. In *The Eye of the Storm*, by contrast, abject corporeality is absolutely central to the novel as narrative events unfold around the dying body of the aged Elizabeth Hunter. Characters in the novel relate to Elizabeth's corporeality in various ways, revealing through their different perspectives the intimate association of abjection with the sacred.

Incorporating the Physical: *Voss* and the Role of Laura Trevelyan

In White's oeuvre, the theme of the acceptance of corporeality is arguably most explicit in *Voss*. Because of its description of a mystical love relationship

---

1 Victor Hugo, "Le crapaud" ("Pas de bête qui n'ait un reflet d'infini; / Pas de prunelle abjecte et vile qui ne touche / L'éclair d'en haut, parfois tendre et parfois farouche"), in Hugo, *La Légende des siècles*, original preface by Charles Baudelaire, preface by Didier Hallépée (1859–83; Paris: Collection Lettres Classiques, 2015): 182, tr. in Julia Kristeva, *Powers of Horror: An Essay on Abjection*, tr. Leon S. Roudiez (*Pouvoirs de l'horreur: Essai sur l'abjection*, 1980; New York: Columbia UP, 1982): 1.

precluding the literal physical contact of its protagonists, however, *Voss* is often read as exemplifying White's concern with disembodiment. The novel nonetheless emphasizes the interrelated concreteness and mysticism of physicality. It is, moreover, an allegorical text exploring and foregrounding the metaphorical distance between self-enclosed subjectivity and corporeality, a distinction that it ultimately attempts to erode.

Loosely based on the expedition of Ludwig Leichhardt, who embarked on two exploratory journeys from east to west across the Australian continent, finally disappearing during the second in 1848, *Voss* charts the fictional explorer Johann Ulrich Voss's physical, psychological, and metaphysical journey as he and his party of men venture from the fertile outskirts of the Australian continent into its inhospitable desert interior. The journey is hazardous and physically debilitating, but it is Voss's monumental egoism in conditions requiring the acceptance of corporeal fallibility that will harm him the most. In its development of the explorer's monstrous notion of the supreme and disembodied Self, *Voss* depicts the moral failings of European Enlightenment consciousness. Voss is Prussian, and his nationality recalls the identity of the Prussian Enlightenment philosopher, Immanuel Kant.[2] Kant's *Critique of Pure Reason* argues for an a-priori knowledge called the transcendental ego: the self-enclosed consciousness bringing the physical world into being for the perceiver through rational concepts that categorize, order, and thus construct it. Voss embodies the transcendental ego, "sufficient in himself"[3] and distrusting everything "external to himself" (21). For Voss, the "Idea, its granite monolith untouched" (44) is all-important. In Kantian terms, a "concept formed from notions and transcending [...] experience is an *idea* or concept of reason."[4] When Voss refuses to acknowledge "the hindrances the world sets to the pursuit of the metaphysical Ideal,"[5] he subordinates physical reality to a-priori rational concepts, attempting to transcend experience in favor of reason. For Voss, the act of knowing is "a way of possessing or dominating."[6] Yet the physical world, dictating experience and impinging upon his consciousness, asserts its indomitability and ultimately destroys his enclosed subjectivity. Veronica Brady indicates the novel's informing theme: "consciousness is given notice

---

2   Voss's obsession with the will has also drawn comparisons between his character and the philosophies of Nietzsche and Schopenhauer. See Dorothy Green, "*Voss*: Stubborn Music," 304.
3   Patrick White, *Voss*, 15.
4   Immanuel Kant, *Critique of Pure Reason*, 314.
5   Maryvonne Nedeljkovic, "Voss or the Uneasy Conscience," 87.
6   Susan A. Wood, "The Power and Failure of 'Vision' in Patrick White's *Voss*," MFS: *Modern Fiction Studies* 27.1 (Spring 1981): 148.

of its impending defeat,"[7] and the "land, the weather, the inability of bodies to endure the sufferings of the desert demonstrate the limits of rebellion and of the craving for knowledge that lead [Voss] to discover the fallibility of human knowledge."[8] Physicality, in other words, trumps reason. Voss is incorrect in his assumption that it is "not possible" to "damage the Idea";[9] reason does not precede experience and must yield to the exigencies of the flesh and the physical demands upon it. Ultimately, Voss's Enlightenment assumptions are subverted.[10]

Voss situates its protagonist's presumptuously disembodied consciousness within the newly colonized world, thereby associating colonial expansion and Enlightenment notions of the self. As Marcel Aurousseau observes,

> White has endowed the Australian imagination with a symbolic figure of heroic proportions applying its whole strength to the task of learning to know Australia.[11]

Voss is indeed driven by the will-to-power and knowledge that defines both Enlightenment thought and the Imperial project. Yet if the Enlightenment consciousness consists of a-priori knowledge, then Voss attempts to subjugate the continent to his reason. The novel therefore problematizes the notion of the explorer-hero. Voss's project is dangerously hubristic; it is, moreover, White's comment on the fascism of mind over body that has engendered notions of superior rationality and that resulted in the exploitation of the colonies and the rise and terror of Adolf Hitler.[12] As a novel calling for the acknowledgement of corporeality in the post-Enlightenment, twentieth-century context, *Voss* suggests the ethical and political implications of the refusal to do so. Defined, as Keith Garebian observes, by the "radical theme of metaphysical

---

7   Veronica Brady, "The Novelist and the New World," 172.
8   Brady, "The Novelist and the New World," 174.
9   White, *Voss*, 44.
10 Voss's Enlightenment associations are evident in his name. Irmtraud Petersson notes that 'Voss' is pronounced as '*phos*', the Greek word for light: "Once this connection has been recognized, [...] the significance of the title becomes more meaningful because [...] the novel abounds in light symbolism"; Petersson, "New 'Light' on *Voss*: The Significance of its Title," *World Literature Written in English* 28.2 (July 1988): 246. This symbolism gains associations with mystical illumination and Enlightenment rationalism.
11 Marcel Aurousseau, "The Identity of Voss," *Meanjin* 17 (1958): 87.
12 The character of Voss, White informs us, arose from his musings in the Egyptian desert during World War II on the "arch-megalomaniac" of the time ("The Prodigal Son" [1958], in *Patrick White Speaks*, ed. Brennan & Flynn, 15).

completeness,"[13] it confronts the abject in the attempt to diminish the rationalist concern with repudiation and othering, defence mechanisms that secure subjectivity but that split the self from its constitutive aspects. Peter Beatson reads this splitting in gendered terms, arguing that Voss's subjectivity is "aggressively, self-assertively masculine, it holds itself aloof from any involvement with the world of the senses, the pluralistic world of flux."[14] Because it is constituted by aversion, Beatson classifies it as a "neurosis."[15] Brady agrees: Voss's defiance

> generates the monstrous alter ego which condemns him to a state of division between an arrogant and aggressive outer personality and a secret self within longing for communion with others.[16]

Like Beatson, John Coates argues that White's spiritual view is dependent upon his "emphasis on the spiritual androgyny of man [sic]."[17] Aggressive masculinity requires the incorporation of a complementary, modifying femininity to produce an integrated self premised upon the reclaiming of its abjects. Accordingly, *Voss* comprises two intersecting narrative strands. Alternating with the narrative concerning Voss and his expedition is the story of Laura Trevelyan, Voss's spiritual counterpart and Intended.[18] The two meet only briefly in person on three occasions at the beginning of the novel and, after Voss departs on his expedition, Laura remains within the domestic setting of Sydney. She is, however, linked to Voss by the strength of a relationship which, despite little initial interaction, develops into an intuitive and seemingly

---

13   Keith Garebian, "The Desert and the Garden: The Theme of Completeness in *Voss*," MFS: *Modern Fiction Studies* 22.4 (Winter 1976): 557.

14   Peter Beatson, "The Three Stages: Mysticism in Patrick White's *Voss*," *Southerly* 30.2 (June 1970): 114.

15   Beatson, "The Three Stages," 114.

16   Brady, "The Novelist and the New World," 183.

17   John Coates, "Voss and Jacob Boehme: A Note on the Spirituality of Patrick White," *Australian Literary Studies* 9.1 (May 1979): 120.

18   German philosophers and Hitler are not the only progenitors of Voss. The Germanic figure of Conrad's Kurtz, linked to Europe in his relationship to his naively optimistic "Intended," lurks strongly in the shadows of the text. Jeffrey Robinson links *Voss* and *Heart of Darkness* by virtue of their reliance on the "ancient myth of the spiritual journey." However, the two are perhaps more productively compared in the similarity of their protagonists, Voss and Kurtz, both of whom are presumptuously egoistic and exploitative Imperial figures. See Jeffrey Robinson, "The Aboriginal Enigma: *Heart of Darkness*, *Voss* and *Palace of the Peacock*," *Journal of Commonwealth Literature* 20.1 (March 1985): 150.

mystical understanding transcending distance. Laura is an aspect of Voss that he finds compelling yet for the most part repudiates: she becomes increasingly associated with corporeality over the course of the narrative and appears to Voss in his hallucinatory moments of suffering in the desert.

Voss realizes in a dream that it is "the woman who unmakes men, to make saints. [...] Mutual. It is all mutual,"[19] and that his acceptance of the feminine and forfeiture of his self-enclosure will prompt the dissolution of his rationalist masculinism. Laura's role in the novel may be read as transforming it into a "feminine text." Hélène Cixous defines such writing:

> There's *tactility* in the feminine text, there's touch, and this touch passes through the ear. Writing in the feminine is passing on what is cut out by the Symbolic, the voice of the mother, passing on what is most archaic.[20]

Reason submits to the interruptions of the semiotic and disintegrates into White's related concerns with mysticism, corporeality, and the abject.[21] Laura's hallucinatory appearances to Voss in the desert represent this irruption of the irrational, subject-deforming semiotic into the realm of the patriarchal symbolic (the desert entirely occupied by men).

Yet initially Laura is as defined by defensive abjection as her rational counterpart, Voss. This similarity is important because Laura's eventual acceptance of corporeality allows her to become Voss's mystical preceptor and offers his self-enclosed character the possibility of a redemptive openness to others and otherness. At the beginning of the novel, however, they are depicted as mirror images: they are of "equal stature,"[22] share "some guilty secret of personality" (70), and go on to "threaten[...] each other with the flashing weapons of abstract reasoning" (190). Significantly, both are consumed by their loathing for corporeality: Voss had studied towards becoming a surgeon before finding himself "suddenly revolted by the palpitating bodies of men" (13) and Laura, with disgust, rationalizes the initial chasm that she senses

---

19 White, *Voss*, 188.
20 Hélène Cixous, "Castration or Decapitation?" *Signs* 7.1 (Autumn 1981): 54.
21 John Beston identifies in the novel a "struggle for dominance" rather than unification between Voss and Laura. Although his argument approaches the novel far too literally, his point may be extended to the battle between consciousness and corporeality characteristic of White's fiction and the dialectic of the symbolic and the semiotic constituting the signifying process. Ultimately, however, these dualities are revealed as inherently unified. See Beston, "Voss's Proposal and Laura's Acceptance Letter: The Struggle for Dominance in *Voss*," *Quadrant* 16 (1972): 24.
22 White, *Voss*, 69.

between herself and Rose Portion as caused by the presence of the "bodies of these servants" (53).

Laura, an orphan, was adopted by her uncle and aunt, the Bonners, during her childhood. Their house-servant, Rose, is central to the novel's metaphysics. She epitomizes physicality and sexuality, aspects (or a 'portion') of existence that Laura initially repudiates. From the start of the novel, her body intrudes upon Laura's awareness. This is evident in the opening sentences, famous for their stylistic oddity, which literally give Rose the first word and which indicate physicality as the immediate and paramount focus of the text:

> 'There is a man here, miss, asking for your uncle,' said Rose.
> And stood breathing.
> *Voss* 7

The truncated second sentence, beginning *in medias res* and making up an entire paragraph, foregrounds Rose's audible respiration and depicts her as distastefully corporeal in Laura's apparently focalizing perspective. Her heavy breathing pervades the text, emphasized by the opening conjunction, and her body is a disconcerting presence causing the observer to avert his or her gaze:

> Something had made this woman monotonous. Her big breasts moved dully as she spoke, or she would stand, and the weight of her silences impressed itself on strangers. If the more sensitive amongst those she served or addressed failed to look at Rose, it was because her manner seemed to accuse the conscience, or it could have been, more simply, that they were embarrassed by her harelip.
> *Voss* 7

The unusual narration, refusing to commit to any certainty, presents two possible interpretations of Rose and her relationship with Laura: Laura "fail[s] to look at Rose" either because the sight of the servant arouses her guilt or because Rose's facial deformity appals her. In the first half of the novel, then, Laura hovers between two positions—the maintenance of subjectivity via abjection and the possibility of submitting to a compassion dependent on the acceptance of corporeality. Laura's disgust accuses her conscience, and so it would seem that she aspires to a position of acceptance. Either way, Rose's introduction presents her as a disruptive body that Laura must either repudiate or with which she must come to terms.

Laura will eventually incorporate Rose's associations. However, at the beginning of the novel, in contrast to Rose with her harelip and "squat body" (8), she is "flawless" (7). Her character, moreover, exemplifies "White's technique of chiaroscuro portraiture,"[23] is not fleshed out in any specific physical detail. While Rose is presented as heavily embodied, Laura's body remains obscured, first by the dimness of the room, secondly by the description of her clothing, which is itself barely visible in the gloom, and thirdly by the perpetually ambivalent narrative treatment that contributes to her mysterious nature. Attention is diverted away from the centre of her body towards her extremities—her wrists and enigmatic face:

> Her dress, of that very deep blue, was almost swallowed up, all but a smoulder, and where the neat cuffs divided it from her wrists, and at the collar, which gave freedom to her handsome throat. Her face, it had been said, was long-shaped. Whether she was beautiful it was not at first possible to tell, although she should, and could have been.
> *Voss* 9

No real sense of Laura's physicality is tendered. Moreover, she is described as "marble" (7): she is initially another of White's statue-figures, ignoring the corporeal in favor of a rigidly defended incorporeal identity, a combination of Enlightenment rationality and nineteenth-century femininity. In addition to the body, Laura refuses the "fuzz of faith" (9): she has stayed home on a Sunday while the Bonners attend church, thereby refusing religion and inadvertently making herself available for a meeting with Voss. Laura thus initially refuses both body and faith. Her association with rational control and the repression of a troubling animality is referred to later in the novel when she sits "sculpturally upon her mastered horse, of which the complicated veins were throbbing with blood and frustration" (109).

As this description suggests, the body is not so easily dismissed or suppressed. Laura must overcome her aversion to her inherent animality in order to accept her love for Voss and to submit to the "fuzz of faith," an overcoming connoted by her increasing affection for Rose. Voss, too, will find that physical aversion precludes the experience of love. He is to some degree aware that his rejection of the physical is to his own detriment, and although he perversely continues to repudiate it, he longs for the human companionship that he associates with materiality. This leads him to think occasionally

> of the material world which his egoism had made him reject. In that world men and women sat at a round table and broke bread together. At times, he admitted, his hunger was almost unbearable.
> *Voss* 36

---

23   Garebian, "The Desert and the Garden," 559.

The disgust that physicality nonetheless evokes in Voss arises from the hubris that defines him. For Voss, flesh is soft, yielding, and weak. So, too, is the selfless emotion of love, of which "he did not expect much [...] for all that is soft and yielding is easily hurt" (41). Flesh becomes a metaphor for mutuality, and Voss shies away from the "flesh of human relationships, a dreadful, cloying tyranny" that threatens the supremacy of the self (112). While flesh is a metaphor for relational affects such as love and compassion, bone symbolizes hard, deathly self-sufficiency. Voss is therefore frequently described in imagery of bone. In his initial meeting with Laura, the cloth is "taut on the man's bony knees," and his "noticeable cheek-bones and over-large finger-joints" are prominent (12). Such imagery, while emphasizing his awkwardness, also portrays him as a hard and "enclosed man" (15), who in his rivalry with God believes that he is able to "dispense with flesh" (34).

Voss's journey towards the acceptance of corporeality cannot be severed from Laura's, and the latter is unable to "dispense with flesh" in its embodiment as Rose Portion. Although she tries to be kind to Rose, Laura initially avoids the slightest physical communication that might elicit a response from the servant. Their interaction is thus greatly inhibited, and Laura is incapable of expressing compassion. It is only with "special effort" that she is able to smile at Rose, because the response of the latter is immediate and off-putting: "Kindness made her whole body express her gratitude, but it was her body that repelled" (52). Laura thus finds herself in a bind, unable to escape her sense of revulsion. This is a central tension for the character, whose responses are contradictory: "Laura Trevelyan had continued to feel repelled. It was the source of great unhappiness, because frequently she was also touched" (53). The ambiguity evident here is again important to an understanding of Laura's transformation from egoistic rationalist to humble saint: as the former, she is repelled and unhappy because Rose, as maidservant, brushes her hair, hence literally 'touches' her; as the latter, her disgust is the source of unhappiness because Rose's predicament 'touches' her: that is, it evokes her compassion. The notion of touch—the "*tactility*" that Cixous identifies as fundamental to the feminine text—is of primary importance to a novel that invests great significance in corporeality and its relation to the affect of compassion. Laura, aware that physicality is her fundamental stumbling-block, explains the issue central to her initial unhappiness: "It is the bodies of these servants, she [tells] herself in some hopelessness and disgust" (53).

Importantly, when the novel opens, Rose as the housemaid introduces and attends to Voss and Laura, the description singling her out as an important symbolic intermediary in their relationship. On a symbolic level, Voss and Laura are drawn to each other *because of* their corporeality and sexuality, which Rose represents. Physical attraction will remain for the most part unacknowledged, until Laura eventually absorbs Rose's associations, but a strong seam of barely repressed sexual energy defines their relationship from the start. Laura denies and projects her yearnings, with the consequence that the bodies of servants are discomfortingly sexual. The loitering presence and languid sexuality of Jack Slipper, the father of Rose's child, is deeply disturbing to Laura until his departure from the Bonners' property, prompted by his arrest for drunkenness. Jack, however, leaves behind him the pregnant Rose, her "breasts moving in her brown dress" (53), a body continuing to disturb and repel because it awakens Laura's attention to sexuality and becomes associated with her disgust at her own incipient physical attraction to Voss. Accordingly, Laura is beset by the image of Rose during the Pringles' picnic, when her affinity with Voss becomes increasingly clear. As Voss stands beside her, it is "by no means disagreeable," and she notices the "little dark hairs" upon his wrists (70), that telling sign, in White's fiction, of sexual attraction. But Mrs Bonner's voice, discussing Rose's fainting spell (the first indication of her pregnancy), intrudes upon Laura's euphoria, and suddenly Rose is tangibly present to Laura, "standing in her brown dress, her knuckles pressed tight together. The harelip was fearful" (70). This disruption of Laura's happiness, the first of the novel's many imaginary apparitions of abject femininity, prompts her to refuse Voss's offer of food and to remove herself from his presence. Watching him, she recalls unwittingly stumbling upon Jack Slipper in the bamboo thicket on the Bonners' property, a dark, secretive, humid setting of illicit sexual encounter:

> Ah, miss, said Jack Slipper, you have come out for a breather, well, the breeze has got up, can you hear it in the leaves? Whatever the source of the friction of the bamboos, it usually sounded cooler in their thicket. But in summer there was also the murmurous voices of insects, and often of men and women, which could create a breathlessness in that corner of the garden. Full moonlight failed to illuminate its secrets. There was a hot, black smell of rotting. The silver flags, breaking and flying on high, almost escaping from their lacquered masts, were brought back continually by the mysterious ganglion of dark roots.
> *Voss* 71

Amidst "murmurous voices," the "breathlessness" of "men and women," and the secret "hot, black smell of rotting," Laura is drawn towards sexuality and death and the compulsion of mystery associated with both. The "mysterious ganglion of dark roots" is an image that will recur throughout the novel, foreshadowing Laura's dark hair sodden with sweat during the hallucinatory illness that constitutes the crisis and climax of the novel and that, as a consequence of delirium, allows the boundary between Voss's desert setting and Laura's Sydney setting to disintegrate. Thus, from the beginning of *Voss*, the "bodies of these servants," so greatly distressing to Laura, are tied to her experience of her own physicality and her fear of acknowledging it.

Rose's sexuality and corporeality are extended into the image of the rose itself as symbolic associations, typically in White's fiction, expand via verbal association, metaphor, and metonymy. The progress of Laura and Voss's relationship is tracked by the transformation roses undergo in the Bonners' garden. During the Bonners' party in the early stages of the novel, for example, when Voss and Laura meet in the garden and cement their erotic and mystical connection, the "big, no longer perfect roses were bursting with scent and sticky stamens" (85), an image suggesting the poetic consummation of their relationship. Moreover, Rose's name and pregnancy recall Kristeva's concept of the abject semiotic as it is evinced in *The Aunt's Story*. An image of pulsating, maternal "roselight" reminiscent of Theodora Goodman's happy memories of a dreamy childhood emerges: the "flesh of rosy light" (179) linking the symbol of the rose to corporeality and the "flesh of human relationships" (112). Rose is the abject maternal in the novel, the subject-deforming matrix that Voss accesses through the intermediary figure of Laura, who herself comes to accept the body through her eventual acceptance of Rose. As Rose's pregnancy progresses, Laura becomes more attuned to the body. She begins to accept her companion, as the imagery of roses suggests:

> Laura herself had not yet grasped the full sense of that season, only that it was fuller than ever before, and that the flesh of roses was becoming personal, as she cut the long, pointed buds, or heavy blooms that would fall by evening. She had to take all, even the big, blowing ones.
> 'Those will make a mess, miss', Rose Portion did protest once. [...] 'All over the tables and carpets. A mess of rose petals.'
> *Voss* 158–159

Rose's observation foreshadows the "mess" she herself will make in giving birth, bringing into the novel the disorder of corporeality and sexuality that Mrs Bonner finds so disturbing. This disorder is already at work in Laura, however. In the garden, she is "dazed by roses" and their fertility:

> She continued to cut the big heads, in which bees were rummaging. She bent to reach others, till roselight was flooding her face, and she was forced to lower her eyes against the glare of roses.
> *Voss* 159

Laura, then, is eventually dazzled by the novel's symbol of corporeality as White's poetic writing harnesses the semiotic. From this point onward, "her faith in reason [is] less" (160) and she begins to merge with the corporeal Rose. She walks in the "overflowing garden, of big, intemperate roses, with the pregnant woman at her side" (160):

> At such times, the two shadows were joined upon the ground. Heavy with the weight of golden sun, the girl could feel the woman's pulse ticking in her own body, and was, in consequence, calmer than she had ever been, quietly joyful, and resigned. As she strolled towards the house, holding her parasol against the glare, though devoured by the tigerish sun, she trusted in their common flesh. The body, she was finally convinced, must sense the only true solution.
> *Voss* 160

Laura's joyful and compassionate acceptance of Rose is a moment of *jouissance* in which the borders of the self disintegrate and she recognizes that they are unified in "their common flesh." The pronouns in the passage are imprecise: "the girl could feel the woman's pulse ticking in her own body" refers to Laura's merging with Rose, but also to Laura's awakening to her own sexuality. Moreover, "*their* common flesh" may refer to Laura and Rose's shared corporeality but also to Laura and Voss's. In this interpretation, the shadows "joined upon the ground," while again ostensibly referring to Laura and Rose's, also allude to Laura and Voss's shadow selves—their previously abjected corporeality, compassion, and sexuality. As the body "sense[s] the only true solution," rationality dissolves—is "devoured"—along with the distinction between self and other and therefore between discrete characters.

As Wilson Harris observes, "Rose's grotesque attachment [is] a compulsive nightmare for Laura."[24] Yet there is freedom in confronting this nightmare. To allow attraction to the abject to prevail, hence to be drawn over the boundary separating the provisional categories of 'self' and 'other', where meaning and order erode, can be of value in the liberation that it offers from socialized identity. According to Kristeva, who herself invokes the imagery of nightmare, one who submits to the abject is

> on a journey, during the night, the end of which keeps receding. He has a sense of the danger, of the loss that the pseudo-object represents for him,

---

24 Wilson Harris, *Fossil and Psyche* (Austin: African and Afro-American Studies and Research Centre, University of Texas, 1974): 6.

but he cannot help taking the risk at the very moment he sets himself apart. And the more he strays, the more he is saved.[25]

Laura embraces the body both literally and figuratively:

> the girl who in the past had barely suffered her maid to touch her, on account of a physical aversion such contact invariably caused, suddenly reached out and put her arms round the waist of the swelling woman, and buried her face in the apron.
> *Voss* 164

In hugging Rose, Laura embraces corporeality just as she draws another human being towards her. Compassion in White's fiction is not merely the reclaiming of corporeality. More than this, it is empathy for another, occurring via the acceptance of the other's physicality and the acknowledgement of the shared experience of embodiment. When Laura feels Rose's pulse ticking in her own body, for example, or begins to experience Rose's pregnancy as her own, what she undergoes is the dissolution of the self allowed by corporeal empathy. Laura's symbolic pregnancy is therefore not merely the dream manifestation of her love for Voss, as it is commonly understood by critics, of whom David Tacey is one example:

> Conveniently, the entire sexual issue is parcelled out to Laura's maid, whose profane coupling with Jack Slipper leads to the timely birth of the unwanted child. Even more conveniently, the mother dies soon after the birth, leaving Laura to cherish her very own spiritual child. The whole episode involving Mercy is an ugly and unnecessary literalization of the 'fruit' of the Voss/Laura marriage, but more to the point it serves to highlight the tremendous gulf between sexuality and love in White's world.[26]

Tacey ignores the accumulation of imagery that presents Rose as a fundamental aspect of Laura's character—her corporeality. If Voss and Laura's relationship is disembodied, it is not because of a "gulf between sexuality and love." On the contrary, White emphasizes dualism in order to undermine it. Voss's love is dependent on his acknowledgement of corporeality and therefore sexuality. Hence, Mercy as the symbolic manifestation of Voss and Laura's 'spiritual' love

---

25   Julia Kristeva, *Powers of Horror*, 8.
26   David Tacey, *Patrick White: Fiction and the Unconscious* (Melbourne: Oxford UP, 1988): 75.

cannot be adequately comprehended without due consideration of Laura's overcoming of her aversion to corporeality and otherness via her relationship with Rose. The necessity of surmounting the enclosure of aversion similarly dominates Voss's metaphysical journey. Beatson summarizes the fundamental significance of Voss and Laura's relationship thus: "Voss had tried to will himself out of the body: Laura, on the other hand, wills herself into the body."[27]

In reclaiming her corporeality, and in her unbidden and seemingly mystical appearances to Voss in the desert, reminding him of the importance of compassion and of acknowledging the flesh, Laura, like Rose before her, becomes tinged with the abject. The "lovely colours of putrescence"[28] are of vital importance in *Voss*, gaining numerous associations as the narrative unfolds: "green and brown, of mud, and slime, and uncontrolled faeces, and the bottomless stomach of nausea" (270) contribute to the novel's indexes of abjection. Rose wears a dress of "brown stuff" (8) and when she collapses "in her brown gown" at the Bonners' table, the first sign of her pregnancy, she "look[s] a full sack, except that she was stirring and moaning, even retching" (50). Moreover, as Peter Beatson observes,

> there is a close link established between Rose and the country: they are both 'brown', 'monotonous', and from both are averted the genteel eyes of those who do not like to see the stark ugliness of their appearance.[29]

Both corporeality and the indigenous landscape are constructed as abject in relation to "genteel," colonial, "English" identity. Laura's acceptance of Rose is therefore her acceptance of the Australian landscape and her first movement towards the white indigeneity that White's fiction conceptualizes as a possibility.

Laura herself is frequently described as clad in "sombre green"[30] and her moments of happiness are indicated in the synaesthesia of her "green laughter" (158). Wearing the green associated with the body, abjection, indigenous Australia, and the poetic dimension of the novel, she enters Voss's experience as the corporeality, irrationality, and feminized indigenous landscape against which he defends himself. A breeze blows through the "shiny indigenous leaves" (198):

---

27 Beatson, "The Three Stages," 116.
28 White, *Voss*, 388.
29 Beatson, "The Three Stages," 120.
30 White, *Voss*, 59.

> All the immediate world was soon swimming in the same liquid green. She was clothed in it. Green shadows almost disguised her face, where she walked amongst the men, to whom, it appeared, she was known, as others were always known to one another, from childhood, or by instinct. Only he was the passing acquaintance, at whom she did glance once, since it was unavoidable. Then he noticed how her greenish flesh was spotted with blood [...].
>
> *Voss* 198–199

Walking among the men, marked with the sign of the body, Laura is familiar to them, "from childhood, or by instinct." Taking on Rose's associations with the maternal matrix, she represents the pre-symbolic, associated with animality, corporeality, and abjection. Laura's green proliferates in the novel as an index of decay and abjection: pot-holes in the desert fester with "green scum" (23); "green mould" grows in houses (30); "green water and rotting fruit" pervade the text (32); "dead green" is a *memento mori* (69), as are "green skeleton ferns" (148). As physical suffering overwhelms the expedition, the men become tinged with green:

> there was scarce one man who was not chafing the shreds of his shivering, flayed flesh, that had first been desiccated to the substance of salt cod. Greenish-yellow teeth were rattling in the skulls, from which men looked out, luminous, but deceived.
>
> *Voss* 267–268

In this intricate pattern of associative imagery, Laura is associated with decay and death, inevitable corporeal processes that Voss is required to accept. Yet the color green is also associated with verdancy, fertility, the living body, and the semiotic dimension of language: "musical green" (197) recurs as a leitmotif throughout the novel, and thought, slipping into irrationality—the abject dimension of language that undermines reason and subjectivity—is described as "disturbing when it lights up the mind by green flashes" (254). Le Mesurier's poetry depicts a storm during which his "skull [is] split open by the green lightning" (297), and imagines his subjectivity dissolving in the realization that "now that I am nothing, I am, and love is the simplest of all tongues" (297). Green is the color of yearning in the dry desert setting, and the poet predicts that his "blood will water the earth and make it green" (296). Harry Robarts' "offending corpse" is described as a "green woman" (389) towards the end of the novel, alluding to Laura and her associations with abjection, decay, and the body. Ultimately, as Laura's oneiric presence in the desert is designed to teach him, when Voss comes to terms with abject corporeality, he will experience the mystical possibilities of "green flesh, watered by the dew [...] shooting nightly in celestial crops" (369). As the novel insists, "divine powers [are] not disguised by the earth-colours" (281).

Perhaps Laura's efforts to "will herself into the body" are best exemplified in the illness that marks the crisis of her mystically shared experience with Voss—the "brain fever," an upheaval of the mind confounding all reason and leaving the Bonners shaken and perplexed. Laura's illness is prefigured by her feigned headache at the beginning of the novel, her excuse for not attending church and therefore associated with her decision to "become what, she suspected, might be called a rationalist" (9). Thus begins the novel's interest in imagery of the head, with its attendant associations of rationality and the subversion thereof. Laura's hair, in her sickness, unfurls like the fronds of unreason and fever. Mrs Bonner has unbraided it, and the "dark, hot hair appear[s] disagreeable to the uncle, who dislike[s] anything that suggest[s] irregularity" (354). "Racked by her fever" (357), Laura imagines that her hair is "cutting her hands" (357); it is burdensome, "hot and heavy" (357), and associated with pain, irrationality, and discomfort. Laura appears to Voss in his moment of shared suffering, their communion indicated by the image of hair:

> His mouth was filled with the greenish-black tips of hair, and a most exquisite bitterness.
> 'You are not in possession of your faculties,' he said to her at last.
> 'What are my faculties,' she asked.
> Then they were drifting together. They were sharing the same hell, in their common flesh, which he had attempted so often to repudiate. She was fitting him with a sheath of tender white.
> 'Do you see now?' she asked. 'Man is God decapitated. That is why you are bleeding.'
> *Voss* 363–364

The "greenish-black tips of hair" are associated not only with unreason but also with physical decay. Laura, we recall, has in one of Voss's earlier hallucinations "bathe[d] her hair in all flesh, whether of imperial lilies, or the black, putrefying, human kind" (188). As Voss "drifts together" with Laura in a dream of "common flesh" (363), a term also used in the description of Laura's merging with Rose in the garden (160), he is infiltrated by the flux of her hair with its associations of flesh, death, and decay. Irrationality is emphasized as Laura loses her faculties, to the extent that she has no knowledge of what they are, her loss of rationality prompting her "drifting together" with Voss. Her closing aphorism is a claim for the "Godliness" of irrationality that occurs with the acceptance of corporeality: "Man is God decapitated," she argues, her words recalling the decapitated Christ of Palfreyman's vision and suggesting that "Man" is an imperfect "God," but, more importantly, that when humanity relinquishes its obsession with reason, when it is "decapitated," then it may attain illumination.

Thus, an interesting process of corporeal acceptance through relations with others shapes the treatment of the body in *Voss*. Rose Portion symbolizes animality, corporeality, and sexuality, aspects of existence repudiated but eventually embraced by Laura Trevelyan, who thereafter becomes associated with the abject herself, arising in Voss's visions to test his self-sufficiency and to threaten the borders of his subjectivity. Laura's appearances to Voss suggest that he should embrace humility in the face of the inconceivable alterity beyond the limits of his consciousness, an alterity seemingly incorporating the physical world, corporeality, notions of the feminine, unknowable regions of the self, and an overwhelming sense of the unrepresentable sacred.

Unmanageable Joy: The Body in *The Eye of the Storm*

While *Voss* demonstrates White's interest in the need to accept physicality, *The Eye of the Storm* best exemplifies (and, in fact, literalizes) the centrality of abject corporeality in White's writing and the somatic spirituality that it engenders. The title evokes the image of a tumult of activity around a still centre. Most obviously, it alludes to the protagonist Elizabeth Hunter's experience of a storm on Brumby Island that is central to her life and therefore to the narrative. As the storm brews, she is slammed and buffeted in modernist prose, "the umbrella of her dress pulled inside out over her head then returned her breasts ribcage battered objects blood running from her forehead."[31] Reduced to a suffering body, she crawls into a small tomb-like bunker before emerging after a few hours into the jewel-like clarity of the storm's eye. Here, among "thousands of seabirds at rest," she is "no longer a body, least of all a woman: the myth of her womanhood had been exploded by the storm" (409). Yet this experience of liberation from the shackles of socialized identity is not to last: the death-cry of a gull skewered on a branch rends the moment of transient peace. The storm passes over, and with "the eye [...] no longer focused on her," Elizabeth returns to "her significance," thereby regaining her subjectivity (410). Correspondingly, language is restored to rational logic; meaning or "significance" is re-established, and she "become[s] a body again" (410–411). Sixteen years later,

---

31 Patrick White, *The Eye of the Storm*, 407.

in the narrative present, Elizabeth prepares for a second important episode of translation: the "miraculous transformation" of death (198). At this pinnacle moment, the imagery deployed in the description of the storm recurs: her body, reduced by the suffering of old age and perched atop a commode, is similarly emphasized and apparently cast off. Transported back to the beach in her increasingly semiotically invested imagination, she again encounters the "dark birds of light" before her bounded subjectivity is dispersed and she is "no longer filling the void with mock substance: myself is this endlessness" (532).

In the description of the storm and of her death, Elizabeth casts aside her identity. Throughout the novel she is depicted as an artist, a wealthy, grand, and consummate actress who over the course of her life has constructed herself as beautiful, desirable, and feminine. Her identity corresponds to the mirror image, or the externalized gaze: "I may never have been beautiful: even in my heyday I was never absolutely sure only of what was reflected in other people's eyes" (41). Mirror imagery is significant in the text, recalling (as indicated earlier) Lacan's theory of the mirror stage which postulates the basis of identity as constituted in identification with the body-image. The mirror image may shape subjectivity, but it also traps the self within the specular relation. Dorothy, like her mother, feels "imprisoned [...] in her own body" when she sees herself "in one of the looking glasses with which her blind mother still kept herself surrounded" (60). The erosion of the constructed body-image is central to the depictions of both the storm and Elizabeth's dying body, which imagine a "calm in which the self had been stripped, if painfully, of its human imperfections" (29). At the height of her experience on Brumby Island, Elizabeth feels that she is "no longer a body" and that the "myth of her womanhood" has been "exploded by the storm" (409). It is only after the eye of the cyclone has passed that she is "reunited with her womanly self" (411), hence re-incorporated into the symbolic where subjectivity is again made possible.

Close to death, Elizabeth is similarly divested of her gendered identity and prepares to cast aside the symbolic order. Language becomes hazy for her as the proximity of death dissolves meaning and invades the limits of circumscribed identity:

> Dead: she used to shy away from the word, saw it as a stone; then it becomes an idea rather, hovering round the body like mist, straying through the skull in unravelled snatches of thought.
> *The Eye of the Storm* 35

Elizabeth's solicitor, Arnold Wyburd, her lover in the distant past, is unsettled by the disintegration of her femininity and sexuality. One of Elizabeth's "non-breasts" has "worked free of the nightdress"—again the "myth of womanhood" is "exploded" (409). His "discomfiture" is "laced with a spirit of horror" (441). Yet this abjection is entwined with the apprehension of somatic spirituality: the observer of Elizabeth's dying body is faced with a vision of unrepresentable alterity. On the borderline between life and death, her body is linked to the inevitable dissolution of identity, inspiring both dread and awe.

Ann McCulloch argues that the "centre of the plot is embodied in Elizabeth Hunter":[32] her dying body is the centre of both the action and the narrative—the "eye of the storm"—literalizing the centrality of the theme of corporeality. Around her aged form the other characters congregate: Basil and Dorothy Hunter/the Princess de Lascabanes (her acquisitive children who are cruelly plotting her banishment to an old-age home); Sisters Manhood, de Santis, and Badgery (her trio of nurses); Arnold Wyburd (her devoted solicitor); and Lotte Lippmann (the German-Jewish chef and former cabaret dancer). Elizabeth's failing body, immobile but surrounded by activity, is thus the centre of the text and, to some extent, the referent of the novel's title. At the age of eighty-six, close to death after a recent stroke, she is bedridden in her opulent house on the edge of Sydney's Centennial Park. The novel is an extended death-scene: for William Walsh, it is "a work saturated with death,"[33] and for Dorothy Green, Elizabeth is an "unconscionable time in dying."[34] Indeed, for some six hundred pages, the novel traces the events of the days surrounding her death, alternating the narrative present with retrospective description. In its concern with narrative detail and its choice of subject-matter, the text evinces White's fascination with both bodily and narrative excess. Both are intimately related to the theme of subjectivity and to the novel's emphasis on the "destruction of the self."[35] Leonie Kramer argues that "White is exercised by fundamental problems about the nature of the self, established in the case of Elizabeth Hunter by minute attention to the mundane details of a long life."[36] The "profusion of surface details" characterizing the novel is, for the most part, corporeal.[37] A number of critics have accordingly commented on the novel's physical fascinations—the "bodily weakness on which White dwells, perhaps to excess"[38]—with varying

---

32   Ann M. McCulloch, *A Tragic Vision*, 111.
33   William Walsh, "Fiction as Metaphor," 198.
34   Dorothy Green, "Queen Lear or Cleopatra Rediviva," *Meanjin* 32.4 (December 1973): 395.
35   A.P. Riemer, "The Eye of the Needle: Patrick White's Recent Novels," *Southerly* 34.2 (September 1974): 258.
36   Leonie Kramer, "Patrick White: 'The Unplayed I'," *Quadrant* 18.1 (February 1974): 67.
37   Manly Johnson, "Patrick White: The Eye of the Language," *World Literature Written in English* 15.2 (July 1976): 339.
38   Riemer, "The Eye of the Needle," 261.

degrees of distaste. Joseph Dewey claims that "White is unsettlingly graphic in recording the physical indignities of [Elizabeth's] deathwatch."[39] For William Walsh, however, White's power resides precisely in his ability "to refine from the grossness of a bodily condition the subtlety of a mental state."[40] Critics have not discussed, however, the pointed thematization of the body in the text, nor its fundamental concern with the dissolution of subjectivity. The novel is full of characters who, like Dorothy Hunter, *"have never managed to escape being this thing Myself,"*[41] and who are driven toward fleeting moments of liberation via their relation to the abject.

As the title suggests, *The Eye of the Storm* is the most anti-linear of White's works. Although constantly returning to Elizabeth's bed and the activities surrounding it, it alternates its attention between Elizabeth and the various characters who arrive at her deathbed as their stories converge at and diverge from this static, corporeal centre. At the height of Elizabeth's experience of the storm, having momentarily shed the impediments of identity, she envisages herself as a "flaw at the centre of [a] jewel of light,"[42] and in many ways the structure of the novel enacts this vision. Elizabeth's character, her narcissism constituting her defining "flaw," is both refracted through the various personae surrounding her and viewed from their multiple perspectives. In other words, characters are emanations of Elizabeth Hunter; conversely, they also attach their own significances to the old woman and her indomitable character. The novel thus comprises both the representation of Elizabeth's fragmented self and the proliferation of differing perspectives and desires; it is a text in which "details [...] grow disorderly as they take it upon themselves to sprout in conflicting directions."[43] Thus, we might read the "storm" of the novel as both centrifugal and centripetal: Elizabeth's influence emanates outward but, always central to the narrative, she is presented through the prismatic lens of the collective perspective of other characters who turn their gaze back upon her. Riemer phrases this differently:

> the structure is diffuse and concentrated at the same time: concentrated because it is located, true to its title, at the still point which represents the last weeks of Elizabeth Hunter's life, and diffuse because the emphasis

---

39 Joseph Dewey, "Patrick White (1912–1990)," in *World Writers in English*, ed. Jay Parini (New York: Scribner, 2004): 760.
40 Walsh, "Fiction as Metaphor," 198.
41 White, *The Eye of the Storm*, 48, emphasis in the original.
42 *The Eye of the Storm*, 409.
43 *The Eye of the Storm*, 418.

does not fall solely or even, perhaps, predominantly on the nominally central character.[44]

It is not necessarily Elizabeth's character that is central to the novel, but her embodiment. Others must respond to her corporeality, which is variously repulsive, mystical, maternal, and aesthetic, always associated with death, and repeatedly emphasized as the abject that both compels and repels.

That White's writing harnesses the disconcerting power of the abject is evident in early responses to *The Eye of the Storm* which reveal what had become readers' standard bafflement in the face of White's seeming over-indulgence in the apparently repulsive. Paul Bailey, reviewing for the *Observer*, was sickened by a novel in which "physical decay and the sordid lusts of the flesh are gloatingly dwelt upon."[45] Cedric Flower of the *Bulletin* was disappointed enough to ask, "Are we in for a bout of Ken Russell like close ups of open pores, dribbling mouths and faulty bowels that made the last two novels so heavy going?" George Steiner saw the novel as a "performance of a craftsman in the grip—entirely private, perhaps—of disgust."[46] Such condemnation overlooks White's complex and ambiguous representations of the body. Elizabeth's body, in its association with death, is linked to some of White's most noteworthy themes: an apprehension of mystery at the centre of existence, the access of the numinous within the boundaries of the ordinary world, the blurring of the binary of abject 'physicality' and sublime 'spirituality', and the suggestion of an excess that attaches to yet surpasses the merely physical, just as it extends beyond the representational capacity of language. Through entwining corporeality and the compelling mystery of death, juxtaposing past beauty and present decrepitude, and representing others' immediate responses to Elizabeth's physicality, the novel depicts the protagonist's body as a seemingly paradoxical site of allure and disgust, vigor and decay, pulsating life and hovering death. As William Walsh has noted, "the absolute intensity of life represented by Mrs. Hunter herself [is] instanced supremely in her dying."[47] Moreover, White, like Kristeva, approaches the abject as an index of the unstable limits of the self.

In her senescence, Elizabeth is the "ruin of an over-indulged and beautiful youth,"[48] suffering "dreadfully increasing accidents" (30). Through slippages between narrative time-frames, White explores the decline of beauty. In the

---

44 Riemer, "The Eye of the Needle," 262.
45 Quoted in McCulloch, *A Tragic Vision*, 147.
46 George Steiner, "Carnal Knowledge," *New Yorker* (4 March 1974): 109.
47 Walsh, "Fiction as Metaphor," 199.
48 White, *The Eye of the Storm*, 12.

narrative present, her body is a "bundle of creaking bones and acerbated flesh" (112). Virtually a shrouded corpse, she is "almost embalmed" (20); accordingly, she is described as an "old *mummy*" (45). The novel makes much of this pun, linking death and the maternal: in relation to the children she has failed to love, she is a "desiccated carcase, blotched with brown, streaked with yellow, scarred by knives; the body from which they had sprung to force their purposes on life" (19). She herself recalls her offspring as "sensations in her womb, then almost edible, comfortingly soft parcels of fat later [...] turned into leggy, hostile, scarcely human beings, already preparing themselves for flight" (197).

The "mummy," as we have seen, constitutes an important psychoanalytic dimension of White's writing. For Basil and Dorothy Hunter, the dying Elizabeth holds the key to the past and to the primal processes that have constructed their poorly formed identities. Accordingly, both characters are enslaved to what their mother's body represents; she remains for them an "enormously enlarged pulse dictating to the lesser, audible valves opening and closing in their own bodies" (399). Both Basil and Dorothy desire a return to the womb and the dissolution of subjectivity. Dorothy's resentment of her symbolic autonomy, which remains tentative throughout the novel, becomes evident in a dream: "When you could have stayed curled indefinitely in Mummy she pitched you out unarmed" (209). Hence her response when she first arrives at her mother's sickbed: "The princess fell against the bed, groping through the scents of Dettol and baby powder, to embrace, deeper than her mother, her own childhood" (45). Basil's feelings are similar:

> He would have liked to flop down, feel the tape closing round his neck, the clean, soft, white bib settling below his chin, then a detached hand feeding him slowly but firmly with spoonfuls of sweetened bread and milk. In such circumstances the mistakes would not yet have been made, and might even be avoided.
> *The Eye of the Storm* 121

Basil yearns to attain a pre-symbolic unity, emphasized in his desire for sleep:

> He anticipated flopping into bed, pulling up the sheet till it became a hood to intensify the darkness, curling as tight as his stubborn bones would allow, as he remembered possums, beans, a foetus in a bottle.
> *The Eye of the Storm* 455

The abject mother compels Basil and Dorothy into a dissolution that also threatens them with obliteration. Accordingly, Basil, oscillating between affects of desire and self-protective revulsion, feels that he must persuade "his mother to die, so that he might survive" (420). Both Basil and Dorothy are, like their mother, consummate performers, their theatricality emphasizing the theme of the spurious nature of identity. Sir Basil Hunter is literally an actor, knighted for his stage performances, and Dorothy, having married and divorced French royalty, is practised in the art of performing cold gentility. Like their mother, these characters reveal identity as built, layer upon layer, over corporeality and the presymbolic. Kristeva observes that abjection, "like *prohibition of incest*, is a universal phenomenon, one encounters it as soon as the symbolic and/or social dimension of man is constituted."[49] Basil and Dorothy's eventual cold and fruitless incest dramatizes their failed attempts to regain presymbolic unity, as does their desire to merge with the abject mother.[50]

Like other forceful central characters in White's oeuvre (most notably Voss), Elizabeth projects her character onto those around her. Others are then taken up within the novel's symbolic schema as fragments of her personality. Leonie Kramer argues, therefore, that the novel's characters are "nearer realizations of ideas, than discoveries of human beings."[51] This may be the case initially: Elizabeth's nurses, Flora Manhood and Mary de Santis, represent her physicality and spirituality respectively, roles, Mark Williams observes, that they accept "with varying degrees of good grace."[52] Yet each character is embroiled in the novel's dialectic and eventual dissolution of binaries: the overtly sensual Flora Manhood gains glimpses of the numinous, while Mary de Santis's repressed sexuality constantly threatens the vulnerable and seemingly incorporeal spirituality that she erects as a protective façade. The implication is that each character needs to harness the aspect of Elizabeth Hunter that she resists within herself. Together, in this allegorical capacity, Flora and Mary form a chiastic relation. Their static relational positions, however, are eventually dismantled by White's disruption of binaries as they become increasingly complex characters: Flora

---

49 Kristeva, *Powers of Horror*, 68, emphasis in original.
50 Raymond Furness argues that the "love of brother for sister is the nearest approximation on earth to the state of androgynous unity. For the issue of one womb are of the same flesh and blood and a union between brother and sister is, in a sense, a re-uniting of the severed hermaphrodite"; Furness, "The Androgynous Ideal: Its Significance in German Literature," *Modern Language Review* 60.1 (January 1965): 61. Basil and Dorothy's incest indeed exhibits White's fascination with androgyny. The androgyne, it should not be forgotten, is understood in psychoanalytic terms as the unification of the pre-symbolic self, prior to language and thus preceding the categorization of sex, and still in a state of amorphous unification with the (m)other.
51 Kramer, "Unplayed I," 68.
52 Mark Williams, *Patrick White* (London: Macmillan, 1993): 123.

discovers that physicality is inseparable from the sacred and Mary realizes that an authentic spirituality necessarily embraces the corporeal. Ultimately, dualism is dissolved.

Throughout the novel, Flora Manhood is an emphatically physical presence. Associated with color and radiance, she makes her first appearance in a boldly colored minidress patterned with great suns. As Elizabeth's daytime nurse, she is starkly contrasted with the demure and dowdy night nurse, Sister de Santis. Flora, who is obsessed with the need to "contemplate her own body," celebrates life's physicality, as her list of favorite things reveals: "rich, yummy food; sleep; cosmetics; making love; not making love."[53] Accordingly, Elizabeth Hunter, her body steadily deteriorating, desires Flora's "animal presence [as] something the mind craves the farther the body shrivels into skin and bone" (82). At one point she literally reaches out to touch this embodiment of throbbing life, gripping Flora's throat in her failing hands, to possess for a moment "this strong vessel of flesh and muscle, inside which, it seemed, the whole of life was palpitating" (82).

Just as Elizabeth perceives in Flora's youthful energy the vigor of her past, Flora views Elizabeth's body as a horrifying sign of her own inevitable degeneration and death. In keeping with her role in the novel's symbolic schema, Flora is the most physically engaged of Elizabeth's nurses. She comes into especially close contact with the old woman's body: massaging her, making her up, attending to her incontinence, and eventually laying out her corpse and plugging her apertures. Her responses to Elizabeth's aged flesh reveal the complexity of corporeality in White's fiction: initially, Flora regards Elizabeth's body with horror. Massaging her back, she is "overcome by a revulsion, almost a paralysis of her strong golden arm":

> Oh God, my life is slipping away! Where the fumes from the alcohol had cauterised her nostrils, and straying farther, exhilarated her thoughts, now they disgusted, though not so much as this loathsome back streaked with sickly brown-yellow, the frail, fluttering ribs, and however clean, the browner cleft becoming a funnel to the anus.
>
> *The Eye of the Storm* 82–83

Confronted with Elizabeth's physicality, Flora is suddenly aware of the limits of her own existence and the inevitability of her own demise. The divide between self and other is dissolved: for a brief moment, Elizabeth's body becomes Flora's inevitability.

---

53   White, *The Eye of the Storm*, 81.

Yet the body's association with death does not limit it to a site of revulsion and horror. Elizabeth allows her favorite nurse to make her up, which Flora does with a rebellious sense of humor, slathering Elizabeth with glittery cosmetics and topping her with lurid wigs until she is transformed into a grotesque parody of her former beauty. The process of transformation is described as a kind of religious ritual. Flora and Elizabeth's shared love of cosmetics unites them in an ecstatic activity that unlocks Elizabeth's body for Flora and the reader as a site of simultaneous horror and wonder, beauty and grotesquerie, spirituality and corporeality:

> In spite of her desire to worship, the younger woman might have been struck with horror if the faintly silvered lids had not flickered open on the milkier, blank blue of Elizabeth Hunter's stare. Then, for an instant, one of the rare coruscations occurred, in which the original sapphire buried under the opalescence invited you to shed your spite, sloth, indifference, resentments, along with an old woman's cruelty, greed, selfishness. Momentarily at least this fright of an idol became the goddess hidden inside: of life, which you longed for, but hadn't yet dared embrace; of beauty such as you imagined, but had so far failed to grasp [...]; and finally, of death, which hadn't concerned you, except as something to be tidied away, till now you were faced with the vision of it.
> *The Eye of the Storm* 116

In relation to Elizabeth's body, Flora sheds her ego: her spite, sloth, indifference, and resentments, as well as her classification of Elizabeth as cruel, greedy, and selfish. Her communion with the abject corresponds to her acceptance of the degradation of corporeality with its plural associations of life, death, and the unnameable "beauty" associated with the dissolution of the symbolic. Flora's transient vision ensures that the binaries that the novel might initially appear to uphold are revealed as arbitrary: inherent in the grotesque is beauty; inseparably entwined with the vision of life is the apprehension of death. Thus, Flora is just as capable of a mystical vision as the character associated with Elizabeth's spirituality, Mary de Santis. Her vision of somatic spirituality locates the "rare coruscation" of unrepresentable sublimity within the body.

In contrast to Flora, who initially appears to represent Elizabeth's physicality, the night nurse, Mary de Santis, seems to symbolize sanctity and incorporeal spirituality in the novel's symbolic schema. Whereas Elizabeth needs Flora's physicality to remind her of the pulse of embodied life, she requires Mary de Santis to help her attain a "state of disembodiment" (13). Both Mary and Elizabeth recognize the exquisite union they are capable of reaching in each other's company. Holding Elizabeth's hand, Mary realizes their "peculiar pitch of empathy," a "world of trust to which their bodies and minds were no more than entrance gates" (11). Elizabeth, too, acknowledges a "state of pure, living bliss she was now and then allowed to enter. How, she wasn't sure. It could depend on Sister de Santis; she needed Mary to hold her hand" (24). While Flora is aligned with Elizabeth's physis, frequently tending to her bodily needs, Mary seems to minister to Elizabeth's spirit. Her love for the old woman resides in the fact that Elizabeth, however brutal and spiteful, is "also a soul about to leave the body it had worn, and already able to emancipate itself so completely from human emotions, it became at times as redemptive as water, as clear as morning light" (12). Although Mary responds to Elizabeth's need for a "high priestess" (14), this role obscures her fear of social interaction and sexuality. It is only during her hours as night nurse that Mary experiences reprieve from the exigencies of everyday life and, most importantly, from the trials of corporeality:

> Doubts seldom arose at night, because love and usage will invest the most material house with numinous forms and purposes, from amongst which an initiate's thoughts will soar like multi-coloured invocations.
> *The Eye of the Storm* 16

Just as night becomes day and the "most material" house is invested with the "numinous," so is the spiritual inseparable from the material, and the abject material at that. Despite her otherworldly night-time experiences, Mary will find herself in the morning, as night fades, "unreasonably pursued by faint faecal whiffs, by the insinuating stench of urine from an aged bladder" (16). The novel suggests, then, that Flora's obdurate physicality cannot shield her from experiencing the spiritual, just as Mary's spirituality is under threat owing to the physicality she represses.

The emphasis on Mary's sexual repression and her association with the abject ensure the foregrounding of her embodiment. She is unable to retain the pitches of seemingly disembodied empathy that she shares with her dying charge. In spite of the supposedly transcendental instances of union that she and Elizabeth occasionally seem capable of attaining, these moments are fleeting and, it is suggested, secondary to another mode of existence that Mary embraces:

> The night nurse might have wished to remain clinging to their state of perfection if she had not evolved, in the course of her working life, a belief—no, it was stronger: a religion—of perpetual becoming.
> *The Eye of the Storm* 11

This "religion" positions Mary within the vast family of White's embodied questers. She is involved in a process of striving which never arrives at an ultimate moment of pure, uncontingent being. As the following bathetic description makes clear, the seeming banality of daytime will always dawn upon the night nurse; the inescapable needs and desires of the body will perpetually return to plague her:

> A glare from furniture and a bed pan scarcely covered by a towel, sprang at the high priestess, stripping her of the illusions of office, the night thoughts, speculations of a mystical turn few had ever guessed at, and certainly, thank God, no one shared, except, perhaps, one old woman. In her daytime form, Mary de Santis of thumping bust and pronounced calves, might have been headed for basketball.
> *The Eye of the Storm* 14

Yet, in the perpetual grind of living, Mary achieves the kind of insight of which White approves. As a character associated with continuation, she can inherit the moments of clarity and selfless insight afforded to Elizabeth Hunter, moments from which the old lady has for the most part failed to benefit over the course of her voraciously selfish existence. Significantly, the novel concludes with an episode in which Mary celebrates the "unmanageable joy" of corporeality amidst the roses in the sun-drenched garden of the recently deceased Elizabeth. An earlier scene prepares for the final episode: as Mary walks among the flowers, a stranger interrupts her "trance of roses" (203), greeting her in her mother's native Greek:

> '*Tí ximaíroma kánomay!*'
> The words went shivering and chiming through her veins. If their meaning was lost on her by now, they echoed through her head in her mother's voice. All the way up the path, the stairs, a melancholy murmuring recurred: of words, and bells, and women's voices rejoicing or lamenting, she could no longer have told which.
> *The Eye of the Storm* 204

The maternal semiotic, eroding "significance" or clear interpretation (410), momentarily floods Mary's consciousness. So often roses represent corporeality in White's writing—"the roses sparkled drowsed brooded leaped flaunting their earthbound flesh in an honorably failed attempt to convey the ultimate" (205). As Mary stares at them, she realizes the meaning of the Greek words: "What a sunrise we are making!" (204). Her interaction with the stranger indicates the illumination of physicality via the transformation of White's symbol of the flesh: sunlight translates the "heap of passive roseflesh back into dew, light, pure colour" (202), pre-empting the novel's closing scene.

Ultimately, the disembodiment of night yields to the physicality of daylight as the incorporeal spirit is exposed as a myth. Before describing the concluding sunlit episode in which Mary features so prominently, it is necessary to focus on another character of symbolic importance in the novel: Lotte Lippmann. Elizabeth's housekeeper and cook, Lotte embodies that aspect of the protagonist facing death. A refugee from Nazi Germany and a survivor of the "ovens" of the Third Reich (79), Lotte has arrived in Australia to take up her brutally ironic role as Elizabeth's chef. Cooking is her art, but it is not her only mode of expression. When she has no appetite for food, Elizabeth requests that Lotte sing or dance, thereby allowing the housekeeper to practise her previous art of cabaret performance (one can hardly resist thinking here of Lotte Lenya). As one of White's signature artist-figures, she reaches after the inexpressible via her particular mode of expression. Her art, as she remembers it, exceeds language:

> I have no voice. Except that of drunkenness. Which is what they have been longing for. It is their need—and mine. They laugh. They wish to touch my hat, my stick, my coat tails of almond velvet. They aspire—to what? to be translated out of themselves? to be destroyed?
> *The Eye of the Storm* 144

Lotte's singing exhibits the "drunkenness" of the semiotic. Moreover, she is always on the border of life's energy (figured in food) and death (symbolized by her bizarre dances of translation and/or destruction). Lotte's irony, satire, and eye for the comedy that is also life's tragedy link her to a liberating laughter that indicates White's interest in *jouissance*—the "unmanageable joy" (589) of the unrepresentable corporeal semiotic. As she dances for the dying Elizabeth,

> Lotte Lippmann, a serious person and satirist, did not know why she was laughing. But her ribs were aching [...]. At least she was liberated. She was free to unite in pure joy with the source of it.
> *The Eye of the Storm* 526

Lotte's dance reflects the erosion of stable meaning, of the "significance" (410) that Elizabeth similarly casts aside during her moment of dissolution in the storm on Brumby Island. Her theatrical make-up, like Elizabeth Hunter's grotesque cosmetic transformations at the hands of Flora Manhood, is expressive of ambiguity and abject sublimity. In particular, it intimates the permeable threshold between the supposed oppositions of comedy and horror. Again, it is Flora who is unsettled, interpreting Lotte's countenance as a joke collapsing into a representation of death. Lotte's lips are

> formally drawn in twin peaks almost as far as the nostrils, with a heavy crimson loop swooning in the direction of the chin. Where lips and cheeks had not burnt through, the skin was whiter than powder could make it [...]. It was a good giggle. Till the nurse took fright. Something in Lotte Lippman's eyes pierced an unhappiness at Flora Manhood's core [...].
> *The Eye of the Storm* 425

Lotte's deathly make-up reveals the intensity of corporeal instinct in the image of "lips and cheeks burning through." Further contributing to the emphasis on her embodiment is her painful, brittle physicality: the "swollen flesh and contorted bones" of her feet, on which she performs her *danse macabre*, have "deformed the scarred, once sprightly, skintight pumps" (425). Such imagery associates her with the inevitable putrescence of the flesh, with death, and, most importantly, with Elizabeth's dying body. Lotte performs twice for Elizabeth. On the first occasion, her body, thrown into the contortions of dance, symbolizes Elizabeth's encounter with death. Her grotesque movements enact the weakness, frailty, and brittleness of the body:

> she stared out of the chalky face at the figure on the bed, or farther, probably much farther. For that reason she could not resist, finally, whatever it was that took place: translation, or dislocation. A whip almost audibly cracked: the limbs twitched into jerky action, the face was split by a patent-leather smile, the more deathly for clenched jawbones and one or two gaps somewhere earwards.
> *The Eye of the Storm* 428

Corporeality is associated with both "translation" and "dislocation": Lotte's dance of death, signifying the unspeakable, exemplifies a moment of apparently mystical translation which would not be possible without the "dislocation" of meaning and the fragmentation of identity associated with the return of the abject—of limbs twitching, of the "deathly" face splitting, of cracking bones, and of the "gaps earwards" that perhaps suggest the failure of the interpretation of language.

Lotte's second performance is the dance that transports Elizabeth into her memory of the storm on Brumby Island, a recollection that eventually dissolves into her death. In the dress in which "Elizabeth Hunter of audacious legs had glided out through the dusty light in the opening steps of the next foxtrot" (524), Lotte, about to embark on her own horrific dance, reflects the protagonist's physical deterioration. Flora, as onlooker, takes note of Lotte's cadaverous back with "all those vertebrae like beads where Elizabeth Hunter's nakedness had been" (525). The juxtaposition of Lotte's emaciated body with Elizabeth's legendary beauty emphasizes the ravages of time. Yet, as Lotte dances, her wasted body, closely detailed, is drawn into relation to the poetry, beauty, and somatic spirituality associated with Elizabeth's dress:

> Balancing on one deformed foot, she stretched a leg, with its knots and ladders of blue veins ending in a scarred pump. If it had not been for the dress she might have flopped down in a heap amongst her own physical shortcomings. But the dress hinted at a poetry which her innermost being might help her to convey; it reflected a faith in love and joy to which she tentatively subscribed.
> *The Eye of the Storm* 526

Poetry, love, and joy—associated with the semiotic, alterity, and *jouissance*—are emphasized in this depiction of embodiment. Looking on, Elizabeth recognizes Lotte's ability to express the mysticism she associates with death, "the inconceivable something you have always, it seemed, been looking for" (526). She recognizes that it is in Lotte's embodiment, essentially in Lotte's dance of failure, that the inconceivable can be glimpsed, however obliquely:

> why you should expect it through the person of a steamy, devoted, often tiresome Jewess standing on one leg the other side of a veil of water (which is all that human vision amounts to) you could not have explained. Unless you were both human, and consequently, flawed.
> *The Eye of the Storm* 526

Indeed, as Lotte dances, "caressing her own arms, her shoulders with hands which could not press close enough, fingers which could not dig deep enough into her dark, blenching flesh" (527), Elizabeth is transported back to Brumby Island and begins to feel herself dispersing, "the fragments the fragments becoming sand" (528). Lotte's dance is embodied ecstasy; it is only through her declining, exaggerated corporeality that she is capable of gesturing at the numinous. As her routine reveals, the more degraded the body and the sharper the confrontation with the abject, the swifter the dissolution of the ego, the submission of the self to somatic spirituality, and the simultaneous and approximate realization of the unrepresentable Other. Instead of a transporting disembodiment, then, the writing strains towards a somatic spirituality, paradoxically writing itself beyond the representable.

The novel's conclusion juxtaposes Lotte Lippmann's eventual suicide with Mary de Santis's ultimate experience of translation in Elizabeth Hunter's garden subsequent to the old lady's death. Each episode represents one of two possible outcomes of the storm of life: devastation and regeneration. However, the scenes should not be read as starkly contrasting with each other. Lotte Lippman's suicide transmutes into poetic ecstasy just as Sister de Santis's "unmanageable joy" (589) among the birds in the garden is a clear expression of somatic spirituality. Furthermore, each scene can be related back to the central figure, Elizabeth Hunter, whose power and mystery are equally represented in her relation to death and to life and thus inherent in her embodiment. Both Lotte and Mary are described in these closing scenes in terms of pulse: Lotte, regarding her "still curiously solid body," has accepted the onset of death and feels, in keeping with her association with irony, the "pulses in her wrists [...] winking at her" (588). The blood coursing through her veins is inseparable from death: "all this time her fate had been knotted in her wrists. She cut each knot of veins with care" (588). Mary, by contrast, feels "her veins, her heart [...] throbbing with life" (588). Her pulsating, living body, firmly weighted on the earth, is imbued with grace:

> The hem of her nightdress soon became saturated, heavy as her own flesh, as she filled the birds' dishes. Reaching up, her arms were rounded by increasing light.
> *The Eye of the Storm* 589

White's poetic language compares Mary's dress to flesh, thereby pointing up the embodiment of the scene. As her dress pulls downward, moreover, her arms extend upward: rooted in the flesh, her body extends into illumination. While Lotte's blood-filled bath becomes a "flush of roses, of increasing crimson" (585), Mary decides that she will pick the last rose of the season for her new patient. Death and life, flesh and spirituality, conclusion and regeneration are inextricably implicated. The scene recalls Lotte's song lyrics (translated from the German), "The roses can never wither / Love lets them be resurrected" (430), and Mary's interpretation of the rose as a symbol resolving "the dichotomy of earthbound flesh and aspiring spirit" (203), "Love," then, is once again associated with the disintegration of conceptual boundaries. Moreover, Mary's joy in the garden among her own "dark birds of light" recalls Elizabeth's moment of translation in the storm, firmly embedding it in embodied experience.

The novel concludes with the realization of Elizabeth's prior wishes: "to make her acquaintances as drunk as she with sensuousness" (32). While the novel's final episode incorporates the transcendent imagery of wings, it locates this transcendence within the physical, natural world:

> She poured the remainder of the seed into the dish on the upper terrace. The birds already clutching the terracotta rim, scattered as she blundered amongst them, then wheeled back, clashing, curving, descending and ascending, shaking the tassels of light or seed suspended from the dish. She could feel claws snatching for a hold in her hair.
> She ducked, to escape from this prism of dew and light, this tumult of wings and her own unmanageable joy.
> *The Eye of the Storm* 589

The concluding scenes of Lotte's suicide and Mary's becoming—descriptions which clearly support each other and which cannot be read in isolation—suggest that corporeality is always expressive of death and of life, exceeding the body image and linguistic categorization in the direction and signification of both. Manly Johnson argues that these scenes provide "another note in an incessant counterpoint of struggle to escape the degradation of the flesh."[54] White, however, is entirely unconcerned with an "escape" from the body, depicting instead the alchemical illumination characteristic of his fiction when his characters are depicted as accepting corporeality. Moreover, the perennial excess of energy and oblivion inherent in the body, and in White's philosophy of becoming, pushes his language beyond the merely significatory into the mystical, the poetic, and the affective—the "unmanageable joy" of physicality. Ultimately, the acceptance of the corporeal results in the transformation of identity. The novel's final sentences illuminate Mary's metamorphosis and posit the possibility of a subjectivity that embraces corporeality, abjection, and dissolution, however disturbing these concepts may be:

> Shortly after she went inside the house. In the hall she bowed her head, amazed and not a little frightened by what she saw in Elizabeth Hunter's looking glass.
> *The Eye of the Storm* 589

---

54 Johnson, "The Eye of the Language," 355.

The Eye of the Storm, as Patricia Morley argues, is a "celebration of life"[55] that strains the representative capacity of language: abject corporeality is depicted as beyond the limits of representation and as engendering a liberating *jouissance*. The novel, like White's oeuvre as a whole, is fascinated by "mysterious otherness."[56] Sublime alterity may be gleaned in the significantly communicative moments of embodiment that White's characters share, the overwhelming corporeal affect that is part of their becoming, the patterning of the texts themselves, and the poetic resonances of White's literary language.

55   Patricia Morley, "'The Road to Dover': Patrick White's *The Eye of the Storm*," *Humanities Association Review* 26 (1975): 109.
56   White, *The Eye of the Storm*, 222.

Conclusion: Unifying the Fragments

No mind can engender till divided into two.[1]

∵

This book has contended that White emphasizes dualism, only to problematize and subvert it. By way of conclusion, and to unify, as it were, the fragments of White's writing and the elements of my discussion, I argue that his fiction conceptualizes characters as fragments of the self or the literary text rather than as figures complete in themselves. This is not to say that they remain flat: they are frequently provided with compelling histories while manifesting complex responses to their present. Moreover, they are presented as embodied figures deeply implicated in the vicissitudes of their environments, both social and natural, and shaped by their affective relations to others. Nonetheless, White's writing dramatizes personality as founded upon the disavowal or acceptance of aspects of the self traditionally denied or downplayed in Western epistemology. In particular, his writing elaborates the mind/body schism central to philosophical discourse since Plato and particularly important to post-Enlightenment conceptions of subjectivity subsequent to Descartes' radical separation of consciousness (*res cogitans*) from corporeality (*res extensa*). White's fiction, as I have argued, is thus deeply concerned with the dynamics of abjection. The modern belief in and psychoanalytic construction of ontological disembodiment is a frequent focus of his writing, contributing to his critique of modernity and his consistent interest in his characters' differing relations to the body. Further, his interest in these relations is dramatized as the potentially contrasting responses of the self to its inevitable corporeality.

These inconsistent responses have been theorized. Peter Brooks, for instance, takes as examples the multiple ways in which the body is described in language, arguing that attitudes to embodiment are peculiarly changeable: we are, "in various conceptions or metaphors, in our body, or having a body, or at one with our body, or alienated from it."[2] For Anthony Synnott, the "one

---

[1] W.B. Yeats, "The Trembling of the Veil" (1922), in Yeats, *Autobiographies* (London: Macmillan, 1955): 263.
[2] Peter Brooks, *Body Work*, 1.

CONCLUSION: UNIFYING THE FRAGMENTS 245

word, body," may signify "very different realities and perceptions of reality,"³ both to oneself and between different people. Bodies emerge differently in narrative—for Daniel Punday, two of the ways in which the body surfaces as a meaningful narratable object is via the sorting of body types and the degree of embodiment accorded to a character. Punday observes that "every narrative implicitly or explicitly defines a certain range of body types" via the comparison of bodies in the text,

> character bodies primarily enter into semantic relations, since by sorting bodies into types a narrative defines the contrasts that underlie thematic, symbolic, and psychological patterns.⁴

Sorting characters into body types is "one way the body enters into the semantics of the narrative and helps to support the process of characterization" (61). Further, "narratives must define character bodies […] according to the degree to which individuals are embodied" (66). As Punday explains, the degree of embodiment "describes how closely we should associate characters with [their] bodies" (66). He argues that this gradation is essential to narratology:

> the potential distance between body and character is an element of the interpretation of a narrative, just like the potential distance between the viewpoint of a narrator and that of the author. (66)

For White, the sorting of bodies into gradations of embodiment is particularly important, for his fiction both stages and undermines the myth of dualism defining Western assumptions, and his characters are constructed according to this logic of emphasis and subversion, representing and critiquing or affirming differing attitudes to the body.

In their embodiment of different attitudes to physicality, White's characters deny the body, accept it, live it, succumb to it, celebrate it, or move between these various positions. Moreover, they slide along a continuum of masochism and sensuality, sometimes exhibiting both responses to their bodies. As White divulges in *Flaws in the Glass*, "the puritan in me has always wrestled with the sensualist."⁵ "Patrick White," the quasi-fictional "editor" of White's last and most postmodern novel, *Memoirs of Many in One*, similarly admits to

---

3   Anthony Synnott, "Tomb, Temple, Machine and Self," 80.
4   Daniel Punday, *Narrative Bodies*, 61.
5   White, *Flaws in the Glass*, 151.

being both "sybarite and masochist."⁶ In *The Twyborn Affair*, Gravenor accuses Eadith Trist of having "a savage nymphomaniac inside [her], and a stern puritan holding her back."⁷ Such ambivalence dramatizes the opposing attitudes White envisages as constituting the self, suggesting, in addition, the tension between civilized morality and libidinal desire elucidated in the theories of Freud, Norbert Elias, Lacan, and Kristeva. Indeed, White's fiction foregrounds the dynamic interaction of the contrary forces of social law and bodily, libidinal excess defining subjectivity, sometimes dividing characters into those who represent symbolic Law and those who embody corporeal excess. Whatever the relations of White's characters to the flesh may be, these relations define their positions in the narrative, for it is corporeality that ultimately asserts itself and prevails in his fiction. To ignore the body in White, as the object (and abject) of differing attitudes, and as an enduring theme, is to deny a fundamental dimension of the work. Certainly, as this study has argued, White's writing is characterized by an "abject dictatorship of the flesh,"⁸ and constantly foregrounds the significance of corporeality and abjection.

The different relations to embodiment evinced in White's fiction arguably represent the author's own conflicted attitude to his body. In *Flaws in the Glass*, White imagines his writing as an introduction to "the cast of characters of which I am composed,"⁹ claiming that his face is "many-faceted" and his "body protean, according to [...] the demands of fiction."¹⁰ As David Marr's capacious biography reveals, bronchial difficulties and homosexuality placed White in an ambivalent relation to his body. While, as Marr suggests, White masochistically despised his sickliness and resented his status as a social outsider,¹¹ his fiction shows that he sought value in the body, which, despite being the site of social stigma, is also a source of sensuous delight. Moreover, White questioned the metaphysical significance of physicality and found solace in locating significance, sacred and banal, in the flesh, despite, and indeed because of, the historical refusal of Western culture to do so. However, White's writing is not merely a theatrical stage for creative authorial 'selving' and thus for his dramatization of conflicting personal attitudes toward the body. The notion of the extension of the self into the lives of others, which implies the mirroring and contrasting of characters, is thematized in the fiction itself. In *The Living*

---

6   White, *Memoirs of Many in One*, 16.
7   White, *The Twyborn Affair*, 344.
8   White, *The Living and the Dead*, 263.
9   White, *Flaws in the Glass*, 20.
10 *Flaws in the Glass*, 153.
11 David Marr, *Patrick White: A Life*, 75.

and the Dead, Elyot Standish eventually recognizes himself as central to a pattern of the lives of others: "Alone he was not yet alone, uniting as he did the themes of so many other lives."[12] Similarly, Elizabeth Hunter in *The Eye of the Storm* advances the idea that "we are not one but many."[13] This emphasizes the notion that White's characters may reflect disavowed aspects of a self that is often embodied by a significant protagonist—one who must reintegrate the elements of existence that he or she has abjected and that others represent. This clear staging of psychological fragmentation informs what Manfred Mackenzie has identified as the allegorical dimension in White. Mackenzie focuses on Theodora Goodman's tendency in *The Aunt's Story* to invent phantasmagorical characters as the externalization of her troubled and fragmented psyche:

> she selves in this way because she is the typically 'generative' hero of the morally charged allegory, who generates characters that are aspects of himself [sic] and who can only be understood as such.[14]

White's fictions are indeed "morally charged allegories," emphasizing the ethical need to accept the flesh. In their recuperation of abjected aspects of self and society, moreover, they challenge discourses of normality, celebrating the disavowed, transgressive, or ignored aspects of existence: physicality, sexuality, or sensual immersion in the landscape. Further, White's fiction challenges the narcissism (based on abjection) that corresponds to the idea that the self is a disembodied entity merely tied to, and thus always superior to, the material world. To counter the notion of the transcendental ego, his writing revolves around the human body, consistently returning to corporeality as a focus of narrative drive and interest. The body assumes particular significance in the ethical realm, compelling characters and reader alike to locate value—often spiritual—within embodied existence.

Nonetheless, White's fiction contends with a history of manichaeanism that would dismiss the body as a mechanism or shell and, at most, as a prison-house of corruption. It appears to acknowledge this philosophical position in order to highlight and contest it. Conflicting attitudes toward the body are therefore often quite explicit, evident, for example, in the contrasting characters of Waldo and Arthur Brown, or Elyot and Eden Standish, or Laura Trevelyan (initially) and Rose Portion, as this study has argued. The inevitable return of the body

---

12   White, *The Living and the Dead*, 18, 357.
13   White, *The Eye of the Storm*, 100.
14   Manfred Mackenzie, "Patrick White's Later Novels: A Generic Reading," *Southern Review* (Adelaide) 1.3 (1965): 9.

to those who deny it is a common theme in White's writing, and his novels of fragmentation thus depict those aspects of the self that require integration.

Body-denying characters are important in such fiction of psychological fragmentation. They promote a rational, dualistic view of the world, which the texts consistently work to subvert. Elyot Standish of *The Living and the Dead*, Johann Ulrich Voss and Laura Trevelyan of *Voss*, Waldo Brown of *The Solid Mandala*, Hurtle Duffield of *The Vivisector*, and Austin Roxburgh of *A Fringe of Leaves* variously attempt to dissociate themselves from the body. They may—like the bloodless, Casaubonish intellectuals Elyot, Waldo, and Austin—view it as inessential yet threatening to the notion of the self. Elyot privileges the mind over the body, promoting the "intellectual puzzle as a substitute for living."[15] His desire to "take refuge behind what people told him was a scholarly mind"[16] arises from a fear of death that paradoxically resolves itself as a kind of alienating death-in-life. Waldo Brown, like Elyot, repudiates the flesh signified by his brother, Arthur, in favor of a spurious, narcissistic intellect and the "cultivation of personal detachment."[17] Voss maintains a state of corporeal aversion: he is "revolted by the palpitating bodies of men,"[18] and convinced in his transcendental egoism that he can "dispense with flesh."[19] Laura, before her values change and she challenges herself and Voss to accept the body, is devoted to the rational logic of Enlightenment thought, spending her leisure time working "fanatically at some mathematical problem, just for the excitement of it, to solve and know."[20] Austin Roxburgh rejects what he perceives as his wife's distasteful sexuality and prefers to view death merely as a "literary conceit."[21] Each of these characters reacts masochistically to any surrender to sensuality. For Voss, it is "wrong to surrender to sensuous delights" and he must "suffer accordingly."[22]

White's body-deniers, particularly his most notable egoists, Voss and Duffield, may also objectify the body. As the title of *The Vivisector* proposes, the artist works invasively upon the living body, scrutinizing it to further his art, despite the suffering such objectification may cause. In objectifying the body, White's characters diminish its importance and hubristically elevate the

---

15   White, *The Living and the Dead*, 174.
16   *The Living and the Dead*, 176.
17   White, *The Solid Mandala*, 177.
18   White, *Voss*, 13.
19   *Voss*, 34.
20   White, *Voss*, 9.
21   White, *A Fringe of Leaves*, 54.
22   White, *Voss*, 129.

apparently disembodied consciousness. Consistently, White associates egoism with body-denial: Voss, for example, is forced into confrontation with "the material world which his egoism ha[s] made him reject."[23] Narcissistic enclosure in the self is presented as evil in White's writing—hence his devotion to materiality, which assists in what Eden Standish in *The Living and the Dead* endorses as the "escape from the disgusting, the nauseating aspect of the human ego."[24] Within fiction intent upon the destruction of foreclosed, transcendental subjectivity, characters like Voss and Duffield cannot maintain their idealism and will have to face the fact, as it is wryly phrased in *The Vivisector*, that "much more depend[s] upon the bowels than the intellect [is] prepared to admit."[25] As it is with the cynical intellectual Le Mesurier—who mirrors that aspect of Voss that deifies the mind and diminishes the flesh—the "throbbing" body becomes a "deafening reality":[26] persistently, it returns to White's body-denying characters as the ground-tone of existence.

White's characters who repudiate the body may exhibit an unconscious longing for the flesh, looking to seemingly more embodied characters, sometimes with revulsion, but also frequently with envy or the gaze of a potential acolyte. In *Voss*, for example, Laura looks to the heavily embodied Rose Portion to help her re-integrate the physical aspect of her character that she denies, and, indeed, Rose's surname suggests that she embodies part of Laura's character. Austin Roxburgh in *A Fringe of Leaves*, "far removed from his physical activity,"[27] looks to the "mystery of virility as embodied in his brother Garnet,"[28] hoping "to borrow some of Garnet's health and strength";[29] he also appreciates, although he tries hard to deny it, his wife's rude country strength. Most conspicuously, Waldo Brown is drawn to, yet resists, his brother Arthur's 'animality' and bodiliness. *The Solid Mandala*, with its emphasis on the symbol of its title, a Jungian image of totality, underscores White's interest in the notion of the integrated self. Body-denying characters are balanced with body-affirming characters, and the need for the former to incorporate the latter's attitude or perception is frequently rehearsed.

In contrast to White's deniers of corporeality, other characters are aligned with the body usually in one of four discernible ways, although these categories

---

23 White, *Voss*, 36.
24 White, *The Living and the Dead*, 168.
25 White, *The Vivisector*, 396.
26 White, *Voss*, 35.
27 White, *A Fringe of Leaves*, 41.
28 *A Fringe of Leaves*, 198.
29 *A Fringe of Leaves*, 15.

are not necessarily neatly distinct. The first set of body-promoting characters lives comfortably as physical entities, conscious of a world of tangible objects, including the body, that are invested with spiritual significance. These characters of an "empirical nature"[30] are accorded a high degree of embodiment: they are frequently strongly associated with their solid, emphatic bodies, from which they cannot or do not distinguish themselves. Julia Fallon of *The Living and the Dead*, Stan Parker of *The Tree of Man*, Judd and Rose Portion of *Voss*, Ruth Godbold of *Riders in the Chariot*, and Mary de Santis of *The Eye of the Storm* fit into this category. Judd, for example, is comfortable within his physical limits: having weathered the tortures of convict life, he has learned physical endurance and come to terms with his body. Unlike the explorer, Voss, he does not aspire to transcendental apotheosis and is instead (like a true explorer) "intensely interested in natural forms" and "wedded to earthly things,"[31] rather than desiring to rise above and subjugate them. The physical being of Judd, who is always presented as a stalwart presence in the material world, is compared to that of a tree or a rock. He is a

> union of strength and delicacy, like some gnarled trees that have been tortured and twisted by time and weather into exaggerated shapes, but of which the leaves still quiver at each change, and constantly shed shy, subtle scents.
> *Voss* 133

Upon looking at him, moreover, Voss recalls a "mass of limestone, broken by nature into forms that were almost human, and filled with a similar, slow brooding innocence."[32]

"Slow brooding innocence" indeed exemplifies this group of characters—an innocence of humility reflected in material objects and the natural world, both free of the egoism of human consciousness. Like Judd, Ruth Godbold of *Riders in the Chariot* is described in imagery of rock, emphasizing her solid physical presence. She embodies permanence and biology, and is the most physically tangible of the novel's four visionaries. In the flux of modern life, she is a reliable point of stability: "Permanence enclose[s] her, like stone."[33] This imagery not only suggests her endurance but also evokes her reliability and duty. Her employer, Mrs Chalmers–Robinson, contemplates her as "some substance

---

[30] White, *Voss*, 176.
[31] *Voss*, 243.
[32] White, *Voss*, 135–136.
[33] White, *Riders in the Chariot*, 301.

CONCLUSION: UNIFYING THE FRAGMENTS

that would not give way beneath her weight and needs, like the elastic souls of human beings."[34] Ruth's reliability is a function of her maternal presence, emphasized by her nursing of others, her most recurring duty of faithfulness. As a solid physical presence concerned with the care of others' bodies, and as a character consistently aligned with spirituality and the abject semiotic, Godbold possesses a faith that is itself personalized—given body—as bodily and maternal:

> Faith is not less persuasive for its fluctuations. Rather, it becomes like a living thing, like a child fluttering in the womb. So Mrs Godbold's faith would stir and increase inside the grey, gelatinous envelope of morning, until, at last, it was delivered, new-born, with all the glory and confidence of fire.
> This almost biological aspect of his wife's faith was what the husband hated most.
> *Riders in the Chariot* 301

In *The Eye of the Storm*, Mary de Santis continues Ruth Godbold's associations of body and faith. A "votary of life"[35] and one of Elizabeth Hunter's nurses, she, too, is a figure of reliability and duty, linked to the care of the body, though her self-characterization, as befits her pursuit of a spiritual vocation and in contrast to Godbold, hovers above substance:

> I've only wanted to serve others—through my profession—which is all I know how to do. Oh, and to love, of course [...] but that is so vast it is difficult to imagine—how—how to achieve it.
> *The Eye of the Storm* 156

Mary does, however, understand love, at least as it is promoted in White's fiction: "'love is a kind of supernatural state to which I must give myself entirely, and be used up, particularly my imperfections—till I am nothing'."[36]

It is not surprising that Judd is eventually the only survivor of Voss's expedition: his association with the body links him to life, as do Ruth Godbold's and Mary de Santis's corporeal relations. Both *Riders in the Chariot* and *The Eye of the Storm* conclude by focusing respectively on these characters. Their endings emphatically celebrate the living body through their focus on these figures of

---

34   *Riders in the Chariot*, 315.
35   White, *The Eye of the Storm*, 154.
36   *The Eye of the Storm*, 157.

embodiment and their final affirmations of existence. *Riders in the Chariot* concludes with Ruth Godbold's "own vision of the Chariot":

> her very centre was touched by the wings of love and charity. So that she closed her eyes as she walked, and put her arms around her own body, tight, for fear that the melting marrow might spill out of it.
> *Riders in the Chariot* 640

Here, the metaphysical image of the Chariot is located within the body itself and White's famously alchemical imagery locates golden value in fluid and subject-engulfing corporeality. In the final words of the novel, moreover, Ruth's feet remain "planted firmly on the earth,"[37] suggesting that meaning resides in embodied existence rather than in transcending the material world. The closing sentence describes her "breathing heavy, for it was a stiff pull up the hill, to the shed in which she continued to live."[38] Mary de Santis, too, is associated with life and continuation. At the conclusion of *The Eye of the Storm*, her "veins, her heart, were throbbing with life" and she "continue[s] throbbing, flickering, inside her clumsy flesh."[39] In what is arguably White's most poetic episode, as she feeds birds in the garden, she is trapped in "this prism of dew and light, this tumult of wings and her own unmanageable joy."[40] Her presence at the conclusion of the novel, after the death of Elizabeth Hunter and Lotte Lippmann, affirms the sensual ecstasy of embodiment and locates worth in the corporeal, libidinal excess of *jouissance*, a transcendence of subjectivity that is nonetheless an immersion in physicality. This group of body-promoting characters, then, although they often struggle with their corporeality, are for the most part—or ultimately—content in their bodies. Like Amy Parker in *The Tree of Man*, they "hold[…] the slow throb of [the] heart in […] folded arms."[41]

The Tree of Man is interested in the contrast of "the nostalgia of permanence and the fiend of motion,"[42] a distinction that can be observed in White's body-promoters. While those who live comfortably as embodied entities personify permanence, the second group of characters aligned with the body is associated with motion—with corporeality as a powerfully destructive yet intuitively creative force, opposed to Enlightenment notions of rationality and aligned

---

37 White, *Riders in the Chariot*, 643.
38 *Riders in the Chariot*, 643.
39 White, *The Eye of the Storm*, 588.
40 *The Eye of the Storm*, 589.
41 White, *The Tree of Man*, 112.
42 *The Tree of Man*, 8.

with poetry, nature, and the unconscious. These characters often run against social norms via various modes of bodily transgression, figured in their physical 'otherness', their inability to uphold the heteronormative values of Western culture initially dictating their identity, or their associations with the transgressive, corporeal instances of poetic language that White foregrounds. His writing often emphasizes the materiality of signification by collapsing the distinction between representation and the body. Reciprocally, this foregrounds a sense of heightened, poetic meaning inherent in the body itself. Terry Eagleton defines poetry thus:

> language which draws attention to itself, or which is focused upon itself, or (as the semiotic jargon has it) language in which the signifier predominates over the signified.[43]

In other words, it is "writing which flaunts its material being, rather than modestly effacing it before the Holy-of-Holies of meaning."[44] White's fiction indeed promotes the materiality of language, and language and the body are often analogous in its conception; a concern with the materiality of the body is also a concern with the materiality of language. White frequently posits what we may call the physicality of words (as affirmed by Gordon Collier's book-title, taken from "the rocks and sticks of words" in White's seminal essay "The Prodigal Son") and is often concerned with this aspect of language rather than with what language alludes to—its various meanings or referents. Thus, for example, General Sokolnikov's lips, in a Whitean reification of a physical human feature,

> would fan out into a rubber trumpet down which poured the rounded stream of words, which he would pick up sometimes and examine through his little rimless spectacles.
> *The Aunt's Story* 149

For Himmelfarb at prayer, "the words that fell from his mouth were leaping crystals, each reflecting to infinity the words contained within the words."[45] White's fiction is self-consciously aware of the endless deferral of meaning in language. In its constant attempts to gesture towards notions of meaning and truth—to capture a sense of 'infinity'—his language proliferates. Layer upon

---

43   Terry Eagleton, *How to Read a Poem* (Oxford: Blackwell, 2007): 41.
44   Eagleton, *How to Read a Poem*, 42.
45   White, *Riders in the Chariot*, 521.

layer of text accumulates in a kind of narrative excess that often correlates with an aesthetic of corporeal excess in the fiction. For this, White has been criticized. According to A.L. McLeod, for example, he is "often prolix: the simple statement seems unknown to him." Thus, "he can write the simple sentence, but he can't write the short, simple, straightforward novel."[46] Arguably, however, White's language performatively enacts, first, the intractable materiality of language itself and, second, the elusiveness of meaning that his writing constantly conveys. Occasionally, as indicated with serious wittiness in *The Tree of Man*, words will "rise to the occasion and disgorge whole worlds."[47]

Through his transgressive characters in particular, White's writing displays a language of physicality, of embodiment. Characters such as Catherine Standish in *The Living and the Dead*, Theodora Goodman in *The Aunt's Story*, Elizabeth Hunter in *The Eye of the Storm*, and Ellen Roxburgh in *A Fringe of Leaves* experience the engulfment and dissolution of their socialized identity within and by their corporeal, libidinal selves. Each of these characters subverts societal roles (in particular, the construction of femininity) through bodies that are variously unacceptable, or are becoming unacceptable, to normative Western society. But it is perhaps E. Twyborn of *The Twyborn Affair* who best embodies White's critique of gender constructions. He refuses the seemingly natural yet socialized correlation between his male body and masculine gender, defying via transgender the discursive law that requires him to adopt and perform masculinity. Other characters, such as Theodora Goodman of *The Aunt's Story*, the four "riders" of *Riders in the Chariot*, Arthur Brown of *The Solid Mandala*, and Rhoda Courtney of *The Vivisector*, trouble the social order because of their physical ugliness or their status as outsiders. In the patterning of White's narratives, the corporeality of these characters often extends into the pervasive theme of mysticism. Contrasted with those who deny the body, whose closed perspective on the world corresponds to their abjection, White's corporeally invested and often afflicted characters reach into and open up to the world, their otherness reflecting the sense of mystery that White imputes to physical existence.

The last two ways in which White's characters may be aligned with the body are incommensurate neither with the two categories mentioned thus far nor with each other: characters may exist in an intensely embodied communion with the natural landscape (Judd in *Voss*), and they may appear as heavily embodied owing to intellectual incapacity (Arthur in *The Solid Mandala*). White's characters are frequently a "reflection of Dostoevsky's 'idiots': the humbly

---

46   A.L. McLeod, "Patrick White: Nobel Prize for Literature 1973," 443.
47   White, *The Tree of Man*, 18.

good, the divinely crazed."[48] Mary Hare of *Riders in the Chariot* is both saintly and mad. Moreover, she merges with the landscape, even representing the possibility of white indigeneity: she is "speckled and dappled, like any wild thing native to the place,"[49] and her moments of spiritual illumination—which occur, it is suggested, during seizures—are described in terms of her metamorphosis from a human individual into an element of the landscape: "her thoughts would sprout in tender growth of young shoots, or long loops of insinuating vines."[50]

Being both mad and simple, Mary Hare is perhaps more complex than White's more typically simple-minded characters. The embodiment of the latter is presented more directly, as it itself provides a clear window onto the simple affective intensity experienced by these characters. When upset, for example, Bub Quigley in *The Tree of Man* is described as running "up and down on his long, clothes-prop legs," his "dribbly desperation [...] terrible in the landscape."[51] Because of their heavy embodiment, White's slow-witted characters are always figures of heightened affective and empathetic intuition. Again, we are reminded that compassion increases when the narcissism White associates with reason diminishes. Bub, with his "child's face on a young man's body" (48), looks into the "faces of people with such candour" that it is "obvious he [is] mingling with their thoughts" (84). Moreover, he exemplifies the humility and goodness of one whose simplicity renders him passive and receptive, rather than active and ego-bound.

∙∙∙

In conclusion, this book has argued that White's fiction promotes the ethical, metaphysical, affective, and ontological acceptance of the body. Although the writing focuses intensely on corporeality, this is not because of a fascinated and dismissive disgust. Rather, it stems from White's interest in endorsing an integrated self that incorporates its 'others' and that extends into the physical world. This is a self of humility and simplicity defined by compassion rather than hubristically elevated by means of repudiation, repression, and abjection. It is a self stripped of its heteronormative, colonial assumptions and extending into the world of others.

---

48   Ingmar Björksten, *Patrick White: A General Introduction*, tr. Stanley Gerston (St Lucia: U of Queensland P, 1976): 2.
49   White, *Riders in the Chariot*, 18.
50   *Riders in the Chariot*, 46.
51   White, *The Tree of Man*, 48.

As I hope to have shown, White's fiction works towards integration through its emphasis on and subversion of dualism, its concern with corporeality and affect, its presentation of a poetic language of physical intensity, its dissolution of static images of socialized identity into the flux and formlessness of pre-symbolic corporeality, and its promotion of the sacredness of the flesh. Moreover, its emphasis on the felt experience of the body provides access to a relation to the world beyond the limitations, prohibitions, and self-enclosure of the symbolic order. Literature, deployed to emphasize the sensory, may replicate this felt experience. It may promote an intellectual readerly engagement that nonetheless stimulates the senses, thereby performatively enacting the dissolution of the binary of mind and body. While White's fiction strives to dissolve dualism, it does not diminish the importance of cognitive ability. Instead, its complex prose promotes reflection and thus a cerebral activity that *embraces* the physical. Reading, therefore, may become a process of intellectual yet embodied engagement with the physical world, and literature that foregrounds materiality—like White's—facilitates this process.

White's pro-body stance is of literary-historical significance, opening the way for experimental postmodernism, the postcolonial concern with alterity and difference, and contemporary ecological concerns. Awareness of the bodily aspect of his writing also encourages renewed and contemporary theoretical readings of White: in many ways, his interest in dissolving binaries pre-empts poststructuralist thought. White's fiction may elucidate such theory just as the theory may illuminate the fiction, a textual dialogue that I hope to have illustrated in my application to his work of Kristevan psychoanalysis. An interesting extension of this project would be a comparative study of White and contemporary authors who have taken his concerns into postmodernism while being directly influenced by poststructuralist philosophy: J.M. Coetzee and David Malouf, for example, have both expressed their admiration for White. Such authors transform White's somatic maximalism into a pared-down contemporary prose that retains its interest in the corporeal while eschewing White's intense abundant descriptions and sometimes reactionary emphasis on the abject. Accumulation of detail and recurrent conceptual density, however, are important to White's writing. They self-reflexively replicate the nineteenth-century novel in style and therefore emphasize White's literature of the abject as a critical counterpoint to repressed and repressive Victorian and colonial values. Moreover, as I have argued, White's constant, repetitive interest in materiality and the body, reflected in the length of his narratives, emphasizes physicality in novels that, for the most part, trace the living years of their protagonists.

Finally, then, although many of White's fictions drive the narrative towards death, this does not bespeak White's desire to free his characters from the

CONCLUSION: UNIFYING THE FRAGMENTS

'prison-house' of the flesh. On the contrary, White's representations of death coexist with an intensely focused celebration of corporeal existence, the specificity of the material world, and the *jouissance* inherent in submitting to physicality. The close of *The Tree of Man* provides one of the best examples of White's commitment to life and the body coinciding with intensely sensory language. After Stan Parker's death, a brief chapter concludes the novel. It is devoted to the experience of Stan's grandson, one of White's poet-seers. The boy wanders around the bush behind the house, where his own "scraggy" physicality reflects the indigenous gum trees and "mass of scrub."[52] He is seized with ennui, wondering how to capture and express meaning. His solution is typically Whitean: he will "write a poem" (499). At first, he decides that this will be a "poem of death" (499). However, he changes his mind when he realizes that "death is faintly credible because it is still smelling of life" (499). Thus, we are precipitated into White's vision of living, physical detail. The boy's poem "of life, of all life" (499), as yet unwritten, will treat the following:

> Of all people, even the closed ones, who do open on asphalt and in trains. He would make the trains run on silver lines, the people still dreaming on their shelves, who will wake up soon enough and feel for their money and their teeth. Little bits of coloured thought, that he had suddenly, and would look at for a long time, would go into his poem, and urgent telegrams, and the pieces of torn letters that fall out of metal baskets. He would put the windows that he had looked inside. Sleep, of course, that blue eiderdown that divides life from life. His poem was growing. It would have the smell of bread, and the rather grey wisdom of youth, and his grandmother's kumquats, and girls with yellow plaits exchanging love-talk behind their hands, and the blood thumping like a drum, and red apples, and a little wisp of white cloud that will swell into a horse and trample the whole sky once it gets the wind inside it.
>
> *The Tree of Man* 499

The boy experiences this unwritten poem as a physical, affective welling-up inside of him: "As his poem mounted in him he could not bear it, or rather what was his impotence" (499), and the novel closes with the poem in gestation rather than fulfilment. The boy returns to the house, carrying with him "his greatness, which was still a secret" (499). So, "in the end there were the trees" (499), the novel concludes—emphasizing physicality over language and the physicality of *White's* language—and the boy "putting out shoots of green

---

52   White, *The Tree of Man*, 498.

thought" (499) that promote the novel's recognition of physical detail, down to "the blood thumping like a drum." Ultimately, White's fiction is "committed to the flesh,"[53] embracing the living, sacred details of corporeality and the material world and rendering them in the imagistic excess of his sensory prose. At the end of *The Tree of Man*, life and death are contrasted, yet White's novels insist that, "in the end, there [is] no end."[54] The blood-beat goes on; the body prevails.

---

53   White, *Riders in the Chariot*, 139.
54   White, *The Tree of Man*, 499.

Works Cited

Abram, David. *The Spell of the Sensuous* (New York: Vintage, 1996).
Abrams, M.H., with Geoffrey Galt Harpham. *A Glossary of Literary Terms* (Boston MA: Thomson Learning, 8th ed. 2005).
Ashcroft, Bill. "More than One Horizon," in *Patrick White: A Critical Symposium*, ed. Ron Shepherd & Kirpal Singh (Adelaide, SA: Centre for Research in the New Literatures in English, 1978): 123–134.
Ashcroft, Bill. "The Presence of the Sacred in Patrick White," in *Remembering Patrick White: Contemporary Critical Essays*, ed. Elizabeth McMahon & Brigitta Olubas (Cross/Cultures 128; Amsterdam & New York: Rodopi, 2010): 95–108.
Aurora, Gursharan. "The Unity of Being—Synergies between White's Mystic Vision and the Indian Religio-Spiritual Tradition," in *Patrick White Centenary: The Legacy of a Prodigal Son*, ed. Bill Ashcroft & Cynthia vanden Driesen (Newcastle upon Tyne: Cambridge Scholars, 2014): 319–338.
Aurousseau, Marcel. "The Identity of Voss," *Meanjin* 17 (1958): 84–87.
Austin, J.L. *How to Do Things with Words* (Oxford: Clarendon, 1975).
Bakhtin, Mikhail M. *Rabelais and His World*, tr. Hélène Iswolsky (*Tvorchestvo Fransua Rable*, 1965; tr. 1968; Bloomington: Indiana UP, 2nd ed. 1984).
Barker, Francis. *The Tremulous Private Body: Essays on Subjection* (London & New York: Methuen, 1984).
Barnes, John. "New Tracks to Travel: The Stories of White, Porter and Cowan," *Meanjin* 105/25.2 (Winter 1966): 154–170.
Barthes, Roland. *The Pleasure of the Text*, tr. Richard Miller (*Le plaisir du texte*, 1973; New York: Hill & Wang, 1975).
Barthes, Roland. *Writing Degree Zero*, tr. Annette Lavers & Colin Smith (*Le degré zéro de l'écriture*, 1953/64; New York: Hill & Wang, 1968).
Beatson, Peter. *The Eye in the Mandala: Patrick White: A Vision of Man and God* (London: Paul Elek, 1976).
Beatson, Peter. "The Three Stages: Mysticism in Patrick White's *Voss*," *Southerly* 30.2 (June 1970): 111–121.
Becker–Leckrone, Megan. *Julia Kristeva and Literary Theory* (New York: Palgrave Macmillan, 2005).
Ben-Bassat, Hedda. "To Gather the Sparks: Kabbalistic and Hasidic Elements in Patrick White's *Riders in the Chariot*," *Journal of Literature & Theology* 4.3 (November 1990): 327–345.
Bernstein, Michael Andre. *Bitter Carnival: Ressentiment and the Abject Hero* (Princeton NJ: Princeton UP, 1992).

Beston, John B. "Patrick White, *The Twyborn Affair*," *World Literature Written in English* 19.2 (August 1980): 200–203.

Beston, John B. "Voss's Proposal and Laura's Acceptance Letter: The Struggle for Dominance in *Voss*," *Quadrant* 16 (1972): 24–30.

Beston, Rose Marie. "More Burnt Ones: Patrick White's *The Cockatoos*," *World Literature Written in English* 14.2 (July 1975): 520–524.

Beston, John B., & Rose Marie Beston. "The Black Volcanic Hills of Meroë: Fire Imagery in Patrick White's *The Aunt's Story*," ARIEL: *A Review of International English Literature* 3.4 (October 1972): 33–43.

Beston, John B., & Rose Marie Beston. "The Theme of Spiritual Progression in *Voss*," ARIEL: *A Review of International English Literature* 5.3 (July 1974): 99–114.

Björksten, Ingmar. *Patrick White: A General Introduction*, tr. Stanley Gerson (St Lucia: U of Queensland P, 1976).

Blake, William. *The Marriage of Heaven and Hell* (1790–93; Oxford: Oxford UP, 1975).

Bliss, Carolyn. *Patrick White's Fiction: The Paradox of Fortunate Failure* (London: Macmillan, 1986).

Bonaventure, Saint. *The Life of Saint Francis*, tr. Ewart Cousins (New York: Paulist Press, 1978).

Bottomley, Frank. *Attitudes to the Body in Western Christendom* (London: Lepus, 1979).

Bourdieu, Pierre. *The Logic of Practice*, tr. Richard Nice (*Le sens pratique*, 1980; Stanford UP: Stanford CA, 1990).

Bourdieu, Pierre. *Outline of a Theory of Practice*, tr. Richard Nice (*Esquisse d'une théorie de la pratique*, 1972; Cambridge: Cambridge UP, 1977).

Brady, Veronica. "*A Fringe of Leaves*: Civilization by the Skin of Our Own Teeth," *Southerly* 37.2 (June 1977): 123–140.

Brady, Veronica. "'Down at the Dump' and Lacan's Mirror Stage," *Australian Literary Studies* 11.2 (October 1983a): 233–37.

Brady, Veronica. "*The Eye of the Storm*," *Westerly* 4 (December 1973): 60–70.

Brady, Veronica. "Glabrous Shaman or Centennial Park's Very Own Saint? Patrick White's Apocalypse," *Westerly* 31.3 (September 1986): 71–78.

Brady, Veronica. "The Novelist and the New World: Patrick White's *Voss*," *Texas Studies in Literature and Language* 21.2 (Summer 1979): 169–185.

Brady, Veronica. "The Novelist and the Reign of Necessity: Patrick White and Simone Weil," in *Patrick White: A Critical Symposium*, ed. Ron Shepherd & Kirpal Singh (Adelaide, SA: Centre for Research in the New Literatures in English, 1978): 108–116.

Brady, Veronica. "Patrick White and the Question of Woman," in *Who Is She?* ed. Shirley Walker (St Lucia: U of Queensland P, 1983b): 178–190.

Braunstein, Nestor. "Desire and Jouissance in the Teachings of Lacan," in *The Cambridge Companion to Lacan*, ed. Jean–Michel Rabaté (Cambridge: Cambridge UP, 2003): 102–115.

Brisbane, Katherine. "Australian Drama," in *The Literature of Australia*, ed. Geoffrey Dutton (Harmondsworth: Penguin, 1976): 248–289.

Brooks, Peter. *Body Work: Objects of Desire in Modern Narrative* (Cambridge MA & London: Harvard UP, 1993).

Brooks, Peter. *Reading for the Plot: Design and Intention in Narrative* (Cambridge MA: Harvard UP, 1992).

Brown, Norman O. "The Excremental Vision" (1959), in *20th Century Literary Criticism: A Reader*, ed. David Lodge (London: Longman, 1986): 509–527.

Burgess, O.N. "Patrick White, His Critics and Laura Trevelyan," *Australian Quarterly* 33.4 (December 1961): 49–57.

Burkitt, Ian. *Bodies of Thought: Embodiment, Identity and Modernity* (Thousand Oaks CA & London: Sage, 1999).

Butler, Judith. *Bodies That Matter: On the Discursive Limits of "Sex"* (London: Routledge, 1993).

Butler, Judith. *Gender Trouble: Feminism and the Subversion of Identity* (1990; London: Routledge, 1999).

Butler, Judith. "Imitation and Gender Insubordination" (1990), in *The Judith Butler Reader*, ed. Sara Salih (Malden MA: Blackwell, 2004): 119–137.

Certeau, Michel de. "Mystique," in *Encyclopédie universalis* (Paris: Encyclopaedia Universalis, 1978), vol. 2: 522.

Cixous, Hélène. "Castration or Decapitation?" *Signs* 7.1 (Autumn 1981): 41–55.

Coad, David. "Patrick White: Prophet in the Wilderness," *World Literature Today* 67.3 (Summer 1993): 510–514.

Coad, David. "Patrick White's Castrated Country," *Commonwealth: Essays and Studies* 15.1 (1992): 88–95.

Coates, John. "Voss and Jacob Boehme: A Note on the Spirituality of Patrick White," *Australian Literary Studies* 9.1 (May 1979): 119–122.

Coetzee, J.M. "Introduction" to Patrick White, *Voss* (New York: Penguin, 2008): xi–xx.

Colebrook, Claire. *Gilles Deleuze* (London: Routledge, 2002).

Collier, Gordon. "Metonyms of Mood and Condition: The Semiosis of Habitation in Selected Australian Fiction Since Patrick White," in *The Cross-Cultural Legacy: Critical and Creative Writings in Memory of Hena Maes–Jelinek*, ed. Gordon Collier, Geoffrey V. Davis, Marc Delrez & Bénédicte Ledent (Cross/Cultures 193; Leiden & Boston MA: Brill | Rodopi, 2017): 255–293.

Collier, Gordon. *The Rocks and Sticks of Words: Style, Discourse and Narrative Structure in the Fiction of Patrick White* (Cross/Cultures 5; Amsterdam & Atlanta GA: Rodopi, 1992).

Colmer, John. "Duality in Patrick White," in *Patrick White: A Critical Symposium*, ed. Ron Shepherd & Kirpal Singh (Adelaide, SA: Centre for Research in the New Literatures in English, 1978a): 70–76.

Colmer, John. *Riders in the Chariot: Patrick White* (Melbourne: Edward Arnold, 1978b).
Colmer, John. *Patrick White* (London: Methuen, 1984).
Core, George. "Poetically the Most Accurate Man Alive," *Virginia Quarterly Review* 53.4 (Autumn 1977): 766–772.
Cranny–Francis, Anne. *The Body in the Text* (Melbourne: Melbourne UP, 1995).
Darwin, Charles. *The Descent of Man, and Selection in Relation to Sex*, intro. John Tyler Bonner & Robert M. May (1871; Princeton NJ: Princeton UP, 1981).
Davis, Charles. *Body as Spirit: The Nature of Religious Feeling* (New York: Seabury, 1976).
Deleuze, Gilles. *Empiricism and Subjectivity: An Essay on Hume's Theory of Human Nature*, tr. Constantin V. Boundas (*Empirisme et subjectivité*, 1953; New York: Columbia UP, 1991).
Deleuze, Gilles. "Ethology: Spinoza and Us," in *Incorporations*, ed. Jonathan Crary & Sanford Kwinter (New York: Zone, 1992): 625–633.
Derrida, Jacques. "Following Theory," in *life.after.theory*, ed. Michael Payne & John Schad (London: Continuum, 2003): 1–51.
Derrida, Jacques. *Limited Inc.*, ed. Gerald Graff, tr. Jeffrey Mehlman & Samuel Weber (Evanston IL: Northwestern UP, 1988).
Derrida, Jacques. *Of Grammatology*, tr. & intro. Gayatri Chakravorty Spivak (*De la Grammatologie*, 1967; Baltimore MD: Johns Hopkins UP, 1997).
Descartes, René. *Discourse on Method and the Meditations*, tr. F.E. Sutcliffe (*Discours de la méthode*, 1637; Harmondsworth: Penguin, 1968).
Dewey, Joseph. "Patrick White (1912–1990)," in *World Writers in English*, ed. Jay Parini (New York: Scribner, 2004): 747–765.
Docker, John. "Patrick White and Romanticism: *The Vivisector*," *Southerly* 33.1 (March 1973): 44–61.
Douglas, Mary. *Natural Symbols: Explorations in Cosmology* (London: Barrie & Rockliff, 1970).
Douglas, Mary. *Purity and Danger: An Analysis of Concepts of Pollution* (London: Routledge & Kegan Paul, 1966).
During, Simon. *Patrick White* (Oxford: Oxford UP, 1996).
Dutton, Geoffrey. *Patrick White* (Melbourne: Oxford UP, 1971).
Eagleton, Terry. *How to Read a Poem* (Oxford: Blackwell, 2007).
Edgecombe, Rodney. "Faith, Pride and Selfhood in Patrick White's *Voss*," *English Studies in Africa* 27.2 (1984): 133–145.
Elias, Norbert. *The Civilizing Process*, tr. Edmund Jephcott (*Über den Prozeß der Zivilisation*, 1939; tr. 1984; Oxford: Blackwell, 1994).
Éluard, Paul. *Œuvres complètes* (Paris: Gallimard, 1968).
Epictetus. *The Discourses*, tr. P.E. Matheson (New York: Heritage, 1968).
Foucault, Michel. *Discipline and Punish: The Birth of the Prison*, tr. Alan Sheridan (*Surveiller et punir: Naissance de la prison*, 1975; Harmondsworth: Penguin, 1991).

Freud, Sigmund. *Case Histories 1: 'Dora'* [1901] *and 'Little Hans'* [1909], ed. James Strachey with Angela Richards, tr. Alix Strachey & James Strachey (Pelican Freud Library 8; Harmondsworth: Penguin, 1977).

Freud, Sigmund. "The Ego and the Id" ("Das Ich und das Es," 1923), in *The Standard Edition of the Complete Psychological Works of Sigmund Freud*, vol. 19: *The Ego and the Id and Other Works (1923–1925)*, gen. ed. James Strachey (London: Hogarth, 1961): 12–69.

Furness, Raymond. "The Androgynous Ideal: Its Significance in German Literature," *Modern Language Review* 60.1 (January 1965): 58–64.

Garebian, Keith. "The Desert and the Garden: The Theme of Completeness in *Voss*," MFS: *Modern Fiction Studies* 22.4 (Winter 1976): 557–569.

Gatens, Moira. "Privacy and the Body: The Publicity of Affect," in *Privacies: Philosophical Evaluations*, ed. Beate Rössler (Stanford CA: Stanford UP, 2004): 113–132.

Giffin, Michael. "Four Approaches to Patrick White," *Quadrant* 50.12 (December 2006): 70–75.

Giffin, Michael. "Judaism between *Torah*, *Haskalah* and *Kabbalah*: The Revealed Imagination in the Novels of Patrick White," *Journal of Literature and Theology* 8.1 (March 1994): 64–79.

Giffin, Michael. *Patrick White and the Religious Imagination: Arthur's Dream* (Lewiston NY: Edwin Mellen, 1999).

Graham–Smith, Gregory. "Against the Androgyne as Humanist He(te)ro: Patrick White's Queering of the Platonic Myth," in *Remembering Patrick White: Contemporary Critical Essays*, ed. Elizabeth McMahon & Brigitta Olubas (Cross/Cultures 128; Amsterdam & New York: Rodopi, 2010): 163–179.

Green, Dorothy. "Queen Lear or Cleopatra Rediviva," *Meanjin* 32.4 (December 1973): 395–405.

Green, Dorothy. "*Voss*: Stubborn Music," in *The Australian Experience: Critical Essays on Australian Novels*, ed. W.S. Ransom (Canberra: Australian National University, 1976): 284–310.

Grosz, Elizabeth. "The Body of Signification," in *Abjection, Melancholia and Love: The Work of Julia Kristeva*, ed. John Fletcher & Andrew Benjamin (London: Routledge, 1990): 80–103.

Grosz, Elizabeth. *Sexual Subversions: Three French Feminists* (Sydney: Allen & Unwin, 1989).

Grosz, Elizabeth. *Volatile Bodies: Toward a Corporeal Feminism* (Bloomington: Indiana UP, 1994).

Hadgraft, Cecil. "The Theme of Revelation in Patrick White's Novels," *Southerly* 37 (1977): 34–46.

Hagstrum, Jean H. "Christ's Body," in *William Blake: Essays in Honour of Sir Geoffrey Keynes*, ed. Morton D. Paley & Michael Philips (Oxford: Oxford UP, 1973): 129–156.

Hansson, Karin. "The Indigenous and the Metropolitan in *A Fringe of Leaves*," *World Literature Written in English* 24.1 (April 1984): 178–189.

Harries, Lyndon. "The Peculiar Gifts of Patrick White," *Contemporary Literature* 19.4 (Autumn 1978): 459–471.

Harris, Wilson. *Fossil and Psyche* (Austin: African and Afro-American Studies and Research Centre, University of Texas, 1974).

Hassall, A.J. "The Making of a Colonial Myth: The Mrs Fraser Story in Patrick White's *A Fringe of Leaves* and André Brink's *An Instant in the Wind*," *ARIEL: A Review of International English Literature* 18.3 (1987): 3–28.

Herring, Thelma, & G.A. Wilkes. "A Conversation with Patrick White," *Southerly* 33.2 (June 1973): 132–143.

Heseltine, Harry. "Patrick White 1912–1990," *Contemporary Literary Criticism* 69 (1992): 392–397.

Horkheimer, Max, & Theodor W. Adorno. *Dialectic of Enlightenment: Philosophical Fragments*, ed. Schmid Noerr Gunzelin, tr. Edmund Jephcott (*Dialektik der Aufklärung*, 1944, rev. 1947; Stanford CA: Stanford UP, 2002).

Hugo, Victor. *La Légende des siècles*, original preface by Charles Baudelaire, preface by Didier Hallépée (1859–83; Paris: Collection Lettres Classiques, 2015).

Hulbert, Ann. "*The Twyborn Affair* by Patrick White," *New Republic* (3 May 1980): 37–38.

Johnson, Manly. "Patrick White: The Eye of the Language," *World Literature Written in English* 15.2 (July 1976): 339–358.

Johnson, Manly. "Twyborn: The Abbess, the Bulbul, and the Bawdy House," *MFS: Modern Fiction Studies* 27.1 (Spring 1981): 159–168.

Jung, C.G. "The Symbolism of the Mandala," in Jung, *Psychology and Alchemy*, tr. R.F.C. Hull (*Collected Works* 12; London: Routledge & Kegan Paul, 1953): 95–223.

Kant, Immanuel. *The Critique of Pure Reason*, tr. Norman Kemp Smith, intro. Howard Caygill (*Kritik der reinen Vernunft*, 1781, 2nd ed. 1787; New York: St Martin's, 1965).

Keen, Suzanne. *Empathy and the Novel* (Oxford: Oxford UP, 2007).

Kiernan, Brian. "The Novels of Patrick White," in *The Literature of Australia*, ed. Geoffrey Dutton (Harmondsworth: Penguin, 1976): 461–484.

Kiernan, Brian. *Patrick White* (London: Macmillan, 1980).

Kiernan, Brian. "Patrick White: The Novelist and the Modern World," in *Cunning Exiles: Studies of Modern Prose Writers*, ed. Don Anderson & Stephen Knight (Sydney: Angus & Robertson, 1974): 81–103.

Klopper, Dirk. "The Body in Biography," *Social Dynamics: A Journal of African Studies* 30.1 (June 2004): 84–94.

Kramer, Leonie. "Patrick White: 'The Unplayed I'," *Quadrant* 18.1 (February 1974): 65–68.

Kristeva, Julia. *Powers of Horror: An Essay on Abjection*, tr. Leon S. Roudiez (*Pouvoirs de l'horreur: Essai sur l'abjection*, 1980; New York: Columbia up, 1982).

Kristeva, Julia. *Revolution in Poetic Language*. tr. Margaret Waller (*La Révolution du langage poétique: L'Avant-garde à la fin du XIXe siècle*, 1974; New York: Columbia UP, 1984).

Lacan, Jacques. *Écrits: A Selection*, tr. Alan Sheridan (New York: W.W. Norton, 1977).

Laidlaw, R.P. "The Complexity of *Voss*," *Southern Review* (Adelaide) 4.1 (1970): 3–14.

Lawson, Alan. "Bound to Dis-integrate—Narrative and Interpretation in *The Aunt's Story*," *Antipodes* 6.1 (June 1992): 9–15.

Lechte, John. *Julia Kristeva* (London: Routledge, 1990).

Lechte, John, & Maria Margaroni. *Julia Kristeva: Live Theory* (London & New York: Continuum, 2004).

Leitch, Vincent B., ed. *The Norton Anthology of Theory and Criticism* (New York & London: W.W. Norton, 2001).

Lever, Susan. "*The Twyborn Affair*: Beyond the Human Hierarchy of Men and Women," *Australian Literary Studies* 16.3 (May 1994): 289–296.

Lodge, David, ed. *20th Century Literary Criticism: A Reader* (London: Longman, 1986).

Loney, Douglas. "Theodora Goodman and the Minds of Mortals: Patrick White's *The Aunt's Story*," *English Studies in Canada* 8.4 (December 1982): 483–500.

Lucy, Niall. *A Derrida Dictionary* (Malden MA: Blackwell, 2004).

Lupton, Deborah. *The Emotional Self* (Thousand Oaks CA & London: Sage, 1998).

MacAinsh, Noel. "Voss and his Communications—A Structural Contrast," *Australian Literary Studies* 10.4 (October 1982): 437–447.

Mackenzie, Manfred. "The Consciousness of 'Twin Consciousness': Patrick White's *The Solid Mandala*," *Novel: A Forum on Fiction* 2.3 (Spring 1969): 241–254.

Mackenzie, Manfred. "Patrick White's Later Novels: A Generic Reading," *Southern Review* (Adelaide) 1.3 (1965): 5–18.

McCann, Andrew. "Decomposing Suburbia: Patrick White's Perversity," *Australian Literary Studies* 18.4 (November 1998): 56–71.

McCann, Andrew. "The Ethics of Abjection: Patrick White's *Riders in the Chariot*," *Australian Literary Studies* 18.2 (October 1997): 145–155.

McCredden, Lyn. "'Splintering and Coalescing': Language and the Sacred in Patrick White's Novels," in *Patrick White Centenary: The Legacy of a Prodigal Son*, ed. Bill Ashcroft & Cynthia vanden Driesen (Newcastle upon Tyne: Cambridge Scholars, 2014): 43–62.

McCredden, Lyn. "*Voss*: Earthed and Transformative Sacredness," in *Remembering Patrick White: Contemporary Critical Essays*, ed. Elizabeth McMahon & Brigitta Olubas (Cross/Cultures 128; Amsterdam & New York: Rodopi, 2010): 109–123.

McCulloch, Ann M. *A Tragic Vision: The Novels of Patrick White* (St Lucia: U of Queensland P, 1983).

McFarlane, Brian. "Inhumanity in the Australian Novel: *Riders in the Chariot*," *Critical Review* (Melbourne) 19 (1977): 24–41.

McLeod, A.L. "Patrick White: Nobel Prize for Literature 1973," *Books Abroad* 48.3 (Summer 1974): 439–445.

Maes–Jelinek, Hena. "Fictional Breakthrough and the Unveiling of 'unspeakable rites' in Patrick White's *A Fringe of Leaves* and Wilson Harris's *Yurokon*," *Kunapipi* 2.2 (1980): 33–43.

Margaroni, Maria. "'The Lost Foundation': Kristeva's Semiotic *Chora* and Its Ambiguous Legacy," *Hypatia* 20.1 (Winter 2005): 78–98.

Marr, David. *Patrick White: A Life* (London: Jonathan Cape, 1991).

Marx, Karl. *Capital*, vol. 1 (Moscow: Progress, 1968).

Meister Eckhart. "About Disinterest," in *Meister Eckhart: A Modern Translation*, tr. & intro. Raymond Bernard Blakney (New York: Harper & Row, 1941): 82–91.

Menninghaus, Winfried. *Disgust: Theory and History of a Strong Sensation* (Albany: State U of New York P, 2003).

Moi, Toril, ed. *The Kristeva Reader* (Oxford: Basil Blackwell, 1986).

Morley, Patricia. *The Mystery of Unity: Theme and Techniques in the Novels of Patrick White* (Montreal & Kingston, Ontario: McGill–Queen's UP, 1972).

Morley, Patricia. "'The Road to Dover': Patrick White's *The Eye of the Storm*," *Humanities Association Review* 26 (1975): 106–115.

Morris, Pam. *Literature and Feminism: An Introduction* (Oxford: Blackwell, 1993).

Myers, David. *The Peacocks and the Bourgeoisie: Ironic Vision in Patrick White's Shorter Fiction* (Adelaide SA: Adelaide UP, 1978).

Nandan, Satendra. "Patrick White: The Quest of the Artist," in *Patrick White Centenary: The Legacy of a Prodigal Son*, ed. Bill Ashcroft & Cynthia vanden Driesen (Newcastle upon Tyne: Cambridge Scholars, 2014): 110–124.

Nedeljkovic, Maryvonne. "Voss or the Uneasy Conscience," *Commonwealth: Essays and Studies* 9.2 (1987): 84–91.

Nochlin, Linda. *The Body in Pieces: The Fragment as a Metaphor for Modernity* (London: Thames & Hudson, 1994).

Nussbaum, Martha. *Upheavals of Thought: The Intelligence of Emotions* (Cambridge: Cambridge UP, 2001).

Oliver, Kelly. "Conflicted Love," *Hypatia* 15.3 (Summer 2000): 1–18.

Penwarden, Charles. "Of Word and Flesh: An Interview with Julia Kristeva by Charles Penwarden," in *Rites of Passage: Art for the End of the Twentieth Century*, ed. Stuart Morgan & Frances Morris (London: Tate Gallery, 1995): 21–27.

Petersson, Irmtraud. "New 'Light' on *Voss*: The Significance of Its Title," *World Literature Written in English* 28.2 (July 1988): 245–259.

Plato. *The Collected Dialogues*, ed. Edith Hamilton & Huntington Cairns (Princeton NJ: Princeton UP, 1963).

Plato. *Phaedo*, tr. & ed. David Gallop (Oxford: Clarendon, 1975).

Punday, Daniel. *Narrative Bodies: Toward a Corporeal Narratology* (New York: Palgrave Macmillan, 2003).

Ratcliffe, Sophie. *On Sympathy* (Oxford: Oxford UP, 2008).

Riemer, A.P. "Back to the Abyss: Patrick White's Early Novels," *Southerly* 47.4 (December 1987): 347–369.

Riemer, A.P. "Eddie and the Bogomils—Some Observations on *The Twyborn Affair*," *Southerly* 40.1 (March 1980): 12–29.

Riemer, A.P. "The Eye of the Needle: Patrick White's Recent Novels," *Southerly* 34.2 (September 1974): 248–266.

Robbins, Ruth. *Literary Feminisms* (Basingstoke: Macmillan, 2000).

Robinson, Jeffrey. "The Aboriginal Enigma: *Heart of Darkness*, *Voss* and *Palace of the Peacock*," *Journal of Commonwealth Literature* 20.1 (March 1985): 148–155.

Rooney, Brigid. "Public Recluse: Patrick White's Literary-Political Returns," in *Remembering Patrick White: Contemporary Critical Essays*, ed. Elizabeth McMahon & Brigitta Olubas (Cross/Cultures 128; Amsterdam & New York: Rodopi, 2010): 3–18.

Ross, Robert. "Patrick White's *The Twyborn Affair*: A Portrait of the Artist," *Commonwealth Novel in English* 2 (1983): 94–105.

Roudinesco, Élisabeth. *Our Dark Side: A History of Perversion* (Cambridge: Polity, 2009).

Salih, Sara. *Judith Butler* (London: Routledge, 2002).

Schaffer, Kay. "Australian Mythologies: The Eliza Fraser Story and Constructions of the Feminine in Patrick White's *A Fringe of Leaves* and Sidney Nolan's 'Eliza Fraser' Paintings," *Kunapipi* 11.2 (1989): 1–15.

Schaffer, Kay. *In the Wake of First Contact* (Melbourne: Cambridge UP, 1995).

Scheick, William J. "The Gothic Grace and Rainbow Aesthetic of Patrick White's Fiction: An Introduction," *Texas Studies in Literature and Language* 21.2 (Summer 1979): 131–146.

Sedgwick, Eve Kosofsky. *Epistemology of the Closet* (Berkeley: U of California P, 1990).

Seigworth, Gregory J., & Melissa Gregg. "An Inventory of Shimmers," in *The Affect Theory Reader*, ed. Melissa Gregg & Gregory J. Seigworth (Durham NC & London: Duke UP, 2010): 1–25.

Shepherd, Ron. "An Indian Story: 'The Twitching Colonel'," in *Patrick White: A Critical Symposium*, ed. Ron Shepherd & Kirpal Singh (Adelaide, SA: Centre for Research in the New Literatures in English, 1978): 28–33.

Singh, Kirpal. "The Fiend of Motion: Theodora Goodman in Patrick White's *The Aunt's Story*," *Quadrant* 19.9 (December 1975): 90–92.

Spargo, Tamsin. *Foucault and Queer Theory* (Cambridge: Icon, 1999).

Steiner, George. "Carnal Knowledge," *New Yorker* (4 March 1974): 109–113.

Steven, Laurence. *Disassociation and Wholeness in Patrick White's Fiction* (Waterloo, Ontario: Wilfrid Laurier UP, 1989).

Synnott, Anthony. "Tomb, Temple, Machine and Self: The Social Construction of the Body," *British Journal of Sociology* 43.1 (March 1992): 79–110.

Tacey, David. *Patrick White: Fiction and the Unconscious* (Melbourne: Oxford UP, 1988).

Teresa of Avila. *The Way of Perfection*, tr. E. Allison Peers (*El camino de perfección*, 1583; Garden City NY: Doubleday Image, 1964).

vanden Driesen, Cynthia. "Patrick White and the 'Unprofessed Factor': The Challenge before the Contemporary Religious Novelist," in *Patrick White: A Critical Symposium*, ed. Ron Shepherd & Kirpal Singh (Adelaide, SA: Centre for Research in the New Literatures in English, 1978): 77–85.

vanden Driesen, Cynthia. *Writing the Nation: Patrick White and the Indigene* (Cross/Cultures 97; Amsterdam & New York: Rodopi, 2009).

Walsh, William. "Fiction as Metaphor: The Novels of Patrick White," *Sewanee Review* 82.2 (Spring 1974): 197–211.

Walsh, William. *Patrick White's Fiction* (Hornsby, NSW: Allen & Unwin, 1977).

Walsh, William. "Patrick White's Vision of Human Incompleteness: *The Solid Mandala* and *The Vivisector*," in *Readings in Commonwealth Literature*, ed. William Walsh (Oxford: Clarendon, 1973): 420–426.

Weil, Kari. *Androgyny and the Denial of Difference* (Charlottesville: UP of Virginia, 1993).

White, Patrick. *The Aunt's Story* (1948; London: Vintage, 1994).

White, Patrick. *The Burnt Ones* (1964; Harmondsworth: Penguin, 1984).

White, Patrick. *The Cockatoos* (1974; Harmondsworth: Penguin, 1979).

White, Patrick. "Credo" (1988), in *Patrick White Speaks* (1992). ed. Brennan & Flynn, 197.

White, Patrick. *The Eye of the Storm* (1973; London: Penguin, 1987).

White, Patrick. *Flaws in the Glass: A Self-Portrait* (London: Jonathan Cape, 1981).

White, Patrick. *A Fringe of Leaves* (1976; London: Vintage, 1997).

White, Patrick. "In the Making" [as "Patrick White"], in Craig McGregor, *In the Making* (Melbourne: Nelson, 1969): 218–222. Repr. in *Patrick White Speaks* (1992), ed. Brennan & Flynn, 19–23.

White, Patrick. "In This World of Hypocrisy and Cynicism," *Arena* 68 (1984): 7–13. Repr. in *Patrick White Speaks* (1992), ed. Brennan & Flynn, 151–158.

White, Patrick. *Letters*, ed. David Marr (London: Jonathan Cape, 1994).

White, Patrick. *The Living and the Dead* (1941; Harmondsworth: Penguin, 1977).

White, Patrick. *Memoirs of Many in One* (London: Jonathan Cape, 1986).

White, Patrick. *Patrick White Speaks*, ed. Paul Brennan & Christine Flynn (1989; London: Penguin, 1992b).

White, Patrick. "The Prodigal Son," *Australian Letters* 1.3 (1958): 37–40. Repr. in *Patrick White Speaks* (1992), ed. Brennan & Flynn, 13–17.

White, Patrick. "The Reading Sickness" (speech, Mitchell Library, Sydney, 19 September 1980), in *Patrick White Speaks* (1992), ed. Brennan & Flynn, 73–78.

White, Patrick. *Riders in the Chariot* (1961; New York: New York Review of Books, 2002).

White, Patrick. *The Solid Mandala* (London: Eyre & Spottiswoode, 1966).
White, Patrick. *Three Uneasy Pieces* (1987; London: Jonathan Cape, 1988).
White, Patrick. *The Tree of Man* (1955; London: Eyre & Spottiswoode, 1956).
White, Patrick. *The Twyborn Affair* (1979; London: Vintage, 1995).
White, Patrick. *The Vivisector* (1970; Harmondsworth: Penguin, 1985).
White, Patrick. *Voss* (1957; London: Vintage, 1994).
Wilding, Michael. "Patrick White: The Politics of Modernism," in Wilding, *Studies in Classic Australian Fiction* (Sydney Studies; Sydney: Shoestring, 1997): 221–231.
Wilkes, G.A. "Patrick White's *The Tree of Man*," in *Ten Essays on Patrick White*, ed. G.A. Wilkes (Sydney: Angus & Robertson, 1970): 21–33.
Williams, Mark. *Patrick White* (London: Macmillan, 1993).
Wolfe, Peter. *Laden Choirs: The Fiction of Patrick White* (Lexington: UP of Kentucky, 1983).
Wood, Susan A. "The Power and Failure of 'Vision' in Patrick White's *Voss*," *MFS: Modern Fiction Studies* 27.1 (Spring 1981): 141–158.
Yeats, W.B. *Autobiographies* (London: Macmillan, 1955).
Žižek, Slavoj. *The Plague of Fantasies* (London: Verso, 1997).

Index

abjection 1, 3, 4, 7, 8, 10, 11, 13, 16, 18–21, 24, 26, 29, 31–36, 38, 39, 44, 50, 52, 54–56, 59, 62, 64, 65, 67–69, 72–75, 77, 81, 91, 95, 99, 104, 106–109, 116, 125, 128, 129, 131–133, 139, 144, 146, 152–155, 158–160, 163, 168–170, 175–179, 184–189, 191–195, 197, 200, 201, 203, 204, 206–208, 211, 212, 215–217, 220–222, 224–227, 229–233, 235, 236, 238–240, 242–244, 246, 247, 251, 254–256
Aboriginals, Australian 4, 36, 37, 63, 139, 204, 205, 209, 210
Abram, David 120, 183–185
Abrams, M.H. 125
acceptance, bodily 10
Adorno, Theodor W. 9, 82–84, 86
affect 2, 5, 7, 19, 21, 27, 37, 42–47, 49, 50, 62–64, 77, 95, 99, 100, 105, 106, 112, 114, 115, 121, 122, 124, 126, 134, 167, 187, 190, 219, 242–244, 255–257
ageing 4, 13, 18, 154, 155, 161, 169, 171, 212, 228, 229, 231, 234, 236
"Age of a Wart, The" (White) 39, 45, 79
Alacoque, St. Margaret-Mary 56
alterity 35, 191, 197, 204, 227, 229, 240, 243, 256
ambiguity 2, 4, 11, 20, 21, 24, 34, 89, 93, 118, 130, 131, 140, 141, 152, 158, 163, 165, 168, 171, 177, 179, 180, 210, 219, 231, 238
ambivalence 11, 72, 73, 164, 179, 246
androgyny 69, 131, 163–165, 167, 171, 175, 179, 215, 233
Angela of Fuligno, St. 56
animality 5, 10, 29, 52, 62, 66–69, 73, 75, 76, 110, 120, 135, 145, 146, 182, 184–188, 207, 210, 218, 225, 227, 249
antisemitism 78
Apollonian–Dionysiac binary 109
Artaud, Antonin 34
asceticism 55, 56
Ashcroft, Bill 6, 40, 54, 113
Augustine, St. 55
Aunt's Story, The (White) 4–6, 10, 18, 36, 39, 40, 42, 51, 52, 63, 91, 93, 94, 113, 114, 117–121, 129, 140, 142–144, 162, 163, 165, 166, 168, 171, 172, 174, 180, 183, 184, 221, 247, 253, 254
Aurora, Gursharan 89
Aurousseau, Marcel 214
Austin, J.L. 169
aversion
    physical 55, 208, 215, 218, 223, 224, 248
    to sexuality 248
awkwardness 5, 46, 114, 140, 141, 152, 166, 203, 219

Bailey, Paul 231
Bakhtin, Mikhail 8, 12, 15, 57, 70–73
Barker, Francis 57
Barnes, John 148
Barthes, Roland 103, 104, 126
Beatson, Peter 2, 87, 215, 224
becoming, White's philosophy of 9, 94–99, 126, 198, 203, 236, 242, 243
Ben-Bassat, Hedda 181
Bentham, Jeremy 141
Bernstein, Michael Andre 21
Beston, John B. 140, 169, 177, 216
Beston, Rose Marie 124, 169
Björksten, Ingmar 255
Blake, William 171, 181, 199
Bliss, Carolyn 12, 89
bodiliness 21, 26, 40, 41, 49, 73, 103, 108, 110, 129, 153, 167, 178, 187, 188, 191, 200, 249
bodily fluids 43
bodily waste 32
body
    cosmetic marking of 122–126
    denial of 8, 15, 25, 30, 33, 59, 66–68, 73, 74, 77, 83, 88, 108, 147, 153, 160, 207, 248, 249
    mechanization of 50, 137, 157, 158, 184, 247
    open vs. closed 70, 71, 73, 96
    permeability of 46
    and pleasure (Barthes) 126
    as prison 51
    social and physical (Douglas) 136, 158
body image 6–8, 15, 29, 48, 54, 128, 129, 152, 167, 179, 189, 242

Bonaventure, St.   55
borders, permeability of   43
Bottomley, Frank   54
Bourdieu, Pierre   9, 136
Brady, Veronica   12, 92, 93, 103, 153, 167, 168, 184, 195, 213–215
Braunstein, Nestor   34, 35
Brisbane, Katherine   198
Brooks, Peter   11, 13, 14, 117, 122, 126, 134, 135, 137, 143, 156, 244
Brothers Karamazov, The (Dostoevsky)   68
Brown, Norman O.   23
Bunyan, John, *Pilgrim's Progress*   93
Burgess, O.N.   103
Burkitt, Ian   73, 150–152
Burnt Ones, The (White)   10, 147–152, 175
Butler, Judith   9–11, 93, 128, 137, 149–151, 169–172, 176, 177

cannibalism   192, 205, 207–211
carnivalesque, the   11, 57, 70, 71
Céline, Ferdinand   34
Certeau, Michel de   193
Chaucer, Geoffrey   72
"Cheery Soul, A" (White)   10, 175, 185
chora (Kristeva)   9, 130–136, 142, 154
Christ   10, 182, 189, 196, 198–202, 205, 227
civilization   52, 62, 77, 82, 211
civilized self   40, 57, 153, 246
Cixous, Hélène   216, 219
Classical thought   50, 51, 53, 56, 57, 62–64, 70, 73, 77, 92, 96, 105, 164
Classical veranda, in *The Solid Mandala*   73, 74, 77
"Clay" (White)   148–150
Coad, David   87, 88, 116, 164
Coates, John   215
Cockatoos, The (White)   3, 4, 122–124, 147
Coetzee, J.M.   104, 256
Colebrook, Claire   95–97
Collier, Gordon   65, 67, 74, 75, 97, 104, 108, 109, 162, 253
Colmer, John   12, 87, 88, 93, 98, 103
colonialism   10, 15, 85, 91, 143–145, 162, 163, 169–176, 180, 214, 224, 255, 256
communion   4, 8, 188, 197, 202–204, 207, 208, 215, 226, 235, 254
compassion   8, 10, 18, 19, 25, 28, 30, 36–44, 49, 51, 63, 76, 82, 85, 92, 146, 178, 182, 187, 189–191, 194, 204, 210, 217, 219, 222, 224, 255
confinement   10, 110, 123, 178
Conrad, Joseph   139, 215
control   18, 20, 39, 55, 57, 60, 66, 108–110, 122, 136–139, 141, 142, 147, 148, 150, 154, 166, 167, 169, 176, 218
Core, George   40
corporeality   1–7, 9–21, 23–29, 31, 32, 35–42, 44–50, 52, 54–60, 62, 64, 66–70, 72, 74, 77, 80, 81, 85, 86, 88, 90, 95, 98–100, 103–105, 107–119, 121–126, 128, 130, 131, 134–136, 139, 141–148, 151–157, 159–162, 164, 166, 167, 172, 177–180, 182, 184–188, 190–210, 212–214, 216–219, 221–227, 229–231, 233–240, 242–244, 246–249, 251–258
Cranny-Francis, Anne   136
"Credo" (White)   190
crucifixion, mock, in Riders in the Chariot   78, 84, 200
cruelty   79, 85, 168, 177, 187, 235

dance   109, 129, 135, 143, 144, 146, 199, 200, 229, 238–240
Dante Alighieri
   Divine Comedy   93
   The Inferno   156
Darwin, Charles   61
Davis, Charles   55
"Dead Roses" (White)   147–148, 150–152
death   1, 4, 8, 13, 14, 16, 18, 20, 25–32, 36, 39, 42, 53, 55, 68, 69, 72, 75, 76, 80, 91, 94, 96, 99, 112, 117, 123, 130–133, 135, 136, 145–147, 156, 162, 163, 168, 190, 191, 208, 209, 211, 212, 220, 225–229, 231, 232, 234–236, 238–242, 248, 252, 256, 258
   denial of   30
death drive   112
death-in-life   28, 38, 248
death wish   105
decapitation   62–64, 200, 202
decay   28, 177, 201, 202, 225, 226, 231, 234
defensive instinct   3, 23, 25, 39, 69, 74, 86, 158, 187, 216
Deleuze, Gilles   45, 95–97, 136
denial   249
   physical   245
Derrida, Jacques   9, 90, 91, 96, 136

Descartes, René 8, 47, 50–52, 57–59, 61, 63, 70, 72, 90–92, 137, 184, 244
desire 14, 21, 23, 25, 29, 31, 53, 55, 58, 59, 67, 100, 106–110, 112, 114–126, 143, 145–147, 150–152, 164, 168, 176, 187, 193, 210, 232, 233, 235, 246, 248, 256
Dewey, Joseph 230
dialectical method 93–95, 110, 233
discipline, social 137, 138
disease 13, 43, 110, 177
disembodiment 2, 3, 8, 10, 28, 54, 59, 63, 64, 68, 73, 86, 91, 92, 100, 182, 185, 201, 204, 212–214, 223, 235, 236, 238, 241, 244, 247, 249
disgust 2, 6, 11, 20, 21, 24, 25, 27, 29, 36, 39, 41, 44, 52, 56, 66, 67, 87, 99, 115, 122, 144, 170, 177, 178, 194, 206–208, 211, 216, 217, 219, 220, 231, 233–235, 249, 255
disintegration
    of boundaries 42, 97, 196, 221, 241
    of ego 6, 38, 40, 68, 116, 121, 130, 133, 135, 187, 194, 225, 229, 230, 239, 240
    of language 66, 134
    of sexual identity 228
disorder 19, 20, 24, 27, 33, 107, 109, 130, 147, 230
dissolution 4, 6, 10, 19, 23, 24, 27, 28, 31–33, 40, 42, 45, 51, 56, 59, 67, 97, 99, 110, 133, 134, 147, 179, 185, 188, 191, 194, 207, 210, 216, 223, 229, 230, 232, 233, 235, 238, 240, 242, 254, 256
Divine Comedy (Dante) 93
Docker, John 153
dogs 29, 78, 79
    significance of 10, 68, 69, 118, 185–187
Dostoevsky, Fyodor 34, 254
    The Brothers Karamazov 68
double telling, in *The Solid Mandala* 65, 74
Douglas, Mary 9, 12, 136, 137, 150, 158
dualism 2, 7–11, 19, 27, 28, 47, 50–53, 56, 58, 62–64, 70, 86–90, 92, 93, 99, 105, 108, 109, 137, 164, 165, 181, 182, 191, 193, 195, 216, 223, 234, 244, 245, 248, 256
During, Simon 153
Dutton, Geoffrey 77

Eagleton, Terry 253
ecstasy 5, 33–35, 41, 109, 198, 204, 235, 240, 241, 252

Edgecombe, Rodney 183
Elias, Norbert 57, 246
Éluard, Paul 181
emasculation 69
embarrassment 57, 66, 175
embodiment 4, 7, 8, 10, 25–28, 37, 43, 48, 54, 63, 65, 69, 70, 75, 78, 80, 82, 85, 92, 95, 99, 100, 109, 113, 130, 136, 140, 141, 145, 153, 154, 161, 168, 169, 171, 186, 189, 195, 196, 199–202, 206, 208, 212, 218, 219, 223, 231, 234–237, 239–241, 243–247, 249, 250, 252, 254–256
empathy 15, 37, 41–43, 47, 65, 75, 76, 114, 124, 187, 223, 236, 255
Englishness 163, 169, 173, 224
engulfment 3, 6, 8, 10, 21, 33, 35, 36, 56, 71, 80, 107, 116, 139, 155, 182, 194, 252, 254
Enlightenment 3, 51, 52, 59, 60, 66, 69, 71, 73, 77, 83, 84, 86, 92, 94, 105, 183, 193, 213, 214, 218, 244, 248, 252
epilepsy 134, 135, 255
epistemophilia (Brooks) 117
Eucharist 10, 182, 202–204, 209
excess 1, 2, 14, 15, 28, 29, 35, 43, 46, 57, 59, 71–73, 81, 99, 113, 117, 122, 125, 126, 151, 163, 177, 180, 182, 229, 231, 242, 246, 252, 254, 258
excrement 1, 12, 21, 38, 92, 182
excretion, art as 100, 102, 110
externalization, of inner states 48, 100, 123, 247
Eye of the Storm, The (White) 4, 6, 10, 11, 18, 39, 51, 71, 72, 95, 123, 132, 133, 152, 191, 192, 212, 227–243, 247, 250–252, 254

fascism 83, 214
femininity 27, 59, 69, 75, 109, 131, 138, 143, 153, 164, 165, 171, 172, 176, 178, 179, 205, 216, 219, 227, 228
"Five-Twenty" (White) 4, 122–126
Flaws in the Glass (White) 108, 111, 162–164, 195, 245, 246
flower symbolism 5, 95, 122–125, 148, 166, 168–171, 201, 206, 221, 237
Flower, Cedric 231
fluidity 9, 10, 26, 43, 105, 109, 131, 142, 153, 176, 252
flux, material 5, 9, 28, 33, 42, 50, 58, 59, 65, 94, 96, 126, 128, 131, 147, 167, 215, 226, 250, 256

focalization, in narration   65, 74, 110, 116, 134, 141, 150
foetus, image of   135, 166
formlessness   27, 28, 32, 36, 41, 42, 59, 131, 256
Foucault, Michel   9, 11, 57, 136–138, 141, 148
fragmentation   6, 9, 22, 23, 48, 49, 63, 66, 94, 101, 114, 129, 134, 135, 153, 165, 179, 216, 230, 239, 247, 248
Francis of Assisi   55
free indirect discourse   11, 26
Freud, Sigmund   14, 22, 61, 106, 117, 165, 171, 246
Fringe of Leaves, A (White)   3, 4, 115, 138, 139, 142, 152, 192, 205–211, 248, 249, 254
Furness, Raymond   233
Fuseli, Henry   63

garden, as significant locus   6, 123–125, 166, 170, 180, 220–222, 226, 237, 241, 252
Garebian, Keith   214, 215, 218
Gatens, Moira   42
gender constructions   5, 10, 69, 131, 148, 162, 164–166, 168–176, 180, 254
gendered identity   128, 149, 150, 157, 161, 163–165, 169–172, 179, 215, 228
Giffin, Michael   12, 77, 88, 92
God   2, 4, 10, 54, 55, 81–83, 89, 96, 102, 120, 169, 183, 185, 188–190, 192, 195, 196, 198, 199, 203, 219, 226, 227
Gothic imagery   63, 71–73
Graham-Smith, Gregory   163
green, as index   225, 226
Green, Dorothy   181, 213, 229
Gregg, Melissa   45, 49, 95
Grosz, Elizabeth   12, 20, 22–24, 29, 47, 52, 89, 90, 96, 105, 136, 159
grotesque, the   1, 8, 11, 13, 57, 70–75, 77, 84, 122, 160, 222, 235, 238, 239
group identity   83, 138, 157–161, 206

habitus (Bourdieu)   136
Hadgraft, Cecil   2, 60
Hagstrum, Jean H.   199
hair/hairiness, as index   31, 48, 85, 115, 133, 135, 148, 197, 198, 219, 220, 226
hallucination   27, 63
Hansson, Karin   209
Happy Valley (White)   95
Harries, Lyndon   102
Harris, Wilson   222

Hassall, A.J.   205, 209–211
hatred   45, 64, 78, 80
Heart of Darkness (Conrad)   215
Hegel, G.W.F.   93
hermaphroditism   69, 164, 165, 233
Herring, Thelma   107, 112
Heseltine, Harry   46
heterosexuality   139, 151, 152, 173–176, 178, 179
Hiroshima   79
Hitler, Adolf   84, 85, 214, 215
Holocaust   80, 81, 83, 85
Homer, *The Odyssey*   93
homophobia   177
homosexuality   107, 139, 140, 149, 163, 164, 176, 177, 246
Horkheimer, Max   9, 82–84, 86
horror   20, 21, 26, 29, 30, 32, 33, 36, 37, 42, 53, 74, 75, 79, 81, 99, 116, 155, 159, 160, 171, 186, 201, 234, 235, 239, 240
Hugo, Victor   212
Hulbert, Ann   15
humors, theory of   43
hypocrisy   15, 72
hysteria   165

illness   18, 189, 220, 226, 231, 232
illumination   36, 41, 42, 56, 93, 99, 195, 196, 199, 201, 207, 214, 227, 238, 241, 242, 255
Imaginary, the (Lacan)   21–23
immanence   88, 93
inarticulate, the   30, 102, 130, 134, 183
incorporeality   2, 3, 8, 11, 53, 54, 59, 62, 67, 68, 145, 185, 218, 233, 235, 238
indeterminacy   93, 99, 171
indigeneity   144, 210, 224, 255
   Australian (landscape etc.)   168–170, 174, 224, 257
inexpressibility   40
infancy   9, 21, 110, 132, 133, 162, 166
Inferno, The (Dante)   156
insanity   13, 166
interior *vs.* exterior   32, 47, 57, 90, 97, 197
"In the Making" (White)   12, 102, 106
"In This World of Hypocrisy and Cynicism" (White)   140
introjection   34, 48
intuition   11, 28, 49, 66, 106, 130, 164, 255
Irigaray, Luce   136
irony   1, 62, 68, 69, 175, 192, 238

irrationality   56, 60, 66, 69, 73, 94, 111, 114, 118, 135, 175, 180, 200, 202, 216, 224–227

Johnson, Manly   178, 229, 242
jouissance   8, 34–36, 56, 99, 144, 194, 207, 211, 222, 238, 240, 243, 252, 257
Joyce, James   112
Jung, Carl Gustav   181, 199, 249

Kafka, Franz   34
Kant, Immanuel   8, 59–61, 183, 213
Keen, Suzanne   43
Kiernan, Brian   12, 86, 264
Klopper, Dirk   47
Kramer, Leonie   229, 233
Kristeva, Julia   3, 7, 9–11, 19–24, 27, 32–36, 38, 44, 49, 50, 56, 99, 104–109, 111, 112, 128, 130–134, 142, 158, 159, 166, 177, 185, 188, 194, 195, 197, 212, 221–223, 231, 233, 246

Lacan, Jacques   6–8, 15, 21–23, 34, 35, 54, 56, 97, 128, 177, 228, 246
Laidlaw, R.P.   202
landscape   15, 38, 42, 65, 97, 168, 169, 205, 210, 224, 247, 254, 255
language of flesh   4, 5, 9
language, nature and function of, in White   100–126
Lautréamont   34
Lawson, Alan   94
Lechte, John   104, 105, 131
Leichhardt, Ludwig   213
Lever, Susan   179
Living and the Dead, The (White)   1, 7, 18, 19, 24–30, 33, 34, 36, 38, 41, 42, 44, 54, 59, 65, 69, 78, 79, 107, 112, 152–158, 190, 195, 196, 246–250, 254
Loney, Douglas   93
love   15, 31, 32, 35, 39, 40, 42, 43, 45, 52, 55, 59, 64, 65, 68, 96, 109, 129, 166, 167, 171, 178, 185, 187, 188, 191, 194, 195, 200, 201, 212, 218, 219, 223, 225, 232, 233, 236, 240, 251, 252, 257
Lucy, Niall   91
Lupton, Deborah   43, 60, 70, 71, 136
Lyotard, Jean-François   136

MacAinsh, Noel   106, 111, 112
Mackenzie, Manfred   65, 247

madness   6, 255
Maes-Jelinek, Hena   210
Malouf, David   256
mandala   109, 199
Margaroni, Maria   104, 130–131
marginalization   13, 37, 142, 157, 160, 161
Marr, David   139, 140, 246
Marx, Karl   61, 157
masculinity   69, 109, 115, 133, 149, 164, 165, 171, 176, 178–180, 215, 254
materialism   48, 85, 86, 181
materiality   4, 9, 15, 28–30, 32, 54, 57, 95, 100, 101, 103, 106, 112, 122, 126, 142, 168, 181, 183, 184, 186, 188, 194, 196, 200, 201, 203, 218, 249, 253, 254, 256
maternal, the   9, 11, 20, 116, 130–133, 154, 162, 166, 167, 179, 195, 221, 225, 231, 232, 237, 251
McCann, Andrew   12, 13, 78, 159
McCredden, Lyn   6, 7, 40, 64, 182
McCulloch, Ann M.   86, 108, 200, 229, 231
McFarlane, Brian   37, 43
McLeod, A.L.   129, 254
meaninglessness   27, 30
Medusa   63, 156
Meister Eckhart   55, 181
Memoirs of Many in One (White)   106, 168, 193, 245, 246
Menninghaus, Winfried   131, 133
metaphysical value   4, 36, 60, 82, 85, 86, 90, 91, 101, 137, 205, 210, 213, 214, 224, 246, 252, 255
metaphysics of presence (Derrida)   9, 17, 90, 96
Miller, Henry   63
mimicry, colonial   172
mind–body binary   3, 4, 8, 11, 12, 18, 26, 27, 29, 39, 47, 50–53, 55–59, 61–64, 66, 68, 69, 71, 73, 86, 87, 89–94, 96, 100, 101, 105, 106, 140, 141, 150, 185, 186, 188, 201, 205, 214, 225, 226, 234, 244, 248, 249, 256, 257
mind, self-sufficiency of   59
mirror stage (Lacan)   6, 7, 15, 21, 22, 54, 128
mirror topos   6, 59, 64, 68, 125, 152, 156, 177, 201, 216, 228
misogyny   152
Möbius strip   89, 96
modernism   63

modernity   3, 8, 13, 15, 51, 52, 56, 59, 60, 62, 63, 69–73, 77, 78, 80, 86, 137, 193, 244
Morley, Patricia   108, 243
Morris, Pam   171
mortality   8, 24, 26–30, 32, 33, 75, 76, 144, 146, 154, 186, 199, 204
mother–child binary   105, 116, 131, 163, 166, 223, 232
mother–daughter binary   6, 135, 140, 147, 150, 166, 168, 170
mother–son binary   30, 69, 116, 132, 148, 149, 154, 165, 179
music   9, 42, 96, 107, 109–115, 129, 143, 170
Myers, David   13, 124, 125
mysticism   8, 10, 19, 35, 56, 60, 85, 101, 104, 134, 181, 182, 184–186, 188, 190, 192–201, 206, 207, 210, 212–214, 216, 221, 224, 226, 231, 235, 237, 239, 240, 242, 254

Nandan, Satendra   38
narcissism   3, 8, 19, 38–40, 51, 52, 64, 65, 69, 77, 82, 85, 195, 212, 230, 247, 248, 255
National Socialism   82
Nedeljkovic, Maryvonne   195, 213
New Criticism   86
Nietzsche, Friedrich   61, 213
Nochlin, Linda   63
normativity   8, 78, 159
   social   10, 13, 128, 129, 136, 139, 142–144, 152, 158–160, 163, 165, 166, 169, 170, 172, 175, 176, 254
nostalgia   63, 252
Nussbaum, Martha   43

Odyssey, The (Homer)   93
Oliver, Kelly   104
orgasm
   art as   111
   music as   112
othering   21, 159, 215
otherness   3–5, 10, 15, 18–21, 23, 26, 29, 31, 33, 35–37, 39, 40, 42, 43, 45, 49, 52, 58, 61, 64, 66–69, 78, 81, 84, 88, 90, 91, 95, 96, 107, 109, 112, 119, 141, 142, 157, 159, 162, 163, 166, 172, 176, 180, 182, 185, 186, 189, 191, 192, 204, 210, 214, 216, 219, 222–224, 228, 229, 233, 234, 236, 240–243, 253, 254
outsider status   5, 129, 158, 178, 193, 246, 254

panopticon (Bentham)   141
penal system   138
performativity, discursive   149, 154, 170, 173
permanence   93, 94, 98, 250, 252
Petersson, Irmtraud   214
physicality   1, 2, 4–8, 10, 13, 15, 16, 18, 20, 21, 23, 25, 28, 36–38, 41–43, 45, 46, 48, 49, 51, 53–56, 59, 60, 64–67, 70, 71, 78, 81, 82, 86–89, 92, 96, 98–101, 103, 106, 112, 115, 118–126, 135–137, 139–145, 147, 152, 154, 156, 158, 168, 169, 171, 176, 177, 180–184, 187–191, 195–205, 208, 213, 214, 217–221, 223, 225–227, 229–231, 233–236, 238–240, 242, 245–247, 249–258
Pilgrim's Progress (Bunyan)   93
Plato   8, 50, 53, 54, 61, 90, 130, 244
poetic language   11, 37, 100, 106, 222, 241, 253, 256
pollution   53
poststructuralism   91, 92, 94, 97, 136, 169, 256
prejudice   19, 78, 178
pre-symbolic   9, 22, 103, 116, 130, 131, 135, 142, 225, 232, 233, 256
"Prodigal Son, The" (White)   112, 188, 214, 253
Proust, Marcel   34
psychoanalytic approach   7, 9, 11, 12, 63, 193, 210, 232, 233, 244, 256
psychosis   35
Punday, Daniel   11, 14, 15, 23, 245
purification   34, 50, 99, 158
puritanism, Australian   72, 245, 246
purity–corruption binary   2, 8, 54, 55, 178
Pushkin, Alexander   102

Ratcliffe, Sophie   43, 44
rationalism   3, 4, 8, 11, 28, 35, 36, 44, 49, 59, 60, 62, 63, 65–68, 70, 72–74, 83–86, 91, 94, 99–101, 105, 106, 108, 111, 121, 123, 125, 130, 182, 184, 185, 187–190, 193, 200, 201, 205, 207, 208, 213–216, 218, 219, 226, 227, 248
rationality   15, 44, 52, 54, 62, 63, 66, 68, 69, 72, 77, 99, 101, 104, 108, 110, 121, 123, 127, 132, 146, 207, 214, 218, 222, 226, 252
"Reading Sickness, The" (White)   72
Real, the (Lacan)   21, 22
reason   3, 5, 8, 10, 11, 28, 39, 53, 60, 62–64, 67, 69, 70, 75, 82, 83, 85, 88, 91, 92, 101, 105,

107–109, 111, 119, 129, 131, 132, 175, 179, 183, 184, 202, 207, 213, 214, 222, 225–227, 255
redemption   3, 4, 6, 10, 13, 16, 23, 32, 34, 38, 42, 51, 65, 69, 85, 129, 147, 182, 185, 191, 198, 205, 216, 236
regression, infantile   131–133
reification   77, 148, 149, 182, 248, 253
restraint, bodily   5, 57, 70, 71, 110, 135–139, 142, 148, 167
revelation   3, 32, 35
Riders in the Chariot (White)   5, 11–13, 36–38, 42, 45–48, 51, 54, 62, 70, 78, 81–85, 92–94, 97, 99, 110, 111, 122, 129, 130, 135, 141, 157–159, 162, 191, 196, 198, 200, 250–255, 258
Riemer, A.P.   2, 3, 129, 130, 178, 229–231
Robbins, Ruth   106
Robinson, Jeffrey   215
Rooney, Brigid   46, 47
Ross, Robert   177
Roudinesco, Élisabeth   10, 12, 188–190, 192–194, 207

sacredness   7, 40, 182, 256
sacred, the   5–8, 10, 31, 34, 35, 54, 56, 68, 69, 77, 99, 130, 182–185, 187, 188, 190, 191, 197, 202–205, 207, 212, 227, 234, 246, 258
Salih, Sara   93
Saussure, Ferdinand   105, 133
scatological, the   12, 92, 103, 107
Schaffer, Kay   205, 209
Scheick, William J.   72, 73
Schopenhauer   213
second-person narration   26, 154
secularism   85
Sedgwick, Eve Kosofsky   176
Seigworth, Gregory J.   45, 49, 95
self-control   57
selflessness   38, 39, 185, 187, 194, 219, 237
self-loathing, of White   140
semiotic (Kristeva)   9, 104–109, 111, 112, 120, 121, 127, 130–133, 154, 166, 167, 198, 216, 221, 222, 225, 237, 238, 240, 251
Semmler, Clement   192
sensuality   108, 112, 113, 123–125, 245, 248
sexuality   5, 78, 95, 107, 111, 116, 117, 119, 121, 122, 124, 136, 139, 143, 145, 147, 152, 154, 162–164, 171–179, 182, 192, 201, 217, 219–223, 227, 228, 233, 236, 247, 248

Shakespeare, William   72
shame   57, 67, 74, 75, 186, 187, 203
Shepherd, Ron   87
silence   3, 4, 30, 47, 74, 75, 200
Singh, Kirpal   129
skin, as indexical surface   47, 67, 79, 85, 112, 117, 138, 148, 155, 160, 169, 177, 197, 201, 239
social gaze   10, 139–142, 217, 228, 230, 249. *See also* panopticon (Bentham)
socialization   8–10, 22, 31, 35, 128, 130, 131, 138, 143, 144, 147, 150, 162, 163, 165, 176, 179, 205, 206, 211, 222, 227, 246, 254, 256
solidity   28, 32, 42, 58
Solid Mandala, The (White)   8, 12, 14, 64–69, 73–77, 80, 81, 95, 102, 108–110, 159–162, 164, 165, 181, 186, 194, 199, 200, 248, 249, 254
solipsism   39, 45, 92
somatic, the   2, 7, 10, 18, 39, 42, 44, 45, 48, 51, 85, 86, 94, 123, 165, 182, 196, 202, 203, 205, 212, 227, 229, 235, 240, 241, 256
Spargo, Tamsin   176
spirituality   1, 7, 8, 10, 15, 38, 39, 41, 42, 44, 51, 54–56, 60, 63, 68, 85, 86, 88, 89, 93, 94, 102, 142, 181, 182, 190–192, 195–200, 202–205, 208, 212, 215, 223, 227, 229, 231, 233, 235, 236, 240, 241, 247, 250, 251, 255
statue, as image for social constraint   70, 142–147, 150, 167, 218
Steiner, George   231
Steven, Laurence   87, 93
stranger, the   25, 26, 41, 48, 68, 124, 167, 237
subjectivity   3–13, 18–20, 22, 23, 30–32, 35–38, 40–42, 45, 47, 48, 50, 56, 59, 63, 69, 70, 91, 95–97, 99, 104, 112, 116, 121, 127, 128, 130, 131, 133, 135, 137–139, 142, 145, 147, 148, 150, 152, 154, 155, 158, 160, 162, 169, 170, 182, 184–187, 189, 195, 204, 206, 208, 210, 213, 215, 217, 225, 227–229, 232, 242, 244, 246, 249, 252
sublime   6, 16, 23, 30, 31, 35, 56, 99, 183, 185, 188, 189, 195–197, 203, 207, 231, 235, 238
suburbia   13, 33, 48, 62, 73, 75, 77, 78, 80, 83–86, 158–161, 191
suffering   15, 37, 42, 43, 64, 75, 76, 78, 80–82, 89, 95, 114, 146, 176, 182, 188, 190–192, 199–201, 216, 225–227, 231, 248

INDEX

symbolic order   5, 9, 19, 20, 105, 133, 150, 164, 194
symbolic order (Kristeva)   4, 5, 9, 19, 20, 22, 24, 27, 33, 63, 66, 76, 104–109, 111, 119, 128, 130–133, 138, 142, 144, 148, 150–152, 164–168, 170, 174, 180, 194, 198, 200, 202, 204, 210, 216, 228, 232–235, 238, 246, 256
Symbolic, the (Lacan)   21, 128
symbols, artist's search for   16
sympathy   30, 37, 43, 177, 186
synaesthesia   99, 123, 125, 224
Synnott, Anthony   11, 53, 55, 56, 61, 137, 198, 244, 245

Tacey, David   223
Teresa of Avila   55
third-person narration   117
Three Uneasy Pieces (White)   39, 79
totalitarianism   83
touch, as index   5, 31, 51, 119–121, 124, 167, 208, 216, 219, 223, 234, 238
transcendence   6–8, 19, 24, 31, 34, 38, 39, 45, 52, 53, 55, 59–62, 88, 93, 94, 104, 128, 129, 131, 142, 181–183, 193, 199, 203, 204, 213, 236, 242, 247–250, 252
transgender   69, 109, 163, 165, 173
transgression   73, 75, 106, 118, 123, 144, 151, 152, 155, 157, 163, 170, 173–175, 186, 192, 194, 247, 253, 254
transvestism   69, 165, 171, 173, 179
Tree of Man, The (White)   3, 4, 6, 10, 13, 32, 40, 48, 51, 54, 60, 62, 102, 114, 142, 144–147, 154, 184, 186, 192, 193, 200, 203, 204, 250, 252, 254, 255, 257, 258
Trembling of the Veil, The (Yeats)   244
twin consciousness   65, 67
twinship   65
Twyborn Affair, The (White)   3, 10, 14, 15, 46, 47, 55, 109, 110, 116, 124, 132, 162–168, 171–180, 192, 246, 254

ugliness   13, 16, 31, 45, 160, 169, 224, 254
unification   3, 6, 8, 12, 15, 20, 22, 23, 31, 36, 42, 81, 93, 96, 108, 128, 164, 165, 179, 204, 210, 216, 222, 233, 235, 236

vanden Driesen, Cynthia   88, 210
Vivisector, The (White)   1–2, 14, 16, 38, 55, 79, 102, 110, 111, 113, 131, 132, 134, 182, 192, 248, 249, 254
Voss (White)   3, 4, 6, 7, 10, 13, 14, 30, 31, 34, 48, 51, 52, 59, 61, 63, 72, 83, 94–96, 98, 100, 101, 106, 112, 115, 121, 123, 132, 133, 138, 140, 141, 153, 182–184, 187–190, 193–195, 198, 200–202, 204, 205, 210–227, 233, 248–251, 254

Walsh, William   2, 12, 65, 129, 160, 229–231
Weil, Simone   92, 164
White, Patrick, *works*
  "The Age of a Wart"   39, 45, 79
  The Aunt's Story   4–6, 10, 18, 36, 39, 40, 42, 51, 52, 63, 91, 93, 94, 113, 114, 117–121, 129, 140, 142–144, 162, 163, 165, 166, 168, 171, 172, 174, 180, 183, 184, 221, 247, 253, 254
  The Burnt Ones   10, 147–152, 175
  A Cheery Soul   10, 175, 185
  "Clay"   148–150
  The Cockatoos   3, 4, 122–124, 147
  "Dead Roses"   147–148, 150–152
  The Eye of the Storm   4, 6, 10, 11, 18, 39, 51, 71, 72, 95, 123, 132, 133, 152, 191, 192, 212, 227–243, 247, 250–252, 254
  "Five-Twenty"   4, 122, 123, 126
  Flaws in the Glass   108, 111, 162–164, 195, 245, 246
  A Fringe of Leaves   3, 4, 115, 138, 139, 142, 152, 192, 205–211, 248, 249, 254
  Happy Valley   95
  "In the Making"   12, 102, 106
  "In This World of Hypocrisy and Cynicism"   140
  The Living and the Dead   1, 7, 18, 19, 24–30, 33, 34, 36, 38, 41, 42, 44, 54, 59, 65, 69, 78, 79, 107, 112, 152–158, 190, 195, 196, 246–250, 254
  Memoirs of Many in One   106, 168, 193, 245, 246
  "The Prodigal Son"   112, 188, 214, 253
  Riders in the Chariot   5, 11–13, 36–38, 42, 45–48, 51, 54, 62, 70, 78, 81–85, 92–94, 97–99, 110, 111, 122, 129, 130, 135, 141, 157–159, 162, 191, 196–198, 200, 250–255, 258

White, Patrick, *works* (*cont.*)
  The Solid Mandala 8, 12, 14, 64–69, 73–77, 80, 81, 95, 102, 108–110, 159–162, 164, 165, 181, 186, 194, 199, 200, 248, 249, 254
  Three Uneasy Pieces 39, 79
  The Tree of Man 3, 4, 6, 10, 13, 32, 40, 48, 51, 54, 60, 62, 102, 114, 142, 144–147, 154, 184, 186, 192, 193, 200, 203, 204, 250, 252, 254, 255, 257, 258
  The Twyborn Affair 3, 10, 14, 15, 46, 47, 55, 109, 110, 116, 124, 132, 162–168, 171–180, 192, 246, 254
  The Vivisector 1–2, 14, 16, 38, 55, 79, 102, 110, 111, 113, 131, 132, 134, 182, 192, 248, 249, 254

Voss 3, 4, 6, 7, 10, 13, 14, 30, 31, 34, 48, 51, 52, 59, 61, 63, 72, 83, 94–96, 98, 100, 101, 106, 112, 115, 121, 123, 132, 133, 138, 140, 141, 153, 182–184, 187–190, 193–195, 198, 200, 202, 204, 205, 210–227, 233, 248–251, 254
Wilding, Michael 84
Wilkes, G.A. 40, 107, 112
Williams, Mark 12, 233
Wolfe, Peter 12, 24, 89, 198
Wood, Susan A. 213

Yeats, W.B. 244
yellow, as index 30, 168, 169

Žižek, Slavoj 143, 144